INSIGHT GUIDE

SICILY

APA PUBLICATIONS

Part of the Langenscheidt Publishing Group

INSIGHT GUIDE
SICILY

ABOUT THIS BOOK

Editorial
Project Editor
Jeffery Pike
Managing Editor
Emily Hatchwell
Editorial Director
Brian Bell

Distribution

UK & Ireland
GeoCenter International Ltd
The Viables Centre, Harrow Way
Basingstoke, Hants RG22 4BJ
Fax: (44) 1256 817988
United States
Langenscheidt Publishers, Inc.
46–35 54th Road, Maspeth, NY 11378
Fax: (1) 718 784 0640
Canada
Thomas Allen & Son Ltd
390 Steelcase Road East
Markham, Ontario L3R 1G2
Fax: (1) 905 475 6747
Australia
Universal Press
1 Waterloo Road
Macquarie Park, NSW 2113
Fax: (61) 2 9888 9074
New Zealand
Hema Maps New Zealand Ltd (HNZ)
Unit D, 24 Ra ORA Drive
East Tamaki, Auckland
Fax: (64) 9 273 6479
Worldwide
**Apa Publications GmbH & Co.
Verlag KG (Singapore branch)**
38 Joo Koon Road, Singapore 628990
Tel: (65) 865-1600. Fax: (65) 861-6438

Printing

Insight Print Services (Pte) Ltd
38 Joo Koon Road, Singapore 628990
Tel: (65) 865-1600. Fax: (65) 861-6438

©2001 Apa Publications GmbH & Co.
Verlag KG (Singapore branch)
All Rights Reserved
First Edition 1993
Third Edition 2000, reprinted 2001

CONTACTING THE EDITORS
We would appreciate it if readers
would alert us to errors or out-
dated information by writing to:
**Insight Guides, P.O. Box 7910,
London SE1 1WE, England.
Fax: (44) 20 7403 0290.**
insight@apaguide.demon.co.uk

www.insightguides.com

This guidebook combines the interests and enthusiasms of two of the world's best-known infor-
mation providers: Insight Guides, whose titles have set the standard for visual travel guides since 1970, and Discovery Channel, the world's premier source of nonfiction television programming.

The editors of Insight Guides provide both practical advice and general understanding about a destination's his-
tory, culture, institutions and people. Discovery Channel and its website, www.discovery.com, help millions of viewers explore their world from the comfort of their own home and also encourage them to explore it first-hand.

This fully updated edition of

Insight Guide: Sicily is structured to convey an understanding of the island and its culture, and to guide readers through its many attractions:

◆ The **Features** section, indicated by a yellow bar at the top of each page, covers the rich history and culture of Sicily in a series of informative essays.

◆ The main **Places** section, with a blue bar, is a complete guide to all the sights and areas worth visiting. Places of special interest are coordi-
nated by number with the maps.

◆ The **Travel Tips** list-
ings section, with an orange bar, provides a point of reference for information on travel, hotels, restaurants, shops and more.

EXPLORE YOUR WORLD

Discovery
CHANNEL

The contributors

This edition of *Insight Guide: Sicily* was edited by **Jeffery Pike**, a London-based editor, supervised by managing editor **Emily Hatchwell** at Insight Guides. The book has been completely updated with the help of a number of people.

The principal contributor, as in earlier editions, was **Lisa Gerard-Sharp**, a writer and broadcaster with a special interest in Italy. Having contributed to Insight guides to Tuscany, Florence and Naples, she steadily gravitated southwards to Sicily. In compiling the earlier editions of this book, she found herself intrigued by the clash between the legendary immutability of Sicily and the apparent striving for change, especially among the young. For this edition, she returned to the island twice, spending time exploring the major sights and the many out-of-the-way treasures, to produce a thoroughly revised Places section.

Most of the History chapters were written by **Rowlinson Carter**, an Insight stalwart with a passion for Classical history. He was fascinated by the Sicilians' early experiments with democracy, but equally intrigued that "the democratic interlude soon gave way to a race of full-blooded tyrants".

The chapters on Food and the Egadi Islands were contributed by **Mary Taylor Simeti**, an American writer who divides her time between Palermo and her farm in Alcamo. The feature on Women in Sicily was revised and augmented by **Clare Longrigg**, a journalist on *The Independent* in London and author of the revealing book *Mafia Women*.

The new chapters on the Aeolian Islands and Sicily's Wild Places were written by **Jenny Bennathan**, who combines a love of wildlife with a fondness for the Aeolians. In 1999 she moved to Alicudi, to become the island's 101st resident.

The Travel Tips section was completely revised and updated by **Mariella d'Amato**, a freelance translator based in Palermo, who frequently works with a local company producing documentaries on nature, tourism and cultural events.

Thanks are due to various tourist offices in Sicily for the enthusiastic support they offered to Gerard-Sharp in her researches, and especially to **Italiatour** for their help with travel arrangements.

Thanks also go to **Susannah Wight** for proofreading, to **Cynthia Howell** for meticulously checking the maps, and to **Penny Phenix** for indexing this latest edition.

Map Legend

▬ ▪▪ ▪	International Boundary
▬ ▬ ▬	Province Boundary
▬ ▪ ▬ ▪	National Park/Reserve
▬ ▬ ▬	Ferry Route
✈ ✈	Airport: International/Regional
🚌	Bus Station
❶	Tourist Information
✉	Post Office
✝ ✝ ✝	Church/Ruins
✝	Monastery
☪	Mosque
✡	Synagogue
🏰 🏚	Castle/Ruins
∴	Archaeological Site
∩	Cave
𝚰	Statue/Monument
★	Place of Interest

The main places of interest in the Places section are coordinated by number with a full-colour map (e.g. ❶), and a symbol at the top of every right-hand page tells you where to find the map.

CONTENTS

Hoping for a catch at Siracusa.

Travel Tips

Places

THE SHAPING OF SICILY

Sicily's complex history has produced an island with a unique character – proud, brooding, enigmatic and irreverent

Sicily may be Italian, but the islanders are Latin only by adoption. They may look back at Magna Graecia or Moorish Sicily but tend to be bored by their exotic past. Mostly, they sleep-walk their way through history, as if it were a bad play in a long-forgotten language. Floating not far beneath the surface is a kaleidoscope of swirling foreignness against a backdrop of Sicilian fatalism.

This is the legacy of a land whose heyday was over 700 years ago. It is most visible in the diversity of architectural styles, brought together under one roof in a remarkable mongrel, Siracusa Cathedral. Yet Sicilians themselves, as they often boast, are *bastardi puri* ("pure bastards"), the product of racial overdose.

The assumption that people want overt power, leadership, laws, equality, a democratically calibrated society is laughably unSicilian. The Greeks' lessons in democracy fell on stony ground: the Sicilians responded with a race of full-blooded tyrants. The Mafia, with greater superficial sophistication, showed equal disdain for democratic niceties: their shadowy state within a state became more effective than the pale, public model. Sicilians dismiss democracy as a system only suitable for "Nordic" countries. Until recently, most landed, educated Sicilians declined public office, preferring private gain to public good. As the Prince says in Lampedusa's *The Leopard*: "I cannot lift a finger in politics. It would only get bitten."

Poor Sicilians knuckled under or emigrated, often flourishing on foreign soil. Millions have conquered the United States with a classic Sicilian combination of contacts, cuisine and cunning, symbolised by the Pizza Connection, the Mafia's imaginative drugs cartel. The heroin distribution and money-laundering ring operated in the guise of an international pizza chain. This is the deadly product served by Sicilian history. As the writer Leonardo Sciascia says: "History has been a wicked stepmother to us Sicilians." Yet it is this heritage of doom, drama and excess that draws visitors to an island marooned between Europe and Africa.

Goethe, too, found Sicily intoxicating, from the Classical temples and Etna's eruptions to the volcanic nature of the Sicilians. "To have seen Italy without seeing Sicily," he wrote, "is not to have seen Italy at all – for Sicily is the key to everything." ❏

PRECEDING PAGES: the Doric temple at Segesta; at anchor off Panarea in the Aeolian Islands; the hilltop town of Centúripe, "the balcony of Sicily"; Norman nobility represented in traditional puppets.
LEFT: a headless Roman and a thoughtful citizen in Catania.

Decisive Dates

20,000–10,000 BC Old Stone Age settlers live in caves on Monte Pellegrino and the Egadi Islands.
4,000–3,000 BC New Stone Age settlers from the eastern Mediterranean arrive on Sicily's east coast.
3,000–2,000 BC Settlers from the Aegean bring metalwork and domesticated animals (Copper Age).
2,000–1,000 BC Bronze Age Sicilians start trading with Mycenean Greeks.
c1250 BC The Siculi (Sicels), Sicani (Sicans) and Elymni (Elymians) settle.
c860 BC Carthaginians (Phoenicians from North

Africa) establish trading sites at Panormus (modern Palermo), Solus (Solunto) and Motya (Mózia).
c734 BC Naxos, the first Greek colony in Sicily, is founded by Chalcidians.
c733 BC Greeks from Corinth found Siracusa.
730–700 BC Other Greeks establish colonies at Megara Hyblaea, Gela, Selinus (modern Selinunte) and Akragas (Agrigento).
5th century BC Height of Greek civilisation in Sicily. Siracusa rivals Athens in power and prestige.
c485 BC Gelon of Gela captures Siracusa; he and Theron of Akragas now control most of Greek Sicily.
480 BC Gela, Akragas and Siracusa defeat the Carthaginians at the battle of Himera.
c450 BC A revolt led by Ducetius, a Sicel, is crushed – the end of native resistance to Greek rule.
415 BC Athens' naval expedition, which besieges Siracusa, is humiliatingly defeated.
409–7 BC Carthage sacks Selinus, Himera, Akragas and Gela. Dionysius takes charge in Siracusa. Plague forces Carthaginians to withdraw.
405–367 BC Dionysius I is Tyrant of Siracusa.
344 BC Corinth sends troops to defend Siracusa: they defeat Carthaginians at the River Crimisus.
310 BC Agathocles of Siracusa defeated by Carthaginians at Ecnomus.
289 BC Mamertini (mercenaries from Campania) seize Messina.
278–275 BC Pyrrhus tries in vain to unite Sicily.
269 BC Hieron II defeats Mamertini, declares himself king of Sicily.

ROME AND BYZANTIUM

254 BC Palermo falls to Rome.
227 BC Sicily is made a Roman province.
218 BC Siracusa supports Carthage against Rome.
212 BC Siracusa falls to the Romans; all of Sicily now ruled by Rome.
138–131 BC Syrian slave Eunus leads first slave revolt against the Romans.
104–99 BC Trifon leads second slave revolt.
44–36 BC Pompey's son, Sextus Pompeius, controls Sardinia, Corsica and Sicily with his fleets.
2nd century AD Spread of Christianity in Sicily.
324–327 Reign of Constantine the Great. The capital of the Empire is moved to Constantinople.
395 Sicily becomes part of the Western Roman Empire.
410 Rome is attacked by the Visigoths.
468 Vandals from North Africa invade Sicily.
493 Sicily is overrun by the Ostrogoths.
535 The Byzantine general Belisarius conquers Sicily for Emperor Justinian of Byzantium.
651 First major Arab raid on Sicily.
726 The Byzantine emperor confiscates all Papal property in Sicily.

ARABS AND NORMANS

831 Palermo falls to the Saracens (Arabs).
842–859 Arabs capture Messina, Modica, Ragusa and Enna.
878 Siracusa is taken by storm and destroyed.
902 Taormina, the last Byzantine stronghold, falls to the Arabs.
965 All of Sicily under Arab control. Palermo is second largest city in the world (after Constantinople).
1061 The Normans land in Sicily: the beginning of 30 years of struggle against the Arabs.

1072 Norman Count Roger de Hauteville (Altavilla) takes Palermo "for Christendom".
1091 Noto, the last major Moslem stronghold, falls to the Normans, who now control all Sicily,
1130 Count Roger's son, Roger II, becomes King of Sicily. Palermo is one of the finest cities in Europe.
1198–1250 Emperor Frederick II rules Sicily.
1266 Charles of Anjou is crowned King of Sicily. (Angevin rule until 1282.)
1282 The Sicilian Vespers. Popular Sicilian uprising against the French.

SPANISH RULE

1302 The Aragonese begin 200-year domination.
1442 Alfonso V, King of Aragon reunites Naples and Sicily and takes the title King of Two Sicilies.
1502 The Spanish crown assumes control of Sicily, but the Barons retain much power.
1513 The Spanish Inquisition visits Sicily.
1647 Anti-Spanish uprising in Palermo is quickly repressed.
1669 Etna erupts, destroying Catania and east coast towns.
1693 Massive earthquake strikes the east.
1713 Treaty of Utrecht. Victor Amadeus II of Piedmont-Savoy becomes King of Sicily.
1720 Duke of Savoy surrenders Sicily for Sardinia. Austrian Viceroys rule.
1734–1860 The Spanish Bourbons rule Sicily through Viceroys.
1759 The Kingdom of Naples and Sicily passes to Ferdinand IV.
1798 Lord Nelson is given the Duchy of Bronte.
1806–15 The British occupation of Sicily.
1814 English-owned distilleries in Marsala begin producing a sherry-like wine.
1816 The Kingdom of the Two Sicilies is created under the Bourbons.

REVOLUTION AND UNIFICATION

1848–49 Sicilian Revolution.
1860 Garibaldi and his *Mille* (1,000) land at Marsala, and force the Bourbons off Sicily.
1861 Sicily joins Kingdom of Italy.
1900 Emigration is the highest in Europe.
1908 Messina destroyed by an earthquake, which leaves around 84,000 victims.
1911 Population census finds that 58 percent of Sicilians are illiterate.

PRECEDING PAGES: a German map of Sicily from 1650. **LEFT:** a gleeful Greek gorgon from Gela. **RIGHT:** Ferdinand I, King of the Two Sicilies, in 1816.

1915 Italy joins the Allies in World War I.
1922–43 Fascism in Italy under Benito Mussolini.
1943 Invasion of Sicily by the Allies.
1946 Sicily is granted regional autonomy by the Italian Parliament.
1950 Land reforms: estates over 300 hectares (740 acres) are seized and redistributed as small-holdings.
1951–75 One million Sicilians emigrate to northern Italy and northern Europe.
1957 Italy becomes a founder member of the EEC.
1968 Disastrous earthquake in the Belice Valley.
1973 Parliamentary anti-Mafia Commission set up.
1982 Mafia kills General dalla Chiesa. The "super-

grass" Tommaso Buscetta first denounces Cosa Nostra to Sicilian anti-Mafia pool of judges.
1986 The Mafia maxi-trials (*maxiprocessi*) indict hundreds.
1992 Mafia assassinations of two judges and Euro MP Salvatore Lima. Eruption of Mount Etna.
1993 Arrest of Totò Riina, the Sicilian Godfather.
1995 Giulio Andreotti, seven times Prime Minister of Italy, is brought to Palermo to face charges of collaborating with the Mafia.
1996 National election won by the Left, after 50 years in opposition. The dome of Noto Cathedral collapses.
1999 After a four-year trial, Andreotti is acquitted of Mafia involvement. ❑

BEGINNINGS

The early history of the island is the story of conflicting tribes

with diverse origins – divisions that amazingly survive in modern Sicily

Sicilian history is a cavalcade of invasion. The Sicani, Siculi, Elymni, Carthaginians and Greeks were the first. The invasions continued with the second wave of Carthaginians followed by Romans, sundry Italians, mercenaries and myriad slaves, Jews, Vandals, Saracens, Normans and Spaniards. Some, like the Vandals, did little more than vandalise, but the majority remained for long periods, adding another rich layer to Sicily's extraordinary fusion of genes and culture.

The islanders may not have been great shapers of their own destiny but the powers of Sicilian subversiveness were substantial. In response to invasion, Sicily proved itself to be a ball and chain around its conquerors' necks: sullen, slothful, uncooperative, a millstone dragging its rulers into futile conflict while leaving noble Sicilians free to live in their own luxurious private theatre.

Strategic Sicily

Children spot Sicily on a map as the "ball" at the toe of the "boot" of Italy. But their grasp of Classical history would be better served by reflecting on the closeness of Cap Bon, the tip of North Africa. The sea is only 160 km (100 miles) wide; from high ground, one can gaze across to ancient Carthage, where Tunis now stands, and contemplate a long-dead rival.

The straits separating Sicily from Africa are a bottleneck. The Mediterranean Sea is therefore not round but kidney-shaped. When the known world was limited to the lands lining the Mediterranean, the boundaries were Phoenicia, modern-day Lebanon, and the Straits of Gibraltar. Sicily was not only in the centre but divided "the world" into two. The ancient superpowers could settle for domination of one side of the sea or the other. To control both, they had to possess Sicily.

Sicily's size is diminished by notions of a

LEFT: a Phoenician head from the 6th century BC found on Mozia. **RIGHT:** even older – anthropomorphic dancers in a Stone Age cave drawing.

soccer ball. In modern terms it is not huge: a third the size of Ireland, a quarter of Cuba; but to the ancients it was almost a continent. Ancient Sicily was big enough for enemies like the Phoenicians and Greeks to occupy separate parts. There were even cases of two unrelated wars being fought on the island at the same

time. Yet Sicily was never quite big enough to be a power in its own right, even though Siracusa (Syracuse) was once the greatest city in Europe. The island has always been at the mercy of larger forces swirling around its shores, and has been dragged into practically every major Mediterranean war as an adjunct to one or other of the adversaries.

All nations around the Mediterranean (and others too) have shaped Sicilian history; all the languages spoken around the Mediterranean have been spoken in Sicily. Most historians agree that Sicily has been subjugated and plundered for its strategic site, fertile lands, art treasures, and endless supply of slaves, mercenaries and feudal peasants. Yet the image of a pathetic Sicilian scapegoat should not go unchallenged. A more radical line of historical enquiry might be: did she fall or was she pushed?

To most foreign historians, she was pushed, forced to cohabit with brutal foreign bedfellows. But, as Voltaire suggested, perhaps she even jumped willingly into the conqueror's arms. Sensing a slight to macho Southern pride, modern Sicilian historians have fought back. They cite instances of spirited resistance: the Great Slave Revolts against the Greeks and Romans and the infamous Sicilian Vespers, the uprising against the French. More dubiously,

the rise of the Mafia has also been credited to Sicilian resourcefulness.

Yet sleeping with the enemy is the classic Sicilian defence. The Phoenician temple priestesses in Erice did it literally. Later Sicilians have been more subtle. The Mafia cooperated fully with the American landings in 1943. In the same year, the Italian army, the Communists and the Mafia buried the hatchet and formed an unholy alliance against the threat of Sicilian separatism. But this is not common prostitution: it is the arrogance of a courtesan who can retreat into the purity of her head while the sordid world flounders below.

Much like aggrieved native Americans on

Columbus Day, the Sicilians do not accept that they were "discovered" by the ancient Greeks. The controversy has reverberations to this day. Depending on where Sicilians live, there is still an identification with one or other of the early racial groups. Ancestry matters in Sicily, even if larded with two millennia of intervening myth.

As a new land open to conquest, Sicily was the America of the ancient world. It was invaded in turn by Phoenicians, Greeks and Romans. But it was also a land with a disgruntled indigenous people who did not take kindly to being swamped by a refined yet more powerful culture. The native Sicilians had their own deities, it was just that the Greeks marketed their gods better.

Mythological tales have Sicily founded by Vulcan's forge, by the Promethean god Hephaestus or by the winged Daedalus from Crete. But more significant is the cultural distinction between Siculi and Sicani, Sicily's foremost native peoples. This ancestral mystique is still at the heart of the islanders' *Sicilianità*, their innate "Sicilian-ness".

Racial splits

There were three indigenous groups with separate cultures and languages. The Elymni (Elymians) held sway in the northwest; also in the west were the Sicani (Sicans); and the east was home to the Siculi (Sicels). While the Sicani were the most hostile to Greek settlers, the Siculi and even the Elymni were Hellenised by contact with the Greeks. The natives were united only in mutual dislike.

The Sicani were an ancient Semitic race, possibly immigrants from Libya and Syria.

TROJAN REFUGEES?

The Elymni are the most mysterious of the early Sicilians. Present from the Iron Age onwards, they were based around Segesta and Erice, where their city walls remain. Their origins are disputed, with conflicting claims linking them to Mycenaean or Minoan civilisations and even to Asia Minor. According to the Greek historian Thucydides, the Elymni were refugees from Troy, who escaped from the city when the Greeks took it with the Trojan Horse. The Elymni were clearly the most open to Phoenician culture but found it expedient to accommodate the Greeks, with the exception of the hated colony at Selinunte.

Their main colony was Sant'Angelo Muxaro in Agrigento province, where myth and history merge. Daedalus supposedly escaped Crete by making waxen wings and arrived in Sant'Angelo to a red-carpet welcome from King Kokalos of the Sicani. What is beyond doubt is that this belligerent race resisted Greek influence and fought against such Hellenised cities as Akragas (Agrigento).

The Siculi came from Liguria or Latium in the 13th century before Christ. According to Thucydides, they "defeated the Sicani in battle, drove them to the south and west of the island, and renamed it Sicily instead of Sicania". These seafarers and farmers were gradually Hellenised by the Greek settlers on the eastern coast. However, in Dorian Greek settlements such as Siracusa, the Siculi were reduced to serfdom. Even the Ionian settlements rarely granted them Greek citizenship.

Still, in exceptional cases the Greeks elevated the Siculi from the status of barbarians (non-Greeks) to persons qualified to marry Greeks, the ultimate accolade. The Siculi worshipped pan-Hellenic gods, as witnessed by a temple to Demeter at Morgantina near Enna. Sicily abounds in Siculi settlements, with the best one in Ispica.

Phoenicians from Africa

Sicily was the exception to the rule that these seafarers, having founded Carthage, were keener on trading than colonising. The old Carthaginian sector occupied northwestern Sicily and was closely involved with the neighbouring Sicani race. They only fortified their settlements at Solunto, Motya (Mozia) and Panormus (Palermo) when their livelihood was threatened by Greek expansion.

The Phoenicians became "Carthaginians" as their North African colony prospered and eclipsed their Levantine home. Northern Sicily is dotted with Punic (Carthaginian) remains. Erice has the base of a Phoenician temple and shrine to Astarte, the goddess of fertility, while commemorative steles and stonework remain

LEFT: tombs excavated by the Sicani around 1100 BC, near modern Caltabellotta. **RIGHT:** the earliest Carthaginian tomb, discovered on Mozia.

TOMB DIGGERS

One of the earliest and grandest achievements of the Siculi was the vast necropolis of Pantálica, near Siracusa, which has 5,000 burial chambers, the oldest dating from the 13th century BC.

at Solunto. Lilybaeum, modern Marsala, boasts a necropolis and a sophisticated Punic ship.

On the island colony of Motya (modern Mozia), the base for attacks against the Greeks, is a Punic harbour as well as the notorious sacrificial altar. Undoubtedly, there were sensationalist aspects of their culture, such as sacred prostitution and human sacrifice. The jars of charred infants would imply that Motya was not an ideal place to bring up a baby.

Since then, the balance of power has swung

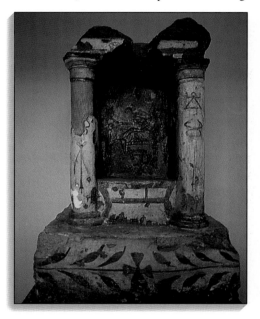

from Siculi to Sicani and back again. In black and white terms, it is a split between Greek Eastern Sicily and Arab Western Sicily. During Hellenisation, the Siculi, the most recent settlers, triumphed as the dominant culture. However, under Roman rule, the Sicani in the west bounced back. Under the Byzantines, the "Greek" east of the island was in the ascendant while with the advent of the Arabs, Western Sicily had its revenge.

Today, the racial split affects everything, from manners and morals to modern trade and the Mafia. Since Sicily is now named after the Hellenised Siculi race, it is clear that Greek culture ultimately triumphed, in name at least. ❏

MAGNA GRAECIA

In the 6th and 5th centuries BC, Sicily saw a flowering of Greek civilisation that rivalled the achievements of Athens and Corinth

The Sicily of Magna Graecia ("Greater Greece") had a population of more than 3 million – a greater number than Athens and Sparta combined. The islanders, even the smouldering Sicilians and Phoenicians who monopolised cities like Panormus (Palermo), spoke Greek and practised Greek art. Agriculture flourished and the island became the granary of the Mediterranean. Athenian prosperity, then paying for the building of the magnificent Acropolis, depended on funds siphoned off from Sicily.

But none of this promise was self-evident when the Greek migrants drifted to Sicily, more as an escape from civil strife than as part of a master plan for domination of the West. Sicily's eastern flanks were settled by Ionian-speaking Greeks from the Peloponnese while Dorian colonies favoured the south coast. They were unaware that there were already Phoenician settlements on the western shore.

The first colony was Naxos (734 BC), founded by Chalcidian Greeks. After Naxos came other east coast colonies also with Ionian links: Zankle (Messina), Leontinoi (Lentini) and Katane (Catania). On the south coast were Dorian colonies settled by Greeks from Rhodes and Crete: Gela, Akragas (Agrigento), Selinunte and Heraclea Minoa. Syrakusai, the greatest colony of all (Siracusa to the Italians or Syracuse to us) was founded by Corinthians a year after Naxos.

Centuries of warfare

These colonies were ruled by "tyrants", a term that in its original sense simply meant men who seized power instead of inheriting it. In so far as the colonists stayed in touch with home, it was with a specific city or island. So Sicilian settlements living cheek by jowl often had conflicting loyalties, which erupted whenever

LEFT: Venus Anadiomene, a Roman copy of a Greek original, in the Museo Archeológico, Siracusa.
RIGHT: the Trinacria, the ancient symbol of Sicily, on a bowl in the same museum.

Greek fought Greek at home, as they often did.

Sicily's first sharp taste of what the rest of its history would be occurred in 480 BC, when the Carthaginians mounted a massive attack on Greece's western flank – which included Sicily. The Carthaginian commander Hamilcar set sail for Sicily with an army of 300,000 mercenaries

in 200 galleys and 3,000 transport ships. He besieged Himera (Termini Imerese) by land and sea, prompting the resident tyrant Theron to appeal for help from Gelon, his counterpart in the powerful Greek city of Siracusa.

Gelon's forced march through the mountains with 50,000 men and 5,000 cavalry is a minor military epic, and he was soon in a position to throw a cordon around the Carthaginian siege. Hamilcar, meanwhile, had asked Selinunte, "the unfaithful (Greek) city of the west", to back up his forces.

Sicilian military history is full of trickery, and Gelon set the standard with a Trojan Horse approach: his cavalry masqueraded as Hamilcar's reinforcements from Selinunte. The Carthaginian ranks opened up, allowing Gelon's interlopers to charge the beached Carthaginian ships and torch them. The column of smoke was Gelon's signal to bring his men storming down; 150,000 Carthaginians were slain in the battle.

Hamilcar died a Phoenician death at Himera: "He spread out his arms and prayed to the setting sun, and threw himself into the flames upon the altar the last and noblest burnt-offering of his own sacrifice." To celebrate his vic-

COINCIDENCE

Gelon's astounding military victory over Hamilcar took place on the same day in 480 BC as the equally unlikely triumph of the Greek fleet over the Persians at Salamis.

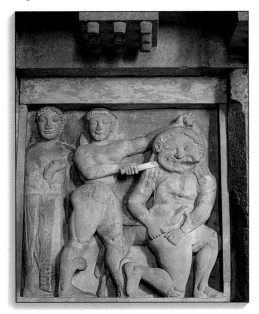

tory, Gelon built the temples of Demeter and Persephone in Siracusa on the strength of Carthage's cash indemnity. Carthage did not attack again for 70 years.

The victory confirmed Gelon as the most powerful figure in the Greek world. After Himera, he adopted a conciliatory attitude towards Phoenician settlements on Sicily, notably Panormus (Palermo) and Motya (Mozia). In return, the Carthaginians were required to build two temples to Athene and to sacrifice animals rather than human babies. But babies were sacrified long afterwards: the archaeological evidence comes from the Tophet (sacrificial cemetery) excavated at Motya.

Fun and games

Gelon's successor, Hieron I (478–466 BC) basked in his glory and forged unity among some Greek Sicilian city states. The Sicilians, especially Siracusa, dominated the Olympiads, excelling at chariot races and mule cart racing. Officially the athletes competed for token prizes, but sponsorship was as lucrative then as now, so a winner could expect to enjoy free housing forever. Victory celebrations lasted a year, and the foremost poets of the day were commissioned to compose verses in the victor's honour. The poet Simonides felt his muse leave him when asked to write an ode to a victorious mule. He managed an opening line, "All hail, ye daughters of wind-swift mares", and went on to finish the poem with no further references to the beast.

The temples of Selinunte, Segesta and Agrigento, which are the lasting monuments of this Golden Age of Tyranny, did not match the architectural subtlety of the Parthenon in Athens, but are splendid nonetheless. The ruins of Selinunte, south of Marsala, are the remains of seven temples, which fell like dominoes after an earthquake.

The dawn of democracy

The Greek tyrannies collapsed, said Aristotle, because in the absence of orderly rules of succession they fell victim to dynastic struggles. Within a few years of Hieron I's death virtually every city had sacked its tyrant, and the island moved *en bloc* into an experiment with a new form of government: democracy.

The democracy in question was hardly a multiparty system, majority rule, one-man, one-vote – still less, one-woman, one-vote. Only an elite qualified for the vote. Slaves, even freed men, were definitely out, as were the Sicilian-born descendants of immigrants. Nor did children of foreigners married to bona-fide citizens qualify.

But Greek-style democracy was present in Sicily. Public debate was lively and free, and the island produced orators of whom the mainland Greeks were envious. The ballot box

LEFT: Perseus slays Medusa, from Temple C at Selinunte. **RIGHT:** detail from an Attic vase in the Museo Archeológico at Gela.

existed, in that a stipulated proportion of enfranchised citizens could write down the name of someone they thought ought to be banished for a fixed term for the public good.

Great slave revolts

The Sicilian experiment with democracy lasted 70 years and stirred long dormant instincts. The Hellenised but still distinct native inhabitants felt aggrieved. They never attained citizenship so could not aspire to being second-class citizens. "Sicilian Power" was born, personifed by Ducetius around 450 BC.

The native Sicilians had been pushed back into the interior by Greeks who liked living on the coast. Ducetius popped up as the self-proclaimed "King of the Sicilians". Within six years he had persuaded several Siculi towns to back him. Growing militancy led to an armed attack on Enna and Akragas. The rebels enjoyed modest success before being overwhelmed by a punitive expedition despatched by Siracusa.

Ducetius was spared on condition that he left town; the city offered him a pension to live in Corinth, "home" to most Siracusans. He cut an exotic figure in exile, and such was his appeal that Corinthians joined him in a clandestine

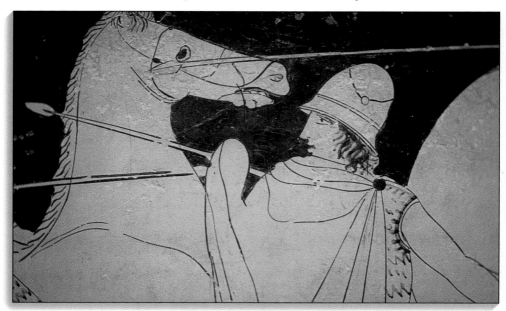

COMIC DEATH OF TRAGIC WRITER

The lure of quick commissions attracted the finest Greek literary and artistic talents to affluent Sicily. The founder of Greek tragic drama, the Athenian playwrite Aeschylus, was among them, although he probably left Greece downcast after losing the tragedy-writing competition to his young rival Sophocles. In any case he died an extraordinary death at Gela in 456 BC.

An eagle seized a tortoise and, looking down from a great height for a rock on which to drop and break it, mistook Aeschylus's bald pate for a polished stone. That was the end of the tragedian, who was given a moving funeral and monument by the people of Gela.

return to Sicily, with the aim of founding a colony on Sicilian Liberation lines. But when Akragas was attacked by his rebels, the fear that Siracusa was involved led Akragas to declare war on the senior city.

Athenian adventures

Sicilian cities were always ready to fight at the drop of a hat. The Athenians were only too happy to intervene for their own ends, particularly as Siracusa emerged as a rival. But remoteness from Greek mainland politics meant that Sicilians avoided alignment with either the Dorian (Spartan) or Ionian (Athenian) factions. Athens had a political stake in

Sicily and, after defending its colony of Leon-tinoi against Siracusa in 427 BC, desired further influence. The quarrelsome Sicilian cities of Selinunte and Segesta provided a pretext. When Selinunte asked Siracusa for help, Segesta went running to Athens, offering to pay the costs of military aid, plus a handsome premium. Prudent Athens sent representatives to look into Segesta's creditworthiness.

They were received in Segesta with a show of breathtaking splendour. They were led up to the temple of Aphrodite on Mount Eryx (Erice) above Drepanon (Trápani) and shown a vast collection of sacred vessels made of gold and

silver and dripping with precious stones. The treasures were too sacred, they were told, to be touched or even to be viewed except from a reverential distance. The ambassadors were then marched off to sumptuous banquets, everywhere eating off gold and silver plate.

In Athens, the ambassadors had no hesitation in recommending that ships be put at the disposal of Segesta. On the question of hard payment, the city had admittedly given them only enough to cover the cost of the first month but there could be no doubt that the balance would be forthcoming. Unfortunately, the temple treasures were fakes. The gold and silver plate was a single, recycled set borrowed from the Siculi.

As for the silver bullion provided as a deposit, that was also borrowed. However, the fraud was not exposed and the 250 ships which sailed from Piraeus with 25,000 men was the largest Greek armada to have set forth.

But the commanders dithered, disappeared in search of booty and only after two years at sea did they finally reach Siracusa. So many men had sickened, died or jumped ship that morale was woeful. In the meantime, Sparta had sent troops to Siracusa to organise defences. The battle for control of Siracusa's great harbour took place in 413 BC and was the greatest victory of Greeks over Greeks.

The Athenians were humiliated and never returned home. The generals were executed and the 7,000 captured troops were lowered by crane into the stone quarries of Siracusa, a sheer drop of 30 metres (100 ft) into a hell which was stifling hot by day and freezing at night. They were held there for 10 weeks, after which the survivors were sold into slavery.

Carthage strikes back

It was second nature to the Sicilian Greeks that, once the Athenian threat was seen off, they reverted to fighting among themselves. It was equally in character that two wars should be going on at once. One was a continuation of the wounds opened by Ionians against Dorians on the Greek mainland; more predictably, the other was between Segesta and Selinunte, implacable enemies.

Segesta turned to Carthage for help, thus triggering the second Carthaginian invasion. Hannibal, grandson of Hamilcar, had no grudge against Selinunte, but he had a score to settle with the Greeks, in particular with Himera, the city where his grandfather died. In 409 BC Hannibal arrived with a mercenary force at Lilybaeum, where Carthaginian invaders landed almost as a routine. He made quick work of Selinunte. In fact, it ceased to exist as a city from that day.

Then Hannibal turned his attention to personal vengeance and breached Himera's defences. "A massacre of course began," says the historian Edward Freeman. "But a mere massacre was not what he wanted." The 3,000 male survivors were taken to where Hamilcar had died, where they were tortured and offered as sacrifices to the memory of the dead general.

On his return the following year, Hannibal

attacked Akragas, second only to Siracusa among Sicilian cities but rusty in war. The ensuing siege was interrupted by Hannibal's death. In the course of digging trenches, the Carthaginians exposed corpses. A plague swept through the camp, and Hannibal was one of the casualties. Hostilities were suspended for a decent burial, and demoralised Carthaginians revived only when Hannibal's successor, Himilkon, showed that he meant business by sacrificing his own son to their beloved god Moloch.

EUREKA!

The Greek mathematician and engineer Archimedes was born in Siracusa in 287 BC. He was killed by the invading Romans in the same city in 212 BC.

out the military mess. He immediately crossed the Straits to Leontini to round up all men under 40 to serve as his bodyguards. Siracusa had another tyrant.

Dionysius I reorganised the army, but nothing could stop the Carthaginian advance on Siracusa. The city was only saved by a return of the plague among the Carthaginian forces. With over half the army dead, the vanquished force slunk home to Africa. Dionysius strengthened his position by capturing and destroying the Phoenician base at Motya.

Akragas's pampered soldiers lasted surprisingly well, and the city fell after an eight-month siege. While a huge amount of art and treasure was shipped back to Carthage, the city was not gutted like Himera. Akragas was a byword for luxury in Magna Graecia so it was reward enough to raid the temples and drain the legendary wine cellars dry.

The Siracusan generals were blamed for Akragas's defeat in speeches by a spirited demagogue, one Dionysius. Almost inevitably, in 405 BC, Dionysius was given full powers to sort

LEFT: a stylised Greek bust. **ABOVE:** bronze ram found in Siracusa, now in the Museo Archeológico, Palermo.

After a reign of 38 years, Dionysius' death was followed a chaos of disputed succession. Timoleon (345–336 BC) restored some sort of democracy to the island, and imported settlers from Italy and Greece. But a later tyrant, Agathocles (315–289 BC) took Sicily back to the bellicose old days, seizing portions of Sicily still occupied by Carthaginians, and waging wars on the Italian mainland and in North Africa.

Finally Hieron II (265–215 BC) brought some measure of stability, calming the warring Sicilian cities, striking a treaty between Siracusa and Carthage, and eventually making an alliance with the new, fast-expanding Mediterranean superpower – Rome. ❑

BUILDING FOR POSTERITY

The Ancient Greeks who held sway in Sicily left the island with a heritage of noble buildings and domestic architecture that is unrivalled anywhere

Of the three great ancient civilisations that held sway in Sicily, it is the Greeks who left the most enduring architectural legacy. The buildings and artifacts of the Carthaginians were largely destroyed by Greeks – an exception being the remains at Mozia, including fine pebble mosaics (left).

And little remains of Roman temples and public buildings – ironically because of Rome's more sophisticated building technology. Where the Greeks built with solid stone, the Romans used cement within brick casings and faced buildings with a veneer of high-quality stone or marble. Once this was plundered by later generations, the cement and brick soon crumbled to dust. The most enduring Roman remains include indestructable amphitheatres built into hillsides (e.g. Siracusa) and lavish additions to Greek buildings (e.g. the theatre at Taormina).

The Greeks built most of their public buildings in the Doric style, with simple, austere lines and a perfect harmony of proportion. The earliest large-scale temple (575 BC) is at Siracusa. Its imposing design was reproduced, with variations, over two centuries at Himera, Segesta, Akgragas (Agrigento) and elsewhere, but most splendidly at Selinunte, where at least nine majestic temples were built in the period 580–480 BC.

△ **SEAT WITH A VIEW**
Segesta's wonderfully situated Greek theatre (3rd century BC). The tiers of seats face west, towards the Bay of Castellamare.

▽ **RECENTLY RESTORED**
Temple E at Selinunte, dedicated to Hera in around 480 BC, was toppled by an earthquake but re-erected in 1957.

△ **KING OF THE CASTLE**
The mighty Castello Eurialo, northeast of Siracusa, was part of the city's defences built by Dionysius the Elder.

◁ **STONE SPOUT**
A carved stone lion's head water-spout from the 5th-century BC Temple of Victory at Himera.

◁ **WELL-KEPT SECRET**
The Temple of Concord (with modern Agrigento in the background) is one of the best preserved of all Greek temples, anywhere. It was built around 430 BC.

▽ **PLAY TIME**
The theatre at Taormina was built by Greeks for drama, but later enlarged by Romans who used it for circus games.

▽ **FALLEN GIANT**
The Temple of Olympian Zeus at Agrigento once had 38 of these colossal *telamones* (giants) set on its outer wall.

Sicily's archeological museums are rich with artifacts from many periods and many cultures – Bronze Age, Phoenician, Greek, Roman, Etruscan, and more besides.

Palermo's Museo Archeológico contains Carthaginian and Egyptian remains, some Roman sarcophagi (above) and sculptures, notably a huge Emperor Claudius enthroned like Zeus, Greek vases and statues, and art from various temples (the friezes from Selinunte are particularly fine).

Siracusa's museum probably has Sicily's most diverse collection, featuring sensual statues, gruesome theatrical masks, huge burial urns and poignant sarcophagi.

Agrigento's museum has intriguing Bronze-Age finds, painted Attic vases, carvings and statues, and Roman tombs and mosaics. The highlight is a huge *telemon* from the Temple of Zeus.

△ **SPECIAL EFFECTS**
The Roman amphitheatre at Siracusa, carved partly from the hillside. The central pit was for stage machinery for spectacles.

▷ **MUSEUM PIECE**
A red-figure Attic *krater* from Palermo's superb collection of Greek vases.

ROME AND BYZANTIUM

Sicily was the first Roman province, and remained under Rome's sway for seven centuries, until the Eastern Empire brought Greece back to the island

I n 264 BC the Punic Wars triggered momentous changes in Sicily. Thanks to a treaty with Carthage, Siracusa escaped the horrors of the First Punic War but northern Sicily was not spared. With Rome's support, Messina tried to evict the local Carthaginian garrison, thus invoking the wrath of Carthage. The ensuing

clash between Carthaginians and Romans was the start of the Punic Wars, which ceased only when Carthage was obliterated.

Sandwiched beween the rival powers, Sicily was the battleground. Popular images of the Punic Wars tend to be dominated by Hannibal's elephantine attack on Rome but the preliminaries to the finale in Carthage were fought in Sicily. When it was over, Sicily was firmly within the Roman Empire.

Rome's takeover during the wars was typically methodical. Akragas (Agrigento) fell in 261 BC and 25,000 of its inhabitants were sold into slavery. Camarina, Panormus (Palermo) and Selinunte followed over the next decade.

During the 30 years that Hannibal the Great was at large in Italy with his army and his single elephant, Sicily was the vital link between Europe and North Africa. The Carthaginians fought tooth and nail for Sicily, relying on traditional west coast sympathies to support its forces. Carthage had 40,000 troops and 200 ships on the island but ultimately, after a two-year siege, Siracusa fell to Rome in 212 BC.

Vast quantities of art and statuary were torn from temples, public buildings and private houses in Siracusa and elsewhere and shipped back to Rome. The Greek mainland had by then been overrun by semi-barbaric Macedonians; Athens was in decline, and Sicily had the finest collection of Greek art anywhere. According to Livy, the wide-eyed excitement caused by the booty unwrapped in Rome was the beginning of Rome's infatuation with Greek civilisation.

In 210 BC, by which time Akragas had fallen, the Roman commander reported that not a single Carthaginian remained in Sicily. The island became Rome's first province (as opposed to being incorporated in the republic) because it was too Hellenised.

Roman rule

Sicily was later described by Cato as "the Republic's granary, the nurse at whose breast the Roman people is fed". But the Romans did not operate a scorched-earth policy against the earlier cultures. Greek language and traditions prevailed despite Latinisation. Even old Phoenician-Carthagian traces remained in Roman Sicily, notably the cult of sacred prostitution at the temple at Eryx (Erice).

The province was governed by a praetor answerable only to the Roman Senate. He was not allowed to buy slaves in his province except to replace those who died. (The ordinary citizen probably kept about 200 slaves.) The governor was not to engage in business, and he could neither marry a local woman nor bring a wife out to join him. Administration went on much as before with many Greek features retained.

The Romans accepted that all Sicilians spoke

Greek and did not attempt to force Latin down their throats. The Roman administrators used interpreters. Sicily retained the Greek calendar with its festival days, and the records of the Olympic Games show that the odd Sicilian was still winning events.

In 138 BC, one of the richest men in Sicily was Damophilus of Enna, a ruthless slave master. Whipped up by Eunus, his Syrian court jester, 400 slaves rioted, murdered their master and joined other dissident slaves. Eunus was hailed king and forced slave owners to manufacture weapons for the rebel cause or to face execution. Eunus was joined by Cleon, and the two rebels commanded more than 100,000 men. They brushed aside the Roman militia and won control of Morgantina and Tauromenium (Taormina) as well as Enna.

Cleon was declared commander-in-chief while Eunus enjoyed kingship, complete with diadem and his own coinage. Eunus's "reign" lasted seven years but Rome finally sent an army of 20,000 against him. The slaves resisted at Tauromenium (Taormina) and Enna but thousands were captured and thrown from the battlements. Yet the Romans were lenient with Eunus who was merely imprisoned. Although rebels were executed, Rome limited its revenge in order to conserve the supply of slave labour.

Revolt of the freemen

The second Sicilian revolt occurred in ironic circumstances. In 104 BC, Rome was under attack by Germanic tribes and needed fighting men, but slave hunting had caused a shortage of this prime resource. To help, the Senate freed slaves throughout the Roman provinces – and in Sicily they promptly rebelled. Although 4,000 newly enfranchised Roman soldiers defected, the revolt failed. The captured rebels were shipped to Rome to fight wild animals for the entertainment of spectators at the circus.

Far more damaging to Sicily was the civil war between Octavian (the future emperor Augustus) and Sextus Pompeius, who seized the island in 44 BC. He blockaded Italy, interrupting Sicily's vital grain exports and crippling the island economically. When Sextus was finally defeated by Octavian's admiral Vipsanius Agrippa in 36 BC, the new emperor's retribution on the Sicilians was severe.

After the defeat of Antony and Cleopatra, veterans discharged from the victorious army of Augustus Caesar were given smallholdings in Sicily and undoubtedly added to the process of Latinisation. Moves to make Sicilians full Roman citizens were dropped when they ran into stiff (Roman) opposition. The compromise was to give certain cities a higher standing than their

REBEL WITH A CAUSE

The slave uprising of 104 BC attracted 90,000 rebels in Italy. The gladiator Spartacus, their leader, was immortalised on film centuries later by Kirk Douglas.

country cousins. Palermo, Agrigento and Catania gained influence and industry but Segesta lost favour, despite the continued existence of its fabled sacred prostitutes.

The first tourists

History is silent about the next five centuries of Roman rule. In common with the rest of the Empire, Sicilians became full Roman citizens in AD 212 – a sign that the island was, in Roman eyes at least, simply an extension of Italy. It acquired a reputation as a Roman tourist resort; the emperor Caligula was especially fond of it. A tantalising glimpse of Sicily as the playground of rich Romans is the Imperial Villa

LEFT: a spirited Roman fresco in Palermo archaeological museum. **RIGHT:** part of a Roman mosaic, Marsala.

at Casale (*see page 215*). Enough survives to give a vivid impression of a pleasure palace of 50 rooms on four levels. Mosaics show a phantasmagoria of bathing, dancing, fishing, hunting, wine-pressing, music and drama – a vision of paradise as a wealthy, contented pagan would see it while relaxing on holiday.

Heathen hordes

Whoever was occupying the Villa at Casale in the 5th century may well have had to leave in a hurry because the tranquillity of *Pax Romana* in Sicily exploded under the onslaught of a people who are remembered as the unmitigated louts of Western history – the Vandals. This infamous tribe, exiled from Germany, first conquered North Africa, then in AD 468 used Sicily as a springboard back to Europe. The Vandals are blamed for a common sight in museums of antiquity, statues with broken noses.

Meanwhile, Rome and the rest of Italy had fallen to another Germanic race, the Goths, who eventually expanded their rule to Sicily, expelling the Vandals. Under the Goths, the Sicilians endured a century of uneasy peace.

When Italy became too chaotic under the Goths to remain the seat of the Empire, the Emperor decamped to Constantinople. Byzan-

UNDERGROUND RELIGION

Christianity on the island probably first took root in the 2nd century AD, among Jewish communities in Eastern Sicily. The first images of the faith appear on tombs in the catacombs of Siracusa. The sculpted sarcophagi found in San Giovanni catacombs suggest a clumsy striving for biblical storytelling.

In AD 313, after Constantine's edict legitimising Christianity, embryonic Byzantine religious art emerged from the darkness of the catacombs to take its place in the churches of Eastern Sicily. St Marcianus of Siracusa and St Agata of Catania were the focus of flourishing cults.

tium, as the Eastern Empire was named, was in a real sense New Greece, and the old empire was abandoned to a long line of foreign occupiers. From here, the Greek Orthodox Church emerged as a spiritual pole to justify Sicilian antagonism to an increasingly secular and rapacious Rome.

Welcome relief

The Byzantine general Belisarius invaded Sicily in AD 535 in the name of Emperor Justinian. The Sicilians, still Greek at heart, looked on the Byzantines both as kith and kin and as welcome relief. Only the Goth garrison in Palermo put up any resistance. Belisarius dealt with them by hoisting small boats full of archers to the mastheads of his ships so that they could fire over the city's low parapets.

In AD 651, Byzantine control was threatened by Arab raids. Pope Martin, who owned vast estates in Sicily, sent troops south to meet the Arabs, who retreated with their booty. The Byzantine Emperor Constans II, at loggerheads with the Pope, contrived to make the Pope's intervention look like collusion with the Arabs. He had the Pope arrested, sent to Constantinople and executed. Constans then took the momentous decision to turn the clock back three centuries and return the capital of the

conquest confirmed Sicily's eastern orientation, symbolised by Greek language and liturgy. Yet, like the Romans before them, the Byzantines exploited the rich Sicilian estates.

Byzantine art

Visitors to Byzantine Sicily noted the women's love of ornament. Their jewels were both a testament to the skills of Byzantine goldsmiths and a worldly counterpoint to the shimmering church mosaics. Contrary to belief, the art of the period is well served by Sicily, which has its share of cupolas emblazoned with austere Greek bishops and inscrutable saints. In church

Empire to the West. His court settled at Siracusa in 662 but Sicilians' visions of glory were soon dispelled. Constans seized property, taxed extortionately and sold debtors into slavery. It was a slave who redressed the balance in AD 668. Constans was being soaped in his bath when the slave picked up the soap box and brought it down on the Emperor's head.

Constans's successor returned the capital to Constantinople for the next 750 years, while Sicily reverted to Papal administration and produced a string of Popes. The Byzantine

apses, Christ Pantocrator offers his benediction in a universe of gold. Early Byzantine art is represented by sarcophagi or frescoes of wide-eyed madonnas languishing on peeling walls. The secular sphere is recalled by Byzantine baths, homes and jewellery but church art and architecture are pre-eminent.

Early Byzantine art is a maze, a question of secrets and ciphers rather than art. More accurately, it is a mosaic, an enigmatic art form beloved by Byzantine craftsmen in Sicily. Arab and native mosaicists created a fusion of Eastern and Christian art that epitomises the rich Byzantine aesthetic. This secret symbolism developed in the deserts of Egypt and Syria.

LEFT: bull mosaic in Imperial Villa, Piazza Armerina.
ABOVE: the splendour of La Matorana church, Palermo.

These early Christians were inspired by mystery rather than a sense of space. Perspective, natural colours and forms were sacrificed to an iconic worship of the mysterious nature of God. The Orient brought the attachment to icons that has never left Sicily.

According to the art historian Egon Sendler, this is "not an opposition of East and West, Orthodoxy and Catholicism, more a case of complementarity". Yet, with the capital of the Empire in Constantinople, Eastern influences predominated.

CHURCH SHAPES

Byzantine basilicas with a typical Greek cross plan are found only in the east of island. More characteristic in Sicily are the cube-shaped churches echoing models in North Africa and Sardinia.

Sicilian Byzantine art, however, is also a stylised variant on Roman art. As it was infused with a new spirituality, it gained in confidence and artistry. New symbolism emerges: pagan themes are erased or simply subsumed. The lyre-playing Orpheus is Jesus the good shepherd while the sacrificial lamb is the love of Christ. The vines representing rites of renewal and Bacchic sensuality symbolise the Resurrection. Imperial triumph becomes Christ in Majesty, with Christ Pantocrator resplendent in blues and golds. The golden backdrop portrays God's grandeur as a stream of light.

In essence, vigorous Classical naturalism ceded to Eastern stylisation, with realism replaced by decorative patterns and increasing abstraction. Symbolism supplanted Greek Classical beauty: three-dimensionality was an irrelevance; faces became inscrutable masks that gazed inward in contemplation. In Sicily's churches, isolated, floating figures are silhouetted against gold backgrounds.

Byzantine architecture used massive domes with square bases, spires, minarets and rounded arches. However, Sicily's rich heritage allows it to bend all the rules. In Catania, the cathedral plunders Roman and Byzantine columns while Santa Maria della Rotonda, a frescoed basilica, incorporates the Roman baths. Whilst there is no early masterpiece to rival the mosaics in Ravenna, Sicily has a wider range of artefacts. Palermo's Palazzo Abatellis has some luminous mosaics, from serene madonnas to stony-eyed saints. There is lavish Byzantine jewellery in Siracusa and Palermo museums.

As the capital of the Byzantine Empire, Siracusa naturally possesses the greatest concentration of art and architecture. San Marziano crypt was used as a Byzantine basilica until the Temple to Athena was converted into a Christian church. In Palazzo Bellomo museum are fragments of frescoes, such as a vivid *Creation of the Birds and Fishes*, a work of swirling shapes and an impassive God. There are faded frescoes of the saints in Santa Lucia, an early basilica. During the Sack of Siracusa in 878, the Arabs captured much Byzantine booty and copied the rest. Nonetheless, Siracusa museum displays Byzantine-style icons dating from the 8th to the 18th centuries. Although the form often degenerated into a shallow sentimentality, these gold-framed madonnas and rich Nativity scenes are a late flowering of Byzantine art.

The style is an icon for many later Sicilian painters. Antonello da Messina, the greatest of Sicilian Renaissance artists, painted a picture of San Zosimo, the first Greek bishop, which is a homage to Byzantium. Even more important is the contribution of the Byzantine style to Arab-Norman art, that glorious Sicilian marriage of East and West. ❏

LEFT: a Greek patriarch in La Martorana church, Palermo. RIGHT: Byzantine mosaic in La Martorana.

ARABS AND NORMANS

*Two hundred years of Muslim domination, then conquest by Norman
defenders of the faith left Sicily with a unique hybrid culture*

Throughout the Byzantine period, Sicily was the target of frequent piratical raids by Syrians, Egyptians and Moors from North Africa. As early as 652, Saracens from Kairouan (in modern Tunisia) made incursions into the island. In around 700, the island of Pantelleria was captured by Moors, and it was only discord among the Arabs that stopped Sicily being next. Instead, trading arrangements were agreed and Arab merchants established themselves in Sicilian ports. Then, in 827, came the fully fledged Arab invasion.

It was sparked off by a failed Sicilian coup against an unpopular Byzantine governor. Euphemius, a wealthy landowner, overcame the imperial garrison in Siracusa, declared himself Emperor and invited the Emir of Tunisia to help him. The response was a fleet of 100 ships and 10,000 troops, mainly Arabs, Berbers and Spanish Muslims. After stiff resistance at Siracusa, the Arabs gained a foothold in Mazara. Palermo fell after a long siege in 831, but Siracusa held out until 878 and pockets of resistance continued for almost a century.

The fall of Siracusa ended its 1,500-year history as the first city of Sicily. It now took second place to Palermo, as Christianity did to Islam, and the Greek language to Arabic. Palermo Cathedral was converted into a mosque and resounded to Muslim prayers for nearly 250 years.

An influx of Arab settlers replaced the massacred citizens. The invaders were known as Saracens, a term that encompassed Arabs, Berbers and Spanish Moors. These masters of the Mediterranean had stamped their authority on southern Spain but, after the initial slaughter, settled down to a benign and liberal regime in Sicily.

As virtually an independent emirate, Sicily played a privileged role as a bridge between

Africa and Europe. Trade flourished and taxation was low. The historian Denis Mack Smith attributes its prosperity to the "immense economic commonwealth which stretched from Spain to Syria".

The tolerant regime allowed subjects to abide by their own laws. Despite freedom of worship,

Christians freely converted to Islam: there were soon hundreds of mosques in Palermo alone.

Arab enlightenment

The Arabs instigated land reforms which boosted productivity and encouraged the spread of smallholdings, a dent to the power of the landed estates. The Arabs borrowed only the best: Roman engineering skills were fine-tuned and Persian irrigation systems adopted. The Arab reverence for water meant the creation of fountains, baths, reservoirs and storage towers that are visible today. Mining techniques were improved. Sulphur, lead, silver, antimony and alum were refined, as was sea salt. The Arabs

LEFT: a Moorish fountain and distinctive honeycomb vaulting in the the palace of La Ziza in Palermo.
RIGHT: an engraving of St John of the Hermits, Palermo, converted into a mosque by the Arabs.

cultivated citrus plantations and introduced sugar cane, cotton, mulberries, palms, melons, pistachio nuts, papyrus and flax. The sumac tree was used in the tanning and dyeing industries. Cotton mills and silk factories abounded, including one in the Emir's Palermo palace.

Ice from Mount Etna was stored and used to make sorbets and sherbets, while sea salt was dried on the salt flats at Trapani. The Arabs introduced coral and tuna fishing, along with the traditions and chants that survive on the Egadi Islands today.

> ### MOORISH MEMORIES
>
> Many Sicilian place names are souvenirs of the Arab occupation, with prefixes such as *calta* ("castle") and *gibil* ("mountain").

contained the Sultan's palace, baths, a modest mosque, the arsenal, government offices and the Sultan's private prison. Palermo was especially well provided with butchers; Ibn Hawqual reckoned 7,000 persons engaged in the trade in 150 shops.

The Arab hallmark was a sophisticated and cosmopolitan society. But among the many charges levelled at the Arabs were the abandoning of olive groves and extensive deforestation, caused by the need to supply Arab countries with timber.

Nor did the Islamic faith deter Arabs from planting *zubbibbu* grapes.

Arabian splendour

A description of Palermo was given by Ibn Hawqual, a Baghdad merchant, who visited the city in 950. A walled suburb called the Kasr ("the citadel") is the centre of Palermo today, with the "great Friday mosque" on the site of the later Norman cathedral. A chest containing the body of Aristotle supposedly answered prayers for rain, good health, and "for every ill that causes man to offer prayers to Allah, whose name be praised".

The suburb of Khalessah (today's Kalsa)

Melting pot

As well as Arabs from Spain, Syria and Egypt, there were Berbers, Black Africans, Jews, Persians, Greeks, Lombards and Slavs. In particular, Western Sicily prospered under Arab rule: Berbers settled in the Agrigento area while Syrians and Egyptians settled in Palermo. But Sicily was not immune to racial rivalry. In succession Sicily was run by the Sunni Aghlabid dynasty in Tunisia and by the Shia Fatimids in Egypt. The Byzantines took advantage of temporary racial discord to occupy the east of the island for several years.

The Saracen rulers of Sicily quarrelled among themselves and with their nominal superiors in North Africa and Baghdad, but their disunity was nothing compared with the Italian dilemma. Norman knights had entered Italy and were in conflict with the Lombards, and the Papacy got itself into such a pickle that in the middle of the 11th century there were simultaneously no fewer than three Popes. Against this chaotic backcloth, backward Western Christendom struggled to respond.

Arab artistry

The Arab domination of the island only served to enhance Byzantine art and architecture. The Emirs employed Byzantine craftsmen, so earlier decorative patterns and stylisation suffused Islamic art. A thousand years of Greek-infused values could not be so easily erased. Compared with the rest of Italy, the Byzantine style lasted longest in Sicily and flowered latest, merging seamlessly into the Arab-Norman style.

Greek craftsmen, heirs to the Byzantine tradition, created cupolas and pictorial mosaics with Cufic or Greek inscriptions. In Cefalù Cathedral, master craftsmen from Thebes and Corinth perfected the art of the mosaic, using burnished stone and marble or glittering glass and gold. The mosaics in Palermo's La Martorana church are in pure Byzantine style – fluid, gracious, subtle and infused with spirituality.

The Arabs absorbed the central enigma of Byzantine church architecture: an aura of mystery created by screens, symbolic colours, contrasts of light and dark. Arab-Byzantine art echoed this theme to perfection, culminating in Palermo's Cappella Palatina. Also in the Royal Palace is Sala di Re Ruggero, a unique example of Byzantine secular art. Santa Maria in Mili San Pietro is reminiscent of the five-domed chapels of Byzantium, but with *mihrab* (niches) of Muslim prayer rooms indicating the direction of Mecca.

Sicilian conservatism made for a smooth transition from Byzantine to Islamic architecture. After the Hegira (Mohammed's flight in 622), the Arabs had mainly occupied Byzantine lands, so they simply transplanted Oriental styles to Sicily. Although many churches were converted into mosques, the Arabs happily encased Byzantine art and symbolism in Islamic ornamentation. Christian and Islamic symbolism were conveniently fused. Peacocks feature often in Islamic art as symbols of the soul or eternal life, an emblem echoed by Christian imagery. The symbol is carved on columns in La Ziza and appears on mosaics in the Sala di Re Ruggero.

Islamic art rests on the negation of naturalism. In its place is fanciful geometry, exuberant embellishment and a maze of detail that offers a coded approach to the mystery of God. The Arabs were masters of decorative devices, from arabesques, zigzags and cunning mouldings to walls encrusted with niches. Other motifs are pointed arches, slender columns,

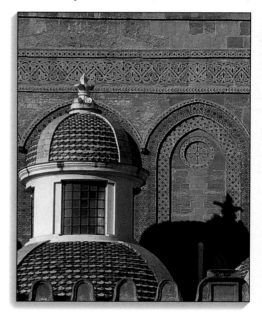

SARACEN SPLENDOUR

Ibn Hamdis, the greatest medieval Arab poet, was driven from Siracusa by the Normans, and his haunting poetry exalts the loss: "Since I have been chased out of paradise, how can I bring you news of it, except in the bitterness of my tears." What he missed in exile were the lush gardens, courtyards dripping with fountains, vivid Moorish domes, sumptuous Saracen palaces with their interiors a shimmering universe of gold, and cool churches afloat with gauzy Byzantine mosaics. He described his beloved Sicily as "a land to which the dove lent its collar, clothed by the peacock from its many-coloured mantle of feathers."

LEFT: decorative Arab script in La Ziza.
RIGHT: Arab-Norman detail on Palermo Cathedral.

double-arched lintels and stepped squinches.

But to Westerners, the most exotic effect is spun by the honeycomb ceilings. Known as *muqarnas* or stalactite work, this beehive design is created by corbelled squinches. The form is borrowed from North African *mihrab* mosques but at its finest, in the Royal Palace, rivals the splendours of Baghdad and Cordova. Iraqi artists from the school of Samarra decorated the ceiling of the Cappella Palatina. This glorious kaleidoscope of interlacing patterns represents the Arab love of

RATHER FINE

The Moorish palace of La Ziza derives its modern name from *aziz* – the Arabic for "splendid".

tament to Arabian craftsmanship, with stalactite vaults, latticework windows, a tiered fountain, and a wind chamber to protect the Emir's family from the enervating *scirocco*.

Such Moorish palaces are significant for their worship of water. In Sicily, fountains and fish ponds, baths and aqueducts frequently have symbolic Arab origins. Donnafugata, a commonplace name, means "enclosed fountain" in Arabic. Abd ar-Rahman, a visitor to King Roger's Norman court, praised "regal palaces in which glory resides"

abstraction – incidentally breaking the Koranic taboo on the depiction of living figures, in true Sicilian style.

The Arab imprint is also present in more humble projects, ranging from rural mosques to the delicate, arched bridge over the river Simeto. Arab urban design took root in Western Sicily, particularly in such towns as Mazara, Palermo and Sciacca. The street plans are based on a traditional "branching tree" design in which secondary roads splinter into blind alleys.

Palermo contains most surviving Islamic architecture. The showcase of the arts is the Moorish palace of La Ziza. It is in itself a testament to Arabian craftsmanship, with stalactite vaults, latticework windows, a tiered fountain, and a wind chamber to protect the Emir's family from the enervating *scirocco*.

in whose "superb gardens lion-headed fountains pour out the waters of paradise".

The most sophisticated Arabian baths are in Palermo province. Cefalù's baths contain a faded Cufic inscription while the walled bathhouse of Cefalà Diana is still more intimate. The restored room is divided by a trio of delicate, slender arches and had pools of different depths as well as niches for cosmetics or unguents.

Arab goldsmiths and sculptors also transformed the "minor" arts. In Palermo, the Treasury contains Egyptian coffers encrusted with gems and ivory, while Palazzo Abatellis displays a Moorish vase and intricate carvings in wood and stone. But the masterpiece is a sculpted door from the Fatimid dynasty, a latticework of wood as intricate as lace.

Palermo's La Martorana church has a richly sculpted door resembling contemporary inlaid work in Cairo. In Palermo Cathedral, a column inscribed with a Koranic text proclaims God's glory: "He shrouds day with night; how can we owe him creation and not pay him homage as Emperor?" By contrast, the Normans worshipped art but paid lip service to God.

Invasion by stealth

The Arabs called the Normans "wolves" because of their ferocity, barbarism and native cunning. Undeterred, the Emirs of Catania and Siracusa invited the Normans to invade. The Emirs were disgruntled by the concentration of Arab power in the west of the island. The Norman Hautevilles, Christian freebooters, needed no encouragement.

But this was no fully fledged invasion, rather a campaign of attrition and conquest by political persuasion. In fact, it was the only option available to conquerors with few forces of their own. Robert Guiscard, a fortune-hunting Norman knight, was living the life of a brigand in Calabria, across the Straits of Messina, when he was joined by his younger brother, Count Roger. Robert gave him 40 men-at-arms with permission to commit unlimited depredations.

While the brothers prospered in crime, the Papacy sank into a morass: Popes were poisoned on taking office and, if they lived, were reduced to selling their vestments to survive. Ultimately, the Papacy reached an accommodation with the unruly Normans, and Robert was proclaimed "future Duke of Sicily". In exchange he swore never to endanger the Pope's "life, limb or liberty". With Papal licence, the brothers confessed their sins, vowed to live Christian lives, and attacked Sicily in 1061.

In 1068, Roger defeated the Arabs at Misilmeri but the crucial step was the siege of Palermo in 1072. Robert urged his men on to seize the city, which was "hateful to God and

subject to devils". The Normans laid loaves of bread out on the ground as bait. Some of the inhabitants ran the risk of dashing out to grab the bread. On succeeding days, the loaves were placed farther away, giving the Normans time to swoop in, capture the wretches, and sell them as slaves.

The great Palermo Mosque was quickly reconsecrated to Christ and a Mass of Thanksgiving held by the Normans. Robert magnanimously shared the spoils with Count Roger, also known as Conte Ruggero and King Roger I. He was an autocratic ruler, buttressed by the Byzantine concept of divine rule and supported

by barons, mercenaries and a strong fleet. Under Arab influence, Roger was transformed from a foolhardy crusader and rough diamond into a cultured figure.

Arab influence did not wane with the Norman conquest. Since the Normans were not an invading force, the local population was spared. The Normans recognised Saracen superiority in culture and commerce, so welcomed Muslim courtiers and merchants. Most Arabs retained their castles, palaces and lands as well as their social prestige. Arab craftsmanship was prized in the conversion of mosques to cathedrals while their administrative skills, erudition and poetry were appreciated at court. The

LEFT: a tablet in La Ziza bears the languages of Arab-Norman study: Arabic, Hebrew, Latin and Greek.
RIGHT: the Normans vanquishing the Saracens, sculpted on the Cathedral of Mazara del Vallo.

Normans were prodigious builders and went on to plant their realm with castles, churches and palaces in Romanesque and Gothic styles, inspired by Northern architecture, but often subverted by Moorish models.

Architectural hybrids

Arabian castles, based on Susa in Tunisia, the point of Arab departure, gave way to pure Norman castles stretching from Enna, in the navel of Sicily, to the majestic castle at Cáccamo in the west. But the Normans built most of their castles to protect the east coast, and here their references tend to be Islamic.

Augusta castle resembles Al-Andarin in Syria, while Catania echoes Farashbend. Like North African forts, these are severe, square castles with Moorish corner towers.

The Romanesque fortress church of San Giovanni dei Lebbrosi was built in 1071 during the Norman siege of Palermo. Cistercian and Cluniac craftsmen were imported to build churches such as San Nicola in Agrigento. But the finest Romanesque church is Palermo's La Magione, which was once a Cistercian monastery. The sobriety of its cloisters is echoed by the gravity of the interior.

Cut off from the architectural mainstream, Norman Sicily looked East. Disentangling the racial strands is difficult since the Normans commissioned craftsmen from Byzantium, the Orient and Italy. It is an inclusive art form, reflecting Norman tolerance and their recognition of Arab artistic supremacy. Stylistic purity is not part of the Sicilian architectural vocabulary. The cosmopolitan nature of "native" architecture makes for an exotic, heady brew. However, the style never sinks to pastiche; the fusion is organic, a result of one civilisation successfully grafted on to another. As the writer Vincent Cronin says: "In Sicily this simultaneity of time constantly bewilders, suggesting that all beauty exists in an eternal present." The Sicilians put it more succinctly: architecturally they are "*bastardi puri*" (pure bastards).

Roger II: King and Sultan

Count Roger died in 1101, leaving Sicily governed by his widow until the coronation of his son, Roger II, in 1130. Although this took place in the Cappella Palatina, La Martorana

---

THREE ARAB-NORMAN MASTERPIECES OF PALERMO PROVINCE

Cefalù Cathedral is seemingly the most "northern", most Gothic of the major churches from this period. Yet even here, the mosaics are pure Byzantine and the decayed cloisters seem Moorish. Cefalù's Christ looks more Oriental than in other mosaics, a depiction of God that fuses East and West, the majesty, authority and asceticism of Islam merging with the humanism and compassion of the Christ figure.

Bishop Gregorovius declared **Monreale Cathedral** "so luminous and bright as to appear unbecoming of a Northern god, though certainly not of a Southern god". The interior is inlaid like a jewel box. Opinion is divided as to whether the glittering mosaics were made by Byzantine,

Arabian or Sicilian craftsmen. The biblical logic is certainly Byzantine, while the leitmotifs and ornamentation are Arab. The cloister's Moorish arches are decorated with mosaic inlays and arabesque carvings.

Palermo's **Cappella Palatina** is the most sublime of Arab-Norman treasures. The magnificent walls are studded with Byzantine mosaics, while the ceiling is a starry sky with 24 small star-shaped cupolas in two lines, part of a honeycomb ceiling. This is a pageant of scenes – the earliest datable series of Islamic paintings in existence – in which musicians, dancers, hunters, royal beasts and Imperial emblems recreate the luxurious lifestyle of an Arabian Emir.

has a glorious mosaic of him receiving his crown from Christ in a ceremony redolent of Byzantine ritual.

As King of Sicily, Puglia and Calabria, Roger extended his empire southwards to Malta and Africa, threatening Constantinople. He was guided by George of Antioch, his Grand Vizier or "Emir of emirs". Roger himself acted as an Oriental sultan, so much so that monks declared him a Muslim in Christian clothing. For their part, Muslim scholars adapted to the new life at court, not least to "the abundance of golden wine".

Revelling in glory, Roger spent lavishly on palaces, mosques, gardens and education. As the richest king in Christendom, he fully indulged his love of Arab art and culture. He also patronised astronomers and astrologers, Koranic scholars and Sicilian poets. This charismatic king was well versed in three languages. His cosmopolitan court was home to French *jongleurs* and balladeers who followed the itinerant Norman knights.

As in Arab times, liberalism decreed that "Latins, Greeks, Jews and Saracens be judged according to their own laws". Norman French, Greek, Arabic, and Latin were all spoken. Even so, cultural and economic pressures led the Arabs gradually to retreat inland, away from the coastal cities.

The Latinisation of Sicily

Only the Normans were granted fiefdoms and, with this, the Arabs' attempts to dismantle the great estates were undone. The rise of the baronial class was the most dubious Norman legacy, but these rugged kings also bequeathed an efficient administration and a relatively liberal regime. In its day, this melting pot of racial talent made for the most culturally creative society in Christendom.

Yet Latinisation under Norman rule should not be underrated. Immigration meant an influx of Pisans, Lombards and French. In time, educated Arabs emigrated, seemingly excluded from the emerging northern *mores*.

Roger was succeeded by King William I, posthumously nicknamed "the Bad" because he aroused jealousies by being "more a

LEFT: the Moorish arches of Monreale Cathedral's cloisters. **RIGHT:** Roger II receives a petitioner in Palermo's Capella Palatina.

Mohammedan than a Christian in belief, in character and in manners". He lived like an Arab Emir in a palace that contained a bodyguard of black slaves and a harem under eunuch management. His lifestyle was a matter of taste, not faith, because he had no qualms about raiding the Muslims in North Africa on behalf of the Pope.

Jealousies in Palermo erupted and the sybaritic court was sacked. A mob raided the harem, raping the women and killing the eunuchs. The King survived and a semblance of order was restored. William quietly stocked another harem, and a riot re-occurred, sparking

off fighting between Christians and Muslims until the whole country was tired of slaughter, and sank, with its sovereign, into apathy.

His son, William the Good, was only 14 when crowned in 1166, and his reign was guided by Walter of the Mill, the English Archbishop of Palermo and architect of Palermo Cathedral. The English connection was strengthened when William's successor, the bastard Tancred, was married to Joanna, King Richard the Lionheart's sister. Richard raided Messina while on his way to the Crusades but did at least present Tancred with Excalibur, King Arthur's sword, a fitting tribute to the end of a legendary line of warrior kings. ❑

EMPERORS, KINGS AND VICEROYS

*For nearly 700 years, Sicily was ruled by a succession of foreign
powers – Germans and French, Spanish kings and Hapsburg emperors*

The death of William the Good in 1189 without an heir sent the succession reeling back through Tancred, Roger's bastard grandson, and thence into the House of Hohenstaufen, which produced the Prussian kings, the Aragonese and Holy Roman Emperors. The brain-numbing genealogy after Roger boils

down to the fact that apart from several interludes, Norman and Spanish blood reigned over Sicily until 1860.

The Holy Roman Empire

The Germanic Hohenstauen dynasty supplied the next wave of invaders. In 1194, after Roger's line petered out, Henry VI, the Holy Roman Emperor, moved in. Henry sifted through the treasures and chose which to send back home north of the Alps, and the Vienna museum thus became the repository of King Roger's cloak and William the Good's embroidered tunic and leggings.

The authoritarian Emperor built the palace of La Cuba and mopped up the House of Tancred, either murdering them or sending them to slavery in Germany. After dying of dysentry, Henry was buried in a magnificent tomb in Palermo Cathedral: space was made for him by tossing out the bones of various Tancreds.

Henry's son, Frederick I of Sicily, was confusingly crowned Emperor Frederick II in 1220. Born in Palermo of a Norman mother, he never considered himself Sicilian yet was known as a "baptised Sultan", thanks to his predilection for a *seraglio* and Saracen pages. Despite an Arabian lifestyle, Frederick chose a centralised, Western European policy which sealed the grim fate of Saracen Sicily.

First, he had to contend with a Muslim backlash, mobilising the barons against the Arabs. Muslims were discriminated against and transplanted to the mainland. Under Frederick's autocratic regime, rural settlements gave way to baronial estates. On his death in 1250, the empire was left in chaos, with family vendettas filling the void created by the collapse of royal authority.

Stupor Mundi

Nonetheless, Frederick's talents were enough for him to be dubbed "wonder of the world". In between empire-building, he founded a school of Sicilian poetry, wrote a book on falconry and created travelling zoos. He also studied science, pondering such arcane questions as the workings of Mount Etna and the precise location of hell. Yet while the barons found Sicily paradise, his other subjects might well have located hell in Sicily.

Frederick fortified all of eastern Sicily from Messina to Siracusa. He sacked Catania in 1232 and then built castles to control his rebellious subjects. Castello Ursino in Catania is one of the finest bastions, a lava-stone moated fort with four corner towers. Despite his reputation, Frederick loved Sicily. As an artistic memorial, he left such lovely churches as the Alemanni and Badiazza in Messina, as well as the Swabian mosaics in Monreale.

Successors like Charles of Anjou called themselves King of Sicily, using the title as an adornment as they pursued greater ambitions abroad. This Loire Valley dynasty had royal links and pretensions. The Angevins defeated the Swabians on the Italian mainland and claimed Sicily in 1266. Backed by the Pope, Charles plundered the island and taxed so punitively that rebellion hung in the air, provoked by Charles moving the capital from Palermo to Naples.

Revolt against the French

The Easter rebellion in 1282 was the most significant uprising in Sicily's history, both a patri-

weapons. As the bell was calling the faithful to Vespers, the French captain drunkenly ordered his men to search the women as well. "He himself laid hands upon the fairest, and pretending to look for a knife upon her he thrust his hand out to her bosom."

She fainted in the arms of her husband, who let out the ringing cry: "*Moranu i franchiski*" (Death to the French) and the French officer was struck down dead at the feet of the woman he had insulted. The incident led to a riot, which in turn, with the encouragement of the local aristocracy, became an all-out revolt. The uprising spread from Palermo throughout

otic insurrection and a revolt against feudalism. But far from freeing Sicilians from a foreign yoke, it led directly to the War of the Vespers, a confused 20-year conflict between French (Angevin) and Spanish (Aragonese) houses, which finally left Sicily in Spanish hands.

It all began when Palermo's traditional Easter Monday procession was joined by French soldiers from Charles's garrison. The festive mood turned to sullen silence as the Sicilians were searched by the French troops for concealed

LEFT: Frederick II in the arms of his mother, the Norman Queen Constance Hauteville.
ABOVE: the court of Frederick II, *Stupor Mundi*.

Sicily, and in the massacre that followed no Frenchman was safe. Any doubt about race was settled by a knife placed at the suspect's throat and the order to say *"ciceri"* ("chickpeas" in dialect), a word the French supposedly could not pronounce.

The nobles of Palermo invited Peter II of Aragon to intervene on their behalf, and the Spaniard readily agreed, accepting the title King of Sicily while promising to respect the freedom of Sicilians. The people of Palermo were unimpressed by their Spanish liberators "and in their hearts did not believe that such men could deliver them from King Charles". But Charles withdrew from Sicily, and

French influence on the island had effectively come to an end.

The war between the Angevins and the Aragonese rumbled on, mainly waged in sea battles and in Spain, until the Peace of Caltabellotta in 1302. Robert of Anjou, Charles's successor, took Naples while Sicily was ceded to Peter's son, Frederick of Aragon, on the condition that on his death the kingdom would return to Robert – an agreement the Aragonese later chose to ignore.

TWO SICILIES

For centuries, the kingdom of Naples was known by the name *Regnum Sicilae*. To avoid confusion, the island of Sicily was designated as *Trinacria* (three-cornered) in the treaty of 1372.

The Spanish in Sicily

Friction between the Aragonese in Sicily and the Normans in Naples frequently erupted into open warfare until, in 1372, Naples agreed to Sicilian self-rule provided that the Sicilian ruler paid an annual tax to Naples and recognised the dominance of the Pope.

Alphonso of Aragon united the crowns of Naples and Sicily in 1442 and tried to reduce baronial power. More significantly, his reign ushered in the foreign viceroys who were to

SAFE AS HOUSES

The 14th century saw the spread of Catalan-Gothic, a brief architectural golden age. In return for their support, the Aragonese rulers were obliged to enlarge the feudal privileges of the barons, who celebrated by building grand private castles. The Chiaramonte, the dominant feudal dynasty of the century, gave its name to the architectural style, in which fortresses doubled as palaces, with decorated facades, vaulted rooms and lavish, painted ceilings. In Palermo, the austere beauty of Palazzo Chiaramonte and Palazzo Sclafani represent the perfection of the Chiaramonte style. Similar tower houses exist in Enna, Randazzo and Taormina.

govern over the next four centuries. But Sicilian independence was submission under a new guise. The unification of Castile and Aragon in 1479, followed by the expulsion of the Moors from the Spanish peninsula, meant that Sicily dwindled in importance to the Spanish monarchs. The island, under the rule of a series of viceroys, was little more than a source of revenue for Spain, and was drained to fund the *Riconquista* and wars against the Turks.

The Inquisition

After 1487 the Inquisition was powerful in Sicily. Palermo retains the severe palace that housed the Inquisition headquarters. The

Spanish spy system used a grim police force to expel all Jews. Intellectual and cultural life suffocated under the burden of fear and conformity. The system enforced the nobles' loyalty to the Spanish crown and supported baronial privileges that were being swept away elsewhere. Sicilian grandees were indulged by the Spanish and, with no freedom from feudalism, the peasants reverted to banditry. Popularly perceived as honourable lawlessness, brigandry was the breeding ground for the Mafia and was tacitly supported by the barons.

Spanish rule did not go completely unopposed. In 1647 a revolt in Palermo, spearheaded

Treaty of Utrecht of 1713, when it was awarded to the northern Italian House of Savoy.

Victor Amadeus, Duke of Piedmont-Savoy and the new king of Sicily, arrived in an English ship, Britain having decided that Sicily should be given to a weak Italian power rather than to the Austrian Habsburgs, who retained Naples. The Sicilian nobility hoped the Duke would restore the gold and glitter of the Spanish court. They were nonplussed when the new king appeared in clothes made of undyed wool. The king's survey of the economy underlined how far Sicily had degenerated. Why were there so many palpably unemployed people in Palermo,

by two commoners, was quickly suppressed. And in 1674 Messina rose against the Spanish, with aid from the king of France. Spain did not recapture the city until four years later.

House of Savoy

After Charles II of Spain died in 1700, Sicily could do little but sit back and watch as the Wars of the Spanish Succession involved several contending European powers. The island was little more than a bargaining counter in the

FAR LEFT: Charles of Anjou. **LEFT:** Catania in 1669, before the disastrous earthquake. **ABOVE:** an 18th-century engraving of the Quattro Canti, Palermo.

the King wanted to know, when agriculture was crying out for labour? Agriculture in Sicily had dwindled so seriously that cereals had to be imported. Tax collection was put out to commercial tender, and the highest bidder unleashed a private army of thugs to recoup the cost.

In 1718 the Spanish invaded Sicily to recover their former land. The Sicilians, smarting from austerity measures, welcomed the 20,000 troops. Anticipating a return to unfettered privilege, Sicilian grandees brought their Spanish finery out of mothballs. Austria declared war on Spain, but it was British ships that sank the Spanish fleet off Sicily, allowing Austrian troops to cross the Straits of Messina. The war between Spain and Austria climaxed in Fran-cavilla, the biggest battle fought on Sicilian soil since Roman times.

The victorious Habsburg Emperor duly became King of Sicily. The regime, adminis-tered as before by viceroys, was unpopular. "The Germans never became familiar with Sicil-ians," wrote Mongitore, "and their barbarous language was unintelligible."

Austrian rule was cut short in 1734 when, in a replay of 1718, a Spanish fleet arrived and

FEUDAL SURVIVORS

Under the Bourbons, the Sicilian nobility – 142 princes, 788 marquesses and 1,500 barons – abandoned their feudal castles for luxury in Palermo, but still owned 280 of the island's 360 villages.

out seriously wealthy aristocrats from counter-feit title-hunters. Sicilian nobles indulged in luxury, gambling and litigation, the Prince of Villadora setting the pace with 22 simultaneous lawsuits.

British sway

After Nelson's defeat of the French in 1798, Ferdinand felt emboldened to attack French forces in Italy but was forced to flee to Palermo under Nelson's protection. The King rewarded Nelson with the Dukedom of Bronte, an estate near Mount Etna.

took Sicily back. The conquest was bloodless, and Sicily was again joined to Naples under Charles of Bourbon, the Spanish infante.

House of Bourbon

When Charles succeeded to the Spanish throne in 1759 he was told he could not keep Naples and Sicily as well, so he handed them over to his son Ferdinand, whose reign lasted 66 years.

The Bourbon rulers are belittled in *The Leop-ard*. The shabby grandeur of their palace is one of "sumptuously second-rate rooms". By con-trast, Palermo boasted more palaces than the entire British Empire. Even grander were the 200 villas in Bagheria, built specifically to sort

Britain retained an interest in Sicily, if only to prevent Napoleon from moving in. In 1806, Ferdinand IV invited Britain to take over Sicily's defence – which made Sicily richer than it had been for centuries. British subsidies encouraged the mining industry and reduced unemployment. While Ferdinand went on hunt-ing trips, the real governor was William Bentinck, the British commander. Still, Britain could never decide what to do with Sicily. The King reluctantly accepted a constitution. "We are living with cannibals," he told Bentinck, only signing on condition that a warship was on standby to spirit him away to a safe haven.

In the event, the Austrian reconquest of

Naples meant that Britain withdrew from the nightmare. In 1816, the Kingdom of the Two Sicilies was created: the kingdoms of Naples and Palermo were unified and Ferdinand became king. He immediately abolished the separate Sicilian flag and retreated to his court in Naples. In 1820, during the St Rosalia celebrations, Palermo rose against him, a rebellion only put down after the arrival of 10,000 Austrian troops. After Ferdinand's death in 1825, the government was equally inefficient, brutal and corrupt.

AMATEUR SAILORS

Garibaldi and his troops arrived at Marsala in two small paddle steamers. They had sailed 960 km (600 miles) with no food or water, and no chart or sextant.

Sicilians desired a federal Italy; the majority merely disliked Naples, which they knew, more than a Northern Italy they did not know except through dim memories of Piedmontese rule.

That was the backdrop to another revolt in Palermo in 1860, which spurred Giuseppe Garibaldi to choose Sicily as the starting point for his unification of Italy. On 11 May, he arrived at Marsala with 1,000 men, with whom he aimed to liberate the island from Bourbon rule in the name of the Piedmont House of

Enter Garibaldi

Palermo provided the flashpoint for a revolt in 1848. In one place the riot was over the price of bread, in another against the town hall. In the aftermath, the King offered a liberal constitution but this was rejected in favour of an independent Sicily. The Bourbon flag was replaced by the tricolour.

But when a Bourbon army landed at Messina, the Sicilians quickly realised that the King would be back. Only a tiny minority of

LEFT: 19th-century rioters take to violence against church and state. **ABOVE:** lithograph showing Garibaldi's troops taking Palermo in May 1860.

Savoy. The recent withdrawal of the garrison from Marsala, Garibaldi's skill at guerilla warfare, and growing support from the Sicilian peasantry, ensured a victory over 15,000 Bourbon troops at Calatafimi. Within days, Garibaldi occupied Palermo. He proclaimed himself dictator, ruling on behalf of Vittório Emanuele of Piedmont. A final victory over the Bourbons at Milazzo decided the issue.

In a plebiscite, Sicilians voted almost unanimously for Unification of Italy. This meant the end of Garibaldi's brief dictatorship and the assumption of power by Count Cavour in Turin. To many Sicilians, that sounded more like annexation than union, a hint of *déjà vu*. ❏

THE ITALIAN FLAG

Becoming part of a united Italy did not solve Sicily's economic and social problems at a stroke – and Mussolini only made things worse

Union with Italy, under king Vittório Emanuele II, did not bring prosperity to Sicily, merely a substitution of Torinese dialect for Neapolitan dialect. The new parliamentary system brought democracy of a sort – but only 1 percent of the island's population was eligible to vote, and most could see no improvement in their lot. Economically, the island's fortunes went from poor to worse.

There were abortive uprisings against the new government – the first, in Palermo, only six years after unification – which were savagely repressed. For most Sicilians the only escape from poverty seemed to be emigration. In the last decades of the 19th century, villages lost their male populations to the United States, Argentina, Tunisia and Brazil. In a single year, Sicily waved goodbye to 20 per cent of its population, although the economic slump was offset by remittances sent back home to relatives.

The 20th century began ominously with the Messina earthquake in 1908, which killed up to 84,000 people and destroyed thousands of homes. Sudden mass homelessness only added to the emigrant flood leaving the island. The economic situation was not improved by Italy's military adventures: the conquest of Libya in 1912 was followed by World War I, which both took their toll on the Sicilian economy.

Il Duce

After 1918, feudal relationships were severely weakened. Returning *americani* came home with self-respect as well as savings. But the cloud on the horizon was Mussolini, who assumed power in Rome in 1922, without much support from Sicily. While the island was not predisposed to Fascism, it was swept along by Mussolini's empty posturing. A magazine called *The Problems of Sicily* was forced to change its name since there *were* no more problems, the dictator declared. A plebiscite in 1934 confirmed his confidence. Only 116 Sicilians

LEFT: Benito Mussolini takes the stage. **RIGHT:** Victor Emmanuel II, the first king of a united Italy.

out of 4 million disagreed that Fascism had been good for them.

The plebiscite was a testament to Mussolini's demagoguery. Three generations after Garibaldi, little had changed. *Il Duce* talked about building dams, supposedly the panacea for Sicily's agriculture, but few materialised. Peas-

ants still lived in one room with their animals. The railways were single track and the extraordinary level of mule ownership was the concomitant of the lack of roads. This was at a time when highways were being cut through the Libyan desert.

Anti-Mafia campaign

In reality, Mussolini's masterplan was to industrialise the influential north and to use Sicily as the provider of raw materials. Projects suited his purposes only if they generated publicity, and Sicily offered one worthwhile cause: bringing the Mafia to heel. Initially the Mafia were all for Mussolini; not so when he despatched

Cesare Mori, an expert in uprisings, to eradicate the scourge.

Inspector Mori started briskly. Various Dons were rounded up, walls were removed from roadsides where they facilitated ambushes, and the carrying of firearms forbidden. Mori made an example of the hill town of Gangi, laying siege to it and then locking up a hundred *mafiosi*, including the formidable "Queen of Gangi", a woman who dressed as a man.

Mussolini announced that the Mafia had been

MILITARY MULTITUDE

When the US 7th Army and the British 8th Army landed in Sicily in 1943, their total forces numbered 160,000 – the largest invading army the island had ever seen.

eliminated. The murder rate, he said, had dropped from 10 a day to only three a week. Mussolini had indeed curbed the Mafia by depriving them of official protection. But the net result was to drive the criminal families deeper underground. Inspector Mori may have been given food for thought when he offered a prize for the best essay by a schoolboy on how to destroy the Mafia. He received not one entry.

War looms

In 1937, when World War II was just below the horizon, Mussolini visited Sicily to review his achievements. He informed his audience that Sicily was poised for "one of the happiest epochs in its 4,000 years' history". If Sicilians knew anything about previous epochs, they could anticipate a grim future.

The Allies chose Sicily as the landing stage for bringing the war against Hitler back to Europe. Mussolini had always said that the Allies would never be able to invade Sicily. This was military madness: the coast was defenceless, the air cover minimal, and even if there had been good roads, most of the artillery was still horse-drawn. Gela found itself yet again playing host to an invading army. The Americans landed there in July 1943 while British and Canadian forces tackled the east coast.

General Patton commanded the US 7th Army in Sicily, running a short and relatively sweet campaign. The German forces and their Italian rump scrambled across the Straits along with most of their equipment, and once more Sicily was detached from the mainland and under foreign control.

The role of the Mafia in the Allied conquest of Sicily was open to attack, given deals struck between Allied military planners and Lucky Luciano in his American prison cell. Vito Genovese, while wanted for murder and other crimes by police in the United States, turned up as a liaison officer attached to an American army unit.

Ironically, the Allies helped restore the Mafia's authority in Sicily and so erased Mussolini's only solid achievement. In the absence of the previous Fascist administrators, the army invited Don Calógero Vizzini to do the job. The Allies, whose principal interest was to keep Sicily quiet, did not look into his background. He had been bankrupted and locked up by Mussolini as one of the most undesirable *mafiosi*.

Separatism

Influential voices in Sicily wished to formalise the division between Sicily and Italy, and there was heady talk of Sicily becoming part of the United States. When the Allies then returned the island to Italian administration, one frustrated group of extremists formed a secret army, raised their own flag, and declared war on Italy.

In 1946, the Italian government granted Sicily autonomy in areas such as agriculture, mining and industry. Separatists still insisted that Italy owed Sicily reparations for misrule since 1861, but this issue soon gave way to the new rhetoric of the Cold War, a contest between Christian Democrats on the one hand and Socialists and Communists on the other.

The balance of power between the two factions lay in the dubious hands of Don Vizzini. For the Mafia, the issue was merely one of choosing political partners in the allocation of building licences, import permits and state contracts. In 1948 Don Vizzini made his choice. The Christian Democrats doubled their number of seats and were comfortably installed as the majority party for the next 40 years. Subsequent demands for government action against the Mafia fell on curiously deaf ears.

In recognition that the Italian government was at last willing to make an effort to close the economic gap between Sicily and the mainland, the United States, the World Bank and later the EC chipped in with support. The most radical transformation was in the thorny business of land ownership. After the war, 1 percent of the population still owned at least half of all agricultural land. The old absentee landownership system was now subject to controls that required that any holding of more than 200 hectares (500 acres) could be expropriated if the owners did not carry out improvements. The number of small and medium holdings rose significantly.

Industrial stagnation

Dams proved as intractable as ever. Some projects had been on the drawing board for 100 years. There was nothing wrong with them except that the Mafia had a line in controlling the water supply and was in no hurry to have the system altered. Dams were half-built and then abandoned, with a stream of water running uselessly into the sea.

Just as it began to look as if the economy was racing to stand still, Gulf Oil struck lucky near Ragusa in 1953 and another discovery near Gela quickly followed. The Cinderella island was suddenly the basis of the Italian oil industry, and by 1966 one of several refineries was

CARELESS CONSTRUCTION

In the building boom of the 1960s safety regulations were often ignored, as revealed by the 1968 earthquake in the Valle di Belice. Although a relatively small quake, it made 50,000 people homeless.

alone handling 8 million tons of crude a year. The petrol industry attracted its chemical derivatives; gas was discovered at the Nelson estate at Bronte; and Sicily at last commanded the power to make industrialisation practicable.

The effect on the topography worked in opposite directions. As a port, once mighty Palermo was eclipsed by Augusta with its oil facilities, while forgotten Siracusa began to emulate the greatness it had known in Greek times. The pattern was the emergence of a new Sicily in the

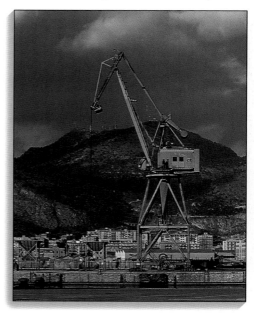

east to replace the domination of the west. Palermo was still the largest city by far, but northern industrialists had no patience with the old mob rule, which could immobilise the place. In 1956 Palermo was crippled by open gang warfare over control of the food markets.

Although conditions improved after the discovery of oil and gas, the island still knew that a job in Northern Italy paid more in a month than a Sicilian could expect to earn at home in a year. Sicily's fortunes have always depended on events overseas, and it is the island's ability to stem the flight of its best people across the Straits of Messina that will write its history for the foreseeable future. ❏

LEFT: Italian troops surrender to the British in July 1943.
RIGHT: Palermo's port is in economic decline.

SICILY TODAY

Recent decades have seen a political shift from the traditional Right, a popular resistance to Mafia influence and a new awakening of civic consciousness

Palermo's popular advertising slogan is: "Invade Sicily, everyone else has." Sicily has never been its own master. Even now, critics call the island an occupied territory, a Roman colony (albeit a heavily subsidised one) subject to the policies of Rome and the European Union. The only homegrown institution that seems to wield any lasting power is the Mafia, an organisation that enriches itself on the island's poverty.

Sicilians express this feeling of powerlessness in no uncertain terms. In the evening, when men gather at the *piazza*, they rail against the government, political parties, the Mafia, anyone they can pin the blame on. They talk about being trapped, paralysed, immobile, frozen. One young teacher compares life in Sicily to a feeling of breathlessness. He calls the sensation *apnea*. "Do you know what *apnea* is?" he asks. "It's when a person can't breathe. That's what it's like. We're suffocating on this island."

Consumerism

Yet relative prosperity is filtering through and *per capita* income has quadrupled since 1950. Up to 20 percent of the workforce are state employees, from lecturers to office workers and museum attendants.

In conversation, an elderly woman talks about the old days, *i tempi di miseria*, the "times of poverty", before World War II when her village was dominated by rich landowners and the peasants had barely enough food to survive. "We don't suffer the way we used to," she says. "We have electricity now, toilets, cars, doctors."

Then she stops talking and looks around as if to size up the effect these things have had on their lives. She looks toward the cafes where unemployed men spend their days playing cards, at the broken fountain at the centre of the *piazza*. "Listen to me," she says. "This is not what we wanted."

Sicily has a population of around 5 million,

making the island the most densely populated region in Italy. Unemployment hovers around 25 percent. Income per capita is little more than half of Northern Italy's. Yet Sicily boasts the best-qualified unemployed: more than 80 percent are graduates. Despite such problems, Sicily received 20,000 Albanian immigrants

in 1991, a figure which has to be juggled with the incalculable numbers of illegal Tunisian and Moroccan fishermen working along Trápani's African coast.

Economic miracle?

Sicilian politicians regularly proclaim the sighting of an "economic miracle". In Mussolini's day it was dams; in the 1960s it was oil; in the 1970s it was greenhouses and reservoirs; in the 1980s it was a building boom; now it is tourism and a bridge across the Straits. Yet the real miracle is that Sicily has an economy at all.

An estimated 40 percent of the population works on the land, producing 20 percent of the

LEFT: rural life in Trápani province.
RIGHT: a corkmaking factory in Castelvetrano.

island's GNP. Sicily also possesses a quarter of Italy's fishing fleet, mostly based on Trápani and Mazara del Vallo. But to surmise that Sicily is an agricultural economy would be wrong. It would be more accurate to talk of an agrarian outlook marginalised by encroaching industrialisation. What the rural hinterland and industrialised coast share is a rootedness in the land.

The traditional crops of olives, grapes and cereals remain vital. The hinterland is a mix of mechanisation and sweated

> ### FRUITLESS TASK
>
> Despite the lush groves in Palermo's Conca d'Oro, bottled orange juice is imported. Israeli and Moroccan fruit is cheaper; besides, Sicilian machinery has trouble extracting the pips.

Sicilian nostalgia for the passing of local cottage industries, such as cheese making. Still, the past is salvaged: *caciocavallo* cheesemakers survive, and Módica herders ride the plains like Wild West cowboys.

And the locals can be enterprising when it suits them. In 1992 EC inspectors were outraged to find they had been fooled by "walking" olive trees. In order to gain extra subsidies, farmers planted their trees in tubs and moved them from field to field as the EC counting team advanced.

Industry

Sicily suffers from the "cathedrals in the desert" syndrome, with the siting of uneconomic plants in empty locations, devoid of infrastructure. These great white elephants have trampled the once lovely coast and polluted the seas. None of these oil refineries or chemical plants is labour-intensive and the profits have been siphoned off to Milan. Heavy industry defaces the coast at Augusta, Gela, Siracusa and Milazzo. But oil, asphalt and petro-chemical plants have failed to bring dramatic prosperity.

Barzini describes the difficulties of building a notional *cassate* factory in Sicily. If created locally, it could be the best in the world – but would never open.

It is easy to criticise Sicilians' lack of entrepreneurial spirit, but the whole business ethos is averse to risk. Private initiative is discouraged by the habit of state support and Pirandellian layers of bureaucracy. Not only are individuals often powerless to act but their projects, or even lives, are endangered if they choose not to fit into the framework. At best, obstacles take the form of incomprehension, bureaucratic delays, and expected bribes. At worst, there are threatening phone calls and *pizzo* (protection money).

brow. While the vast wheatfields are intensively farmed, sights of elderly peasants laden with olives are common, as are burdens of brushwood shared between mules and masters. (*See Rural Life, page 71*.)

In agriculture, Ragusa province is held up as a model, with cattle breeding, market gardening and wine growing. Farmers transformed a once malaria-infested plain into a forest of greenhouses bursting with spring vegetables and hothouse flowers.

Since this is Sicily, there is a downside. Giuseppe Fava, a journalist later murdered by the Mafia, lamented the unaesthetic tracts of glass covering the coastal dunes. He also had a

North versus South

The North is resentful of Sicily, seething at real crime and imagined subsidies. "Our taxes go straight to Rome," a Lombard League member complains, "and Rome moves the money into pointless public projects in the South." Support for Umberto Bossi's separatist party, Lega Nord, is growing, along with similar parties that advocate the dismantling of

Italy into self-governing states. It's not independence the Northerners want so much as freedom from the South.

Sicily is Bossi's *bête noire* and he always raises a cheer by ridiculing Italy's inefficient postal system. Letters between Milan and Turin are sorted in Sicily, thus providing Southerners with hate mail and Northerners with late mail. Such sinecures may be on their way out as the newly moral Italian government indulges in uncharacteristic cost-cutting and nudges industrial fiefdoms towards privatisation.

Young entrepreneurs are struggling to change the business culture and are having some suc-

state pension system, Sicily is now exposed to the chill winds of the market economy. After the planned switch to privatisation, politicians will no longer be able to use the bloated state sector for personal patronage.

Most importantly, however, investors fear the Mafia and the pervasiveness of crime. It's not only the drug trade, extortion rings and street crime but also the Mafia's infiltration of the political system. It is yet another vicious circle. The Mafia cannot truly be beaten until Sicily has a freestanding, vital economy. Yet the more money Rome pumps into Sicily, the stronger the Mafia becomes.

cess in Catania and Siracusa. The "Arab" west of the island is more allergic to private initiative, with the exception of the wine industry.

Corporate investors have been hesitant about setting up in Sicily. They baulk at the lack of infrastructure. There's no sense developing products, investors say, if there aren't reliable highways, railroads, airports and telecommunications to get the products to market.

With the end of subsidies from the Cassa del Mezzogiorno fund and reforms of the abused

LEFT: citrus growers find it hard to compete.
ABOVE: much of the Conca d'Oro, Palermo's "golden shell" of citrus groves, has been built over.

LEAVING HOME

There are at least 5 million Sicilians outside Italy. A million people left the island between 1950 and 1970. Of the 25 million Italians in the US, 18 million are of Sicilian origin and many are married to fellow Sicilians.

Sicilian waiters run Toronto's *pizzerie*. Sicilians from rugged Mussomeli end up in England as gardeners in genteel Woking. Fishermen from Castellammare work as Great Barrier Reef divers. One high-flier became president of Euronews in Lyons.

Of the 500,000 declared Sicilians who live elsewhere in the European Union, most can be found in Germany, France, Belgium and Britain.

A bulging bureaucracy

Fat state contracts, one of the mainstays of Rome's strategy for stimulating development in Sicily, are soaked up by layer upon layer of graft, kick-backs, overbilling and no-show workers. Government rolls are swollen with fraudulent pensions and do-nothing jobs that are doled out by local politicians in exchange for votes. Sicily and Campania compete for the title of graveyard of public works.

The passion for road construction is particularly Sicilian. Such labour-intensive projects are often diverted through fiefdoms, or unnecessarily built on stilts over flat land. Many di Montechiaro, blackspots in the Agrigento backwoods. Palma has the highest child mortality rate in Europe, with *vedove bianche* (grass widows) left pregnant after each fleeting visit from their emigrant husbands in Belgium or Germany. By day, the town is merely depressed, a place partly without running water, sewers or electricity. At night the town is overrun by hungry, marauding dogs; in Palma, individuals own large packs, both for protection and as a symbol of human worth.

Derelict *palazzi* line the bombed centre of Palermo while one boarded-up Catania suburb is known as Little Beirut. Slums without ser-

roads are little more than sets of potholes joined by tar, so badly built – conveniently – as to be in a perpetual state of renovation. Travelling the island, one finds incomplete highways, museums *in restauro* for 20 years, and unfinished housing projects, all testimony to the bureaucratic black holes through which state funds fall.

Many town councils are regularly dissolved for corruption. In industrial Gela, 5,000 citizens converged on the town hall and burnt documents in protest against maladministration in 1983. The town council was again suspended in 1992 after accusations of criminal ties.

Poverty is still endemic in Licata and Palma vices should be demolished under the laws on unauthorised building, but most are not. Tucked out of sight in Messina and many other towns are the tenements or insanitary shacks of the *terremotati*, those made homeless after a series of earthquakes. The squalid living conditions and high crime rate tend to be hushed up.

Despite *miseria*, there is cause for hope, both in individual initiatives and a new political climate. Since the 1950s, when activist Danilo

ABOVE: bizarre roads on stilts were a cover for some unnecessary make-work projects.
RIGHT: 20th-century pollution provides the backdrop for the Temple of Concord, Agrigento.

Dolci set up his Centre for Research in Trappeto, one of the most corrupt and squalid areas in Western Sicily, a persistent effort has been made to expose Sicily's problems. As an advocate of passive resistance, Dolci helped ordinary people reclaim political power, sparking off a wave of reform that is still being felt today.

Political shift

The Christian Democrats (DC) believed they had a divine right to Sicily until the sands suddenly shifted in 1992. A political shift in post-Cold War Italy opened a window of opportunity for reformers. Traditionally considered a bulwark against Communism, the Christian Democrats lost much of their power base in Sicily. Amid accusations of vote-rigging by their opponents, the party was discredited.

La Rete, a new reforming party committed to anti-Mafia and anti-corruption policies, moved to fill the vacuum. According to La Rete's leader, Palermo mayor Leoluca Orlando, the only requirement for party membership is honesty. His campaign against crime and corruption, both inside and outside the political system, was endorsed by the electorate in 1993, when Orlando was re-elected mayor of Palermo by 75 percent of the voters, an unprecedented majority. Having initiated some dramatic reforms designed to banish the economic interests of organised crime in the city, Orlando is under no illusions: the Mafia still has a hold on some of the city's businesses, he concedes, but he claims that it no longer controls Palermo's institutions.

Some people blame Sicily's problems on the so-called Southern mentality: if nothing is done, no one can be blamed, and an ethic of voracious self-interest precludes community effort. Yet, in a place like Sicily, where jobs are scarce and resources are limited, looking out for oneself and one's family isn't just a matter of attitude, it's a matter of survival.

But Elvira Sellerio, a respected publisher from Palermo, is cautiously optimistic: "We Sicilians have always been subjects, never citizens. The awakening of a civic consciousness is new: give us time to learn how to become citizens." If the optimists are right, Sicily may be due for the Renaissance it missed the first time round. ❑

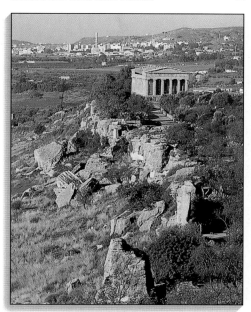

THE TOURIST INDUSTRY

As a potential source of revenue, tourism is being heavily promoted in Sicily, and not just to the familiar markets of Germany, France and Scandinavia. The island's wealth of natural and cultural treasures, and its colourful traditions and festivals, have the potential to attract a healthy income from abroad. Yet a shortage of beds and a lack of infrastructure (such as reliable public transport) mean that tourism is not developing as fast as it might.

The approach to tourism differs dramatically between one region and the next. The tourist offices for the provinces of Palermo, Siracusa and Trápani, for instance, have clear brand images and a warm welcome. Palermo is spending a fortune in establishing itself as a centre for cultural tourism, staging hundreds of musical and theatrical events and restoring many of its historical buildings. Trápani is particularly perceptive about the provision of cultural activities in Classical sites.

By contrast, Agrigento and Caltanissetta province sleep on, oblivious to the new wave of invaders. On a local level, many museums have odd opening times and believe they exist for the benefit of staff coffee breaks.

One small but significant growth area is *agriturismo*, holidays in the countryside, often on a working farm, which bring vital revenue to deprived rural areas.

THE SICILIANS

Brooding, conservative, suspicious and superstitious – or self-confident, sensitive, honest and hospitable? The Sicilians are a mass of apparent contradictions

Luigi Barzini calls Sicily "the schoolroom model for beginners, with every Italian quality and defect magnified, exasperated and brightly coloured." Sicilians also have a reputation for being brooding, suspicious, withdrawn and unfathomable. Closer contact reveals stoicism, stifling conservatism, escapism, spirituality and deep sensibility. This contradictory character does not match the sunny Mediterranean stereotype of *dolce far niente*. But, once over the initial hurdles, outsiders may encounter overwhelming hospitality, boundless curiosity and smothering friendship on the slimmest of pretexts.

Public stage

According to Cicero, Sicily gave the world Rhetoric. The passion for debate remains a Sicilian trait but is a substitute for public initiative. As Vincent Cronin says: "Lack of purpose in life is exalted into a kind of purpose, and lack of action into a mode of action." The writer Bufalino confirms this: "We feel no need to turn our desires into deeds." On arrival in Sicily, King Victor Emmanuel was told the nobility were "work-shy, soft and effeminate". This is more subtle than it seems: "It's best to say no, then one can't be blamed," explains a Palermitan aristocrat and university professor. This passivity springs from an individual's sense of alienation from the state.

In 1814 the British Governor of Sicily was perplexed that "Sicilians expect everything to be done for them; they have always been so accustomed to obedience". His Sicilian minister argued for absolutism: "Too much liberty is for the Sicilians what would be a pistol or stiletto in the hands of a boy or a madman." Critics claim that Sicilians remain sluggish citizens, subsidy junkies with little sense of self-help. Sicilians reply that power and prestige lie elsewhere. History has taught them to have no faith in institutions. This historical hangover has led them into a moral morass in which the illusion of social change is confused with reality.

According to the journalist Giuseppe Fava, "the inability to structure society is the Sicilian tragedy." In the face of this dilemma, the traditional responses are emigration, resigna-

tion, complicity or withdrawal into a private world. Though emigration has been the choice of millions, most Sicilians choose to stay but avoid confrontation with the shadow-state of patronage and the Mafia. They shrink from the public sphere, preferring to live intensely but in private. As a result, their world is circumscribed by the family, the bedrock of island life.

Capital society

Palermo is emblematic of the retreat from the world and also of an ambivalence about class. It goes against the grain of Sicilian sentimentality to admit that the middle classes have fled the historic centre in droves, to settle in leafy

PRECEDING PAGES: a pensioners' club in Mazzarino; social gathering in Messina. **LEFT:** young man in an ancient profession. **RIGHT:** widow's weeds in Naro.

villages or in safe suburbs in the foothills of Monte Pellegrino. Yet even here, many modest homes maintain a level of security more common to a South American dictatorship, with watchmen, electronic gates and savage dogs. Optimists point to a gradual return of the middle classes to the *centro storico*, with one square held up as a shining example, a socially mixed island which could be the city's salvation or Old Palermo's *coup de grâce*.

Elsewhere, gentrification looks a long way

off. Arab and African immigrants occupy derelict buildings by the port while neighbouring quarters are home to the underclass (*sottoproletariato*). Pitiful hovels lurk in the shadow of splendid mansions or villas.

Partly as a result of this social imbalance, Palermo's historic centre tends to be deserted at night. What bars there are usually close around 9pm, although the younger set demand – and find – entertainment in the discos and *birrerie* of the new, northern part of town.

The Sicilian upper classes lead such a separate lifestyle that a social vacuum is inevitable. In rural Sicily, the divide is further consolidated by education, Mafia affiliation and isolation.

The story of private virtues and public vices is linked to Sicilians' hybrid past. As Bufalino says: "The Greeks shaped our sensitivity to light and harmony. The Muslims brought us a fragrance of Oriental gardens, of legendary *Thousand and One Nights*; but they also sowed in us a fanatical exaltation and an inclination to deceit and voluptuousness. The Spanish gave us hyperbole and haughtiness, the magnificence of words and rites, the magnanimity of our code of honour, but also a strong taste of ashes and death." Even today, the Arab west is overladen with Oriental inscrutability, Spanish manners and ceremony. By contrast, the Greek east is more democratic, with closer links to the Italian mainland.

Giuseppe Fava sees Palermo as the *alter ego* of Catania: where Palermitani are noble, bureaucratic, parasitic, indolent and decadent, Catanesi are *popolare*, commercial, industrious, cunning and cynical. Citizens from Siracusa, the quintessentially Greek southern city, are perceived of as cultured, educated, open, honest but *babba* (naive).

Culture and language

Sicily's miscegenation lives on in the language. *Cristiani* (Christians) is a generic word for people, just as *turchi* (Turks) refers to heathens. Appearances matter in Sicily: the word *azzizzare* (to beautify) comes from the Arabic; *orfanità* is Spanish-Palermitan dialect for looking good; *spagnolismo* (Hispanicism) naturally means seeming better than you are.

The hybrid Sicilian dialect has no future tense, a sign that nostalgia shapes the culture. Bufalino laments the passing of a "poorer but kinder" Sicily. "Where are the knife-grinders, the blacksmiths, the carters, the tanners, the tooth-pullers, the wandering storytellers, the singers of serenades… the matchmakers, the fortune-tellers?"

Sicilian culture feels intellectually out on a limb yet is curiously smug for being so. Norman Lewis refers to the "sullen mental climate" but the culture is visceral and exotic rather than moribund. Gagini's pure white marble

LEFT: hard bargaining over the price of squid.
RIGHT: the family is at the heart of Sicilian society.

Madonnas contrast with the archetypal sly Sicilian in Antonello da Messina's *Portrait of an Unknown Man*. Modern art encompasses Guttuso's rural landscapes and Francesco di Grandi's morbid paintings capturing the moment of death.

Private theatre

Within a cocoon of personal loyalty to friends and family, individuals cultivate their patch. "Anything that slights our prestige is regarded as an outrage that sometimes not even revenge can assuage." Bufalino's view is widely shared, especially among the upper and lower classes.

In a traditionally oppressed culture, one's word is one's bond; lives have depended on a *parola d'onore,* so promises must be kept. But in the eyes of a pessimistic or powerless individual, betrayal can happen only too easily, sparked off by a casual rebuff. Any rejection of hospitality is seen as a betrayal. As a Palermitan lawyer says: "For us, hospitality is a joy and a duty with obligations on both sides. A refusal is not just rude but fuels our *complessi di tradimento* [betrayal complex]."

According to Bufalino, "pride conducts the orchestra of our feelings" – especially sensuality and sex. Sicilian men of all classes

THE MUSIC OF THE ISLAND

Palermo is officially the noisiest city in Europe, yet even the traffic cannot drown the Sicilians' passion for music. The Teatro Mássimo, which reopened in 1997 after being closed for 23 years, is the venue for operatic productions and classical concerts from October to June.

Vincenzo Bellini, the father of *bel canto*, was born in Catania, where his music is celebrated in the newly restored Teatro Mássimo Bellini (it opened in 1890 with a performance of his best-known opera, *Norma*) – as well as in *pasta alla Norma*.

Eclectic home-grown music also embraces Gregorian chant, Scialpi's romantic ballads and Kunsertu's wailing Arab chants. But at its heart is music drawn from plaintive Greek or Arab laments, played on the shepherds' *scaccia-pensieri* ("worry chaser"), a curious mouth organ.

The traditional instruments used to accompany country dances include the *ciarameddu* (goatskin bagpipes), *friscalettu* (reed pipe) *tamureddu* (skin drum) and *marranzanu* (Jew's harp).

There are still a few surviving *cantastorie* – itinerant minstrels who travel from town to town with a guitar, singing haunting folk songs steeped in memories of poverty, lilting ballads, bawdy ditties and heroic tales of banditry and vanquished law makers.

mythologise their virility. "We males of Catania are generally thought capable of making our wetnurses pregnant," boasts a character in Lampedusa's *The Professor and the Siren*. Yet Bufalino reveals the dark side of Sicilian *machismo*: any sexual slight "causes a turmoil of depression and black rage in our blood that tilts our minds towards the tragic".

In rural Sicily, Verga's 19th-century views on the "ideal female" would not seem out of place today: "She is a short person who busies herself weaving, salting anchovies and producing children as a good housewife should." His novels present a typically bleak view of

relationships: "A woman at the window is a woman to be shunned"... "married couples and mules like to be alone." In his *Sicilian Uncles*, Leonardo Sciascia is more sophisticated yet equally sombre: "The more distant she was from me, the more she pretended desire. She was a good wife."

Sicilian heroes tend to be dead, ideally martyred like St Agata. However, the cult of the anti-hero and the underdog gives prime place to the bandit Giuliano, the incarnation of rebellious bravery. By contrast, state-sanctioned heroes like Judge Falcone are honoured too late; and Leoluca Orlando, his anti-Mafia successor, had to work hard and long to gain the respect of the Palermitans. Any genuine hero trying to change the system is scorned with the ultimate insult: *"idu nu du è"* (he's a nobody). The *disfattista* temperament, full of destructive criticism, is also brought to bear on new initiatives.

Island between heaven and hell

Perhaps the natives' sombre temperament is the product of insularity. To Sciascia, "Sicily has always symbolised a vanquished island as opposed to the victorious insularity of England." To Bufalino, Sicily is "a stone's throw from Africa… a paradise disguised as hell, a hell disguised as paradise." The island offers sweet solitude and self-sufficiency, which can sour into enforced exile or solitary confinement.

Yet despite their melancholic immutability, Sicilians have a passion for the present. Thanks to a heightened sense of history, the islanders attach supreme importance to time. It is not a question of punctuality but of a commitment to the present that cannot be bartered. Sicilians play for keeps, with strong convictions and a serious view of life.

They see themselves as volatile forces of nature, as violent as Etna, but imbued with a sense of the sacred. Spirituality is expressed in spontaneous church services led by lay women. In festivals, Classical polytheism merges with Christianity. But the everyday intimacy of the relationship with God implies a chatty equality and an acceptance of Him in any guise. As Sciascia says, "Sicily exists on the plane of fantasy. How can one live there without imagination?"

Superiority complex

"If we're going to be criminals, then we're the best of all," claims an honest housewife proudly. Bourbon arrogance can make a moody Sicilian feel like a god. Bufalino eulogises: "In no other country is the individual so unrepeatable, so unique."

Lampedusa's *The Leopard* is illuminating in unravelling this state of being Sicilian: "Sicilians never wish to improve for the simple reason that they believe themselves perfect. Their vanity is stronger than their misery. Every invasion by outsiders…upsets their illusion of achieved perfection, and risks disturbing their self-satisfied waiting for nothing at all." ❑

LEFT: a break for *bocce* (bowls).

Rural Life

Secrecy and melancholy are palpable in rural Sicily, where the scruffy one-horse towns have a suspicion of outsiders. A lone woman traveller can expect to be welcomed as if she were a creature out of *Alien*. All rooms in the one deserted inn are inexplicably declared full. The air smells of woodsmoke and incense, inside and out. While wizened men crowd the malodorous bars, widows in black fill the churches with spontaneous services.

But even the most secluded villages are building bridges to the future. Travellers may notice certain technological incongruities: fancy sports cars racing past donkeys laden with bushels of firewood; apartment buildings towering over the clay-tile roofs of ancient cottages.

Most villages are neither wholly traditional nor wholly modern. They are caught in the middle, adrift between the feudal past and high-tech future. Fifty years of government aid have raised the standard of living in the villages, but have done little to encourage lasting economic change. A generation ago, basic services like electricity, plumbing, medical care and education were a luxury. Today, these are taken for granted. The traditional peasant dream of buying land and farming for oneself is being supplanted by the desire for a colour television or a new car.

But, while consumerism is on the rise, there is little evidence that any deep-seated changes have taken root in the countryside. Villages are being subsidised, both by government funds and immigrant remittances, just enough to give them a taste of the North's wealth, without fostering economic self-sufficiency.

Underemployed and undercapitalised, many people still have to piece together a livelihood from a variety of jobs. It is not unusual for a family to farm one or more tiny parcels of land, sharecrop another, own a stake in an olive press or harvesting machine, and take occasional construction work or other state-funded jobs. Competition is stiff, and shrewdness, or *furberia*, is considered an asset, especially in business. "Better to be a devil with a pocketful of money," the saying goes, "than a fool with a few lire." A man is expected to take care of his family, to take advantage of opportunities – and, if necessary, other people – without worrying too much about ethics.

Generosity and kindness are only considered virtues to a point. Villagers generally agree that a person can be too kind-hearted for his own good. They call this type of person *fesso* (simple), an easy target. Again, the proverb says it all: "The man who makes himself a sheep will be eaten by the wolf."

The success of the family is not measured solely by wealth, but by the accumulation of influence and prestige. In a land where government is historically weak, personal power is highly valued. The man who is able to take care of his own affairs is someone who commands respect, a man of honour. And this man of honour is not only in a position to help his family, but his friends as well. *Clientelismo* (patronage) is the only sure way of getting ahead.

Family loyalty extends to the village as a whole, too, especially when villagers are confronted by out-

siders. It's not unusual to hear people refer to themselves first as members of a village, Stefanesi, Sciaccatani, Caltabellotesi, and only then as Sicilians or, less commonly, Italians. Such feelings are natural enough. Small villages tend to be dominated by three or four surnames and, after years of intermarriage, the entire village may seem like an extended family.

As in an extended family, everybody knows everybody else's business, and keeping up appearances is absolutely essential to family pride. This involves dressing and behaving well, performing religious duties, maintaining the appearance of modest wealth and fulfilling family obligations. In short, it means making a *bella figura*, a good impression. Gossip is a great leveller. ❏

RIGHT: subsistence farming in the countryside.

A WOMAN'S PLACE

Matriarchs who control the family, or helpless subordinates to the all-powerful Sicilian male? The role of women is changing...

In 1989 Lara Cardella, a 20-year-old Classics student, caused a sensation with her book *Volevo I Pantaloni* (*I Wanted to Wear Trousers*). Although unnamed, the setting is undoubtedly Licata, the backward Sicilian town in Agrigento province where the writer was born. The novel highlights the bigotry and prejudice directed against the girl who longs to wear trousers but who becomes ostracised and branded the town *buttana* (*puttana* or whore in dialect) through refusing to conform.

"Only men and prostitutes wear trousers," she is told. But a *buttana* is not so much a prostitute as a label for someone who transgresses the peasant code. The story confirms outsiders' views of Sicilian women as underdogs: "We are dogs looking for an owner to cuddle, beat and above all, protect us," the narrator laments. "But who will protect us from our owners, our parents?"

This narrative has a chilling echo in real life. In the early 1980s, a girl from a small village in western Sicily was gang-raped by a group of young, mostly teenage boys, several of whom she knew from school. When she tried to press charges, the boys' families closed ranks against her, portraying her as the village tart (or *puttana*) who had "asked for it" and was trying to get their sons into trouble. The girl was subjected to a hate campaign and forced to take refuge with a women's group in northern Italy.

Parental pressure

Young women in Sicily, particularly outside the major cities, are subject to strict moral codes. Parents exercise a moral patronage over their children that holds tremendous authority, even in a court of law. This authority is exercised in the public eye – parents have to be seen to be acting correctly, even if the best interests of the girl are sacrificed in the process.

In the past, courtship was a secret affair: Mario Puzo describes how young women would sit sewing in the windows where passing young men could only see their profile (no brazen eye contact was allowed). But now that all state schools are mixed, and boys and girls associate freely, and teenage couples can be seen taking the evening *passeggiata* arm in arm or kissing on the seat of a Vespa at the local beauty spot.

But there the "freedom" ends. Sons and daughters of all social classes live with their parents until they are married, and virtually no one cohabits. Parents therefore still exercise a degree of control. In a typical incident, the daughter of a bourgeois family in Siracusa got pregnant by her boyfriend at 17 and ended up engaged "*in casa*", living with her parents-in-law. She had merely swapped one housebound existence for another. Her father and brothers were very disappointed that she was forced to abandon her schooling and any prospect of a college education or career, yet they sanctioned absolutely her transition to teenage housewife.

In some working-class families, again

LEFT: a young couple encounter a priest in Palazzo Adriano. **RIGHT:** the evening *passegiata*.

outside the major cities, girls are taken out of school after the age of 12. The principal reasoning behind fathers not wanting their adolescent girls to go to school is that they don't want them mixing with boys in an environment beyond their control.

Keeping up appearances

Protecting the family's *figura* (image) and *roba* (property) remain fundamental to individual prestige. A man is expected to take care of his public image. As a character in one of Leonardo Sciascia's novels explains: "the only institution in the Sicilian conscience that really counts is the family. The family is the Sicilian's State. The State, as it exists for us, is extraneous to them, merely a *de facto* entity based on force. [The Sicilian] may be carried away by the idea of the State and may even rise to being Prime Minister; but the precise and definite code of his rights and duties will remain within the family."

This thinking lies at the core of Sicilian society. Parents, and more particularly the mother, provide the moral reference point for the Sicilian. There is a word for it: *mammismo*, an infantile dependence on one's mother, particularly prevalent among the urban upper classes. The writer Vincent Cronin calls Sicily "a

ACCEPTABLE ELOPEMENTS

The *fuitina* (lovers' flight) is one of Sicily's more curious phenomena, and is still a reality among the working classes. The *fuitina* takes place when a teenage couple fall in love but cannot be seen together – usually because of the girl's brothers or father exhibiting over-zealous "jealousy" (a demonstration of protectiveness that they feel society requires of them).

The young couple's flight signifies their serious intentions both to the families concerned and to society, and they will be given a room in a relative's house in which to consummate their "marriage". When they are older and self-supporting, their union will be legalised.

The point of the *fuitina* is to save the girl's honour for, if she were to sleep with the boy without family sanction, she would be considered a *puttana*.

There is also a seductively practical reason: it saves money. This way, the couple can be together publicly, the family incurs no shame, but does not have to go to the expense of a lavish wedding.

Unfortunately many of these premature "marriages" end in a disastrous, bitter, housebound existence for the girl, since the teenagers have hardly had time to get to know each other before circumstances force them to take matters in hand.

benevolent pedocracy; a society in which children hold the dominant power". His logic is that children are prized for their youth and beauty, and so "being the most loved, are the most powerful". But the reality is more sinister than this. That a mother can exonerate her child of wrongdoing simply because he is her child indicates an alarmingly amoral system.

The moral authority of a mother is taken as a positive influence and guarantee of her son's good behaviour. In 1996, when police arrested the 20-year-old eldest son of Totò "the Beast" Riina, formerly boss of bosses of the Sicilian Mafia, the boy's mother interceded. In a letter

of family values. Many Sicilians do not like to believe that a woman, particularly a mother, can possess a criminal mind. By championing the mother-child bond, the Mafia scored a major victory in public opinion, which astonishingly, turned against the magistrates who had ordered the boy's arrest.

The importance of public image and prestige also explains the *mafioso*'s traditional chauvinistic behaviour. For far from inhabiting a parallel universe, the Mafia exists within Sicilian society and mores, not outside or in spite of them. Mafia families generally mix only with their underworld friends and relations, and

to *La Repubblica* newspaper, she wrote: "I have decided to open my heart, the heart of a mother swollen and overflowing with grief at the arrest of my son. Giovanni is a normal, open, happy, easy-going boy. He works hard in the fields all day. We have brought up our children making enormous sacrifices, overcoming tremendous difficulties, giving them every possible love and support. We have raised them to respect the family and love their neighbour."

The letter, a *tour de force* of motherly love, was received by many Sicilians as a vindication

tend to demonstrate the deeply conservative side of Sicilian customs and mores.

Family honour

A 15-year-old girl from a working class Palermo family, living on one of the city's grim suburban public housing projects, described in 1992 how her *fidanzato* (fiancé) had forbidden her to go to school, and told her she must not look for work. "He will take care of me," she said proudly.

A man is expected to control his family's behaviour, including his daughter's (and his wife's) sexuality. If his daughter loses her honour he must consider it a personal affront, and

LEFT: volcanic passion near Etna. **ABOVE:** traditional weddings, like this in Caltanissetta, are *de rigueur*.

traditionally he can reclaim *onore* by seeking revenge or forcing the lovers to marry. This attitude is close to the heart of the island's character: it is not sex that the family fears most, but scandal.

Much has been made of the crime of passion or *delitto d'onore*, which is considered entirely understandable, even expected. Until 1975, a man who killed to preserve his honour could expect to receive a short sentence – between three and seven years. But it is a deeply old-fashioned notion, preserved, in the typically pragmatic Sicilian way, only where it suits modern uses. Many a Mafia crime has been

passed off as "*delitto d'onore*" and the police would make no further investigations: if man said he killed because he "had to", society tended to let him off the hook.

What passes as a code of honour has been widely used to exonerate both men and women of crimes. Sicilians' unwillingness to accept that women are capable of criminal behaviour has always worked in the Mafia's favour. Although over 100 women have been arrested for Mafia crimes since 1995, still there are magistrates who refuse to accept that women play an active role in Cosa Nostra. In a landmark ruling in 1983, a judge stated that women were too stupid to get involved in the "difficult

world" of finance, and therefore it was impossible for them to be active in the business of money laundering.

The ruling was all the more scandalous because there were already women of influence in public life at that time: the mayor of Palermo was a woman and, in spite of Sicily's backward reputation in terms of sexual equality, increasing numbers of women were getting university degrees and qualifying for the professions – including the law. Partly as a result of women filtering up through the judiciary, the system has gradually changed from the inside. A senior female Sicilian investigator is far less likely to swallow the argument, often propounded by Mafia lawyers, that women have no option but to obey their husbands.

The 1983 ruling was all the more significant because it enraged a large number of educated Sicilian women and sparked a women's anti-Mafia movement which sought to expose such disastrously old-fashioned views. One woman who joined the ranks of women battling against the Mafia was Piera Aiello, wife of a gangster from Partanna, western Sicily. She became an informer in 1991, and rebutted the image of the helpless, dependent woman in love. In an interview she said: "A wife always knows what is going on. A woman can lead her husband wherever she wants."

Piera Aiello's testimony was of massive importance because it belied the image of the woman as a passive victim. She revealed that women were an essential part of the criminal machinery: most of them knew everything, including the identity of their husbands' associates, and helped hide weapons and plan crimes where necessary. This helped to overturn the familiar view that Sicily is a patriarchy, where women keep their counsel and mutely obey.

Women on top?

Anyone who has got to know a Sicilian family will be aware that there is a strong basis for the belief that Sicily is in fact a matriarchy; that behind the public pretence that the man is boss, the woman is really in charge. Certainly, Sicilian women are far from the quiet, retiring, obedient vessels that we are led to believe.

Yet the familiar postcard image of the men of the town meeting together to play cards or talk at the end of the day is still very much a reality, and in small-town Sicily, one frequently ends up wondering: "Where are the women?"

They are traditionally deprived of that luxury of associating in groups: indoors, the grandmother, mother and daughter will cook, clean and pass the hours together. The bond between them becomes extremely close as a result. But in recent years, political developments have encouraged associations of women who have got together to try to push through changes. The fight against the bomb, against an oppressive male-dominated system and most recently against the Mafia have brought women together in groups of increasing strength and volubility.

Although at present these are largely middle-class, educated women, an increasing number of working-class women, mothers of drug addicts and minor criminals, are getting involved with community and political programmes to improve their children's prospects.

While more women are able to make contact with political groups today, most who want a more progressive existence simply leave the rural areas. The reality is a rural exodus to university in the city. Sicily has a long tradition of girls excelling in higher education. The lure of academia is due not only to high unemployment, but also to a desire for greater autonomy. Study offers many Sicilian girls an escape.

Signs for the future

In some ways, these discussions make Sicily seem more primitive than it is. Catania, Siracusa and Messina, and to a lesser extent Palermo, enjoy liberal lifestyles, at least for the *borghesia* (middle classes). A relatively high proportion of women have careers and independence.

The 1974 divorce law led to a succession of family rights which gave women equal status. Sicilian middle-class women no longer marry young, which reflects in part their strong desire for independence. When they do marry, for the most part they keep their own surnames. Sicily now has the lowest population growth in Europe at an average one child per couple.

The vexed question of whether Sicily is a

> **CITY OF WOMEN**
>
> Women have always been seen as dominant family figures in Cefalù, and in recent years this has extended into public life: most key jobs in the city, including mayor, chief of police and magistrates, are held by women.

matriarchy can be resolved in part by dividing Sicilian life into public and private domains: in public the man runs the family's affairs. But within the home, the woman is in charge, and no longer just of making pasta sauce.

Mary Taylor Simeti, an American who married a Sicilian and whose book, *On Persephone's Island*, describes a year in the life of a Sicilian homemaker, says, "making the year's supply of tomato sauce is the most important domestic

ritual in the Sicilian summer." But increasingly the mothers and grandmothers carry out these duties, and the younger women are happy to take a few jars off them, while buying tinned sauces on their own account.

The majority of forward-looking Sicilians bring up their children with fewer distinctions and privileges between the sexes. True, children stay at home until they are married, even in the most progressive households – but why would they move out? Property is expensive and the family is a tight-knit unit that functions very strongly at all levels and ages. In true Sicilian style, what seems traditional is, for the most part, pragmatic. ❏

LEFT: lacemaking is traditional women's work.
RIGHT: the next generation, Palazzo Adriano.

THE MAFIA

*With its tradition of private justice and its code of silence, the Mafia seemed to
defy authority – until recently, when authority was found to be implicated too*

The Mafia may somehow affect the majority of Sicilians, but local attitudes are changing profoundly. The revulsion of Sicilians over the 1992 murders of Mafia-fighting judges Giovanni Falcone and Paolo Borsellino helped to weaken the Mafia's grip on public opinion, its greatest weapon, and

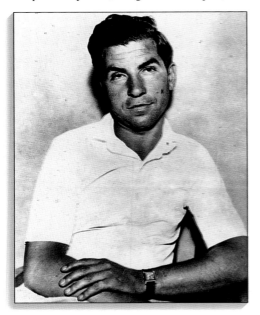

dented the age-old code of silence, or *omertà*. This, coupled with tougher laws and greater police determination, has exposed organised crime as never before.

Murky beginnings

Romantic treatment of what is arguably Italy's biggest blight and its second largest company pins its origins to medieval times and a mysterious religious sect, the Beati Poli, whose hooded members lurked, armed with pikes and swords, in underground passages beneath the streets of Palermo. Some say the word Mafia first appeared in the mid-1600s, meaning a witch; others say it derives from dialectical or

Arabic words meaning "protection", "misery" or "hired assassin". What is certain is that the Mafia as we know it began to take shape in the early 19th century, in the form of brotherhoods, formed to protect Sicilians from corruption, foreign oppression and feudal malpractice. Criminal interests quickly seeped in, corruption became the preferred milieu, and before long the brotherhoods were feeding on the misery from which they pretended to defend their members.

Judges were soon said to be secretly protecting them, nobles to be backing them. The brotherhoods' principal manifestation was as the *gabelotti*, organised minders of the land holdings of an often absent nobility, who distributed jobs and land and policed the countryside.

When Garibaldi set off from Sicily with his redshirts, he did so thanks to the brotherhoods, which lent the support of some 20,000 men. Many were said to be cut-throats, eager to cash in on the spoils of a campaign. Turned back by the troops of Turin, they reorganised to oppose the redistribution to private landlords of nearly half a million acres (200,000 hectares) of Church land in Sicily. These were known as the "agrarian *mafiosi*".

The first godfather

Between 1872 and World War I, poverty and the defeat of agrarian trade unions forced 1½ million Sicilians to emigrate. Most went to the Americas. There, many joined brotherhoods based on those back home and the foundations of Cosa Nostra were laid. Don Vito Cascio Ferro is seen as the father of the modern Mafia and is the source of misconceptions about the good "old Mafia" and the degenerate "new Mafia". After being accused of committing 20 murders, he fled to New York in 1901 and founded the American Mafia.

In 1925, Mussolini, appalled at the Mafia's new importance as a surrogate state, set out to bring it to its knees. He sent his prefect Cesare Mori to Sicily, with almost unlimited powers. By 1927, victory was proclaimed for Mori's heavy-handed tactics, which entailed throwing thousands into prison, and laying siege to towns to flush out the Mafia bosses. But Mori was also a threat to powerful agrarian *mafiosi*. Soon Sicily's landed interests struck a deal with the Fascists, and Mori left the island. In return, the agrarian *mafiosi* saw to it that Sicily's more criminal Mafia elements were almost wiped out.

BOOZE BOON

Prohibition in the 1920s was a boon to the American Mafia. By controlling bootleg liquor supplies, the mob graduated into a sophisticated urban organisation.

They won a reprieve in 1943, when they were given the job of clearing the way for the Allied invasion. Fearing the effects that war between the US and Italy would have on their interests, Italian-American mobsters such as Lucky Luciano had struck a deal with US authorities in 1940. In return for their help they were to be left alone. The operation, overseen by Don Vito Genovese, a Naples thug wanted for murder in the US, went well: the Allies hardly fired a shot.

Local *mafiosi*, re-armed with weapons taken from Italian forces, and their dons – such as Don Calógero Vizini (39 murders, six attempted murders) – were installed by the Allies as mayors of key Sicilian towns.

After the war, organised criminals began supporting Sicily's pro-separatist movement backed by agrarian interests. Together with the authorities, the Mafia joined in the suppression of banditry, which had made inroads into its territory during the Fascist siege.

Gangland massacres

In the 1950s a war of attrition was fought between Don Genco Russo's "country" Mafia dei Giardini who dominated Palermo province, and the "city" Mafia dei Cantieri. The former were old-time spivs who controlled the citrus groves, markets, building industry, water supplies and public appointments. The latter were modern-day gangsters who ran the docks, distribution, contraband cigarettes and most industries. By the end of the decade, it was these, led by the La Barbera brothers and Luciano Liggio, who were dominant over Don Genco Russo's "country" Mafia. When Lucky Luciano died in 1962, Liggio became the new Godfather.

LEFT: Lucky Luciano, who forged links between the Sicilian and American Mafias. RIGHT: the arrest of Luciano Liggio, his successor as Godfather.

In 1957 the American and Sicilian Mafias met in Palermo's Hotel des Palmes, a summit called to create the *Cupola* or Commission and to establish the Sicilians' heroin franchise. The result was a criminal organisation with a clear pyramid structure. The island's *mammasantissima* also had the satisfaction of securing the import and distribution of all heroin in the US. It was known as the Pizza Connection since pizza parlours were a cover for the money laundering. Sicily emerged as a strategic centre for drugs,

arms and international crime, confirming the shift of the Mafia's economic centre of gravity from the country to the city.

Luciano Liggio, a pitiless peasant and undisputed *padrone* of Corleone, was confirmed as the leader of the new Mafia. He was a fast learner: when arrested, he was found reading Kant's *Critique of Pure Reason*. On his capture he announced: "If you want me to survive, I'll need a soft bed, a meat diet, and summer holidays by the sea." From 1974, the semi-invalid ran the Mafia from a prison cell equipped with a personal bar and an entourage of lawyer, barber and doctor. His Corleonese family, led by his lieutenants Salvatore "Totò" Riina and

Bernardo "The Tractor" Provenzano, rose to the top of the heroin trade and to the pinnacle of the Cosa Nostra pecking order by breaking almost the entire codex of Mafia laws.

Clan warfare

The tactics of the Corleonesi were simple: the removal of any *mafioso* who coveted power or caused trouble. The Mafia clan war of the early 1980s left Palermo's streets strewn with blood and the Corleonesi undisputed victors. Riina's name has been linked to some 1,000 murders.

Not all the victims were *mafiosi*. In response to the drugs trade that had prompted the car-

could shed light on their illegal activities. In 1982 La Torre was ambushed and gunned down in Palermo city centre.

One of the mourners at his funeral was General Carlo Alberto Dalla Chiesa, the *carabiniere* who had vanquished the terrorist Red Brigades before being sent to Palermo as chief prefect, promising new action against the Mafia. He had begun digging into Sicily's huge building industry, an easy area in which to invest profits from drugs, and appeared to have stumbled on a minefield – the question of who in the highest political circles protected, or possibly even issued orders to, the Mafia. This

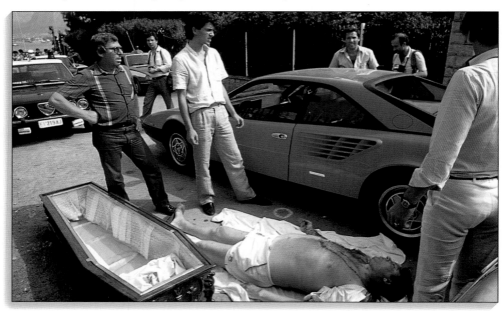

nage, a parliamentary anti-Mafia committee had been established; in reply, the Mafia instituted a campaign of terror in which top officials, the police and politicians were targeted. In 1971, Palermo's chief prosecutor Pietro Scaglione was the first in a long list of *cadáveri eccelenti* (illustrious corpses), allegedly murdered by Liggio, Riina and Provenzano. But anti-Mafia measures continued to be discussed, and sometimes even implemented.

Pio La Torre, the Sicilian regional Communist Party leader, proposed a government dispensation to allow lawyers access to private bank accounts – a measure that would expose Mafia bosses to financial investigation that

suspected complicity was to become known as the "Third Level".

One hundred days after the murder of La Torre, Dalla Chiesa and his wife were murdered in Palermo's Via Carini. Italy was shocked, and questions were asked, not for the first time, about how committed the national government really was to rooting out Mafia crime. Nando Dalla Chiesa, the murdered prefect's son, accused the leaders of the Christian Democrat party – including prime minister Giulio Andreotti – of isolating his father.

ABOVE: a victim of Mafia feuding. **RIGHT:** the maxi-trials of the mid-1980s brought many *mafiosi* to court.

The maxi-trials

In response to strong public feeling, and to counteract accusations of government inertia or complicity, a dramatic crackdown on the Mafia was launched. La Torre's law was rushed through parliament, thousands of suspects were rounded up and an anti-Mafia pool of magistrates, which included Giovanni Falcone and Paolo Borsellino, started their investigations.

Their star witness was the high-ranking *mafioso* Tommaso Buscetta, who was arrested in Brazil in 1982 and, after a failed suicide attempt, agreed to give state's evidence. The testimony of Buscetta and other *pentiti* (penitents) who followed his lead was vital in a series of *maxiprocessi* (maxi-trials) in the mid-1980s. The largest of these trials began in February 1986 and lasted 18 months. In a specially built high-security bunker adjoining the Ucciardone prison in Palermo, 460 *mafiosi* stood trial. Of these, 18 received life sentences, and 338 other sentences totalling 2,065 years. Many others were released when they agreed to give evidence against their former accomplices.

In spite of their obvious success, the anti-Mafia pool of magistrates was mysteriously disbanded in 1988. Judge Falcone had feared the state would wash its hands of him: "First they said, 'Go to war, we're all with you.' Now they say, 'Go to war, but don't bother us.'" His Sicilian pessimism proved correct.

After his investigations were thwarted in Sicily, Falcone moved to Rome as Director of Penal Affairs and lobbied for a force with powers similar to the American FBI. In May 1992, he was on the point of being nominated *super-procuratore*, its head, when the Mafia took their revenge. As he drove with his wife, Judge Francesca Morvillo, along the *autostrada* from the airport to Palermo, their car passed over a remote-controlled mine. The two judges and their three-man escort were killed instantly, their cars reduced to twisted burning metal, and a huge crater blown in the motorway.

Two months later, fellow-magistrate Paolo Borsellino, Falcone's boyhood friend and obvious successor, became another "illustrious corpse". He had just arrived at his mother's home when an 80 kg (175 lb) bomb in his car was detonated. The explosion left virtually no trace of his body, killed his five bodyguards,

and broke windows several blocks away.

His family refused a state funeral, implicitly accusing the government of failing to protect a state servant. "Better one day as Borsellino than a hundred as *mafiosi*," screamed the Palermitan crowds at his funeral.

The terror continued in 1993 with bombs in Milan and Rome that killed bystanders and devastated churches; an explosion at Florence's Uffizi Gallery destroyed minor masterpieces. But the Mafia miscalculated. The assassinations of the two Palermo judges and the attempt to destroy the nation's cultural treasures only served to tighten the resolve of the Italians and their government against the Mafia.

THE PRICE OF PENITENCE

Tommaso Buscetta, who died in April 2000, claimed that his motives in testifying against the Mafia were to bring down an organisation that had betrayed its principles. "It is necessary to destroy this band of criminals," he declared, "who have perverted the principles of Cosa Nostra and dragged them through the mud." No doubt personal revenge was a motive, too: some of his close relatives had been killed by the Corleonese family in the recent clan wars. After Buscetta turned *pentito* and began talking to the prosecutors, Mafia hit men killed his wife, his sons, his parents, his aunts and uncles and several nephews and nieces – 33 relatives in all.

Bedsheet protest

In Sicily the atrocities of 1992 sparked an immediate popular backlash against the Mafia's excesses. On the evening of Falcone's assassination, three Palermo sisters and their daughters hung bedsheets with anti-Mafia slogans from the balconies of their neighbouring apartments. Soon other Palermitans joined in. The bedsheet protest caught on until it seemed that most of Palermo was making a personal stand against the Mafia. As anti-Mafia mayor Leoluca

Francesco Madonia, the second most feared Mafia boss, was arrested in 1992; the courts confiscated his 62 legitimate businesses and property worth $400 million. But the ultimate prize was the Godfather himself, captured in Palermo in 1993 after 23 years on the run. Known as *la belva* (the beast), "Totò" Riina's philosophy shows his shrewd peasant origins: "If someone's finger is hurt, it's better to be safe and cut off his arm." But instead of a monster, Italians were shocked to see a podgy 62-year-old diabetic oozing false

Orlando said later, "On certain days, you could look up at an apartment building and see where the Mafia don lived – it was the apartment without a sheet hanging from the window."

The *Comitato dei Lenzuoli* (Committee of the Sheets) was more than just a short-term reaction to tragedy. It grew into a well-organised and skilful campaigning organisation, using T-shirts, pamphlets, television appearances and public meetings to keep public attention focused on Mafia activities and official attempts to curb them. The bedsheet protest was followed by marches, demonstrations and sit-ins.

In response to sustained public pressure, the authorities had to be seen to be acting.

humility. At his televised trial for ordering political murders, Riina claimed never to have heard of Cosa Nostra, except on television: "I was all house, work, family and church."

Indeed, he had not strayed far from home during his 23 years "on the run". He had lived openly with his family in Corleone, registering his children in local schools and hospitals and generally coming and going as he pleased. Inevitably, citizens wondered how it was that the authorities were seemingly ignorant of the whereabouts of Italy's most wanted man. The question of Mafia complicity at the "Third Level" was raised again.

No amount of political patronage could

prevent Riina and 23 other leading *mafiosi* being sentenced to life imprisonment in 1994. But the can of worms had been opened, and investigations began into the involvement of senior figures in Mafia activities. By 1995 more than 6,000 Italian bureaucrats, corporate executives and politicans (including a staggering 438 deputies and senators) were under investigation or had been indicted on corruption charges.

Right to the top

In September 1995, Giulio Andreotti, 76, seven times prime minister and one of Italy's most respected elder statesmen, shuffled into the courtroom of the Ucciardone prison in Palermo. He was accused of being a protector and friend of the Mafia in return for votes. In a separate trial the following year, Andreotti was accused in Perugia of having been instrumental in the murder of Mino Pecorelli, an investigative journalist killed by Mafia gunmen in 1979. Most of the evidence against him was the testimony of *pentiti*, challenged at every stage by Andreotti's defence team. In fact, delays and legal niceties stretched the trial out for four years. Finally, in October 1999, Andreotti was found not guilty on all counts because of insufficient proof or contradictory evidence.

But the message was clear to *mafiosi* and politicans alike: henceforth no one could be considered "untouchable". Another former prime minister and media tycoon, Silvio Berlusconi, had his business dealings investigated by an anti-Mafia police unit in 1998, though he stoutly denied charges of money-laundering for Cosa Nostra.

Meanwhile, more senior *mafiosi* were rounded up: Leoluca Bagarella, Totò Riina's successor and brother-in-law, in 1995; Giovanni Brusca, one of the organisation's most ruthless killers and the mastermind behind Falcone's assassination, in 1996; two other bosses, Vito Vitale and Mariano Troia, in 1998.

A new Mafia?

No one, even Palermo's successful anti-Mafia mayor Leoluca Orlando, pretends that Cosa Nostra has disappeared. The Mafia is changing. In 1995 it fell into debt, as income fell

(fewer public works and confiscation of Mafia property) and costs rose (mainly legal fees). As the old Mafia guard languish in jail, a more sophisticated organisation, based on "old Mafia values", is believed to be filling the power vacuum. The new-generation gangster is likely to be as ruthless on the stock exchange floor as on the streets of Palermo, be armed with a computer, and be adept at surfing the Internet – the favoured new medium for laundering money.

Along with drugs, extortion and property speculation, Mafia activities now include trading arms, nuclear and conventional, between Eastern European and Middle Eastern and other

embargo-covered countries. Investment features as much in Moscow as it does in Palermo.

But in Sicily, the greatest change has been in public attitudes. Where once *mafioso* activity was seen as revolt against the state, justified by centuries of foreign oppression, today the population is less tolerant. The revelations of political complicity at the highest level has destroyed any fanciful notion that the Mafia somehow represented the private citizen against the forces of authority. While there is no doubt that Sicily still harbours some dangerous criminals, they can no longer rely on support, or even consent, from most Sicilians. The *mafiosi* are no longer untouchable. ❏

LEFT: a threatening gesture made by one of the accused in a maxi-trial. **RIGHT:** former prime minister Giulio Andreotti, accused of Mafia connections.

FOOD AND WINE

*Sicily's fertile volcanic soil and teeming seas have supplied
the island with a rich and varied diet. The wines aren't bad, either*

One of Sicily's best-kept secrets is its ancient and distinguished gastronomic tradition. Only a few Sicilian dishes, such as the eggplant pickle known as *caponata* or the sweet ricotta-filled *cannoli*, have crossed the Straits of Messina to find fame and fortune abroad. Even Sicilians are often unaware of how history seasons their favourite foods.

The Greek colonists who arrived in the 8th century BC were astonished at the fertility of Sicily's volcanic soil, and with such abundance on the doorstep, Siracusa soon became the gastronomic capital of the Classical world.

In the 5th century BC the city gave birth to the first cookbook written in the West, Mithaecus's *Lost Art of Cooking*, and to the first school for chefs. It was apparently a rich and elaborate cuisine: in the 4th century BC, a Sicilian poet, Archestratus, author of a cookery book in verse, complained of an excessive use of fancy sauces, and Plato condemned the court of the Siracusan tyrant Dionysius for the same culinary crime.

Cosmopolitan cuisine

We know too little of the Classical dishes to trace direct descendants in modern Sicilian cuisine, but many sweet-and-sour dishes, such as *caponata*, have a vinegar-based sauce similar to ones described by Archestratus. Classical authors describe cakes that sound like modern *mustazzoli* (biscuits sweetened with a syrup made from grape must) or *regina* biscuits rolled in sesame seeds and sold in Sicilian bakeries today. *Cuccia*, a sweet pudding made from wheat berries, which western Sicilians eat on St Lucy's Day, has echoes of the ritual dish of boiled seeds with which the ancient Greeks marked the onset of winter.

The Arabs brought innovative agricultural and culinary techniques and introduced crops that enriched Sicilian cooking: citrus fruits, rice

and aubergines became staples. They also made Sicilian cuisine sweet and spicy. Cane sugar was introduced, accompanied by a Middle Eastern taste for sumptuous sweets, which is still a Sicilian trademark. The most famous dish of the Arab legacy is *cassata siciliana*, the spectacular and overpoweringly sweet sponge filled

with ricotta cream and decorated with almond paste and candied fruit.

By the end of the Saracen occupation, the mould of Sicilian cooking had been set. The Normans employed Arab chefs and, until the Renaissance, Sicily exported luxury foods (pasta, sugar, confectionery and citrus fruits) to Northern Italy. Although the Spanish brought chocolate and tomatoes from the New World and French chefs were fashionable in the 19th century, significant developments in Sicilian cuisine followed class lines.

The poor survived on bread and wild greens; the aristocracy enjoyed the costly and conspicuous dishes of the *cucina baronale*. As for the

PRECEDING PAGES: olives for sale at Palermo's Vucciria Market. **LEFT:** a Siracusa *formaggeria* (cheese shop). **RIGHT:** *pasta reale*, traditional marzipan fruits.

emerging *borghesia,* it borrowed from both classes to create what is essentially contemporary Sicilian cooking. In essence, it is a flexible cuisine: extravagant in its festive dishes, straightforward in its daily fare, but always dedicated to exalting the extraordinary flavours of the island.

For starters

Trays of *caponata* vie with *sarde a beccafico*, sardines rolled in breadcrumbs, with a pine-nut and currant filling and baked with bay leaves and orange juice, or *involtini di melanzane*, stuffed aubergines (eggplant) in tomato sauce.

may be a classic *insalata di mare* (seafood with oil, lemon and herbs), the *pesce spada affumicato* (smoked swordfish), or a fry of tiny cuttlefish, each no bigger than a thumbnail.

Rice, introduced by the Arabs and cultivated until the 18th century in the Lentini area, survives in *arancine* snacks. In Catania, rice features in a cheese and meat timbale or in *crespelle*, sweet, honey-dipped fritters.

However, most Sicilians feel pasta to be the proper first course. Under Arab rule, Sicily was arguably the first place to produce dried pasta on a commercial scale. Today's best pasta dish is the simple but sublime *pasta con*

These *antipasti* stars share the high table with humbler but equally delicious snacks beloved of Sicilian students and workers: chickpea fritters (*panelle*); potato croquettes (*crocche di patate*); fried rice balls filled with chopped meat and peas (*arancine*); even miniature versions of *pani cu la meuza*, bread rolls stuffed with sautéed beef spleen.

In the mountain towns of the Madonie and Nébrodi, rustic products are served as *antipasti*. These include salami, cow's milk cheeses (*caciotta* and *caciocavallo*), sheep's milk cheeses (*tuma, primosale* or *primiticcio*), sun-dried tomatoes and wild mushrooms *sott'olio*. On the coast, the sea provides the inspiration. It

le melanzane, known in eastern Sicily as *pasta alla Norma* (after the Catanian composer Bellini's operatic heroine). Here, sun-ripened fresh tomatoes, basil, fried aubergines and a sprinkling of salted ricotta melt into a magical blend.

Tomatoes are an essential ingredient in dishes such as the *pasta alla carrettiera* ("carter-style") in which raw, ripe tomatoes are pounded in a mortar with garlic, red pepper and olive oil, then poured uncooked over hot pasta. The celebratory *pasta al ragù* also uses a tomato sauce, this time made with *'strattu*, tomato paste dried in the sun to the consistency of clay, in which pieces of pork or beef have been simmered.

A fancy *ragù* might have sausage, meat balls and a stuffed beef roll. In Enna at Christmas, it is spiced with cinnamon, cloves and bitter cocoa powder. At weddings in the area between Syracuse and Ragusa, *ragù* is served *'ncaciata*, baked with layers of cheese and hard-boiled eggs in a casserole lined with fried aubergine (*melanzane*).

A host of vegetables are served with pasta, ranging from fancy preparations like *fritella*, a spring sauté of new peas, baby fava beans and tiny artichokes, to simpler combinations of pasta garnished with sautéed courgettes or boiled with wild borage or mustard greens. A

fennel. In the east, a potent sauce of anchovies and breadcrumbs is still popular (*anclova e muddica*). In spring, when tuna and swordfish are available, small pieces are stewed with tomatoes and mint and served with pasta. In another dish, smoked tuna roe is grated over spaghetti mixed with olive oil and parsley.

In the Trápani area, where the Arab influence is strongest, a local version of *couscous*, steamed in a fish broth, is a substitute for pasta. The interior boasts a survivor from Classical times: *maccu*, a thick purée made from dried fava or broad beans flavoured with oil and wild fennel seeds.

typical summer dish in western Sicily is *pasta cui tenerumi*, spaghetti broken up into short lengths and cooked with tender sprouts of the vines on which the long thin, pale green *cucuzza* marrow grows. It is topped with raw tomatoes, chopped up with garlic and basil.

Western Sicily's most famous pasta dish is made with fish. Legend has it that the exotic *pasta con sarde* was invented in the 9th century by the cooks of the invading Arab army who used whatever was at hand: sardines, saffron, pine nuts, dried currants and sprigs of wild

LEFT: herbs, tomatoes and peppers on sale in Lípari.
ABOVE: fresh fish and seafood in Sferracavallo.

FAST FOOD AL FRESCO

Sicily's street food is worth investigating, although the timid may prefer to seek it out in *tavola calda* bars rather than try it on the street. In western Sicily, fritters and croquettes are popular, along with squares of an oily, spongy pizza called *sfincione*. From street stands in Palermo one can buy *stigghiola*, goat intestines filled with onions, cheese and parsley, then grilled. *Panelle*, fried chickpea squares, are common street food. The east favours a bread dough wrapped around a meat, cheese or vegetable filling, then baked or fried. The names and shapes vary, but requesting an *impanata* ("in breadcrumbs") usually produces something good.

Fishy meat

Often meat as a main course is disappointing. Beef can be tough and tasteless, except when stuffed and braised in tomato sauce (*bracialone* or *farsumagru*) or skewered and grilled (*involtini alla siciliana*). An exception is the excellent lamb and pork raised in the mountain pastures and oak forests of the Madonie and Nébrodi. Pork sausage, often sprinkled with wild fennel seeds, is uniformly good. However, to the *contadini* (peasants and farmers), the daily *bistecca* is a sign of their new prosperity.

Poor meat is compensated for by exceptionally good seafood. Fish, whether fried, grilled

or simmered *alla ghiotta* with tomatoes, capers and olives, is popular in the Messina area. Siracusa favours a sweet and sour *stemperata* made of Sicilian fish which, although expensive, is usually fresh and tasty.

Given the superb quality of the vegetables, it is hard to forgive restaurants for relying on an undistinguished *insalata mista* to accompany the main course. *Melanzane alla parmigiana* was a Sicilian invention, after all, and there are myriad ways of preparing this delicious vegetable. Artichokes may be fried, stuffed, roasted on coals, or braised with oil, parsley and garlic *alla viddana*. Bright green cauliflower is boiled and served with oil and lemon, or cooked with anchovies, cheese, olives and red wine.

Markets are the place to admire Sicilian vegetables. Palermo's Vucciria and Ballarò are famous for brilliantly coloured and beautifully displayed abundance.

Sweets

Choice becomes hardest towards the end of a meal. The Arabs introduced sorbets, to the Sicilians' eternal gratitude. Etna provided snow throughout the summer and its preservation and sale was the lucrative monopoly of the Bishop of Catania.

The habit of mixing sugar and jasmine essence in a glassful of snow also dates from Arab times. Sicilians, rich and poor alike, have had a passion for ice cream since the 18th century. Home-made ice cream, in a bewildering and tantalising variety of flavours and shapes, is available in bars and restaurants everywhere.

Then there is the gamut of Sicilian pastry, from the chewy *mustazzoli* biscuits or the nut- and fig-flavoured *buccellato* or *cuddureddu* of classical origins, to the opulent Arab tradition of *cassata* and *cannoli*. For centuries, the chief pastry producers were nuns: Palermo alone boasted more than a score of convents, each famous for a particular sweet. A few convents, in Agrigento, Sciacca or Palma di Montechiaro, still sell their pastries. Elsewhere, as in Erice, the tradition is carried on by women who learned their trade in convent orphanages.

On All Souls' Day, Sicilian children traditionally awake to find sugar dolls and baskets of fruit at the foot of their beds, left there by "the souls of their forefathers". The fruit is made of marzipan, known as *pasta reale* or *martorana*, one of Sicily's most delightful culinary traditions. Nowadays, *pasta reale* is readily available all year round in the standard forms of fruits and vegetables, or in the Paschal lambs and flowered hearts that Maria Grammatico of Erice learned to make from the nuns.

Marzipan aspires to an art form in the fanciful creations of Luigi Marciante of Siracusa, Giuseppe Chemi of Taormina and Corrado Costanzo of Noto. Delicious, decorative and durable, marzipan gives a lingering taste of Sicily, one you can take home with you. Visitors with more salacious tastes can be transported

LEFT: fish stew, Catania style, in Aci Trezza.
RIGHT: Marsala dominates this display of Sicilian wines.

by the nuns' sweet triumphs: virgins' breasts (*minni di vergini*) or chancellors' buttocks (*fedde del cancelliere*) could only be Sicilian.

Wine

Grapes and wine have always formed a major part of the Sicilian economy. In the more recent past they had little more than commodity value, being despatched to bump up the strength and colour of insipid offerings from further north, for traditional, low, bush-trained vines can develop prodigious amounts of sugar under Sicily's powerful sun. In the past couple of decades, though, there has been a full-scale return to producing wines for drinking, not blending, and to harnessing native grape varieties to that end.

Surprisingly, it is the white wines that have taken the lead. From grapes wire-trained not too close to the heat-reflecting soil, astutely pruned, harvested before their acidity drops too low, then carefully fermented at cool temperatures to conserve their aromas, light, dry, delicately floral white wines emerge that can rival some better known names of the wine world as well as being ideal for drinking with Sicilian dishes in a Sicilian climate.

The Count's Wines

The Regaleali estate, near Vallelunga in Caltanissetta province, is fascinating, both for its wines and as an insight into local wine-growing traditions. The estate is owned by the Conte Tasca d'Almerita, one of the Sicilian aristocrats who has best used the wine trade to adapt itself to the modern world.

The Count's vineyards lie between 450 and 650 metres (1,500–2,100 ft) above sea level, which together with the strong, cooling breezes they attract and their distance from the sea give very cool nights to balance warm days – almost ideal conditions for vine growing.

The estate has been in the hands of the Conte Tasca family since 1834. It was originally planted mainly with grain: the changeover to vines has been slow and steady, and is continuing. It was Regaleali that led the way back to quality winemaking in the quantity-dominated post-war years and the wines are still among Sicily's leaders.

Straight Regaleali white, red and rosé are not

to be sneezed at; there's also a pair of elegant sparkling wines and a clutch of wines from fashionable, imported grape varieties.

But the estate's reputation hangs on two others. Nozze d'Oro, ("Golden Wedding") is a white, first made in 1985 to mark the Count's 50th wedding anniversary. Now produced in years when weather conditions are particularly favourable, it is refined, rounded, herby, buttery and long-ageing. The Count's favourite, however, is Rosso del Conte, made from the Nero d'Avola and Perricone grapes. Intense, full and powerful, it too ages slowly. Examples from the early 1990s are really exciting.

Wines from elsewhere

A market leader is Terre di Ginestra, from its high (900 metres/2,900 ft) vineyards above San Cipirello, behind Palermo. The grapes are grown on north-facing slopes to avoid excess sun and handled with extreme skill to produce excellent crisp whites.

The locals cannot agree as to which of the two popular indigenous grapes, Catarratto or Inzolia, makes superior white wine. The producer Tenuta di Donnafugata has chosen Inzolia. Try Vigna di Gabbri (a refined wine made from Inzolia grapes) or the standard white, Donnafugata Bianco (a Catarratto-Inzolia blend).

Duca di Salaparuta, also keen on Inzolia,

produces wine under the Corvo label (*corvo* means crow). The producer is based at Casteldaccia, just east along the coast from Palermo, and buys grapes from numbers of small growers. The basic but good drinking wine is Corvo Bianco. But the star is the premium Colomba Platino ("platinum dove"). Even finer is the oak-matured Bianca di Valguarnera, made from Inzolia grapes.

Further west, behind the town of Alcamo, lie huge wine estates under the name of Alcamo, a controlled *Denominazione di Origine Controllata* (DOC) area. Try any wines under the Rapitalà estate label.

Marsala master Marco De Bartoli (see page 91) also works on the island of Pantelleria. Bukkuram (Father of the Vine) estate is named after the zone where the grapes grow on the island. The grapes used are the Moscato variety, locally called Zibibbo, trained as low, individual bushes against the incessant winds. Try the delicate but sweet Moscato di Pantelleria or the classic, rich Moscato Passito di Pantelleria, from grapes that have been left to dry and concentrate rapidly in the sun after picking.

The Aeolian island of Salina has a similar tradition but with Malvasia rather than Moscato vines. Try wines from the estates of Carlo Hauner; Caravaglio and Cantine Colosi.

Wines from the slopes of Etna tend to have a heavier and fruitier flavour than those from other parts of the island. In theory, Etna should produce Sicily's best red wines but the expertise in the west of the island is often lacking in the east. An exception should be made for the white and red Murgo wines from the estate of Barone Scammacca.

Cerasuolo di Vittoria (*cerasuolo* means cherry-coloured) is found in the southeast around Vittória. The wine is another of Sicily's scarce DOCs, made from a blend of the red variety, Nero d'Avola, and the best local variety, Frappato.

It would be a mistake to overlook Sicily's rosés. Made predominantly from Nerello Mascalese, a light-coloured red grape ideally suited to making delicately fruity pinks, they are often the ideal accompaniment to many of Sicily's classic dishes. ❏

LEFT: grapes grown on the slopes of Etna produce rich, fruity wines. **RIGHT:** roasting artichokes on hot ashes is a popular part of a Sicilian picnic.

SICILY IN THE MOVIES

With its dramatic scenery, passionate population and history of crime and corruption, Sicily has attracted more than its fair share of film makers

Sicily is a self-conscious movie in the making. As well as being intensely visual, it is an island of extremes, of exquisite morality and cold-blooded Mafia murder. As a place of passion, where life and death embrace, it writes its own melodramatic script. The island is a gift to directors, from Luchino Visconti,

Franco Zeffirelli and the Taviani brothers to Italian-Americans such as Michael Cimino and Francis Ford Coppola.

Hollywood's infatuation with the glamour of gangsterland has presented American audiences with a biased picture of Sicily, one not pleasing to the Palermo tourist board. The Mafia capital, Corleone, also lends its jagged rocks and sullen populace to *The Godfather* trilogy. The mountains around Montelepre, once the home of Giuliano, Sicily's Robin Hood, echo to the sound of banditry in several action movies. Mount Etna doubles as the Holy Land in biblical epics like *Barabbas* and *The Ten Commandments*. Taormina is the setting for

romantic soap operas. Offshore, on Strómboli, volcanoes erupt violently.

Stromboli: Terra di Dio (1950), set on one of Sicily's barren islands, chronicles the torrid passion between a Lithuanian refugee and a fisherman. *Stromboli* sparked off the romance between Ingrid Bergman and director Roberto Rossellini, an affair as doomed as the brooding melodrama of the movie. In the film, Bergman's character goes into hysterics with each volcanic eruption while in real life the lunar landscape ruined her hairstyle and humour: volcanic dust was a passion killer.

Giovanni Verga's realism has long attracted admirers. Visconti's *La Terra Trema* (*The Earth Shook*, 1947) is based on Verga's *I Malavoglia*, a tale of poverty, misfortune and destiny in a benighted fishing community near Catania. Naturally, the cast were real fishermen with impenetrable Sicilian accents.

Francesco Rosi's *Salvatore Giuliano* (1961) is a story of genuine passion, the tragic fate of Sicily's greatest folk hero. After robbing the rich to feed the poor in the wild landscape west of Palermo, Giuliano was idolised as a freedom fighter by the peasants but condemned as a bandit before being betrayed and murdered in 1950. The film has the grandeur of a Greek myth: the slow looks, stylised gestures, and the scenes of peasants grouped like a classical chorus presages the inevitable funeral cortege.

The Sicilian (1988) directed by Michael Cimino and based on a pulsating novel by Mario Puzo, retells the Giuliano story. But despite looking like a Greek god, the bandit, played by Christopher Lambert, is a pale shadow of Giuliano himself.

By contrast, *The Leopard* (1963), Visconti's epic, is worthy of Lampedusa's masterly novel. Italian film purists question the choice of Burt Lancaster as Prince Salina but few movie buffs find fault with the setting. The film exudes lushness, faded grandeur and decadence. Palermitan locations are used to great effect, especially Palazzo Gangi Valguarnera's glittering hall of mirrors for the Ponteleone ball.

Wolf whistles

The Taviani brothers' *Kaos* (1984) transports the audience to rural Sicily, a chaotic Pirandellian universe of legends and lost loves. Pirandello's stories cover emigration and death, mother love and ties with the land, as well as lycanthropy. One of the tales is a cruel story of a mother's love for an uncaring son who emigrates to America and her rejection of a loving but illegitimate son in Sicily. In another saga, a full moon rekindles sexual desire and turns a peasant into a

CLUB PARADISO

The original Cinema Paradiso that inspired Giuseppe Tornatore's autobiographical film has recently re-opened as a nightclub in Bagheria.

bitter-sweet humour that mocks the grinding poverty. In America, it broke box office records for foreign films. Gabriele Pampinella, a former projectionist, recalls the time he and Tornatore had to call the police to control a riotous audience watching *The Ten Commandments*.

Egidio Termine's *Per Quel Viaggio in Sicilia* (*Journey to Sicily*, 1992) is also an attempt to avoid clichés, "subjects like social degradation and the Mafia". Directed by a young Palermitan well versed in dialect theatre, the film

wolf. The village witnesses his battles between fear and lust on moonlit nights. Despite their distinctly odd subject matter, the stories have the same cathartic effect as the classics.

Cinema Paradiso (1988) is a nostalgic slice of Sicilian history. Giuseppe Tornatore's touching film follows the arrival of the Talkies in small-town Sicily. The cinema's fortunes are seen through the eyes of a young projectionist who eventually abandons his stifling home town for fame abroad. This autobiographical film celebrates Sicilian exuberance with a

has a feel for Sicilian pride and honour but uses teasing irony to undermine the concept of marital fidelity.

Il Postino (*The Postman*, 1994) is a romantic tale of island life in the 1950s, based on a story by Antonio Skarmeta and shot on the Aeolian island of Salina, which lends a beautiful melancholy to the story. The eponymous postman, played by Massimo Troisi, is a fisherman's son who is hired to deliver mail to the island's newest inhabitant, the exiled Chilean poet Pablo Neruda. Over time, he develops an appreciation of poetry (which helps him to win the heart of the local beauty) and of Neruda's Communism (which finally gets him killed). It is a

LEFT: Ingrid Bergman and Mario Vitale in *Stromboli*.
ABOVE: the lavish ballroom scene in *The Leopard*.

touching story, beautifully photographed and deservedly nominated for half a dozen Oscars in 1995. It was Troisi's last film: he died the day after shooting finished.

Mafia in the movies

There is no mistaking the most popular theme in the Sicilian film canon. Leonardo Sciascia's anti-Mafia fiction has long inspired directors. Many stories are potential films, with strong plots, character conflict and a moral dilemma. *Il Giorno della Civetta* (*Day of the Owl*, 1968) is based on his

MOB MONEY

After permitting a Mafia wedding to be shot in their scenic church for *The Godfather*, the citizens of Sávoca used the film makers' fee to repave their streets.

tale of Sicilian sceptism in the face of official justice. The immutable landscape and classic inertia convey quiet desperation.

Yet the finest Mafia portrayal is, heretically, American. Coppola's *The Godfather* trilogy is a modern masterpiece. Part I (1972) is based on Mario Puzo's novel, itself inspired by the internecine Mafia wars in Castellammare in the 1950s. The infamous town of Corleone lent its name to the Godfather, a part played with relish by the celebrated Hollywood Don, Marlon Brando.

fast-paced detective novel of the same name. Franco Nero plays a *carabiniere* captain out to prove the complicity of a Mafia boss in an unsolved murder.

The famous Neapolitan director Francesco Rosi is Sciascia's greatest fan, drawn to his punchy plots. Rosi's *Il Caso Mattei* (*The Mattei Case,* 1971) and *Cadaveri eccellenti* (*Illustrious Corpses,* 1976) are pure Sciascia. Director and writer share the same perceptive, painful and poetic vision. Rosi describes the writer as "the chronicler of discredited institutions, powerless citizens and corrupt bosses".

Emilio Greco's *Una Storia Semplice* (*A Simple Story,* 1991) uses Sciascia's last novella, a

The scale, atmosphere and power of the images make for an operatic intensity. Familiar initiation ceremonies and surreptitious meetings add to the atmosphere. But *The Godfather, Part II* (1974) ends in a bleak moral vision. The closing scenes show the desolation of Michael Corleone as he chooses hegemony over honour and family loyalty.

The Godfather, Part III (1990) traces the story of Michael Corleone as a partly reformed but now ailing gangster. However, Coppola's third bite at the cherry suffers from a sense of *déjà vu*, with damnation rather than salvation on the cards for Michael.

Life on location was chaotic, with 30 script

rewrites in total. Coppola's daughter Sofia was controversially cast in a starring role as Mary Corleone. On the film set, Al Pacino (Michael) and Diane Keaton, fictional partners and real-life lovers at the time, split up because of the strain. During the filming in Palermo, local street urchins would shout out, *"Dov'è Al?"* ("Where's Al?") The answer was never far away: an unreformed Al Pacino was squandering his dollars with shady characters in a seedy gambling den. On the Sicil-

> ### MUSICAL MAFIA
>
> The oddest film with a Mafia theme must be *Tano da Morire* (*To Die for Tano*, 1997), a surreal mixture of documentary and high-camp farce, in which *mafiosi* break into song and occasionally Seventies-style disco dancing.

Goodfellas and *Mobsters* (1992). While *Goodfellas* succeeds, *Mobsters* is a cliché of cretinous casting: hoodlums in trench coats and "Sicilian" moustaches fire both machine guns and speech in the style of Silvester Stallone.

The German director Margarethe von Trotta's *Il Lungo Silenzio* (*The Long Silence*) dealt in 1993 with the anti-Mafia magistrates and, at the Palermo premiere, received applause from Mafia widows. *Vendetta* (1995), directed by the Swedish

ian set, Michael's redemption comes too late.

The film ends with a family gathering in Palermo's Teatro Massimo. The opera is Mascagni's foreboding *Cavalleria Rusticana*, a pastoral melodrama inspired by Verga. The opera is spliced with synchronised slaughter: Coppola, the visionary maverick, orchestrates Sicily in celluloid.

Other Sicilian gangster movies include

LEFT: Christopher Lambert (right) played bandit Salvatore Giuliano in *The Sicilian*.
ABOVE: Massimo Troisi and Philippe Noiret in *Il Postino*.
RIGHT: Rosi's *Cadaveri Eccellenti*, is based on a Sciascia Mafia story.

Mikael Håfström, is another blood-and-guts yarn in which two Swedish businessmen are kidnapped in Rome by the Mafia, held captive in Sicily and finally rescued by the clean-cut hero amid a hail of bullets.

In a classic case of Sicilian irony, sons of Mafia bosses are now turning their sights towards film directing. Their genre? Mafia movies, what else? The crossover between showbiz and crime was evident in the 1992 trial of John Gotti, the "dapper Don" of New York gangland. Movie stars such as Sylvester Stallone, Bruce Willis and Anthony Quinn attended the trial – perhaps in search of ideas for the inevitable movie: *The Dapper Don, Part II.* ❑

SICILY'S WILD PLACES

*The island's lush green interior and beautiful seashore are at last receiving
some protection from development, as regional parks and natural reserves*

Increasingly the wild areas of Sicily's countryside and coast are being protected and made more accessible to the visitor. Since the 1980s more than 80 reserves have been created and laws drawn up to protect natural habitats and control development. This has not always been a straightforward process. The ingrained Sicilian suspicion of authority and government, plus economic hardship and lack of employment opportunities, has often meant local opposition to the protection an area of natural importance, and the accompanying restrictions on development.

The *Forestale*, the authority responsible for the care and development of reserves, are also effectively building control officers, a difficult dual role made more complicated by regional divisions and poor communication between local authorities and residents. Local agreements over grazing of sheep and cattle on environmentally sensitive areas may have been traditional for generations, and those affected by limits on land use can often see little benefit to themselves and their dependants.

More positively, there is a fierce pride in the wild natural beauty of Sicily and a strong tradition of rural pursuits and small-scale agriculture, which are gradually beginning to work in harmony with the ideals of the reserves. The reserves and parks view the traditional crafts and products as an important part of the culture of the region and seek to promote them, as well as providing new employment in the work of the park itself. The small reserve at Zíngaro, for example, employs more than 200 people.

Rich diversity

Sicily's hot summers and mild winters, combined with a mineral-rich soil, provide an ideal environment for a wide variety of flora and fauna, and in spring and autumn the region provides an important staging post for tens of thousands of migrating birds. These, as well as the

native species, are benefiting from the protection of their environment and controls on hunting and fishing.

Along with flowers and plants also found elsewhere in Europe, the island is host to a number of successful "invaders", like the huge prickly pear (known locally as *fici d'India*), the

riverbed-loving oleander, the carob (particularly around Ragusa), the eucalyptus and the umbrella pine, which produces the delicious pine nuts used in making pesto sauce. Indigenous plants include *erba bianca* (woody absinthe), myrtle, arbutus (the strawberry tree), lentisk and tree spurge.

The scuttle of bright lizards dashing off the stones as you walk, the dramatic silhouette of an eagle wheeling round the steep rocks, or the flash of a dolphin leaping out of the bright blue sea add so much delight to an exploration of Sicily. For enthusiasm, it's hard to beat this extract from the guide to the Zingaro reserve: "With silence as your companion, you climb

---

LEFT: a windmill in the Trápani *saline* (salt pans).
RIGHT: convolvulus, woody absinthe and prickly pear.

up steep slopes and down crests and valleys, then climb and descend again. At every step you throw your heart forward, reach it and then throw it even higher and get it again. And you do this all the time as you walk along, so that it is like being able to reach the spirit which in places like this flies away unexpectedly; as sure and as delicately as a bunting or nightingale. And the road doesn't tire you; maybe this is what flying is like. And the enormous everyday task of placating the monsters fiercely eating away at you inside, day after day all your life, is lightened here by a mysterious, arcane autonomous mechanism of defence."

For the keen naturalist, or the interested visitor, exploring the wild places of Sicily will certainly prove a restorative and delightful experience. Taking one of the many excellent guides to Mediterranean flowers and birds may add to your enjoyment.

There are three types of protected area, the regional parks, the natural reserves, and the sea reserves. All three categories are further subdivided into zones, designated A, B, C or D, which define the level of protection and therefore the nature of activities permitted in the zone. Though the niceties of these differences affect residents more than the visitor, the

BIRDS TO SPOT IN SICILY

More than 150 species of birds, both migratory and nesting, have been logged on the island. The notable predators include the golden eagle and the peregrine falcon. Until recently the magnificent peregrines were threatened by levels of insecticide in the environment, but happily they are on the increase again and can be seen singly or in pairs near cliffs.

They are not the only birds of prey sustained by the island's numerous small mammals and lizards: you may see Bonelli's eagles, red kites, marsh harriers, European sparrowhawks and a variety of owls (long-eared, little, scops, tawny and barn). Besides the familiar blackbirds,

crows, robins, skylarks and thrushes, you may spot the hoopoe, red-billed chough, nuthatch, coal tit, Sicilian long-tailed tit, redstart, blackcap, greenfinch, quail and cirl bunting.

On summer evenings swifts, swallows and martins join the bats swooping round the terraces. You may be startled by the sudden flight of the large European woodcock, which bursts out of the undergrowth virtually under your feet. Near fresh water, as in Nébrodi National Reserve, look out for the Sicilian marsh tit and the wonderfully named *Tachybaptus ruficolis*. The Latin means "fast-bathing red stomach", an apt description of the little grebe.

general regulations, available at every park office and information point, are most important for safety and the protection of the environment and should be carefully followed. Most of these are common sense, but it is particularly important to be aware of such problems as the high risk of fire. It is also useful to note that access to some areas is extremely difficult without a car, and camping is forbidden.

There are organised walks in some parks and details of these, along with maps, and excellent books on the flora, fauna and history of the region, can also be obtained from information points.

The regional parks

Parco dei Nébrodi is Sicily's largest park, covering an enormous sweep of the mountainous region from Santo Stefano di Camastra, roughly halfway along the northern coast, right across to the foot of Etna. Nébrodi was designated a reserve in 1993.

The area includes a number of towns and villages and areas of ancient beech and oak woodland. There are a number of lakes that provide important habitats, particularly Biviere di Cesarù. Note that this park is so large that exploring without a car is difficult.

The **Parco delle Madonie**, established in 1989, lies to the west of Nebrodi and similarly takes in beautiful wooded mountainous countryside, well known for skiing in the winter. Smaller and higher, Madonie is also more easily accessible without a car. Buses run from Cefalù, Castelbuono and Petralia, and there is good accommodation available. Pony treks and organised walks are also offered in the summer.

Perhaps the best-known area of Sicily, Etna's dramatic mountain and crater became a park in 1987. The **Parco dell'Etna** offers many long and short organised treks, including the five-day *Grande Traversata Etnea,* and these provide the best options for exploring. Good walks are also possible from a number of bases in the foothills, some accessible by bus. Hiking in the higher areas is not possible in the winter, due to snow and bad visibility.

Most remarkable about the park is its variety, from lush citrus groves and bananas on the lower slopes, through mixed woodland to pine

and finally volcanic desert, sustaining only small hardy plants and flowers, such as the Etna violet, that can survive the extremes of temperature.

The natural reserves

To date there are a gratifying 83 reserves in Sicily, a testament to the determination of those involved in the movement to protect the natural beauty of the region and encourage environmentally sensitive development and tourism. However, many of the reserves have yet to establish any clear definition or boundaries that are obvious to the visitor, and lack facilities or

information. Ten of the better established and better known reserves are listed here, plus the two major sea reserves.

The **Riserva Naturale dello Zíngaro**, a section of coast and hills near Castellammare del Golfo, between Trápani and Palermo, deserves special mention as the pioneer of Sicilian reserves. In response to plans to build a main road along this section of unspoilt coast in 1980, a massive campaign was launched including support from national newspapers and impressive ranks of scientists. Public support soon followed and in May 1980 a peaceful march of 6,000 people was held. Their efforts were recognised by the Regional Assembly and

LEFT: an umbrella pine springs from Etna's lava slopes. **RIGHT:** the peregrine falcon breeds on cliffs.

the following year national legislation was passed, securing the future of parks and reserves in Sicily.

Zíngaro is exceptionally well planned, allowing easy access for all levels of ability, though it might be too much for all but the most intrepid of wheelchair users. Its five exquisite beaches, ancient dwellings and beautiful landscape are a delight, and the facilities include a natural history museum, a marine laboratory, a visitor's centre and an archaeological museum, all housed in carefully

> ### VARIED VEGETATION
>
> More than 700 species of plant can be found within the Zíngaro Natural Reserve, including exotic imports such as the dwarf palm, agave and prickly pear.

restored existing buildings. The reserve is easily reached on public transport or by car and there are plenty of places to stay in nearby Scopello. The tiny beaches get busy in July and August, but by September you can have them to yourself.

Just north of Palermo, the huge rocky mass of **Monte Pellegrino** juts up from the bay. In striking contrast to Zíngaro, the reserve is shared by the shrine of St Rosalia, the patron saint of Palermo, and a collection of associated souvenir shops, and serves as a popular picnic place for families from the city. However there are excellent views, particularly on the road up to the mountain, and walks on the rocky peak. It is about 15 km (9 miles) from Palermo and buses are readily available up to the shrine.

The **Ficuzza** reserve is near Marineo, 35 km (22 miles) south of Palermo. It centres on the tiny hamlet of Ficuzza, a tranquil spot below the woods on Rocca Busambre. Though it's undoubtedly easier to reach by car, buses from Corleone to Palermo do run past. There are a few trattorias in Ficuzza for lunch.

Created as a reserve in 1984, the salt marshes of **Vendicari** support a highly specialised population of plants and animals. The autumn or winter is the time to visit, when thousands of waders and ducks arrive to take advantage of its sheltered waters, along with flamingos, storks and egrets. The remains of a 15th-century tower and ancient Greek fish-processing tanks can be seen. Take binoculars. Vendicari is about 45 km (28 miles) south of Siracusa, and accessible only by car.

Newly defined as reserves, **Necropoli di Pantálica** and **Valle dell'Anapo** accommodate extraordinary Bronze Age cave dwellings, and walks along the Anapo river valley, alongside dramatic gorges and canyons. You can also walk over 13 km (8 miles) along the abandoned Siracusa–Ragusa railway amid wooded hills. The area is rich in wildlife. The area is about 40 km (25 miles) west of Siracusa, and accessible only by car.

Another new reserve, **Gole dell'Alcantara** is not for the faint-hearted. Exploring it can include wading through the freezing waters of the river among the rainbows of colour produced by droplets of spray deep in the rocky

> ### ANIMALS OF THE ISLAND
>
> Though some creatures such as the wolf have vanished, the crested porcupine is still resident, as are the red fox, hare, wild cat, pine marten, weasel and edible dormouse. Among the island's eight species of bat are the mouse-eared bat and the rare Kuhl's pipistrelle and Savi's pipistrelle. Reptiles include the common green lizard, black snake, dark green snake, grass snake and viper, and nocturnal geckos attracted by any outside light. The shy land tortoise is around, but hard to spot with its excellent camouflauge. In fresh water you may see the European pond turtle. Amphibians include the common toad, edible frog, tree frog and painted frog.

gorge, an exhilarating hour of rock and water. There are some bus services from Taormina, approximately 15 km (9 miles) away.

Isola di Mozia, **Lo Stagnone** and **Saline di Trápani** make up the protected area around Mozia. Part of the Phoenician trading route in the 8th century BC, this tiny island is one of four set in the slow-moving waters off the extreme west coast of Sicily, 15 km (9 miles) south of Trápani.

The lagoon itself has been a reserve since 1984, and its salty waters, once used for salt extraction, have a rich marine life including over 40 different kinds of fish. The striking pinks

marine life make swimming and diving a joy, and the smaller islands of Lévanzo and Maréttimo are quiet even in the summer season. The main island of Favignana is flat and easily explored by bicycle.

All the islands have footpaths leading to many of the more secluded areas, but they may be difficult to follow. If you do head off exploring, be certain to take plenty of water and be prepared for rocky scrambles in places. You will be rewarded with deserted rocky shores and sublime tranquillity.

Boat trips round the islands and organised visits to Grotta del Genovese, where there are

and white in the waters, and the rich vegetation on the islands make the area a visual delight.

It is possible to get to the reserve by bus from Marsala, about 6 km (3½ miles) to the south, and there are ferries across to the islands.

Sea reserves

The three beautiful **Isole Egadi**, only half an hour's hydrofoil ride from Trápani, are ringed with caves and creeks, tiny bays and miniature beaches. The clarity of the water and variety of

prehistoric cave drawings, are available.

A well-established reserve and centre for marine studies since 1987, **Ustica** offers a chance to explore the fabulously rich sea world of sponges, corals and fish, and to learn more from the extensive aquarium. There are sea-watching trips with expert guidance and even a sub-aqua archaeological trail complete with Roman amphorae. Sub-aqua, and marine biology courses, exhibitions and conferences are held every year on the island. Regular hyrofoil and ferry services connect to Palermo.

For contact details of all these reserves, and environmental agencies that can supply further information, see the Travel Tips section. ❏

LEFT: the gecko is most active at night, when it hunts flies, moths and spiders. **ABOVE:** the tiny island of Mozia is now part of a natural reserve.

PLACES

A detailed guide to the entire island, with principal sites clearly cross-referenced by number to the maps

To Goethe, Sicily was a unique place, "clear, authentic and complete". Modern Sicily has its share of scruffy, one-horse towns, inscrutable hill-top villages and industrial sprawl. As a touchstone, Tomasi di Lampedusa's vision of his homeland is more perceptive: "a landscape which knows no mean between sensuous sag and hellish drought; which is never petty, never ordinary, never relaxed".

Sicilian scenery is gruff but seldom graceless. The granary of the ancient world contains citrus groves, pastureland and vineyards as well as endless wheatfields. Trápani's weird lagoons and salt pans seemingly float in the unrelenting heat. Away from the accessible coast, an intriguing volcanic hinterland unfolds in mountains, gorges and the scars of abandoned sulphur mines. Like a dragon in its lair, Etna's smoking breath threatens vineyards and lava-stone castles.

Still, first impressions are safer. After breakfasting in Taormina, Cardinal Newman found it "the nearest thing to paradise". To most tourists, Taormina is still the acceptable face of Sicily, a place of indiluted pleasure where culture shock is absent.

Outside this cosmopolitan pocket, the adventure begins. Sicily is not what it seems. The souks and inlaid street patterns of Mazara and Sciacca would not be out of place in Morocco. The perfect medieval town of Erice is a shrine to pagan goddesses, Astarte and Venus. In Sicily, all periods are petrified for posterity. The jewel box of Palermo's Cappella Palatina is a fusion of Arab and Christian. The Arab west of the island is overladen with Spanish finery while the Greek east is truest to the pure Classical spirit.

Despite a patina of neglect, Sicily's architectural riches gleam. The island of Mozia retains its Phoenician port and sacrificial burial grounds. Built to "intimidate the gods or scare human beings", the Greek temples of Agrigento, Segesta and Selinunte are a divine reflection of Magna Graecia. The Romans may not have matched these lovely sites but left the vivid mosaics of Piazza Armerina as an imprint of a sated but sophisticated culture.

Cefalù and Monreale Cathedrals are a tribute to Byzantine craftsmanship, Arab imagery and Norman scale. Elsewhere, Moorish palaces, Swabian castles and domed churches are interpretations of this inspired Sicilian hybrid. Baroque, the island's last great gasp, explodes in the theatrical fireworks of Noto and Catania. As the cultural capital of the ancient world, Siracusa presides over Greek ruins and Christian catacombs with a luminous grace all its own. Palermo, its psychic opposite, radiates sultry splendour. ❑

PRECEDING PAGES: the cloud-capped Nébrodi Mountains; almond trees in bloom, Agrigento province; Palermo's ornate Politeama theatre.
LEFT: Caltabellotta, the loveliest village in Agrigento province.

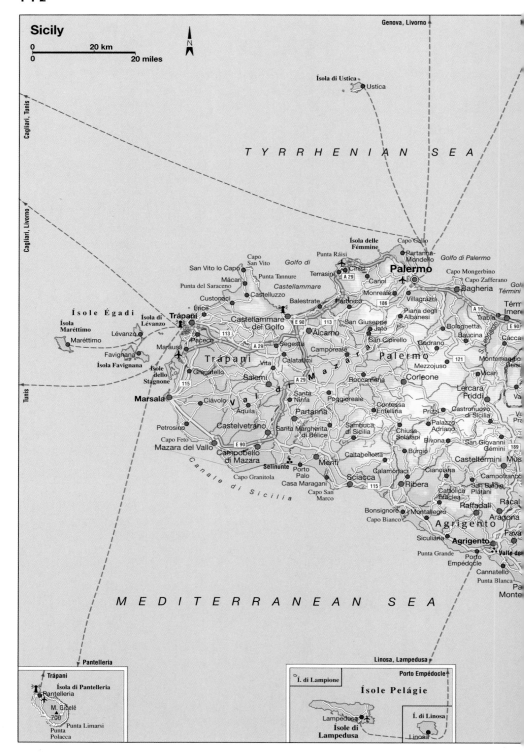

Sicily

0   20 km
0   20 miles

N

Genova, Livorno

Cagliari, Tunis

Cagliari, Livorno

Tunis

Ísola di Ustica

Ustica

T Y R R H E N I A N   S E A

Ísola delle Fémmine
Capo Gallo
Punta Ráisi
Partanna-Mondello
Golfo di Palermo
Capo Mongerbino
Palermo
Capo Zafferano
Golfo di
Capo San Vito
San Vito lo Capo
Terrasini
Cinisi
A 29
Carini
Bagheria
Térmi Imere
Punta Tannure
Monreale
Villagrázia
Térm Imere
Trabia
A 19
Mácari
Castellammare
Partinico
186
Piana degli Albánesi
E 90
Punta del Saraceno
Balestrate
Bolognetta
E 90
Custonaci
Castelluzzo
San Giuseppe Jato
Baucina
Cácca
Érice
113
San Cipirello
Trápani
Castellammare del Golfo
Alcamo
Godrano
Ísole Égadi
Ísola di Lévanzo
Paceco
113
Campóreale
Palermo
Montemaggio Belsi
Ísola Maréttimo
Lévanzo
A 29
Segesta
121
Vicar
Maráusa
Vita
Mazzojuso
Maréttimo
Granatello
Calatafimi
Roccamena
Corleone
Favignana
Salemi
A 29
Lercara Friddi
Ísola Favignana
V a l   d i   M a z a r a
Poggioreale
Va Pra
Ísole dello Stagnone
115
Santa Ninfa
Confessa Entellina
Prizzi
Castronuovo di Sicília
Ciávolo
Partanna
Castelvetrano
Sambuca di Sicília
Palazzo Adriano
San Giovanni Gémini
Marsala
Aquila
Santa Margherita di Bélice
Chiusa Soláfani
Bivona
189
Petrosino
Búrgio
Casteltérmini
Mus
Capo Feto
Santa Margherita di Bélice
Cianciana
Mazara del Vallo
E 90
Menfi
Caltabellotta
Campotranc
Selinunte
Porto Palo
Calamónaci
Ribera
San Blásio Plátani
Campobello di Mazara
Casa Maragani
Capo Granitola
Sciacca
Cattólica Eraclea
Raffadali
Racal
C a n a l e   d i   S i c i l i a
Capo San Marco
115
Bonsignore
Montallegro
Aragona
Capo Bianco
Agrigento
Fava
Siculiana
Agrigento
Valle dei
Punta Grande
Porto Empédocle
Cannatello
Punta Blanca
Pa
Monte

M E D I T E R R A N E A N   S E A

Pantelleria

Linosa, Lampedusa
Porto Empédocle

Trápani
Ísola di Pantelleria
Pantelleria
M. Gibelé
700
Punta Limarsi
Punta Polacca

Í. di Lampione

Ísole Pelágie

Lampedusa
Ísole di Lampedusa

Í. di Linosa

Linosa

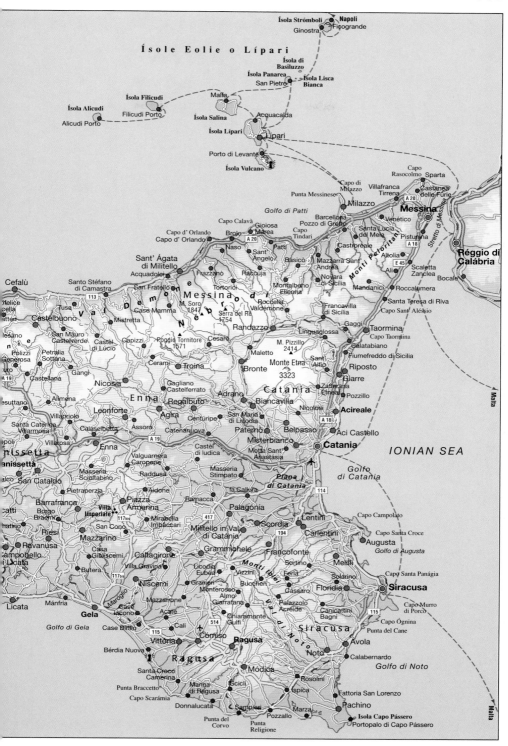

Ísola Strómboli
Ginostra
Napóli
Ficograndé

Ísole Eolie o Lípari

Ísola di Basiluzzo
Ísola Panarea
San Pietro
Ísola Lisca Bianca

Ísola Filicudi
Malfa
Ísola Salina
Acquacalda

Ísola Alicudi
Filicudi Porto
Ísola Lípari
Alicudi Porto
Lípari
Porto di Levante
Ísola Vulcano

Capo Rasocolmo
Sparta
Capo di Milazzo
Villafranca Tirrena
Castanea delle Fúrie
Punta Messinese
Golfo di Patti
Milazzo
Messina
A 20
A 18
Stretto di Messina

Capo Calavà
Gioiosa Marea
Barcellona
Pozzo di Grotto
Venético
Santa Lucia del Mela
Pistunina
A 18
E 45
Réggio di Calábria

Capo d' Orlando
Brolo
Capo Tindari
Castroreale
Altolia
Scaletta Zanclea
Bocale

Sant' Ágata di Militello
Acquadolci
Naso
Sant' Angelo
Patti
Basicó
Mazzarra Sant' Andrea
Novara di Sicilia
Mandanici
Santa Teresa di Riva
Roccalumera

Cefalù
Santo Stéfano di Camastra
Frazzanò
Racuja
Montalbano Elicona
Francavilla di Sicilia
Capo Sant' Aléssio

Tusa
San Fratello
Tortorici
Roccella Valdemone
Gaggi
Taormina

Castelbuono
M. Soro 1847
Case Mamma
Serra del Re 1754
Randazzo
Linguaglossa
Capo Taormina

San Mauro Castelverde
Mistretta
Poggio Tornitore 1571
Cesarò
M. Pizzillo 2414
Galatabiano
Fiumefreddo di Sicilia

Castèl di Lúcio
Capizzi
Maletto
Monte Etna 3323
Sant' Alfio
Riposto

Polizzi Generosa
Petralia Sottana
Cerami
Troina
Bronte
Giarre

Castellana
Gangi
Gagliano Castelferrato
Adrano
Catania
Zafferana Etnea
Pozzillo

Nicosia
Regalbuto
Biancavilla
Nicolosi
Acireale

Alìmena
Leonforte
Agira
Centúripe
San Maria di Licodia
Aci Castello

Villapriolo
Calascibetta
Assoro
Catenanuova
Paternò
Belpasso

Santa Caterina Villarmosa
Villarosa
Enna
A 19
Castèl di Iudica
Misterbianco
Motta Sant' Anastásia
Catania

Valguarnera Caropepe
Masseria Stimpato
IONIAN SEA

Masseria Scioltabino
Raddusa
Aidone
la Calura
Golfo di Catania

Pietraperzia
Piazza
Armerina
Ramacca
114

Barrafranca
Borgo Braemi
Villa Imperiale
117bis
Mirabella Imbáccari
417
Palagónia
Capo Campolato

San Cono
Militello in Val di Catania
Scordia
Lentini
Capo Santa Croce

Riesi
Mazzarino
Grammichele
194
Carlentini
Augusta

Ravanusa
Casa Gibliscemi
Caltagirone
Francofonte
Golfo di Augusta

Campobello di Licata
Butera
Villa Gravina
117bis
Licodia Eubea
Vizzini
Ferla
Melilli
Capo Santa Panágia

Gela
Niscemi
Granieri
Bucchen
Sortino
Solárino
Siracusa

Mánfria
Case Iácono
Mazzarrone
Monterosso Almo
Giarratana
Cássaro
Palazzolo Acréide
Floridia
Capo Murro di Porco

Licata
Acate
Chiaramonte Gulfi
Canicattini Bagni
115
Capo Ógnina

Golfo di Gela
Case Dirillo
Cali
514
Siracusa
Punta del Cane

Vittória
Cómiso
Ragusa
Avola

Bérdia Nuova
Ragusa
Noto
Calabernardo
Golfo di Noto

Santa Croce Camerina
Módica
Rosolini

Punta Bracetto
Marina di Ragusa
Scicli
Íspica
Fattoria San Lorenzo

Capo Scarámia
Donnalucata
Sampieri
Marza
Pachino

Punta del Corvo
Punta Religione
Pozzallo
Ísola Capo Pássero
Portopalo di Capo Pássero

Malta

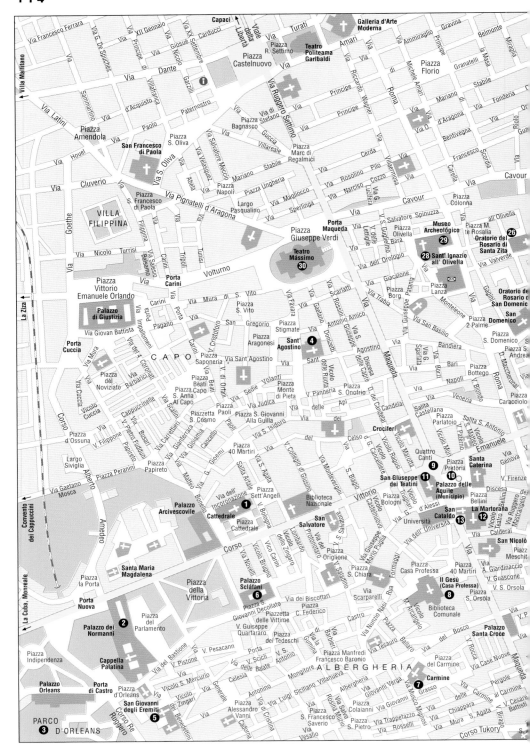

Palermo

N

0   200 m
0   200 yds

T Y R R H E N I A N

S E A

Molo Sud

Via del Mare

Via Sammuzzo

Via Galilei

Via Galvani

Via Patuano

Via Alessandro Volta

Via Ferraris

Via Patti

Via Filippo

Via Crispi

Piazza XIII Vittime

Via CM.8

orgio

rgio
ovesi

Castellamare

V. degli Spersi

Alessandro

Castello

Via Barilai

Via Orlando

V. Ciancialo

V. Cantaleria

Via Sebastiano

Via Tronda

Mercato Ittico

Piazza Cap di Porto

Tavola

Piazza Castello

La Cala

Piazza Fonderia

Via Cesa

Porta Felice

Cala

Cala

La Cala

Piazza F. Matera

Piazza Tarzana

Porta Carbone

Santa Maria della Catena

Via P.to Salvo

Piazza S. Spirito

27

Porta Felice

Foro Italico

22

VILLA

Via Cassari

Via dei Tinti

Via Chiavettieri

UCCIRIA

Corso

Via Bottai

Piazza Marina

17

Santa Maria Emanuele

Piazzetta Dogana

Via della Regia Zecca

V. Niscemi

Vicolo S. Uffizio

Vittorio

Via

23

Palazzo Butera

Butera

A

Via del Parlamento

Oratorio di San Lorenzo

20

San Francesco d'Assisi

21

Santa Maria dei Miracoli

Palazzo Chiaramonte

18

Via V. Aprile

Scopari

Via

Salita Mura di Cattive

MARE

Gricota

Palazzo Mirto

19

Via Merlo

Via dei Papagallo

Vicolo di Blasi

Alloro

La Pietà

Porta Deigreci

Piazza S. Francesco d'Assisi

Via Resuttana

Via Lungarini

V. Català

C. all'Aloro

Alloro

Via Sciara

Palazzo Abatellis (Galleria Nazionale)

16

Via della Savona

Santa Teresa

Piazza della Kalsa

Cassa
armio

Santa
anna

Vicolo dei Correri

Paternostro

Piazza d'Aragona

Via Lungarini

Francesco Riso

La Gancia

Piazza Spasimo

Via S. Teresa

Vicolo del Pallone

Calascibetta

V. Aragona

V.S. Carlo

Via Castro

V. Schiavuzzo

Filippo

V. del Sole

Piazza S. Eumo

Piazza Vetterra

Piazza Ventimiglia

Cervello

Cecilia

Piazza Rivoluzione

V. Garibaldi

dello

Spasimo

L A   K A L S A

Santa Maria d. Spasimo

Porta Reale

Abramo

Lincoln

Foro Italico

Divisi

Via Maestro d'Acqua

Palazzo Aiutamicristo

15

La Magione

14

Piazza Magione

Via

Via

Carmelo Pardi

VILLA GIULIA

Via Monte Santo

Via Garibaldi

Magione

Via della Pace

Via G. Filangieri

C. Rao

Lincoln

Porta Castro Filippo

Gorizia

Corso

Via Milano

Via della Pace

Abramo

Via Paci

Antonio di Rudini

ORTO BOTÁNICO

Via Trento

Via Manzoni

Porta Garibaldi

Via del

Via Rosario Palmieri

Via Balsamo

Piazza Giulio Cesare

Via P. Randazzo

Via Michele Cipolla

Via Antonio

Archirafi

24

a segno

Via Trio

Stazione Centrale

Via Gaspare Ugo

Via P. Randazzo

Bagheria

PALERMO CITY

*Sicily's capital is a synthesis of bomb sites and beauty,
sumptuous Arab-Norman and baroque splendour
interspersed with an intriguing Moorish muddle*

Map
on pages
114–115

Palermo

Palermo is both an essay in chaos and a sensuous spice-box of a city. In Tomasi di Lampedusa's *The Leopard*, the Prince breathes in the orange blossom on a sultry night in Palermo, and is flooded with "the Islamic perfume evoking houris and fleshly joys beyond the grave". Palermo luxuriates in a sultry decadence. In *Persephone's Island*, the writer Mary Simeti, born in America but long based in Sicily, describes her regular return to Palermo in the autumn: "The city awaits us… early persimmons glowing orange amidst pyramids of bright green cauliflowers, smoking tripods of chestnuts roasting at the curbstones, bloodshed and decaying beauty." Like the persimmon, Palermo is tropical, ripe, decadent, the soul of brooding Sicily.

A Phoenician colony existed here from the 8th century BC but not a stone of Punic Palermo remains. The city has also revealed scant Classical remains compared with its cultured east-coast rivals. The only traces of Classical Palermo are in the grid-like urban plan around La Cala, the original harbour. Elsewhere in the historic centre, Palermo is a maze of Moorish alleys, confirming the city's deeper affinities, for it was only with the Arab colonisation that Palermo came into its own. The city was home to Jewish and Lombard merchants, Greek craftsmen and builders, Turkish and Syrian artisans, Persian artists, Berber and Negro slaves. It was the most multiracial population in Europe, and out of such diversity was born the complex city culture that knows many masters.

Under Arab rule the city welcomed 300 mosques and was ringed by pleasure palaces such as La Ziza and hunting lodges like La Cuba. Citizens acquired a love for Arab ornamentation that has never left them. Norman rule coincided with Palermo's golden age, one of expansion, enlightenment, prosperity and cultural riches. The city outskirts were ringed by palms, vineyards, citrus groves, silk farms and rice paddies. Under Spanish rule, the Moorish city was remodelled along grand baroque arteries. This attempt to impose order on the chaotic Arab maze provided a misleading semblance of control. But behind the grand new crossroads of Quattro Canti, the old Moorish city swirled in crooked alleys, lively markets, and poor housing. The urban design formalised the separation of nobles and artisans, rich and poor.

In a sense, little has changed since then, except that many of the middle classes have deserted the city centre in modern times. In 1943, Allied bombs destroyed the port and much of the historic centre, leaving it with gaping holes half-filled with crumbling baroque *palazzi*. The Mafia stepped into the hole, accepting funds from Rome and the EU to rebuild the devastated centre. Instead, corrupt politicians in league with *mafiosi* building contractors siphoned off the funds

PRECEDING PAGES: Palermo harbour. **LEFT:** fountain at Quattro Canti. **BELOW:** the July procession to celebrate Santa Rosalia, the city's patron saint.

for their own illicit ends. Following the Mafia murders of Falcone and Borsellino, high-profile public prosecutors, Palermitans experienced a wave of revulsion, rare in its ability to provoke citizens to public protest.

After a period of political instability, a rare feeling of hope now permeates the air, personified by local boy Leoluca Orlando, the anti-corruption city mayor. Still more significant is the burgeoning sense of civic responsibility felt by citizens, especially the young. This has been formalised into the creation of countless voluntary associations in which disadvantaged, unemployed or under-employed citizens successfully run churches, cultural centres or neighbourhood groups. The Mayor also sees it as his mission to beautify the city, restoring palaces, planting palms and installing period street lights.

Most Palermo churches are now run by associations whose members also act as unpaid guides. In one "adopt a monument" scheme, children from deprived districts are trained to act as guides to a particular local building.

Surreal sights

Palermo is an incredible jumble of periods and styles. Given that the Spanish grid system is subverted by Moorish blind alleys, squalid bomb sites and rampant urbanisation on the outskirts, it is surprising that the city is so legible. Divided by the **Quattro Canti** crossroads, the historic city forms four traditional quarters, with its off-centre heart in the **Kasr**, the great Arab-Norman nucleus. North of Corso Emanuele is the **Capo** quarter, the medieval working-class district behind the Cathedral. West of Via Maqueda and south of Corso Emanuele lies the poor quarter of the **Albergheria**. East of Via Roma lies the **Vucciria**, the dilapidated market district. And to the southeast is the **Kalsa**, a partly restored bomb-damaged quarter with a fine museum and austere Catalan-Gothic *palazzi*.

The Kasr district, named after the Arabic for castle, contains the cathedral and the royal palace, once the upper castle. The **Cattedrale ❶** (daily 7am–7pm) on Corso V. Emanuele, is a Sicilian hybrid: mentally erase the incongruous dome and focus on the tawny stone, sculpted doorway and Moorish decoration on the facade. The peppermint and grey baroque interior is a cool shell, a wanly neutered setting for the royal Norman tombs. Borne by crouching lions, the tombs are made of rare pink porphyry and sculpted by Arab masters, the only craftsmen who knew the technique in Norman times. The treasury contains royal mantles and a Norman crown resembling a bejewelled skull cap. Behind the Duomo emerges the geometric design of the Arab-Norman apses, with black-and-white inlays and blind arches.

Palazzo dei Normanni ❷ (Mon, Fri and Sat 9am–noon), on Piazza Indipendenza, is the eclectic royal palace and centre of power since Byzantine times. Now the seat of the Sicilian Parliament, this cube-shaped palace has walled gardens overgrown with royal orchids, papyrus, hanging banyan trees *ficus belgamine* and kapoks. The African kapoks store water in barrel-like trunks and are a favourite with monkeys, a reminder that the Arab Emirs bred an exotic menagerie here. The most precious trees are the *cicas*, dwarf palms whose leaves take 50 years to grow. An 18th-century carriage drive leads to the Arab-Norman palace that rivalled Cairo and Córdova.

Leading off a lovely loggia is the **Cappella Palatina** (Mon–Fri 9–11.45am, 3–4.45pm), the royal chapel

BELOW:
Palermo cathedral.

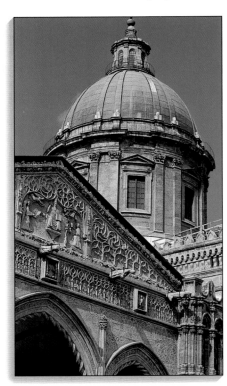

designed by Roger II in 1130 and representing the fusion of Byzantine, Arab, Norman and Sicilian civilisations. The gold mosaics recall the Crusades; Palermo was the port of departure for the Holy Land. In the penumbra, the mystic **Byzantine mosaics** slowly emerge. Christ Pantocrator occupies the cupola, surrounded by archangels and saints. On the walls are sumptuous Biblical scenes framed by Islamic decorative devices with the texture of tapestry.

Individual masterpieces include the delicate marble paschal candlestick, Corinthian capitals, an inlaid Cosmati marble pulpit, marble and porphyry paving underfoot and a treasury containing Islamic caskets. The gold and porphyry throne occupies a dais below a mosaic pointedly entrusting the Norman kings with the Holy Law. The ceiling is unique in a Christian church, a composition of ineffable Oriental splendour. The Normans asked Arab craftsmen to portray paradise and they maliciously obliged with naked maidens that the Normans prudishly clothed and crowned with haloes. Still, the roof remains a paradise of the senses: Persian octagonal stars meet Islamic stalactites. Amid palm trees and peacocks, men play chess, hunt or drink; entwined dancers and female musicians belong to *Arabian Nights* fantasies. On the floor above is the gilded **Parliamentary Chamber** (1350). From the balconies stretch views of the Conca d'Oro, the scenic shell surrounded by lemon groves, the port and hills.

Parco d'Orleans ❸ (daily 9am–1pm, 3–5pm), the lush gardens behind the palace, belong to the Sicilian President. Arabs play cards and chat; mothers play with children; office workers eat ice creams sandwiched into buns, a Palermitan speciality. Like an island in the shark-infested sea of the *centro storico*, the park is an image of Palermo at ease with itself.

The battered **Capo quarter** lies north of the Kasr. Since its origins as the

Map on pages 114–115

A sign outside the Parco d'Orleans specifies that only adults accompanied by children may enter. Shrewd urchins offer their services as "borrowed" kids for the duration of your walk.

LEFT: the ceiling of the Cappella Palatina.
BELOW: Moorish figures on the Porta Nuova.

TIP

An excellent tour led by volunteers shows visitors the underside of the Albergheria. It includes a bird's-eye view of the city from a tower normally closed to the public, a visit to a carob factory or a cart-painter's workshop, hospitality in a cosy inn or sampling street snacks in the Ballarò market. (Albergheria Viaggi, tel: 091-218344)

BELOW:
San Giovanni's exotic gardens and cloisters.

slave-traders' quarter, the Capo has been isolated and slightly menacing. Despite slum clearance, this shack-infested district has featured as a backdrop for Beirut in recent films. Plans to build a city metro were scuppered by fears of subsidence, given the covered rivers and underground passages. The quarter's centrepiece is still **Sant'Agostino** ❹ (Mon–Sat 7am–noon, 4–5.30pm, Sun 7am–noon) the imposing monastery that ran the region in medieval times. Although built in 1275, the sober church was enlarged by the powerful Chiaramonte and Scláfani dynasties. Their crests decorate a delicate portal, which is surmounted by a rose window. Inside are Serpotta frescoes and charming cloisters which were decorated like those at Monreale (*see page 137*).

South of the Corso Emanuele is the ramshackle **Albergheria** quarter, once inhabited by Norman court officials and rich merchants from Pisa and Amalfi. Depending on taste, it is a squalid slum or the old hugger-mugger of backstreet life. Although tottering houses propped up by rotten planks are home to illegal immigrants, a dynamic sense of community prevails over scenes of urban decay.

The romantic **San Giovanni degli Eremiti** ❺ (Mon–Sat 9am–6.30pm, Sun 9am–12.30pm) lies just south of the royal palace. This Byzantine basilica was converted into a Benedictine abbey and a mosque. Byzantine foundations cede to Arab squinches, filigree windows and Norman cloisters overgrown with jasmine. The shape of the early mosque is still visible, as are stiff frescoes and Muslim arches. The garden is enchanting, a riot of acanthus, crab apple and mimosa.

Arab architectural motifs haunt **Palazzo Scláfani** ❻, a fortified Catalan-Gothic *palazzo* north of San Giovanni, built by one of the most powerful feudal families. Further east is the **Carmine** ❼, a Carmelite convent in the heart of the **Ballarò market**, the noisy haunt of artisans and students, housewives and

bootleggers. Currently Palermo's liveliest market, Ballarò is raucous, authentic and sprawling, with the hurly-burly of the exotic food stalls clashing with the second-hand clothes stalls by **Il Gesù** ❽ (daily 7.30–11.30am), also known as **Casa Professa**. This cloistered Jesuitical church has a baroque marble interior that teems with tritons and cherubs.

Map on pages 114–115

Four public faces

Quattro Canti ❾, known as "*il teatro*" (the city theatre), is the central spot offering a cross-section of Palermitan baroque, Arab-Norman splendour and medieval muddle. The four concave-shaped screens of the city conceal chaotic or conflicting districts behind their neat Spanish facades. West of pollution-blackened Via Maqueda, alleys lead back to the battered Capo and Albergheria quarters. Alternatively, the city shows its best public face in **Piazza Pretoria** ❿, which is being restored. The baroque square was originally nicknamed Piazza Vergogna (Square of Shame) after its riot of saucy nude statues cavorting in the fountain, its vast circular basin peopled by tritons, nymphs and river gods. Reputedly, the local nuns chopped off the noses of the nude gods but stopped short of castration.

Adjoining the square is the **Palazzo delle Aquile** (daily 9am–8pm), the mayor's over-restored Gothic city hall, and the towering presence of **San Giuseppe dei Teatini** ⓫ (Mon–Fri 8am–noon, 6–8pm), a theatrical baroque church. The interior is covered in multicoloured marble and is crowned by a cupola with a restored fresco.

On the far side of Via Maqueda lies the Jewish quarter centred on **San Nicolò**, the erstwhile synagogue. It was called *mesquita* since it resembled a mosque but is now less Moorish than the two delightful domed Arab-Norman churches

The multicoloured dome of San Giovanni degli Eremiti.

BELOW: elaborate fountain in Piazza Pretoria.

Il Gesù (Casa Professa) was the first Jesuit foundation in Sicily. The building took over 100 years to complete.

BELOW: grotesque detail in San Giuseppe Teatini.

nearby. **La Martorana** 🄬 (Mon–Sat 9.30am–1pm, 3.30–7pm, Sun 8.30am–1pm) was founded in 1143 by George of Antioch, King Roger's Syrian emir and admiral. Although raised in the Orthodox faith, the Emir planned La Martorana as a mosque. To complicate matters, he chose Greek Byzantine craftsmen to make the splendid mosaics. Baroque additions confirm this as a coded church within a church. The space interweaves Byzantine and Moslem iconography: the Pantocrator is present but so is the figure 8, the Arabic number of perfection.

The triple-domed church of **San Cataldo** 🄭 (Mon–Fri 9am–3.30pm, Sat–Sun 9am–1pm) is one of the last sacred buildings built in the Arab-Norman style. The Oriental impression is confirmed by the brooding Syrian interior. If this exquisite space at first appears sparse, it is only as a reaction to the gilded La Martorana. The subdued light reveals three domes supported by squinches and piers; the Fatimid capitals are so delicate they appear to float. In the crypt are sections of Palermo's Roman walls.

La Kalsa quarter

Meaning "pure" or "chosen" in Arabic, La Kalsa's name became less ironic when Mother Teresa's mission settled off bomb-struck **Piazza Magione**. Well-heeled Palermitans were horrified to be lectured by an Albanian nun, even one incarnating sainthood. Her message was that since Palermo was as poor as the Third World, charity should begin at home. The message seems to have struck a chord since the area is now being regenerated, resulting in a greater sense of safety and belonging, not to mention the cheerful materialism heralded by new bars and *palazzo* restoration, especially close to the gentrified Piazza Marina.

However, this decrepit corner of Palermo houses a wonderful Norman church

as well as the late Mother Teresa's nuns. Moorish filigree windows and blind arcading announce the ancestry of **La Magione** 🄮 (Mon–Sat 8–11.30am, 3–6.30pm, Sun 8am–1pm). This imposing Cistercian church was founded in 1191 and given to the Imperial Teutonic Order by Henry VI. The Arab-Norman interior is plain without being austere. **Palazzo Aiutamicristo** 🄯, on the adjoining square, is a Catalan-Gothic mansion containing a loggia and porticoed courtyard. Just south, in the honeycomb heart of the Kalsa, awaits **Lo Spasimo** (daily 8am–midnight), an open-air cultural entertainment complex set in an atmospheric 16th-century monastery. Concerts are held in the cloisters and the roofless church, which, given a sultry, starry night and swaying palms, creates a romantic, Moorish atmosphere.

Just east, Via Alloro, the city's patrician centre in the Middle Ages, leads to **Palazzo Abatellis** 🄰, a Catalan-Gothic mansion housing Sicily's most endearing art collection, the Galleria Regionale (Mon–Sat 9am–1.30pm, Sun 9am–12.30pm, also Tues, Thur 3–7.30pm). The treasures are matched in scale and quality by the charming setting. Off a Renaissance courtyard and loggia are rich Byzantine mosaics Neapolitan Madonnas, painted medieval crucifixes, sweet Gagini sculptures and soft-hued Renaissance portraits. Other highlights are a serene bust of Eleanor of Aragon; a haunting da Messina Annunciation; and a geometric Moorish door. The undoubted masterpiece is the powerful *Triumph of Death*, a frescoed 15th-century *danse macabre* showing the vanity of human wishes: a skeletal grim reaper cuts a swathe through the nobles' earthly pleasures.

Piazza Marina was a swamp until drained by the Arabs and used as their first citadel. Since then, the square has witnessed the shame and glory of city history. **Palazzo Chiaramonte** 🄳, a Catalan-Gothic fortress, was a feudal stronghold before becoming the seat of the Inquisition in 1598. Carved on the grim prison walls inside is a poignant plea for *pane, pazienza e tempo* (bread, patience and time). Outside, heretics and dissenters were burned. Commonly known as the Steri, the mansion belonged to the Spanish viceroys and the law courts before falling into the hands of the Chancellor of Palermo University. Take the side entrance and, if challenged, be armed with an academic pretext, the price of seeing the gorgeous inner courtyard and the salon with a coffered Moorish ceiling. As the only gentrified square in the old quarter, Piazza Marina is self-consciously proud of its shady **park** and well-tended banyan trees. Around the neat park, bric-a-brac traders vie with energetic waiters in their efforts to drum up trade. Across the square is the charming Renaissance church of **Santa Maria dei Miracoli** (daily 8.30–noon, 4–7pm).

In Via Merlo, just west, is **Palazzo Mirto** 🄳, an unprepossessing *palazzo* with a delightful period interior. Now a museum (Mon–Fri 9am–6.30pm, Sat–Sun 9am–12.30pm), the mansion is a testament to the eclectic tastes of 18th-century Palermitan nobles. Chinoiserie and Empire style clash with neo-Gothic and baroque. Below *trompe l'oeil* ceilings are Louis XVI chairs, rustic panelling, heroic tapestries or crib figures. Best are the secret rooms, and a

Map on pages 114–115

TIP

Unless your hotel has a car park, avoid taking a car into Palermo. There are few safe, supervised parking spots in the city (Piazza Marina and Piazza Bellini are two), and if a foreigner's car disappears, legal redress is in the lap of the gods.

BELOW: the Byzantine glitter of La Martorana.

TIP

Sample such savoury
Palermitan snacks as
deep-fried rice balls
(*arancini*), chickpea
fritters, or broccoli and
artichokes deep-fried
in batter, followed by
marzipan sweets,
prickly pears, water
ices or watermelon
jelly scented with
jasmine. **Il Golosone**
on Piazza Castelnuovo
is a good place for
Sicilian fast food.

BELOW: traditional
grocery shop in the
Vucciria quarter.

chinoiserie salon with lacquered Oriental cabinets, porcelain and pagoda-style seats.

A tip and a smile gain access to **Oratorio di San Lorenzo ⑳** (Mon–Sat 9am–noon) on Via Immacolatella. This whimsical yet overwrought oratory is a Serpotta gem, with every surface awash with cheeky cherubs waving impish bottoms. Close by is **San Francesco d'Assisi ㉑** (Mon–Sat 7am–noon, 4.30–6pm), arguably Palermo's loveliest Gothic church, its austerity softened by a delicate rose window. This northern church once served the Pisan merchants who traded nearby, but the abstraction of the portal reveals an Arab-Norman influence. Opposite the church is **Antica Focacceria**, a legendary Palermitan inn, its battered bow windows matched by marble slabs and a gleaming brass stove. This period piece, which faces an equally good ice-cream parlour, has a reputation for rustic snacks: *panini di panelle*, fried chickpea squares and *pani cu' la meusa*, greasy boiled beef spleen served in a bun.

The **Marina**, due south, was Palermo's grand seafront until the Belle Epoque, was both a public parade and a chance for louche encounters. Now known as **Foro Italico ㉒**, the stark waterfront is home to a scruffy funfair, with Arab and African children riding ponies. The view is overlooked by the newly-restored **Palazzo Butera ㉓**, eulogised by Goethe but bombed by the Allies. Once Sicily's grandest palace, it is now used for receptions and exhibitions. As part of the ongoing regeneration of the area, the council has planted palms along the seafront, created a park and reopened the **Cattive**, a terrace named after the bad-tempered widows and spinsters who once glowered at lovers entwined below.

Next door to the **Villa Giulia** (closed for restoration) is the **Orto Botánico ㉔** (Mon–Fri 9am–5pm, Sat–Sun 9am–1pm), botanical gardens dotted with pavilions, sphinxes and a lily pond. There are clumps of bamboo and bougainvillea, banyans and magnolias, kapoks, pineapples and petticoat palms.

Vucciria quarter

The name is a corruption of the French *boucherie*, thanks to the quantity of flesh on sale in the traditional **Vucciria market**. The stalls straggle along alleys from Via Roma to **San Domenico** (daily 9–11am), a vapid baroque church with an impressive facade. In the 18th century, the Spanish viceroys tried to impose order on Palermo's most chaotic market but failed dismally. The names of the surrounding streets echo their old trades: silversmiths, ironmongers, pastamakers, shoemakers. These colourful alleys display capers and pine nuts, spices and sundried tomatoes, skewered giblets and bootleg tapes, and are particularly charming as night falls and the red awnings are illuminated. However, the ascendancy of Ballarò market means that the Vucciria is only truly bustling on Saturday. If the Vucciria palls, consider a drink in the faded grandeur of **Hotel des Palmes** on Via Roma. Wagner composed part of *Parsifal* in a gilded salon in 1882, while the wartime Mafia boss Lucky Luciano later held court in the dining room.

Sustenance is necessary since between San Domenico and the port is devastation. However, Via Bambinai, a former dollmakers' street, has stayed close to its roots: shops sell votive offerings and

Christmas crib figures. The street contains a baroque jewel in **Oratorio del Rosario di San Domenico** ㉕ (Mon–Fri 9am–1pm, 3–5.30pm, Sat 9.30am–12.30pm), a theatrical Serpotta chapel, where *putti* play cellos amidst seashells, eagles and allegorical exotica. Just around the corner, on Via Valverde, lies an equally celebrated oratory, **Oratorio del Rosario di Santa Zita** ㉖ (Tues–Fri 9am–1pm, 3–6pm, Sat 9am–1pm), reached through lush gardens. The oratories were places the nobles used as social clubs, confraternities, and centres for charitable works, as well as for displays of status and wealth. Here, Serpotta's ravishing stuccowork depicts the intercession of the Virgin in the Battle of Lepanto, with all boats exquisitely differentiated.

Beyond the chapel to the south is **La Cala**, the scruffy portside. Fishing boats bob against a backdrop of bombed *palazzi* whose cellars house immigrant families. However, regeneration is gradually seeping into this semi-derelict quarter, with the restoration of bomb-damaged churches such as **San Giorgio dei Genovesi** (Mon–Sat 9am–1pm, 3–5.30pm), now an exhibition centre. Sandwiched between the port and Piazza Marina is **Santa Maria della Catena** ㉗ (Mon–Fri 9am–1pm), a well-restored Catalan-Gothic church popular with wedding parties. The church, which has early Renaissance elements, is named after the medieval chain that once shut off the port.

From the port, retrace your steps to Via Roma and take Via Bara to Piazza Olivella, part of a charming artisans' quarter of puppetmakers, *pasticcerie* and *trattorie*. The baroque **Olivella** ㉘ church adjoins the **Museo Archeológico** ㉙ (Mon–Fri 9am–1pm, 3–7pm, Sat 9am–1pm), the essence of Classical Sicily encased in a late Renaissance monastery. The inner courtyard is a tangle of lush vegetation and a lily pond. Nearby are inscrutable Egyptian priestly figures

Map on pages 114–115

The Museo del Mare (daily 9.30am–noon), a new maritime museum, is set in the former arsenal on Via Cristoforo Colombo, which has been well restored. There are changing exhibitions and impressive terrace and sea views.

BELOW: Antica Focacceria, the traditional place to devour innards.

The Teatro dei Pupi in Vicolo Ragusi has puppet shows two or three times a week featuring all the traditional characters.

BELOW: one of Serpotta's many cherubs in the Oratorio del Rosario di Santa Zita.

found near Mozia. Anthropomorphic Phoenician sarcophagi stare out of Semitic faces and square bodies. A tablet carved with hieroglyphics, animals and birds vies with an ancient Greek bronze decree from Segesta.

The fabulous **Sala di Selinunte** displays the main frieze from Temple C: Athena protecting Perseus as he battles with the Medusa; and Hercules slaying dwarves. Other stylised friezes portray Hercules tackling a muscular Amazon; Zeus marrying a frosty Hera; and Actaeon attacked by savage dogs. Almost as compelling are the majestic lion-head water spouts and the graceful bronze Ephebus of Selinunte (470 BC). By comparison, the Etruscan friezes look stilted: a mere procession of sleeping warriors, chariots and carved beasts.

Modern quarter

From here, Via Cavour leads west to Piazza Giuseppe Verdi and the well-restored **Teatro Mássimo** ㉚, the city opera house (guided visits Mon–Sat 9am–1pm, tel: 091-334246). The harmonious building, first opened in 1897, was designed by the Palermitan Giovani Battista Basile in eclectic rather than neo-classical style. The portico, graced by Corinthian columns, is of clear Greek inspiration, while the cylindrical shape of the building and the cupola owe more to Roman designs. The interior is equally eclectic: while the grandiose main staircase is baroque, the decor, rich in floral motifs, is decidedly Art Nouveau. This remarkable theatre, which seats 3,400, reopened in 1998 with a glittering production of Verdi's *Aida*, after a scandalous 25-year closure that can be blamed on lethargy, financial shortcomings and political infighting.

The chic shopping street of **Viale della Libertà** disappoints. It was once studded with Art Nouveau villas designed for the *haute bourgeoisie*, but most

have been demolished or disappeared in fires linked to fraudulent insurance claims. The northern end leads to attractive gardens but smart bars and the sophisticated evening *passeggiata* cannot conceal the fact that style has deserted the quarter. Even so, the voluptuously landscaped **Giardino Inglese** makes for a romantic stroll, while **Piazza Castelnuovo**, at the southern end of the street, is the frenetic early evening meeting place for Palermitan youth.

The suburbs

From the scruffy waterfront at Foro Italico, a short drive or stroll southwest leads to a couple of lesser-known Arab-Norman sights. **San Giovani dei Lebbrosi** (Mon–Sat 9.30–11am, 4–5pm) lies on Via Cappello, off Corso dei Mille, one of the city's main Mafia quarters. Built of warm limestone and brick as a castle chapel, this is one of the city's earliest Norman monuments, and was later used as a leper hospital. Nearby is **Ponte dell'Ammiraglio**, a stranded Norman bridge, which straddled a now-diverted river.

Alternatively, a short bus or car journey west from Piazza Castelnuovo leads to Piazza La Ziza, and one of the most impressive legacies of Moorish Palermo. In Norman times, palaces encircled the city "like gold coins around the neck of a bosomy girl". The vivid description by the Arab poet, Ibn Jubayr, conjures up the pleasure dome of **La Ziza** (Mon–Sat 9am–6.30pm, Sun 9am–12.30pm). An Arab arch leads to a palace built on the site of a Roman villa to exploit the existing aqueduct. Fed by canals, the lake was paved with marine-inspired mosaics. La Ziza's most charming spot is the vestibule, adorned by honeycomb vaults, a Saracenic fountain and a glorious mosaic frieze of peacocks and huntsmen. In this breezy chamber, the Emir and his court listened to the lapping of water.

The interior, now a **museum of Arab culture**, is a mixed success. Critics claim that clumsy restoration has ruined the Arab lines and replaced filigree windows with heavy-framed versions. However, some Islamic features remain; the highlights are the mosaics and Cufic script. Beyond the walls is the palace chapel, a domed Oriental affair whose stalactites, squinches and rib vaulting form part of a baroque church.

South of La Ziza is **La Cuba** (Mon–Sat 9am–1pm, 3–6.30pm), the final piece of the Moorish jigsaw. This quaint pavilion lies along Corso Calatafimi, opposite Via Quarto dei Mille, but in Arab times was set in a lovely artificial lake within the luxuriant grounds of La Ziza. Boccaccio set a story from *The Decameron* in this "sumptuous villa", which is now a windowless, roofless ruin, marooned in an army barracks. For those with no taste for the macabre, the return to Palermo is via Porta Nuova, a Spanish gateway decorated with turbaned Moorish giants.

Convento dei Cappuccini (daily 9am–noon, 3–5pm), the grim catacombs, lie on Via Cappuccini, midway between La Cuba and La Ziza. In macabre Sicilian style, superior corpses were mummified here from the 16th century to 1881. In death, the clergy, nobles and bourgeoisie opted for posterity rather than the communal trench. In these galleries, embalmers have stored over 8,000 moth-eaten mummies.

Map on pages 114–115

*Near Piazza La Ziza is the main cultural complex in the north of the city: **Cantieri Culturali alla Ziza**, a former industrial site whose impressive pavilions have recently been turned into functional yet creative exhibition spaces and concert halls.*

BELOW: a cool courtyard in Palermo's Museo Archeológico.

*La Cuba and La
Cubola, pleasure
domes built by
Emperor Henry VI,
once stood in an
artificial lake.*

BELOW: mummified
priest in the
Convento dei
Cappuccini.
RIGHT: waiting
for the bride.

Conca d'Oro

The city outskirts, in the legendary "golden shell" carved into the fold between
coast and mountains, should be carpeted with marigolds and citrus groves but
land speculation and Mafia funding have ensured that Palermo's countryside is
being encased in concrete, with environmental laws flouted by unscrupulous
builders. Yet **Villa Igiea**, Palermo's de luxe hotel on Salita Belmonte, on the east
coast, (tel: 091-540122) is a swan-song to the city's last flicker of greatness.
Ernesto Basile, son of the architect of the Teatro Mássimo, designed it for the
Florio family, Sicily's finest entrepreneurs, who chose an exotic terraced setting
overlooking the sea. The glorious Art Nouveau dining room is a harmonious
composition of elegant cabinets, functional furnishings and ethereal frescoes.

On the northern outskirts lies the **Parco della Favorita**, a neglected Bourbon
park designed by the exiled Ferdinand III. His domineering consort, Maria Car-
olina, conceived of the **Palazzina Cinese** as a Petit Trianon to rival the creation of her sister, Marie Antoinette. This chinoiserie pavilion remains an
inspired folly, with its original 18th-century furnishings. By billeting Allied
troops there during World War II, the villa was spared but now seems destined
for ruination by Palermitan officialdom and neglect. The **Piana dei Colli** villas,
once patrician summer retreats, are sinking under bougainvillaea, oleander and
neglect. Next door is **Villa Niscemi** (villa open Sunday morning; gardens until
sunset daily), whose fate seems assured as an exhibition centre. The villa was
used as Lampedusa's model for Tancredi's home in *The Leopard* and is a recher-
ché film set. Owned by a noble family who came to Sicily with the Normans,
the villa combines elegance with rustic charm.

From the coast, a scenic road climbs **Monte Pellegrino**, passing citrus groves

and shrubland. In these sandstone slopes, the **Addaura caves** have revealed prehistoric drawings. From the terraced slopes, sweeping views span the glinting bay of the Conca d'Oro. **Santuario di Santa Rosalia** (tel: 091-540326 for opening times), a shrine to Palermo's revered patron saint, lies in a mountain grotto on San Pellegrino. Her origins are mysterious but in 1624, while Palermo was in the throes of the plague, her vision instructed a dreamer to hunt for her relics and wave them three times round the city walls. Thus Palermo was saved and devotedly built a sanctuary in Rosalia's honour. Mountain views and an insight into Palermitan sentimentality are the rewards for trailing up to this kitsch spectacle in a damp cave.

Set in the lee of Monte Pellegrino, north of Palermo, lies the fashionable resort of **Mondello**, easily reached by bus from Viale della Libertà. The resort, pioneered by the Bourbons, began as a tuna-fishing village but became a garden suburb under Belgian influence, reaching its heyday in the interwar years. The centre of attraction is the striking ochre and maroon Art Nouveau **pier**, created by a Belgian entrepreneur in the 1890s. All except two beaches are private or charge an admission fee: for free sunbathing, you can choose between the basic official public beach or the Charleston beach, by the pier. The latter is designated "private", but visitors staying in Palermo hotels are entitled to use it free, on provision of a note from the hotelier.

Mondello's attractions are slight but seductive, from summer sea breezes to a ruined medieval watchtower and the odd Belle Epoque villa, not to mention flashy discotheques and decorous dining. The Charleston itself, set on the pier, is one of Palermo's most exclusive seafood restaurants, confirmed by the existence of a spacious summer terrace and a snooty *maître d'hôtel*. ❑

Map on pages 114–115

Patrick Brydone, an 18th-century visitor, believed that the alleged relics of Santa Rosalia were the remains of "some poor wretch that was probably murdered". He was not far wrong: the bones have been proved to be those of a goat.

LEFT: Art Deco nymphs in the Hotel Villa Igiea.
BELOW: sunbathing on a Mondello beach

A FLOWERING OF FLAMBOYANCE

The earthquake of 1693 literally wiped the architectural slate clean in many cities, and gave free rein to the new tastes of the ruling class

The baroque of the 18th century was a golden age for Sicilian architecture, a tantalising game of silhouettes and perspectives, an opportunity for wild ornamentation, with sculpted cornices, fanciful balconies and flowing staircases.

In Palermo, *spagnolismo*, the love of ostentation, found its natural soulmate in baroque taste. Urban planning led to grandiose squares and fancy streets. Convents, churches and oratories sprang up in the historic centre, and city *palazzi* competed for attention. Balconies and cornices were adorned with angels, nymphs, gargoyles and grimacing monsters.

In Bagheria, villas (like the Villa Palagonia, above) acquired opulent staircases and marble-encrusted ballrooms. The distinguished baroque cities of Ragusa and Módica indulged in spatial experiment, theatrical vistas flanked by flights of steps. In Noto, baroque meant spaciousness, symmetry and loftiness. It is a stage set of a city, sculpted in golden stone, exuding *joie de vivre* and ravishing the senses.

▷ **SAINT IN STONE**
St Paul is one of the 12 sculpted apostles who flank the broad staircase leading to San Pietro in Módica, rebuilt after the 1693 earthquake.

△ **MASTERPIECE**
The astonishing stucco work in the Oratorio del Rosario of Santa Zita, Palermo, is Giacomo Serpotta's finest work (*see right*).

▷ **FOUR SEASONS**
The four *palazzo* fronts of Palermo's Quattro Canti include fountains dedicated to the seasons, and statues of Spanish kings and saints.

◁ SIX EXCESSES
Six baroque balconies
with extravagantly
sculpted buttresses adorn
the classical facade of
Noto's Palazzo Villadorata.

▽ HOST OF STATUES
The fountain in Palermo's
Piazza Pretoria has a riot
of nude tritons, nymphs,
gods and goddesses by
two Florentine sculptors.

THE PLASTER MASTER

◁ WEDDING CAKE
San Giorgio in Ragusa is
Rosario Gagliardi's
masterpiece. It took more
than 40 years to complete.

▽ BAROQUE BALLROOM
The salon of Bagheria's
Villa Valguarnera was the
location for the ball scene
in Visconti's *The Leopard*.

▽ TWINING VINES
Palermo's 12th-century
cathedral has many later
additions, including these
ornate baroque pillars.

Giacomo Serpotta, born
in Palermo in 1656,
was a genius in stucco,
who elevated Sicilian
plaster work from a
craft to an art. His most
breathtaking creations
can be seen today in
several of Palermo's
oratories.
   His Oratorio di San
Lorenzo has a fragile
beauty bordering on the
overblown, every
surface festooned with
allegorical stucco
figures. The lavish
Oratorio del Rosario di
San Domenico
combines frothy statues
of the Virtues with a
joyful abundance of
capering cherubs.
   The Oratorio del
Rosario di Santa Zita
(main picture, left) is
Serpotta's masterwork.
A host of exuberant
angels and cherubs
clamber over walls and
window frames,
allegorical statues
seem to float in space,
while an intricate
stucco panel depicting
a sea battle in relief
employs metal wire for
the ships' rigging.

PALERMO PROVINCE

*Leave the raucous capital to explore Monreale's glittering
Arab-Norman cathedral, the Madonie mountains, the
Mafia-infested interior and the marine reserve of Ustica*

Map
on page
138

Outside **Palermo ❶**, the centuries unfurl in a clannish yet sparsely populated countryside. It is a province of extreme light and shade, of esoteric cults and exuberant festivals, of shimmering cathedrals in shady spots. This is the brooding Mafia heartland of gulleys and mountain lairs. Nurtured by the mythology of banditry, the region falls back on ancient suspicion and insularity. Small-town battles and spiritual isolation pervade a wild province. Yet these rural pockets feels far away from the Moorish voluptuousness and sophistication of **Monreale ❷**.

In the words of a Sicilian proverb, "He who goes to Palermo without seeing Monreale leaves a donkey and comes back an ass." Certainly, this sumptuous cathedral is the apogee of Arab-Norman art. The **cathedral** (daily 8am–8pm) and Benedictine monastery were built by William II, allegedly inspired by a vision. In truth, his political rivalry with Walter of the Mill, the Palermitan archbishop, fuelled his desire to build a cathedral greater than Palermo's. Ultimately, William triumphed and his white marble sarcophagus lies in Monreale.

Flanked by severe bell towers, the cathedral is not instantly awe-inspiring yet the details are exquisite. An arched **Romanesque portal**, made by a Pisan master, is framed by a greenish bronze door. The portal displays sculpted bands of garlands, figures and beasts alternated with multi-coloured mosaics. To the left, a Gagini portico shelters another Romanesque **bronze door**, inspired by the delicacy of Byzantine inlaid ivory. The **apses** are the most opulent in Sicily: a poetic abstraction of interlacing limestone and lava arches, sculpted as delicately as wood.

International influences

Monreale drew craftsmen from Persia, Africa, Asia, Greece, Venice, Pisa and Provence. The glistening gold interior fuses Arab purity of volume with Byzantine majesty. The shimmering tapestry of the **mosaics** is unequalled in Europe. It is worth bringing binoculars to admire the Creation series on the upper walls in the right of the nave. The delicacy of the flowers, fruit trees and exotic birds singles out these scenes from Genesis. However, the whole series is a *Biblia pauperum*, a poor man's Bible.

The **Pantocrator** in the apse is an authoritarian God, unlike the softer Christ in Cefalù. Above the royal throne is a mosaic of Christ crowning William the Good, a tribute to the king whose world view embraced concubines, eunuchs and negro slaves. Other delights include Cosmati paving; Roman capitals incorporating busts of Ceres and Proserpine; and a gilded ceiling whose rafters resemble the spines of beautifully bound books.

The **cloisters** (Mon–Fri 9am–1pm, 3–6.30pm, Sat–Sun 9am–noon) express William's love of Islamic art

PRECEDING PAGES:
spring in the hills
near Prizzi.
LEFT: the Arab-
Norman cloisters of
Monreale cathedral.
BELOW: the eight
leaves represent
perfection in Arab
numerology.

TIP

Local treats to look out
for in the *trattorie*
include *pasta con
sarde*, a sardine
speciality, and dry
biscotti di Monreale.
Despite its odd name,
the Baby O Bar
opposite the cathedral
is a pleasant place for
drinks, ice creams or
snacks.

and are the most sumptuous Romanesque cloisters in the world. Every second pair of white marble columns has a vivid zigzag mosaic pattern spiralling up the shaft. The sophistication of these columns suggests a Provençal influence while the Moorish mood, evoked by mosaic inlays or arabesque carvings, conjures up the Alhambra. Many sculptures echo the mosaics but add a personal note, including the name of a mason, or musicians playing Sicilian instruments. The *Allegory of the Seasons*, an enchanting marble composition, depicts tree-planting and pig-killing. In one corner, a loggia creates a *chiaroscuro* effect with a glorious, slightly phallic fountain. Shaped like a palm tree trunk, the shaft is crowned by lions' heads, as at the Alhambra. (Certain columns are now being restored.)

After raucous Palermo, Monreale exudes provincial calm: as a Mafia-controlled town, it is supremely safe for visitors. Sicily's largest Carabinier barracks was built here after *mafiosi* murdered local officers from 1983 to 1984 yet the Mafia remains a potent force.

While the town is an anticlimax after the cathedral's mosaics, a horse and car ride or stroll from the Duomo is a chance to savour the pedestrianised centre with its crumbling baroque churches, and shops selling ceramics or fine ices. **Madonna delle Croci**, set on a hill, offers a last lingering view from the cathedral to the coast.

In the lushly mountainous landscape towards **Boccadifalco** ❸ is the Benedictine abbey of **San Martino** (Mon–Fri 9am–noon), 9 km (5½ miles) west of Monreale along a switchback road. The abbey is known for charitable work among the lay community and for its monumental staircase, monastic library and 18th-century paintings. The surrounding pine forests are a cool escape in summer, unlike the two bandit towns to the west.

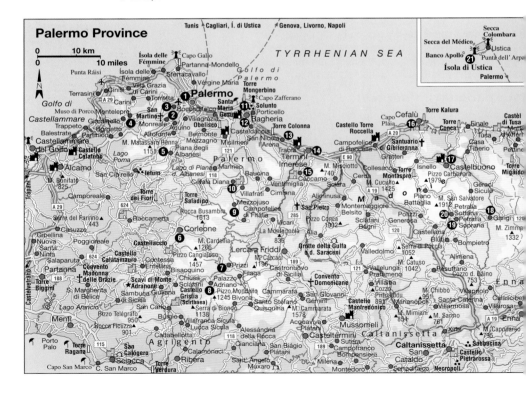

Bandit country

In 1873 John Addington Symonds wrote of **Montelepre** ❹: "The talk was brigands and nothing but brigands." This was especially true on the eve of World War II, when the bandit Salvatore Giuliano reigned over these desolate crags. If the Mafiologists are correct, this is still bandit country. Certainly, local graffiti mention Giuliano's name. Little appears to have changed since Giuliano's mysterious murder in Castelvetrano in 1950.

The medieval heart of Montelepre is enclosed by scruffy alleys and courtyards coiled around the Chiesa Madre. On the edge of town are boulders and cacti; views of deserted farms and fields dotted with boulders indicate that although the feudal estates have gone, little has replaced them. Neighbouring **Partinico** is a byword for urban poverty. In the 1950s Danilo Dolci, Sicily's Gandhi, chose benighted western Sicily to set up his centre.

Piana degli Albanesi ❺, reached along the SS 624, appears suspended above a lake. Lush pastures are encircled by hills, home to 15th-century Greek-speaking immigrants, confusingly designated "Albanians". The community settled here in 1488 after Turkish troops invaded their homeland. Since then, generations have kept their customs and their Orthodox faith in this cheerful town. Marriages and funerals, Epiphany and Easter are times for traditional Byzantine ceremony and folk costumes. The community speaks Greek at home; signs are in Greek as well as Italian. Local cuisine is a cultural stew: *stranghuie* (gnocchi), *brumie me bathé e thieré*, a filling bean casserole, or *dash*, castrated ram, Albanian-Greek style.

Corleone ❻, perched along the rural SS 118, is enfolded in desolate, scorched hills and high verdant plains. The town lies clamped between two rocks, below

Map on page 138

The baroque public fountain erected in Partinico in 1716 is still in use today.

BELOW: a service in Monreale cathedral.

The Saracen castle at Cefalà Diana was once an important stronghold on the Palermo–Agrigento road.

BELOW:
Corleone, where the Mafia still casts a dark shadow.

a weather-beaten escarpment. In the centre looms the **Castello**, a rocky outcrop topped by a Saracen tower. It was a prison until 1976 but is now home to Franciscan friars who take their vow of poverty seriously. Below, the rooftops are stacked in a chromatic range of greys. At first sight, Corleone fails to live up to its infamous reputation. But on closer inspection, an air of watchfulness hangs over the town, with mysterious undercurrents bordering on lawlessness. Madonnas with snapped heads dangle from car dashboards; teenagers toss olive trees over the cliff; grizzled crones carry piles of brushwood for their able-bodied sons; and 12-year-old children in three-wheeled cars speed along cobbled alleys. Nonetheless, the town has a reputation for producing great minds, whether priests, scholars or criminals.

Unlike neighbouring towns, Corleone's shops and businesses pay no *pizzo* (protection money): the town is the stronghold of the most powerful Mafia clan. However, the arrest in 1993 of Totò Riina, the Corleonese *capo di tutti capi*, promised to spell turmoil. When news of his arrest spread, local schoolchildren burst into applause, but the men in battered fedoras stood motionless on the *piazza*. Since then, the mood has changed, particularly among the young, with public-spirited citizens ready to guide visitors around town (tel: 091-8463655).

To the southeast lies **Prizzi ❼**, with its sloping checkerboard of rust-tiled roofs. The town is celebrated for its bizarre Easter festival known as the *ballo dei diavoli* (dance of the devils). Dating back to Sicani times, the dance depicts the eternal struggle between Good and Evil, winter and spring, Christianity and paganism. The gap-toothed devil masks are primitive but menacing while the atmosphere of ritualised violence is echoed by Mafia lore. In this fleeting escape from *miseria*, citizens fall upon Prizzi's cheeses, pastries and wines.

The neighbouring village of **Palazzo Adriano ❽**, 10 km (6 miles) southwest, encapsulates the festering rivalries of these provincial backwaters. Two sombre churches share the main square in mutual antipathy: the Orthodox Santa Maria dell'Assunta scorns the Catholic Santa Maria del Lume. Ironically, the square starred in the warmly evocative *Cinema Paradiso*. From here, the route back to the coast along the SS 188 and SS 121 passes the hilltop village of **Mezzojuso ❾**, snug in the Ficuzza woods. Like many others, the village has mixed Albanian and Arab ancestry and religious frictions. Dell'Annunziata, the Catholic church, is literally overshadowed by the Orthodox San Nicola, home to lovely Byzantine icons. Nearby, the Albanian Santa Maria delle Grazie houses frescoes and the finest iconostasis in Sicily. The adjoining monastery restores and displays precious Greek manuscripts and miniatures. **Cefalà Diana ❿**, just north, is firmly in the Arab camp, with a tumbledown castle and the island's best-preserved Moorish bathhouse.

East from Palermo

From the capital to Cefalù, the coast curves past fishing villages and coves to Capo Zafferano and the ruins at **Solunto ⓫** (Mon–Fri 9am–6pm, Sat–Sun 9am– noon). Set on majestic cliffs, the ruins are less impressive than the wild location. The Phoenician colony of Solus was one of the earliest trading posts on the island and

Map on page 138

urvived until destruction by Siracusa in 398 BC. It was later Hellenised and taken
by Rome, with the result that traces of the three civilisations remain. The highlights
are the floor mosaics and a luxurious villa dwelling with a colonnaded peristyle.
From the agora are stunning views of vineyards, a castle and Cefalù. Beyond the
wizened olive trees and battered boulders are charming swimming spots near the
lighthouse on the cape. **Porticello**, on the shore just below Solunto, is a straggling
fishing village popular with Palermitans for a seafood Sunday lunch.

Just inland is **Bagheria** ⓬, 15 km (9 miles) from Palermo, which developed
during the *Ottocento* vogue for ostentatious summer villas and declined during
the 20th century, thanks to unbridled land speculation. These patrician villas are
mostly in late Renaissance style, with grand staircases and a central body flanked
by sweeping concave wings. The U-shaped lower wings were reserved for ser-
vants, with underground chambers (*stanze del scirocco*) used by the patricians
as retreats from the heat. Villas were encircled by French formal gardens, with
roseraies and *parterres* interspersed with statues and summer houses.

While views of cement works often mar the pastoral idyll, and some villas are
pitiful wrecks, others like the glorious **Villa Valguarnera** remain in noble hands,
albeit with reduced parkland. *Bagheria*, Dacia Maraini's best-known novel,
describes her childhood in this splendid villa. The grandiose **Villa Cattolica**
(Tues–Sun 10am–6pm) houses the bizarre art collection and tomb of Renato
Guttuso, Sicily's best-known modern painter, who died in 1987. A sculptor
friend made him a surreal blue capsule tomb to match the sky, a capsule of
kitsch among the scrubby cacti and lemons.

Villa Palagonia (daily 9am–noon, 4–7pm), the strangest of the villas, was built
in 1715 by the Prince of Palagonia and is now owned by an absentee professor.

*The majestic flight of
stairs splaying open
like a fan, the fake
windows, the fake
balustrades, all of
this to trick the
restless eyes of the
noblemen in
centuries gone by.*
– DACIA MARAINI
BAGHERIA

BELOW:
Capo Zafferano.

One of the grotesque statues at Villa Palagonia, Bagheria.

Arranged around a curved axis, the villa is celebrated for the eccentricity of its grotesque sculptures. A concave wing curves back towards the main *corps* and is topped by a variety of weird Mannerist sculptures: dwarfs, hunchbacks, monsters, dragons, a two-headed dog, and a horse with human hands. Most were created by the surreal imagination of the iconoclastic Prince and are thought to represent his faithless wife's lovers. Sadly, the octagonal entrance is ruined and one approaches from the back. Beside the main entrance, two gargoyles with gaping mouths were used to extinguish the footmen's torches. A flamboyant double staircase ascends to the piano nobile, with the salon's mirrored ceiling representing the sky. The Prince had a clear message engraved over the door: "Mirror yourself in these crystals and contemplate the image of human frailty."

Términi Imerese

San Nicola l'Arena ⓭, 8 km (5 miles) before Términi, is a picturesque fishing village with a 15th-century crenellated castle overlooking the harbour. Now converted into a nightclub, the castle belongs to Palermitan aristocrats. Beside it is a solid brick *tonnara* (cannery), a reminder that the coast was devoted to tuna fishing until recently. **Términi Imerese** ⓮ is an unfortunate jumble of industry, resort and Classical ruins. However, the upper town remains fairly unspoilt, with clumps of Roman remains, from an amphitheatre to city walls, as well as a Greek temple to Zeus. Known to the Romans as Therma Himera, the city was famed for its mineral waters and baths. Just east of town is an impressive Roman aqueduct set in a wild olive grove

Cáccamo ⓯, set inland 10 km (6 miles) along the SS 285, is a dramatic Norman hill fort, the best preserved in western Sicily. The towers, battlements and

BELOW:
Términi Imerese's baroque cathedral.

Map on page 138

ramparts look convincingly medieval, even if parts were redesigned during the baroque period. This well-restored castle can be visited on tours that take in a cluster of churches and a sampling of local dishes (tel: 091-545423 to book).

A return to the coast at **Cefalù** ⑯ is a chance to visit the province's great counterpoint to Monreale Cathedral. Sitting snugly below a headland, Cefalù is Taormina's west coast rival as a tourism centre. The consensus is that, although Taormina has better hotels, nightlife and atmosphere, Cefalù is more compact, peaceful and family-oriented. The **cathedral** (daily 8.30am–noon, 3.30–6pm), built in 1130 by Roger II, has a bold twin-towered facade and a triple apse with blind arcading. The King confidently had porphyry sarcophagi made for posterity but these are now in Palermo Cathedral. Inside, a severe nave is flanked by Roman columns surmounted by Romanesque arches. A sense of space and majesty is created by the concentration of other-worldly **mosaics** in the distant dome, among the earliest created by the Normans yet also praised as the purest extant depiction of Christ. The raised choir represents an Oriental element whereas the gold firmament behind Christ is Byzantine. The open-timber roof has traces of the original Arab-Norman paintings. Below is a Norman font guarded by leopards, the symbol of King Roger's Hauteville dynasty. During ongoing restoration works, the interior is cluttered with tombs and statuary and, more controversially, a huge new window has been installed. Birds often circle the nave, adding a note of life to this pristine temple.

Out of season, **Piazza del Duomo** is a delightful sun trap, with a view of the cathedral at the foot of steep cliffs running up to the fortifications. The square is also framed by the Corso, a Renaissance seminary and a porticoed *palazzo*. Here, the chic Caffe Duomo is the place for an atmospheric *aperitivo al fresco*.

Cefalù's beaches are unremarkable but the better ones are generally linked to specific hotels: Le Calette (tel: 0921-4241444), for instance, offers private access to a delightful rocky cove.

BELOW: Cáccamo Castle, set in rugged terrain.

The Byzantine mosaic of Christ Pantocrator dominates the central apse of Cefalù Cathedral.

Cefalù's **old port**, tangibly Moorish and home to Tunisian fishermen, has been a backdrop in countless films, including *Cinema Paradiso*. A warren of alleys leads west from **Corso Ruggero** and reveals Renaissance facades, Gothic parapets and mullioned windows overlooking tiny courtyards. An underground spring bubbles up in the arcaded Arab baths, sited at the bottom of curved steps. **Via Porto Salvo** passes battered churches and flourishing craft shops. In summer, the town is a delightful tourist trap with quaint craft boutiques selling ceramics and gold jewellery, matched by sophisticated restaurants catering to fastidious French palates. **Porta Pescare**, one of the surviving medieval gates, opens onto a creek, beach and boatyard. In the evening, the seafront, bastion and Corso become a cavalcade devoted to *passeggiate* and *gelati*.

From Piazza Duomo, a steepish hill leads down to **Museo Mandralisca** (daily 9am–1.30pm, 3.30–7.30pm). Apart from several Madonnas, this is a dusty collection, with the shining exception of Antonello da Messina's *Portrait of an Unknown Man*. The painting served as a back door to a pharmacy cabinet on Lipari island until an assistant was unnerved by the sneering face and scratched out the portrait's eyes.

A jagged outcrop overhangs the medieval town and is the site of the **Citadel**, the original Arab town. After the Norman conquest in 1063, the populace left the looming crags for the port below. **Salita Saraceno** leads up through three tiers of city walls to the stone citadel, which occupies a megalithic mound. Two marked walks climb through pine groves to the rocky cliffs and views over rust-coloured roofs. The paths to the top pass ruined water mills, the remains of a Byzantine chapel, a Roman well, water course, battered terracotta pavement and rooms hewn into the rock. Above are traces of a pool, fountain, cistern and

BELOW: the twin towers of Cefalù Cathedral, just visible across the rocky bay.

prison. Set among olive and cypress groves, the muddled ruins are overgrown with euphorbia. Nearby is **Tempio di Diana**, a 4th-century temple to Diana built over a megalithic shrine to a water deity. Unfortunately, forest fires, perhaps started deliberately, ravaged some of the wooded environs of Cefalù in 1999.

The Madonie Mountains

Compared to the Nébrodi (*see page 307*), the Madonie range are more accessible, more open to tourism and less in thrall to the Mafia. Moreover, unlike most of Sicily, the Madonie range have not been scarred by deforestation or urban blight. Piano Cervi and Monte San Salvatore are riddled with aqueducts and streams. Majestic Nébrodi firs have grown on these rugged ridges since the Ice Age and were used to create the roof of Monreale Cathedral. In the remoter regions, wild cats and eagles still thrive.

A day trip from Cefalù visits mountain enclaves and fortified villages linked to the feudal Ventimiglia dynasty. Thanks to low-key tourism, based on outdoor pursuits such as trekking and horse-riding, the Madonie largely escape grinding poverty and rural emigration. In summer, farm stays (*agriturismo*) make an appealing way of exploring the area; the tiny **Piano Battaglia** ski resort is the only winter sports option. Colourful festivals, hearty cuisine and a cultural confidence ensure that the Madonie lack the harshness of the mountainous interior.

After Cefalù, coastal olive groves give way to pine woods and rugged valleys before reaching the impressive site of **Gibilmanna**, with a venerated sanctuary and an underrated museum of rural life and sacred art (daily 10am–1pm, 3–7pm). **Isnello**, 7 km (4 miles) south, reveals a ruined Byzantine castle overlooking majolica-encrusted spires and limestone cliffs. A vastly superior feudal

Map on page 138

At the lower levels of the Madonie olives, hazelnuts and almonds grow; on the higher slopes are beech, holm oak, chestnut and maple, as well as broom, starflower and lentisk.

BELOW: Cefalù's old town and beach.

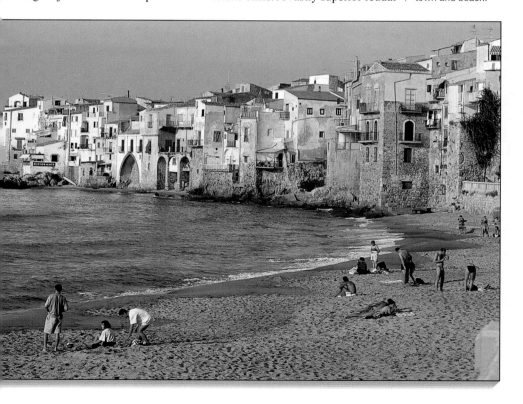

Map on page 138

TIP

One of Sicily's finest gastronomic experiences lies in the centre of Castelbuono: **Nangalarruni** (tel: 0921-671428) is celebrated for its mushroom dishes, roast meats and grilled vegetables.

BELOW: Petralia Sottana rises out of the misty Madonie mountains.

castle towers over **Castelbuono** ⑰, 12 km (7 miles) east, a civilised, prosperous, well-kept place that could be mistaken for Tuscany. Once a fief of the Ventimiglia dynasty but now an enlightened village, Castelbuono lobbied successfully to be an exit point from the new Palermo–Messina motorway. As such, it is reaping the benefits in the weekend influx of visitors drawn to the lively atmosphere, well-restored churches and welcoming restaurants.

The rural route follows the SS 286 south to **Geraci** (22 km/14 miles) and then winds up to **Gangi** ⑱, a tortoise-shaped town with a crumbling watchtower and air of windswept desolation. Although an erstwhile centre of brigandage, the sun-baked town is now a hard-working rural centre smarting from emigration. Below the austere walls stretch the undulating cereal-growing plains and beyond, the grey-green slopes of the Madonie rising to the snow-capped Madonna dell'Alto, the highest peak. **Gangi Vecchio**, on the outskirts, is one of the more charming Madonie haunts for a farm stay (tel: 0921-689191), and also sells wine, oil, cheeses and salami.

Follow the SS 120 west, and the jagged skyline of **Petralia Soprana** ⑲ comes into view. This seemingly prosperous town set on a spur, has covered passageways leading to a belvedere and bracing views, marred by the vast car park on stilts that every up-and-coming hamlet feels obliged to build. Half hidden in alleys are striking mansions with baroque or rococo balconies as well as two watchtowers. **Petralia Sottana** ⑳ ("lower Petralia"), nestling in the wooded hillside, also exudes a quiet ease. Now a mountain resort, this former Norman citadel boasts a trio of Romanesque, Gothic and baroque churches. The Chiesa Matrice is perched on a belvedere and swathed in mist: inside is a precious Arabian candelabra. The road west to **Polizzi Generosa** passes *masserie*, feudal farmsteads that were as self sufficient as most villages. Polizzi is a trekking centre which sustains walkers with pasta and asparagus (*pasta cu l'asparaci*). From here, the fast A19 returns to the coast, as does the winding route via the ski resort of Piano Battaglia.

Diver's paradise

Ustica ㉑, 60 km (37 miles) from Palermo and connected by hydrofoil, can be visited on a day trip but serious divers or underwater photographers will choose to make the island their base. As Sicily's best established marine reserve, Ustica's waters reveal an explosion of colour, from corals, sea sponges and anemones to barracudas, bream, scorpion fish and groupers. This volcanic, turtle-shaped island has tolerated Phoenicians, Saracen pirates and even a penal colony but has flourished as a well-managed marine reserve and resort since the 1960s.

The rugged coastline is riddled with caverns and coves, partly accessible along coastal paths. Land lubbers can visit the fort, lighthouse and aquarium, as well as a marine study centre housed in a watchtower. Sea-lovers will opt for snorkeling and scuba-diving, or even the sea-watching boat, fitted with a transparent keel. Equally novel are the deep-sea archaeological itineraries that explore wrecks and inspect amphorae in their original sites on the seabed.

The High Life

Under Spanish rule, the aristocracy acquired a taste for *spagnolismo*, the pomp and circumstance. Prince Lampedusa's vision of this splendour was one Sicilians would die for: "The ballroom was all golden; smoothed on cornices, stippled on door-frames, damascened pale, almost silvery, over darker gold on door panels and on the shutters which covered and annulled the windows, conferring on the room the look of some superb jewel-case shut off from the unworthy world."

The grandeur intensified under the Bourbons when status-seeking required the purchase of illustrious titles, no matter how undeserved. The puritanical House of Savoy had little effect on patrician tastes in 18th-century Sicily. A palace in Palermo and a villa in Bagheria were the minimum required to keep up appearances. Palazzo Gangi Valguernera's sumptuous interior caused a contemporary English visitor to remark of the Palermitan aristocracy: "Their time is wasted in balls, masquerades and dissipation." Palermo's Gangi palace and Villa Palagonia at Bagheria are equally lavish.

So competitive was the race for status that the nobility pleaded with the King to outlaw the extravagance. They complained that the lower classes were aping them in dowries, funerals and retinues. The government dutifully put a ceiling on such expenditure, but all that achieved was social *kudos* for those who could afford to buy exemptions.

Victor Amadeus's attempt to limit carriage ownership was no more successful, and Palermo had bad traffic jams. Nobles were urged to come into town by horse instead of carriage, but the afternoon carriage drive remained *de rigueur*. On asking why the horse-droppings were never swept up, Goethe was told that the gentry preferred the soft ride for their carriages.

When the hare-brained King Ferdinand II, a hunting fanatic, arrived in Sicily, his first action was to proclaim draconian penalties for poaching on the royal estates. Following his example, the nobility walled off common land near Palermo for their private hunting.

The consumption of ice cream, snow-cooled sorbets and iced drinks was colossal. The snow was collected in March, pounded into balls, and rolled into cool caves. It was then wrapped in straw and salt and brought down on donkeys.

During the 18th century, Palermo's population doubled to about 200,000. The city spent lavishly on public entertainment, with 100 parades a year, including floats, fireworks and masquerades. The grandest one was the festival of Santa Rosalia, Palermo's patron, which lasted five days. A 21-metre (70-ft) *carozza* resembling a Roman galley was pulled by elephants, bears and mules; on top of the contraption sat an orchestra.

In 1783, the Viceroy attempted to shorten the festivities and ordered the savings to be given to poor girls as dowries. No act could have united rich and poor in such outrage and, fearing revolution, the King had to intervene and countermand the curtailment. In July every year, the celebrations today are conducted as zealously as ever. ❑

RIGHT: a mandolin player at Villa Palagonia.

Map on page 152

TRÁPANI PROVINCE

Western Sicily is the most African and most seafaring part of the island, where Moorish and Phoenician culture triumphs over the treasures of Classical Greece

As the least definable yet most varied province, Trápani is a puzzle. This seafaring region represents a swathe of ancient Sicily, from Phoenician Mózia to Greek Selinunte, medieval Erice and Arab Mazara del Vallo. The landscape spans salt pans, vineyards, woods and coastal nature reserves. The province is the most African and Phoenician yet this heart of Muslim Sicily produces alcoholic Marsala. The puzzle continues: as the most Arab of provinces, Trápani has a reputation for being lethargic and morally compromised yet, environmentally, is often at the forefront. Trápani takes a stand against pollution, building speculation and the destruction of coastal salt pans. As triumphs, it claims the setting up of Sicily's first nature reserve and protection of windmills, salt pans and marshes. The year 2000 also witnessed the launch of *pescaturismo*, "fishing tourism", involving excursions with fishermen to discover aspects of the coast and marine parks, as well as learning about fishing,

Trápani city

Apparently Cronos, one of the Titans, castrated his father Uranus with a sickle and threw his genitals into the sea at Cape Drepanum. The result is modern-day **Trápani ❶**. As a seafaring power, its history lies at the heart of the Mediterranean, trading with the Levant and Amalfi, Carthage and Venice. The Arab influence is particularly felt, whether in architecture, attitudes or cuisine: the result is a *couscous* of tastes. It remains an important port and an embarkation point for the Egadi Islands (*see page 165*) and the remote Moorish island of Pantelleria (*see page 168*). Trápani's traditional industries of coral, tuna fishing and salt linger on. The city also has an infamous reputation as a Mafia money-laundering centre, a rumour borne out by the city's countless small banks.

Visually, Trápani is appealing from a distance: a patchwork of shallow lagoons bounded by thin causeways; piles of salt roofed with red tiles. Close up, the spit of the old town has a superficial charm with its 11th-century Spanish fortifications, but even this is marred by the bland urban sprawl. The sights are not monumental but can occupy a morning before a ferry trip to the outlying islands. Apart from a fish and fruit market on **Piazza Mercato di Pesce**, Trápani offers a graceful Gothic church, a fine arts and crafts collection and a cluster of dilapidated baroque *palazzi*. Centred on via Giudecca, the small Jewish quarter has a decayed charm epitomised by the **Giudecca** mansion, while the salty port offers *cuscusu* (fish soup) and lobster in boisterous fishermen's haunts.

About 3 km (2 miles) north of the old town is **Santuario dell'Annunziata** (daily 7.30am–noon,

PRECEDING PAGES: shepherds by the Temple of Segesta. **LEFT:** Trápani fishermen. **BELOW:** old houses in Trápani city.

There are many well-preserved windmills around Trápani.

4–7pm), a Carmelite church in Chiaramonte-Gothic style, and Trápani's main monument. Its charms are a baroque belltower, a Gothic rose window and a doorway decorated in a zigzag pattern. Inside is a rococo nave and a cluster of exotic domed chapels. Dedicated to fishermen, the frescoed Cappella dei Pescatori embraces Byzantine and Moorish elements, as well as a Spanish diamond-point design. Behind the high altar is a lavish chapel containing the **Madonna di Trápani**, a Gothic Pisan statue crowned in jewels. The venerated Madonna is credited with miraculous powers and, as the city symbol, is worshipped by fishermen as well as the proverbial black-clad widows.

Museo Nazionale Pepoli (Mon–Sat 9am–2pm, Sun 9am–1pm), the city's eclectic museum, is housed in the adjoining former convent. Off the cloisters lie Gagini sculptures and sections devoted to the decorative arts. Exquisite craftsmanship is visible in the coral cribs and gilded figurines, the enamelled Moorish lamps and majolica tiles. Gaudiest of all is a coral crucifix, with a salmon-coloured Christ against an ebony and mother-of-pearl cross.

The mystic mountain

Just north is a more enticing base than Trápani for exploring the African Coast. In spring, the winding road climbs past views of acacia, wild gladioli and waxy lemon blossom to the legendary Mount Eryx. Swathed in seasonal mists or in a carpet of flowers, **Erice ❷** is an exquisite medieval walled town. The **Carthaginian walls** survive, rough-hewn slabs inscribed with Punic symbols while nearby is the charming **Quartiere Spagnolo**, the 17th-century Spanish bastion.

This mystical city was founded by the Elymni (Elymians), mysterious settlers of Segesta who worshipped the Mediterranean fertility goddess. She was known

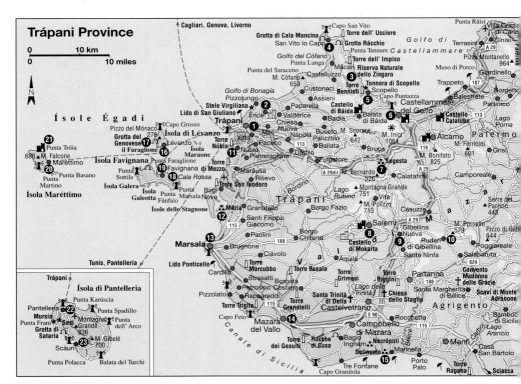

as Astarte to the Elymni and the Phoenicians, Aphrodite to the Greeks, and Venus to the Romans. Each spring, the goddess flew off with an escort of doves to spend time at her shrine in Sicca Veneria, modern El Kef in Tunisia. Her return signalled the reawakening of nature in Sicily. In Erice, the Romans followed earlier customs of worship, including the cult of sacred prostitution at the temple. According to the Sicilian historian Diodorus: "The Romans put aside the gravity of office and entered into play and intercourse with women amidst great gaiety." Despite countless invasions, Erice's sanctuary was inviolate.

Even without a goddess, the views from the **Balio gardens** justify a pilgrimage. Below stretch ragged turrets, wooded groves and vineyards; a tapestry of salt pans and sea slip all the way to the turtle-shaped Egadi Islands and to Cap Bon in Tunisia. As the blunt English poet Fiona Pitt-Kethley concludes: "If you want a good view, go up Eryx, not bloody Etna." Wintry weather is another story. Some older citizens wear a *burdigliuno*, a blue hooded cape worn as a wind shield or for soaking up the first spring rays.

On a rocky outcrop is the **Norman castle** (daily 8am–2pm, 3–6pm) overlooking **Torretta Pepoli**, a Gothic fantasy created by Count Pepoli. Inside the crenellated Norman castle is the **Tempio di Venere**, the battered marble remains of a temple to Venus beside a well. After helping herself to a sliver of marble to bring luck in love, Fiona Pitt-Kethley said: "I expect centuries of lovers have done the same and that's why there's no temple left." Luckily, an enigmatic Greek alabaster bust of the goddess lies in the city museum.

Porta Trápani, a medieval gate, leads to **Via Vittorio Emanuele**, a winding cobbled street lined with medieval palazzi. In Via Chiaramonte, just within the walls of this triangular town, is the severe Gothic **Duomo** (daily 10am–noon, 3–6pm). The crenellated facade is Aragonese and graced by a restored rose window. The blanched interior has fallen under the spell of Gothic Revivalism but is grandly convincing until one considers the original interior lurking under the trickery. At the end of the street is **Re Aceste** (Via Conte Pepoli 45), a typical restaurant.

Virgil compared Eryx to Mount Athos for its altitude and spiritual pre-eminence. Not that Erice remains a sanctuary today. Orphanages and convents have become ceramic and carpet shops or night clubs and chic restaurants. Still, behind this public face lies a private Erice, one of wall-hugging cobbled alleys, grotesque baroque balconies, votive niches and secret courtyards. In keeping with Arab traditions, such courtyards were where women and children could sit in private, working or chatting by the well. Erice is a paradox. In winter, it resembles a windy Umbrian hill town yet in summer bursts with bijou boutiques recalling the Côte d'Azur.

The town is packed in season yet suffers from depopulation. However, the September Festival of Medieval and Renaissance Music is making a name for itself. This sleepy-looking citadel is also home to scientific conferences, centred on the internationally-renowned **Centro Ettore Majorana**, a scientific and cultural institute set in a lovely old convent. Curiously, none of this bustle affects the town's sense of harmony.

Map on page 152

TIP

Coral craftwork is a good buy in Trápani. After inspecting antique coral in the Museo Pepoli, you can buy contemporary pieces from such shops as **Platimiro Fiorenza** (Via Osorio), run by a goldsmith and lecturer in coral.

BELOW: Trápani harbour, with Erice in the background.

Maria Grammatico in her pasticceria in Erice: she learnt her sweetmaking skills from the nuns.

Sweet self-indulgence

Erice has a tradition of *dolci ericini*, excessively sweet cakes. As elsewhere, these were originally made by novice nuns in a closed convent until the convent closed in 1975. Since then, locals lament that the sweets are not as "home-made" as before. Even so, Maria Grammatico vies for the title of best bakery in Sicily in her **Pasticceria Maria** in Via Vittorio Emanuele. She learnt the trade as a novice but fears that there is no one to follow her. Apart from *pasta reale* (marzipan), her sweets have such poetic names as *sospiri* (sighs) and *belli e brutti* (beauties and beasts).

The former convent is in Via Guarnotti but sweet Sicilian memories spill over into the adjoining square of San Domenico. Near the baroque sculpted church is an equally baroque concoction of cakes in **Pasticceria San Carlo**. In **La Pentollacia** (tel: 0923-869099) in Via Guarnotti, one can dine on *couscous* in a former monastery. This grey medieval town is a mistress of sensuality. Yet, as writer Carlo Levi realised, it is also "the Assisi of the south, full of churches, convents, silent streets and of the extraordinary accumulation of mythological memories".

Along the coast to Castellammare

This coast was once noted for its rich tuna-fishing grounds but most *tonnare* (tunneries) have fallen into ruin. However, the sea road passes the **Tonnara di Bonagie** on the way to Sicily's finest nature reserve. The **Riserva Naturale dello Zíngaro ❸** is set on a rocky headland pierced with coves and bays but containing no official roads. The reserve was created with the support of the council, citizens and ecologists but cynics say that it could not have been

achieved without Mafia approval. Locals claim that these sheltered coves continue to be the destination for tiny fishing boats bringing ashore Turkish heroin. Whatever the truth of the matter, the reserve is a glorious home to buzzards and falcons as well as palms, carobs and euphorbia. Human vultures keep a low profile. The continuing success of the reserve causes cynical Sicilians to dismiss Lo Zíngaro as a fabricated Disneyworld, a comparison that escapes foreigners, who are only too delighted to find a semblance of order and efficiency in any Sicilian site.

On the headland lies **San Vito lo Capo ❹**, a burgeoning resort noted for its fine coast, sandy beaches, and lively fish restaurants rather than its sophistication. The northern entrance to Lo Zíngaro lies 11 km (7 miles) southeast, just before the ruins of Torre dell'Impiso. The coastal road south skirts the reserve, passing primeval mountains, shepherds' bothies, abandoned tuna fisheries, ruined towers and ragged rock formations at sea. The ever-changing coastline continues to Castellammare, with the rugged journey made by boat, on horseback or on foot.

Scopello ❺, 10 km (6 miles) before Castellammare, marks the southern entrance to the reserve and has an information desk and car park. This fishing village is based around a *baglio*, an imposing medieval farmstead. Apart from a rustic *trattoria* and a chance to buy farm-fresh cheese, the only site of note is the **Tonnara**, the finest tunnery on the coast, which overlooks the bay and a shingle beach popular with swimmers. The atmospheric complex contains a pink villa, chapel, storerooms and the barracks where the tuna crew stay in the fishing season. Above are a couple of rugged Saracen towers, designed to combat piratical invasions. (A leisurely four-hour marked trail begins in the south, beyond Galleria di Scopello and hugs the coast, passing coves and beaches, until it meets the road at Uzzo, in the northern end of the nature reserve.)

Castellammare del Golfo ❻, an overgrown fishing village, enjoys panoramic views across the gulf and, from the port, a boat ferries visitors to Lo Zíngaro nature reserve (tel: 0924-34222). The sweet, pastel-coloured cottages, castle and idyllic harbour belie the town's bloody past as a Mafia haunt. In the 1950s, around 80 percent of the male population had been in jail and the internecine Mafia wars led the port to become the chief embarkation point to the United States. Today locals joke that so many of the old mafiosi were killed that only dumb innocents remain.

Gavin Maxwell lived among the tuna fishermen in the 1950s, recording their destitution and illiteracy in *Ten Pains of Death*. Yet, even then, there was a clash between old and new lifestyles: "From my eyrie in the castle I watched Castellammaresi women come down to the sea to bathe and swim fully dressed in their everyday clothes, and to meet, while so floundering, bronzed visiting nymphs in bikinis and snorkels."

In rolling countryside south of Castellammare lies **Segesta ❼** (daily 9am–1 hour before sunset), one of the most romantic Classical sites, also reached along the A29 from Trápani. Segesta was founded by the Elymni, a people whose language has yet to be transcribed. The settlers claimed to be refugees who

Map on page 152

A sea of purple and blue and peacock green, with a jagged coastline and great faraglioni [rock towers] thrusting up out of the water as pinnacle islands, pale green with the growth of cactus at their heads.

– GAVIN MAXWELL ON LO ZINGARO

LEFT:
Riserva Naturale dello Zingaro.
BELOW: Castellammare del Golfo.

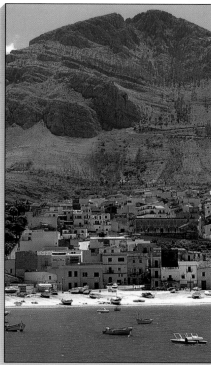

On the salt pans south of Trápani, tiles are used to "roof" the hills of extracted salt, protecting them from rain.

escaped the Fall of Troy but some scholars believe them to be an iconoclastic tribe of Iberian-Ligurian descent. Yet the Trojan link would explain their hatred of the Greeks, an enmity that led to their role in the razing of Selinunte. Segesta itself was sacked by Siracusa in 307 BC.

Crowning a low hill is the roofless **Doric temple**, lacking a *cella* (inner chamber) and fluting on the columns, but no less lovely for that. The **Greek theatre** on the facing hill has an atmosphere of poetic desolation and stages Greek tragedies in the summer. (A minibus service links the temple and theatre.) But Goethe was irritated by Segesta: "The leeches, lizards and snails are no more beautiful in colour than ours; indeed all those I saw were grey."

The earthquake zone

In 1968 a major earthquake struck western Sicily, including Calatafimi, Salemi, Partanna and Gibellina. Over 50,000 people were left homeless and many still live in makeshift accommodation. The reasons are unclear but involve bureaucratic inefficiency and the curious disappearance of funds earmarked for the project. **Salemi ❽**, a benighted hill-top town 30 km (19 miles) north of **Castelvetrano**, is the most intriguing of the earthquake spots. Since the 13th-century castle has been ineffectually propped up, the main interest lies in the narrow, blackened medieval alleys and crumbling churches. Just east lies **Gibellina Nuova ❾**, a strangely ugly new town built after the earthquake flattened the original city, which lies 18 km (11 miles) to the west. The town is dominated by a 1970s conception of futuristic architecture that bears little relation to its history: open-air exhibits such as a petal, plough and tomato overlook lifeless streets. Although Gibellina is trying to position itself as a centre of technology, **Ruderi**

BELOW:
Segesta's beautiful
Greek theatre.

Map on page 152

di Gibellina ⑩, the rubble of a devastated city, has been left as it fell in 1968. A primitive stage has been erected on the ruins and is used for performances of macabre "memorial" concerts, Greek tragedy and contemporary theatre.

The African coast

South of Trápani is the so-called African coast, closer to Tunisia than to mainland Italy. It is known for its **salt pans**, a reminder of an industry that has flourished since Phoenician and Roman times thanks to ideal conditions: low rainfall, regular tides, and the absence of estuaries that would dilute the salinity. The industry represented the mainstay of the local economy between the 14th and 17th centuries. Today's "salt road" (*via del sale*) stretches from Trápani to Mózia, taking in a stretch of saltpans and newly renovated windmills, with the brackish lagoons home to wild ducks, grey herons, common puffins and African cranes. As a result, this coastal area has been declared a nature reserve focused on the workings of the salt pans and the passage of migratory birds. In **Núbia** ⑪, 5 km (3 miles) south of Trápani, is the **Museo delle Saline** (daily 9am–noon, 3–6pm), a working museum rescued as a sea salt-extracting complex, with its scenic windmill and outbuildings.

Further south, a stretch of salt pans and shallow lagoons embrace the marshy but mildly polluted **Saline dello Stagnone**, the largest lagoon in Sicily. Poetic views across the shallow salt pans are intensified at sunset. On the coast facing Mózia is a newer, well-organised salt musem, **Mulina Salina Infersa** (daily 9am–8pm), housed in a converted windmill. From a small jetty here, it is possible to hire canoes to explore the lagoon, or to take the ferry to **Mózia** ⑫, Sicily's chief Punic site. A submerged Phoenician causeway leads across the

Pescaturismo ("fishing tourism") is available from most ports in Trápani, as well as the neighbouring Egadi Islands, which are officially part of the province.

LEFT: Segesta's classical temple.
BELOW: Salemi's castle is held together with metal bands.

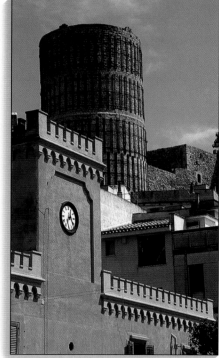

stagnant lagoon to Mozia but most visitors prefer to be ferried across by a local fisherman (tel: 0923-712598 for the custodian if there is no ferry waiting).

Mózia, first known as Motya, looms on the far side of the mosquito-infested Stagnone lagoon. Here, in the 8th century BC, the Phoenicians established a colony in the lagoon, set within a ring of ramparts and towers, and protected by a landward bastion. The trading centre was based on glass, ceramics, ivory, ebony, textiles and metalwork. Within the city, the Phoenicians minted coins depicting the Gorgon's head and worshipped Astarte and Baal, as well as sun and moon goddesses.

During Dionysius I's siege of Motya, a mole was constructed to move the siege engines close to the city walls. Perched on a spindly platform resembling a modern oil rig, his troops had to lean across a sheer drop to do battle with defenders on roof tops: it was a ring of aerial combat that saw citizens plunging to their deaths in the swampy lagoon. Those who survived the massacre or slavery founded a colony at Lilybaeum (Marsala). The island was bought by the Marsala merchant, Joseph Whitaker, who made the excavations his life's work. Since Mózia was never recolonised, Whitaker discovered a secret city more complete than Carthage.

The jetty leads to lush vegetation in an oddly subdued landscape, chosen for its shallow waters and safe anchorage. Plane trees, agaves, verbena and marigolds grow in the swampy soil and are interspersed with monolithic stone blocks. Nearby is the **Cappiddazzu** site, thought to have been a temple. A genteel **museum** of Whitaker's dusty collection conceals one treasure, the Greek statue of the *ephebe*, a sinuous youth in a tunic. The writer Dominique Fernandez waxes lyrical about "the liquid turbulence of the fabric, the firmness of his

Until 1971 it was possible to ride in a horse-drawn cart across the causeway to Mózia – a strange experience, as the causeway lies just below the water, giving the impression that you were riding on the sea.

BELOW:
a cool arcade in Mazara del Vallo.
RIGHT: spreading the word in a square near the Duomo.

buttocks". Close to the museum are crude black and white pebble **mosaics** of a dragon, lion and bull. A path west leads to the **Cothon**, an artificial Punic dry dock with a paved canal running out to sea. It has been dredged after centuries of silt and misuse as a salt pan. A trek north through vines, wild figs and almonds leads to a **necropolis** with stunted tombs and a sacrificial site. Known as the **Tophet**, this is where jars containing the remains of babies were found as well as charred offerings of kids, calves and cats. Sadly, the mosquitoes were not sacrificed and have survived longer than the Carthaginians.

Marsala ⓭ occupies the next cape, 10 km (6 miles) south, and takes its name from the Arabic *Mars-al-Allah*, harbour of God. The view of Capo Boeo was enjoyed by refugees from Mózia in 397 BC and became Carthaginian Lilybaeum, the best-defended Punic naval base in Sicily, and the only city to resist Greek expansion westwards. The site now houses the **Museo Marsala** (daily 9am–1pm, also Wed, Sat, Sun 4–7pm), with a reconstructed **Punic ship** that was sunk off the Egadi Islands during the First Punic War. It was manned by 68 oarsmen and has unrusty iron nails.

In the adjoining **Capo Boeo archaeological zone** (daily 9am–1pm, 4pm–1 hour before sunset) are **Roman mosaics** of a chained dog and a Medusa. Marsala was damaged in 1943 so historic sites are limited to the **Museo degli Arazzi** (Tues–Sun 9am–1pm, 4–6pm), a museum containing richly coloured Flemish tapestries, and to the **cathedral**. It is dedicated to St Thomas of Canterbury and pillars destined for Canterbury Cathedral grace the nave.

The **Stabilimento Florio** (tel: 0923-781111) is one of the most typical of the Marsala distilleries, most of which are set in *bagli*, traditional walled estates with elegant courtyards. The Florio founders are probably Sicily's greatest entre-

Map on page 152

The Marsala Jazz Festival, held in July in the heart of the historic city, is increasingly managing to attract major artists, with concerts sponsored (and fuelled) by Marsala wine companies.

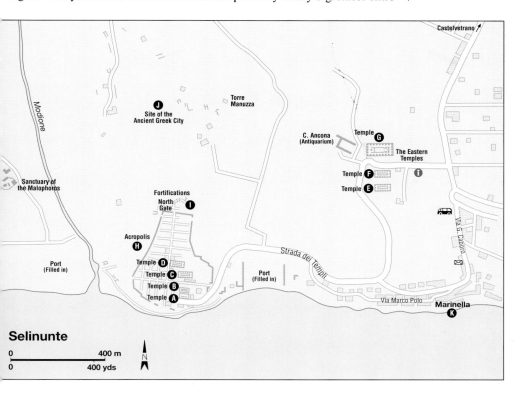

Temple A – what's left of it – stands on the acropolis at Selinunte.

BELOW: Selinunte's Temple E in spring.

preneurs but the amber-coloured dessert wine was pioneered by the British merchants, Ingham and Woodhouse. Woodhouse dealt in sherry and madeira but then discovered the potential of Marsala and established a trading post in the town. *Vergine*, aged in oak barrels, is at least five years old and often drunk slightly chilled. It resembles a medium sherry but leaves an aftertaste of bitter almonds. *Superiore* is similar to sweet Tuscan Vin Santo and drunk as a dessert wine or an aperitivo. The Florio museum has a fine collection of vintages, including illicit bottles sent to the United States during Prohibition, when Florio cunningly labelled the alcohol "seasoning" and "hospital tonic".

From here, the lovely coastal road passes salt pans or marshes south to **Mazara del Vallo** ⓴, a place of moods rather than specific sights. The fishing port feels like a North African town and indeed flourished under Arab rule. A ragged **Norman castle** overlooks the seafront and palm-filled park, while the **Norman cathedral** has been given a baroque veneer and contains two dramatic Roman sarcophagi. However, the best church is at **Porta Palermo**, in the heart of the fishing quarter: the crenellated Norman-Byzantine church of **San Nicolò Regale** overlooks the Tunisian port and contains abstract Roman mosaics. Since the town is now home to one of Italy's largest fishing fleets, the Mazaro river is packed with trawlers all the way to the fish market. **Via Pescatori** is full of Tunisian fishermen but the women are hidden away. Behind lies the **Casbah**, the Tunisian quarter, an intriguing den of arcaded, tapering alleys and backstreet charm. **Piazza Bagno** has a *hammam* with baths and massage. Nearby are a ritual butcher's and several Tunisian cafes with North Africans smoking hubble-bubbles. Locals may refuse to direct women to the Casbah but apart from the occasional drugged youth sitting in a doorway, it feels fairly safe.

Greek glory

As the most westerly Hellenic colony, **Selinunte** , 30 km (19 miles) east of Mazara, is a pocket of Greece in African Sicily. The city was founded in 628 BC by colonists from Megara Hyblaea (*see page 255*) but, as Segesta's sworn enemy, became embroiled in clashes with the Carthaginians and Athenians. After being sacked by Carthage in 409 BC, the city never fully recovered and was destroyed in 250 BC. However, an aerial view of the collapsed columns reveals that they fell like dominoes, evidently the result of an earthquake.

Surprisingly for Sicily, the huge **archaeological site** (daily 9am–7pm) is not overshadowed by building but is left in splendid isolation, flanked by two rivers and ancient ports, both silted up (*see plan on page 159*). The oldest temples, named alphabetically **A**, **B**, **C** and **D**, lie on the acropolis, while the main temples (**E**, **F** and **G**) are set on the eastern hill.

A curious entrance directs visitors through tunnels in sandbanks to the reconstructed **Temple E**, possibly dedicated to Hera (Juno). Its lovely sculptures are in the Palermo museum, much to the chagrin of locals who would like the *metopes* and friezes to return, especially the statue of the *ephebe*, a noble youth, which was unearthed by a local farmer. **Temple F**, built in Archaic style, is the most damaged of the trio, perhaps dedicated to Athena. **Temple G**, probably dedicated to Apollo, is now a vast heap of rubble with one restored raised column. Each column of this temple was built using stone drums weighing 100 tonnes and remained incomplete. Fragments of their painted stucco have been unearthed.

Sited within a walled enclosure, the **acropolis** **H** retains some original **fortifications** **I**, communication trenches and gates. The site is poorly marked but identification is not helped by the confusion of periods: in particular, stone from Temples C and D was raided in the 5th century AD to build a Byzantine village on the spot. North of the acropolis is the ancient **Greek city** **J** and on either side of it lie **necropoli**, quarters that have yet to be excavated.

Selinunte is a tragic yet hauntingly lovely spot. The sight and sound of the waves merge with squabbling magpies and fast yellow-back lizards. In cracks of the ruins grow aromatic wild fennel, parsley, mandrake, acanthus and beds of yellow flowers. It is deeply therapeutic. A lengthy visit to the sprawling site can be followed by a swim along the sandy coast. Framed by temples, the beach at **Marinella** **K** consists of sand dunes and a seaweed-clogged shore, with the seafront lined by lively restaurants.

Just to the south are the **Cave di Cusa**, the Classical quarries whose stone built Selinunte. Set 4 km (2 miles) south of Campobella di Mazara, this charming rural site is always open, and now overrun with goats and wild flowers. Huge column drums lie chiselled, ready to be transported to Temple G at Selinunte, before they were abandoned. The fascination lies in the complex mechanics of construction. Old sketches show how half-carved capitals were levered and pillars were hauled to Selinunte in carts.

The poignancy lies in the fact that all work stopped the moment Selinunte was destroyed. The vanquished city just disappeared under the sands. ❏

Maps
Area 152
Site 159

An immense heap of fallen columns, now aligned and placed side by side like dead soldiers.
– GUY DE MAUPASSANT ON SELINUNTE

BELOW:
the massive slabs in the Cave di Cusa quarries.

THE EGADI ISLANDS

As the easiest offshore islands to visit, the Egadi attract summer crowds, but out of season they offer peace and traditional charm. Much further south lies Pantelleria, Sicily's African island

This small archipelago lying off the western coast of Sicily is totally involved with the sea. And it is a particularly rich and beautiful sea that surrounds Lévanzo, Favignana and Maréttimo: its crystalline and multicoloured waters, teeming with marine life, have provided the islanders with work and nourishment for thousands of years, isolating them in the winter months and, in the calm of spring and summer, carrying off their produce as well as their off-spring. Today the sea is a paradise for sailors and scuba divers (and for those who prefer their fish served on a plate), but also discharges crowds of invaders, tourists brought by ferry and hydrofoil from Trápani, who threaten to over-whelm the peaceful rhythm of island life, especially in Favignana. Fortunately, although the summer weather lasts from mid-May to mid-October, in early and late summer tourism is minimal, and the three islands revert to their traditional patterns. June and September are the best times to discover their subtle charms.

The Egadi have 15,000 years of history and contain the finest prehistoric cave drawings in Italy. The archipelago was once a land bridge linking Africa to Italy and later became the springboard for the Arab conquest of Sicily. Such exotic race memories mean that Arab culture is pronounced, from the guttural local accent to the cube-shaped architecture. Under Norman and Aragonese rule, the Egadi were fortified. The Spanish contributed to the coral industry before selling the islands in 1637 to Genoese bankers, who were granted a barony with feudal fishing rights. The Egadi's lucrative links with Genoa and the Ligurian coast continued when the Florio family bought the islands in 1874.

PRECEDING PAGES:
Favignana port.
LEFT: Forte Santa
Caterina looks
down on tuna
fishermen.
BELOW: a
Favignana sculptor.

Lévanzo

The smallest island, and the one closest to the main-land, bears witness to the islanders' bond with the sea. Much of the coast is still inaccessible, except by boat. The port of **Lévanzo** ⑯ (or **Cala Dogana**) consists of a handful of houses with rooms to let, a couple of small hotels, several cafes and *trattorie*. Its one tarred road turns into a dirt track as soon as it leaves town and winds along a gentle valley between the peaks of the Pizzo del Mónaco and the Pizzo del Corvo. The stony slopes are covered with *Macchia mediterranea*, arid-looking grey-green scrub that turns lush with the winter rains and blooms in late spring. Equally lovely are the lavender, thyme and rosemary; the euphorbia and sea medick flowering in acid yellow; and the bursts of white and purple on the caper plants.

At the head of the valley the track forks: the left-hand path zigzags down the steep coast towards the sea, leading to the **Grotta del Genovese** ⑰, a deep cavern overhanging the rocky shoreline. If the sea is calm and the wind right, you can reach the grotto by

boat, combining the ancient carvings with sailing and swimming from a craft hired at Cala Dogana (or book with the custodian of the caves; tel 0923-924032).

The grotto walls hold Lévanzo's greatest treasure: rock carvings dating from the Mesolithic period. Human dancers and wild animals, especially deer, are depicted in naturalistic poses. In addition, there is a series of rock paintings from the Neolithic period that are less fluid, despite dating from 5,000 years later. These are stylised figures of deities, people, animals and fish. A prominent image is the instantly recognisable tuna, still today the king of the Egadi waters.

Unsurprisingly, fish features heavily in the diet of the Egadi Islands. Recalling the Arab occupation, a fishy couscous is a common dish, as is seafood pasta with tuna, or lobster spaghetti.

Favignana

Facing Lévanzo is the largest and most populous island of the group. Seen from the air, Favignana is shaped like a butterfly poised over the sea, its eastern wing a plain, crisscrossed with roads and pitted with abandoned tufa quarries, its western wing rising to the fortified peak of Monte S. Caterina. More prosaically, Favignana is a land of tuna, tufa and tourism. Ancient tufa-quarrying remodelled the landscape before it was brought to a standstill in the 1950s by the high cost of extracting and transporting the porous limestone.

The island is a homage to stone, its slopes dotted with tufa houses. Even cliffs and caves represent a pleasing spectrum of ochre, russet and cream-coloured rocks. If cyclists pedalling to one of the coves stop to peer over the roadside stone walls, they will discover an abundance of sunken gardens. Sheer stone walls, overgrown with wild thyme and capers, give shelter from the sweeping sea winds to the orange and lemon trees, as well as the figs and tomatoes planted on the floor of the abandoned quarries. Other quarries were carved at the very edge of the sea so that the tufa could be loaded directly onto the boats transporting it

BELOW: the stony slopes of Lévanzo.

to the mainland. Stone from the maze-like **Cala Rossa** ⓲ built entire Moorish cities. The chiselled walls and eroded geometry of seaside quarries such as Cala Rossa and Cavallo make them popular picnic and swimming spots.

On one side of **Favignana port** ⓳, near where the ferry docks, stand beautiful vaulted warehouses in which the big black-bottomed tuna boats, the long nets and huge anchors are stored during the winter. The still waters of the harbour reflect the tiled roofs and stone smokestacks of the **Tonnare Florio**, the former tuna cannery, which closed in the 1990s (processing is now carried out in Trápani). In Florio's time, a day's catch could be as high as 10,000 fish. Today, it has shrunk to under 2,000 a month because of overfishing and deterrents such as pollution, noise and trawling. Even so, the tuna industry survives, with traditional techniques allied to hi-tech sonar detection, used to spot the shoals.

On the peak of the island's one hill looms the Arab-Norman **Forte Santa Caterina**, a political prison in Bourbon times and now a forbidden military zone. **Forte San Giacomo**, formerly a Norman castle and Bourbon prison, performs a similar function today as a maximum-security prison for some of Sicily's *mafiosi*. However, recent protests from inmates about the insalubrious conditions have led to calls for a new prison, a proposal currently blocked by environmentalists.

Maréttimo

The most mysterious, mountainous and greenest of the Egadi lies to the west, separated from her sister islands by a sea rich in sunken treasure. Here lie the remains of the Carthaginian fleet that was destroyed by the Romans in 241 BC. The little port, **Maréttimo** ⓴, has no hotel but a few serviced apartments, and the

Map on page 152

The Palazzo Florio, built in 1876, was once the home of tuna tycoon Ignazio Florio. Today it contains a gallery and cultural centre.

BELOW: Favignana's rocky shore.

Map on page 152

TIP

Hikers should always carry bottled water with them, particularly on Maréttimo: on these parched islands, water is more precious than wine.

BELOW: a Favignana tuna fisherman.

locals happily accept guests in their homes. Peace and natural beauty are what draw visitors here: scuba divers come to explore the 400 caves and grottos scattered along the coast; plant-lovers can study Mediterranean vegetation at its purest; the rest simply want swimming and snorkelling in aquamarine waters, boat trips to limestone caves and walks in spectacular scenery.

Ambitious visitors will climb up to survey the island from **Monte Falcone**. An easier walk is an excursion to **Case Romane**, ruined Roman fortifications not far from the village (from the port, follow directions to Pizzeria Filli Pipitone). Beside the ruins is a crumbling Arab-Norman chapel, thought to have been built by Byzantine monks. An alternative hike leads north along the cliffs and cuts across an isthmus to **Punta Tróia** ㉑, a rocky promontory dominated by a Saracen castle. Originally a watchtower, the castle was enlarged by the Norman King Roger II, and converted by the Spanish into its present form, with an underground cistern that later did service as a dreaded prison. But such sombre thoughts quickly float away on this restful, thyme-scented island.

Pantelleria

Pantelleria is closer to Tunisia than to Sicily, and is reached on a five-hour ferry crossing from Trápani. The island's evocative name probably derives from the Arabic "daughter of the winds" after the breezes that buffet this rocky outpost, even in an African August. The island is dotted with low-domed houses and surrounded by terraces used for growing capers or grapes; even the vines are trained low to protect them from the winds. The landscape is relatively bleak, with jagged rocks and coves instead of beaches, and capers and pines the only signs of classic Mediterranean vegetation.

The volcanic origins of Sicily's biggest island are visible in the presence of lava stone, basalt rock, hot springs, and a landscape pitted with "*cuddie*", small, extinct volcanic craters. **Lago di Venere**, near the hamlet of Bugeber, is a small lake inside a former crater, full of warm, bubbling, sulphurously brown waters, used by local bathers to cure myriad ills. Steam baths can also be taken in the island grottos, such as **Stufa del Bagno di Arturo**, a natural sauna near Siba. As for coastal scenery, the craggy shore is studded with coves, with rocks shaded from red through green to black. For swimmers and divers, the absence of beaches is compensated for by the privacy occasioned by secluded coves and hot springs, and by the quality of the diving, with sightings of ancient wrecks as well as of sea sponges and coral.

Although modern and rather scruffy, **Pantelleria town** ㉒ has a lively air as well as an exoticism encapsulated by the white-cubed houses and restaurants serving fish *couscous*. A rewarding hike from the town to the port of **Scáuri** ㉓ on the southern coast passes traditional *dammusi* houses, terraced vineyards, small settlements and the blackened, lava stone landscape. Dry stone walls enclose orange groves and capers, and are often overlooked by hardy, locally-bred donkeys. The route also passes strange Neolithic dome-shaped funerary monuments, known as *Sesi*, conceivably built by early Tunisian settlers. ❑

The Great Tuna Massacre

Tuna fishing, along with swordfishing, is rooted in the Sicilian psyche. Nowhere is this more so than in Favignana, where it is considered the sea's ultimate challenge to man, as well as the island's traditional livelihood. The tuna's only predators are the killer whale, the Mako shark and man. But their ritual death is gruelling work. As the proverb says: "Tuna fishing shortens your arms and silences your tongue."

The fast-swimming tuna hunt off the coast of Norway but spawn in Sicily's warm spring waters. Here they are captured in a system of chambered nets introduced by the Arabs in the 9th century. The Arabs taught the islanders that tuna refuse to take bait before spawning, so harbour-wide nets were the logical death trap.

The season lasts from May to mid-June, with *la mattanza*, the ritual slaughter, the inexorable fate of a passing shoal. In the past, one day could determine the island's fortune for the rest of the year but numbers are now negligible. Nowadays, this cruel ritual is both a gory tradition and a gruesome tourist spectacle that survives despite conservationists' concerns and the contravention of conventions on driftnet fishing.

Buoys mark out a 330-ft (100-metre) rectangle on the sea; up to 6 miles (10 km) of nets are suspended between the floats. Halfway along lie five antechambers. The innermost section is the *camera della morte*, a death chamber 100 ft (30 metres) deep.

At dawn, or when the winds are right, the black boats set off to check the nets. The helmsman leads the fleet in prayers, aided by an image of the Madonna. The 60-strong crew sings and chants the *cialoma* in guttural Arabic accents. Entreaties are uttered by the *rais*, a Moorish title given to the chief fisherman, who travels in a separate boat and constantly checks the entrance to the *camera della morte*.

The eight black boats encircle the nets. When the *rais* decides that the currents are right, the shoal is steered into the death chamber and the gate closed. As it fills with fish, the floating death trap sags, like a heavy sack. To the command of "*Tira, tira!*" the net is pulled tight. The *rais* chants the fateful battle cry. Each verse of this bloodthirsty sea shanty has a chorus of "*Aiamola, aiamola*", perhaps derived from *Allah! Che muoia!* (Allah, may it die!).

As the net is drawn in to the length of a football pitch, the fish circle frantically in the *sarabanda della morte*, the dance of death. The chanting stops and the slaughter begins. The frantic fish gasp and try to leap to freedom but their attempts are thwarted as they are stabbed and caught behind the gills with long pole-gaff hooks.

Some of the tuna are man-sized and their razor-sharp tail fins can kill. As the silvery fish are pierced, the water is stained red. It takes a frenzied 15 minutes to slaughter about 200 tuna, although some die of heart attacks or over-oxygenation. With true Sicilian logic, the tuna's breeding grounds also become their tragic end. ❑

RIGHT: blood on the quay as the tuna is weighed.

Map on page 174

AGRIGENTO AND THE VALLEY OF THE TEMPLES

The city may be a curious mixture of ugliness and antiquity, of Moorish mazes and modern monstrosities, but the Classical splendour of the Valley of the Temples is pure delight

Siracusa may have been the most powerful city in Greek Sicily but Agrigento (Akragas) was the most luxurious. It was first settled by colonists from Gela in 580 BC, attracted by the abundance of springs and a dreamy, well-fortified site. This most sybaritic of Sicilian cities was run by tyrants and sacked by the Carthaginians in 406 BC (*see page 29*). The city flourished again under the Romans and became the centre of the sulphur mining industry. In AD 535 the Byzantines destroyed all the temples except one, on the grounds that they were pagan. After the medieval city abandoned Akragas, the Classical site was ignored until it was popularised by Goethe and the German Romantics. Winckelmann, the father of modern archaeology, wrote a celebrated book on the wonders of Agrigento, which drew floods of artistic visitors. The wonder was that Winckelmann never set foot in Sicily.

The city abounds in Classical anecdote regarding its fabled wealth. The Tyrant of Akragas kept wine in reservoirs hacked out of solid rock; each giant cellar contained 4,000 litres (900 gallons). Returning Olympic heroes were welcomed by cavalcades of chariots drawn by white horses, which were legendary in the Greek world.

PRECEDING PAGES: the Temple of Olympian Zeus. **LEFT:** the Valley of the Temples. **BELOW:** ancient steps in Agrigento.

Maverick city

Pindar claimed that the people of Akragas "built for eternity but feasted as if there were no tomorrow". The city rivalled Athens in the splendour of its temples, but in its hedonistic lifestyle Akragas was the Los Angeles of the ancient world. Yet the modern approach could not be more disorientating, a sequence of motorway flyovers. At first sight, all that Agrigento seems to share with Athens are nasty industrial outskirts, breeze-block monstrosities and smog.

It is ironic that a Classical city known for its luxurious lifestyle should have fallen so low. Not that the "modern" city is wholly poor, or even modern. As always, Agrigento is a living contradiction. The town's medieval core is a maze of Moorish streets and substandard housing. However, this unaesthetic muddle conceals a fascinating urban mix. By contrast, the new quarter overlooking the temples is an attempt at bourgeois chic, which went horribly wrong when landslides aggravated by overcrowding and shoddy building killed many in 1966.

The scandal was compounded by the discovery that feckless Mafia surveyors had cut corners by not checking for subsidence and that contractors had used poor quality cement. Nowadays, charmless middle-class apartments gaze across at the temples, often

from within the confines of the park. Beyond the Valle dei Templi, the city's glittering shop-window, lies a somewhat soulless town centre, complete with neglected public buildings and a rapacious attitude to tourism. Even so, the image of a parasitical city living off its past glory can be dispelled by a starlit night, a heady southern wine and a stomach full of stuffed swordfish.

Operation Leopard, a major Mafia round-up based in Agrigento, netted 200 suspects in the early 1990s.

City sights

There is a deep hiatus between the present-day city and the city of the past, with an unbridgeable difference between the dreary torpor of compromised modern Agrigento and the inspiring coherence of ancient Akragas. If you are only in the area for a day, head straight for the Valley of the Temples, and restrict your city visit to dinner and an evening stroll. Parking problems and an unreliable public transport system, added to the disparate nature of the archaeological sites and their relative distance from the city, make it inconvenient to combine both places, even for meals. (If you are not staying in a hotel close to

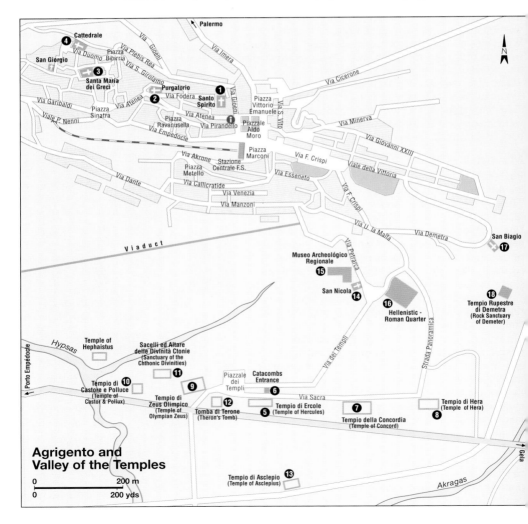

Agrigento and Valley of the Temples

the Valley of the Temples, you should consider taking a picnic lunch to the archaeological sites.)

Map on page 174

Above Via Atenea, the main street as well as the entrance to the historic quarter, stands **Santo Spirito** ❶, a fine Cistercian abbey founded in 1290. Often known as the **Badia Grande**, the complex of cloisters, chapter house and refectory is in Chiaramonte style (*see page 48*). The church has a Gothic portal and rose window, plus a panelled ceiling and baroque interior with stuccos attributed to Serpotta. The vaulted Gothic dormitory leads to a chapter house with mullioned windows and a bold portal, all emboldened with Arab-Norman geometrical motifs. The abbey is undergoing restoration but the commercial spirit triumphs in Agrigento. The sacristan in the house opposite will gladly open the church for a tip, while the Cistercian nuns sell sweet *cuscusu*, almond and pistachio pastries shaped like snakes, shells and flowers. Faced with such delights, the French writer Dominique Fernandez was torn between the "baroque opulence" of the architecture and the "Arab unctuousness" of the cakes. The cakes won.

Dominating Piazza Purgatorio, just off Via Atenea, is the 17th-century church known simply as **Purgatorio** ❷, built on an ancient sacred site, but better known for its riot of baroque allegorical stuccowork by Serpotta, and for its elegant facade. To the left of the church, a stone lion guards an entrance to the ancient underground drinking water and drainage system. Created in the 5th century BC, these were known as one of the wonders of the world. Linked to the underground chamber beneath San Nicola church, the system used conduits and cisterns to channel water to the city. There are plans to open the chambers to the public, including a Roman food store with a lava-stone grinding mill.

Further west is **Santa Maria dei Greci** ❸, a Norman church set among Agrigento's Moorish alleyways, in the heart of the medieval quarter. A Chiaramonte Gothic portal leads to a Norman nave, a coffered ceiling and some Byzantine fragments. Below ground is the greatest surprise: the church is constructed around a 5th-century Greek temple dedicated to Athena. A narrow gallery contains the bases of six fluted Doric columns, the remains of the temple peristyle and stereobate. The sanctuary spans Greek and Christian cults: tradition has it that St Paul preached here.

The **Cattedrale** (Cathedral) ❹, which surmounts a ridge in the west of the city, is designed in eclectic style with Arab-Norman, Catalan-Gothic and baroque elements, from Catalan blind arcading to a Norman belltower. The Norman-Gothic nave boasts an inlaid, coffered ceiling and a section frescoed to simulate a dome. Graceful baroque stuccowork in the choir contrasts with a severe Gothic chapel. Since this is Agrigento, the cathedral naturally occupies a prestigious Greek site: nothing less than the acropolis.

In summer, the Classical city comes alive with open-air performances of drama in tribute to Persephone. The modern city responds with *passeggiate* along tree-lined **Viale Vittoria**. However, like the Classical city, modern Agrigento is both sleek and scruffy. What could be more fitting for a city constructed by Carthaginian slaves yet inhabited by noble girls who built gold tombs for their song birds?

The Norman Santa Maria dei Greci was built over a 5th-century BC Greek temple to Athena.

BELOW: Agrigento in the spring.

Popular dishes on Agrigentine menus are salsiccia al finocchio *(pasta and fennel),* coniglio in agrodolce *(sweet and sour rabbit), and* involtini di spada *(stuffed swordfish). Combinations of shellfish, artichokes, pasta and pilchards are common, as are sweet Arab staples such as* cassata *and* cannoli.

BELOW: this valley once contained Sicily's most luxurious city.

Valle dei Templi

Here, for a fleeting moment, the Classical world comes alive. The Valley of the Temples forms a natural amphitheatre, with a string of Doric temples straddling a ridge south of the city. This is still a valley of wild thyme, fennel, silvery olive groves and almond blossom. An ideal first glimpse of the temples is by night, during a drive along the **Strada Panoramica** and **Via dei Templi**. The temples glow in the black countryside, radiating a sense of cohesion, security and serenity. This crest of temples was designed to be visible from the sea, both as a beacon for sailors and to show that the Gods guarded the sacred city from mortal danger.

An early start guarantees enough solitude to slip back into the Classical world. But unless you plan to view the Temple of Concord from the elegant restaurant in Villa Athena, come armed with a picnic. Otherwise, the on-site snack bar will bring you back to earth with a bump. From the valley, views of the modern town may offend purists. Yet while time cannot stand still, olive and almond groves mask the modernity.

Piazzale dei Templi, the entrance to the main temples, was once the *agora* and is alive to the ancient trading spirit. The local guides now operate a monopoly, refusing to allow unauthorised rivals to present the archaeological park, while small boys demand money to protect tourists' cars from unknown dangers, a feature of Sicilian sites. The park falls into two sections: the enclosed Western Zone (daily 8.30am–7pm) and the unenclosed Eastern Zone (open access), which is best viewed in the early morning or late afternoon; or even from afar, when floodlit at night.

The first treasure visible in the Eastern Zone is the **Tempio di Ercole** (**Temple**

Map on page 174

of Hercules) ❺. Built in 520 BC in Archaic Doric style, this is the oldest temple, second in size to the Temple of Zeus and of roughly the same proportions as the Parthenon in Athens. It once had a gorgeous entablature emblazoned with lions, leaves and palms but now presents an almost abstract puzzle. Although much is in ruins, Alexander Hardcastle performed a truly Herculean task by re-erecting eight columns in 1924.

Villa Aurea, set in olive and almond groves beside the former Golden Gate, belonged to Hardcastle, the Englishman who devotedly excavated the site. The grounds are riddled with catacombs and water cisterns, which run under rocks and orchards the length of the Classical site. A path on the left leads to the **catacombs** ❻, which emerge in a necropolis on the far side of the villa. Now excavated and well-lit, the passages cut through the rock and reveal a cross-section of tombs and fossilised bones. Arches link circular rooms (*tholoi*) containing circular honeycomb cells stacked high with shelf-tombs. Though the oldest tombs here date from the 4th century BC, the main Roman necropoli lie just to the south while Greek burial grounds are scattered around the city.

At the end of the Via Sacra lies the **Tempio della Concordia (Temple of Concord)** ❼, abutting ancient city walls. After the Theseion in Athens, it is the best preserved Greek temple in the world. The pastoral surroundings are at odds with the temple's bloody history: on this bulwark thousands were slain in battle against Carthage. Dating from 430 BC, the temple was saved from ruin in the 6th century by being converted into a church. The peristyle was sealed by dry stone walls, and the cella opened to form twin naves, although sadly the metopes and pediment were destroyed.

The tapering columns tilt inwards imperceptibly, creating an ethereal grace

The Temple of Concord was used as a church for 12 centuries. Mass was celebrated there until 1748, when a local prince obtained permission to return the building to its Classical simplicity.

BELOW: the Temple of Concord.

and airiness that belie the weighty entablature. A further refinement is that the fluted columns have different spacing, narrowing towards the corners. They were originally coated with glazed marble dust to protect the flaky sandstone, then painted with vivid polychrome scenes, predominantly bright blue or blood-red. Now lichen-coated, the temple still represents sheer perfection in line. The only jarring image is the distant cityscape and cemetery but, seen though a heat haze, even that shimmers obligingly. The temple is transformed by light: locals say that one has not lived until seeing Concord changing with the seasons, at dawn and sunset, dusk and moonlight.

Unfortunately, the temple is fenced off and partly propped up by scaffolding, with entry forbidden because of "work in progress", a familiar Sicilian refrain. Moreover, in the year 2000 there was a controversial decision to remove damaged sections of the temple and replace them, temporarily or permanently, with replica columns. The architectural establishment reacted with dismay but, if the temple is to survive for another millennium it might yet be the best solution. Certainly, space to display the originals could be made in the city's well-designed archaeological museum.

The **Tempio di Hera (Temple of Hera)** ❽ surmounts a rocky ridge which formed the city ramparts. Known as Juno to the Romans, Hera was protectress of engaged and married couples. Fittingly, hers is held to be the most romantic of temples, set "high on the hill like an offering to the goddess". Yet Zeus's sister and wife was perceived as a bloodthirsty goddess, to be appeased by sacrifice at an altar beside the walls. Part of the cella and 25 columns remain intact along with the drums of columns; the rest fell over the hill during a landslide. The stones bear reddish traces of fire damage where they were singed by flames.

Scholars disagree over which god the Temple of Concord was dedicated to: the favourite candidate is Demeter, goddess of fertility and peace. The temple's modern name comes from "Concordia" a Latin inscription found nearby.

BELOW: a fallen *telemon* (giant).

Western zone

After retracing your steps to the entrance, cross the road to the **Tempio di Zeus Olimpico (Temple of Olympian Zeus)** ❾. Even at the crest of its golden age, the temple was unfinished. With the area of a football pitch, it was the largest Doric temple ever known. The U-shaped grooves on the stone blocks represent primitive pulley marks formed during construction. Today's fallen masonry is a challenge to the imagination: the best stone was plundered to build the port of Empédocle. A frieze on the east side depicted the battle between Zeus and the Giants, matched by the War of Troy on the western side.

The facade was supported by 38 *telamones* (giant figures) – a revolutionary concept for the time. In this way, the weight of the pediment was shared by the giants and by the columns of the peristyle. The *telamones* also had allegorical and aesthetic functions. They both broke up the uniformity of the peristyle and illustrated the war against Zeus; like Atlas, the defeated giants were compelled to carry the world on their shoulders. A sandstone copy of a *telamon* lies on the ground, dreamily resting his head on his elbows, and one of the originals is on display in the archaeological museum. On the temple, these male *giganti* (also known as *atlantes*, or Atlas figures) alternated with female caryatids and represented the three known racial types of the time: African, Asian and European.

West of the Temple of Zeus is the most confusing quarter, dotted with shrines dating from pre-Greek times. The Via Sacra leads to the **Tempio di Castore e Polluce (Temple of Castor and Pollux, or the Dioscuri)** ❿, spuriously named after the twin sons of Zeus. Although it has become the city symbol, the building is theatrical pastiche, erected in 1836 from the remains of several temples. Even so, it is a graceful and evocative reconstruction. Locally, the temple is known as *tri culonni*, since only three of the four columns are visible from the city. Despite its name, the temple was first dedicated to Persephone and Demeter, Chthonic (Underworld) deities, along with Dionysus.

This theory is supported by the temples in the surrounding area. Known as the **Sacelli ed Altare delle Divinità (Sanctuary of the Chthonic Divinities)** ⓫, the quarter conceals sacrificial altars and ditches, a veritable shrine to fertility, immortality and eternal youth. Pale-coloured beasts were offered to the heavens but black animals were sacrificed to the gods of the Underworld. The altars took the form of flat, concentric circles or deep, well-shaped affairs. Now bounded by a gorge and an orange grove, this sanctuary of death was also the fount of life, with lush gardens and a lake full of exotic birds and fish.

Close to Piazzale dei Templi lies **Tomba di Terone (Theron's Tomb)** ⓬, a tribute to a benevolent Agrigentine tyrant. This truncated tower in Doric-Ionic style is essentially a Roman funerary pyramid, more a celebration of conquest than glory to a local hero. Outside the ancient walls is the isolated **Tempio di Asclepio (Temple of Asclepius)** ⓭, half-hidden in an almond grove. Dedicated to the mysterious god of healing, it lies between the river Akragas and a sacred spring. It is of a curious design, with solid walls and no peristyle, possibly

Map on page 174

A splendid spring like the one which smiled at us this morning at sunrise was certainly never granted to us during our mortal life. The Temple of Concord is just seen peeping out at the southern extremity of this plain which is all green and all flowers.

– GOETHE, 1787

BELOW: traffic on the road to the Temple of Hera.

because the interior housed chambers for dream interpretations as well as wards for recuperation or for taking the waters.

From Piazzale dei Templi, a short drive along Via dei Templi leads to the Villa Athena restaurant (tel: 0922-596288), the archaeological museum, the Hellenistic-Roman quarter and a clutch of pagan shrines. En route are fortifications, a reminder that Agrigento was once enclosed by walls, towers and massive gates, of which the perimeter and craggy foundations remain. The sandy landscape is dotted with olives and pines. Subsidence has created strange slopes and whirling patterns on the soil.

San Nicola ⓮, on Via Petrarca, is a Romanesque church whose severe but grand facade is reminiscent of monuments in ancient Rome. This is not so far-fetched given that the church is built from Greek stone raided from the ruins and also purports to be a Roman temple dedicated to the sun god. The Cistercian church was altered by the Franciscans in the 15th century. A chapel contains the **Sarcophagus of Phaedra**, an exquisitely carved scene of Phaedra's grief at the loss of her lover and stepson Hippolytus.

Next door is the well-presented **Museo Archeológico Regionale** ⓯ (Sun–Tue 9am–1pm; Wed–Sat 9am–1pm and 2–5.30pm) incorporating a church, courtyard and temple foundations. The Graeco-Roman section is the centrepiece, along with a Bronze-Age urn from a Sican tomb and a three-legged Trinacria, the ancient symbol of Sicily. Exhibits include a wealth of painted Attic vases dating from 5th century BC, Greek lion's-head water spouts, an *ephebe* (Classical youth) and a vibrant Roman mosaic of a gazelle. A poignant marble sarcophagus depicts the death of a child amidst weeping. The highlight is a *telamon* in all its massive glory accompanied by other powerful giant heads. Elsewhere

San Nicola was built largely with stone blocks taken from the ruined Temple of Olympian Zeus, which was known as the Giant's Quarry.

BELOW:
San Nicola's
stern facade.

are votive offerings and statues associated with orgiastic rites: phallic donkeys compete with a libidinous pigmy and a hermaphrodite.

The **Hellenistic-Roman Quarter** (9am–one hour before sunset) lies opposite, an ancient commercial and residential area laid out on a grid system. Whereas the Greeks created the grid system, the Romans overlaid with a rational arrangement of public and private space. The well-preserved remains of aqueducts, terracotta and stone water channels are visible, as well as vestiges of shops, taverns and patrician villas. The frescoed villas are paved with patterned mosaics and protected by glass enclosures.

Just east, on the far side of the Strada Panoramica is a stretch of Greek walls and **San Biagio** ⓱, a Norman church perched on a rocky platform. It is carved into an ancient Temple to Demeter and Persephone. Two circular altars lie between the church and another eerie tribute to the goddess of fertility. At the foot of the cliff is the **Tempio Rupestre di Demetra (Rock Sanctuary of Demeter)** ⓲, the oldest sanctuary in the valley, dating from the 7th century BC. Although the church is currently closed, the sacristan, if tipped, is willing to escort visitors to the Rock Sanctuary. A narrow rocky staircase leads down to a damp stone shrine carved into the hillside. A spring flowed into sacred pools here and was used in a water cult. At sundown, the caves conjure up the Underworld only too readily.

Visiting Sicily in 1885, Guy de Maupassant was lucky enough to see the temples without tourists or modern desecration. The writer was struck by their air of "magnificent desolation; dead, arid and yellowing on all sides". Yet with falcons hovering above, lizards scurrying at one's feet, the air heavy with the scent of eucalyptus, today's landscape throbs with life. ❏

Map on page 174

The street plan of the Hellenistic-Roman quarter follows the rules laid down by the Greek town planner Hippodamus of Miletus: parallel main streets (plateiai) intersected at right-angles by secondary streets (stenopoi).

BELOW: the Museo Archeológico.

AGRIGENTO PROVINCE

*This enigmatic southern province embraces everything from
earthquake-struck towns to spectacular hilltop villages,
from spas and coastal forts to the remote Pelagie Islands*

Map
on page
186

People from Agrigento are a mysterious breed, often called *né carne né
pesce*, neither fish nor fowl. Yet this elusive province has produced exceptional Sicilians: Empedocles, the pre-Socratic philosopher; Pirandello,
the playwright; and Sciascia, the political novelist. All were gifted mavericks
who shared a bitter-sweet relationship with their homeland. Empedocles committed suicide on Etna. Pirandello was the master of split personalities. Sciascia called his land a "wicked stepmother" yet rarely left, except to visit Paris.

Outside the capital, Agrigento is barely touched by tourism. There are no
obvious sights in this low-key province. Instead, there are myriad chance dis-
coveries of a lesser order: distinctive hill-top towns; deserted Classical sites;
coastal fortresses; remnants of former feudal estates; Arab-Norman ports; prosperous vineyards. Yet Agrigento also has more than its fair share of unpleasant
surprises: shabby, one-horse towns; suburban sprawl; fields of rotting artichokes; and the scars left by disused sulphur mines. The province is an inward-
looking place whose insularity and lassitude make few concessions to visitors'
demands for charming hotels, reasonable service and unpotholed roads. Agrigento's additional drawbacks are degradation and exceptional poverty, a cluster of Mafia strongholds, and a torpor conditioned by centuries of failure. This
malaise is symbolised by a provincial tourist office
that seems never to be open.

PRECEDING PAGES:
the Moorish port of
Sciacca.
LEFT: mending the
nets, Sciacca.
BELOW: countryside
near Cianciana.

An eastern foray

The route into the hinterland east of Agrigento passes
rugged hill-top towns of Moorish origin, which were
fortified during the Moslem conquest and beyond.
Many of these were sulphur-mining centres until the
early 20th century and, despite a slight agricultural
revival or diversification into wine, have yet to
recover from the collapse of the traditional industry.

Leaving **Agrigento ❶** in the direction of Caltanissetta, follow the SS 122 through the rolling countryside to Favara, a former sulphur centre, with a
medieval castle and baroque main square. From here,
choose the hilly road east to the nearby medieval town
of **Naro ❷**, a far more appealing place, enclosing a
Chiaramonte castle and baroque mansions within battlemented walls.

Follow the SS 410 south to the sea: the rewarding
17-km (11-mile) drive to **Palma di Montechiaro ❸**
affords sweeping views down over the coast. The town
strikes a romantic chord with readers of *The Leopard*.
The novel's Donnafugata is based on a castle founded
here in 1626 by Tomasi, Principe di Lampedusa.
Today the town conjures up a catalogue of Sicilian
ills: disturbing images of grinding poverty, emigration, unemployment, illiteracy, crime, child mortality,

public indifference, despair and dogs. According to recent statistics, 30 percent of children are illiterate and 50 percent leave school at the age of seven.

Lampedusa's once splendid *castello* is crumbling under the burden of serving as a trysting spot, prison and unofficial public lavatory. The town's only dusty glory is the **Chiesa Madre**, decaying under the weight of civic inertia. To qualify for funding, the church steps must be restored in the same stone as before. However, the original quarry is closed so Sicilian bureaucracy decrees that renovation is impossible. About 2km (1 mile) south, the coastal road ends in the resort of **Marina di Palma**. From here, the SS 115 leads back to Agrigento.

However, castle aficionados can follow the same road east to see the remains of a string of fortifications along the coast, notably the striking castles of **Castello di Palma ❹** and, just east, **Torre di Gaffe ❺**. Further east still lies downtrodden **Licata ❻**, marking the eastern confines of the province. Although essentially a working port, Licata also has a 16th-century *castello* and layers of *palazzi*, as well as an almost acceptable beach.

The southwestern coast

Just outside Agrigento city, on the Porto Empédocle road, is Pirandello's birthplace, in the hamlet of **Caos**. The irony was not wasted on Pirandello, who called himself a "son of chaos". Now a small museum (Mon–Fri 9am–one hour before sunset) dedicated to one of Italy's greatest and most wide-ranging writers, this traditional farmhouse was where the "master of the absurd" was born in 1867. In accordance with his wishes, the playwright's ashes were buried under a pine tree on the edge of a cliff. Although this once idyllic spot now overlooks industrial sprawl, Pirandello, whose life was a lesson in defeat

The village of Sant' Angelo Muxaro, north of Agrigento, was once the capital of the Sicani, the indigenous Sicilians who settled the west of the island. As a result, Agrigentines stress their Sicani roots, insisting that they are swarthier than most Sicilians.

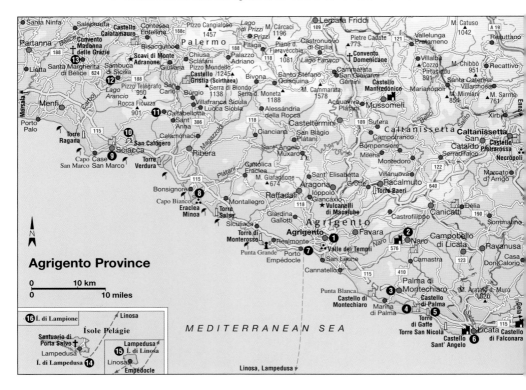

Agrigento Province

0   10 km
0   10 miles

MEDITERRANEAN SEA

snatched from the jaws of victory, would have appreciated his posthumous fall from grace.

Just south (7 km/4½ miles) of Agrigento is **San Leone**, the city's pleasant but unexceptional seaside resort, a humble fishing village until the 1960s. By contrast, **Porto Empédocle ❼**, just west of San Leone, is an unmitigated blackspot, despite its illustrious past. The port quarried the Classical site for stone to build its harbour walls but, perhaps in revenge, the temple gods cursed it with ugliness. The benighted city should be avoided unless a ferry trip to the remote Pelágie Islands (*see page 190*) makes a visit inevitable. Fortunately, the SS 115 soon passes through sparsely populated countryside to the province's most delightful Classical site. En route are views of the coast, which borders a fertile valley and overlooks neat orange plantations and smoothly contoured fields.

The Classical site of **Eraclea Minoa ❽** (daily 9am–one hour before sunset) squats on bleached soil and abuts olive-covered slopes. As one looks down from this idyllic headland, there is a view over white cliffs to the sea, encompassing a crescent of golden sands and pine grove down below. Eraclea was a satellite of Selinunte but suffered a grim fate at the hands of the Carthaginians, when it was depopulated and used as a no-man's-land in Greek and Punic territorial disputes. The name Minoa evokes the legend of King Minos of Crete who pursued Daedalus to Sicily, but the connection is tenuous.

While the site is delightful and the atmosphere therapeutic, the excavations have been laborious and the results far from spectacular. So far, Eraclea has revealed substantial city walls, a Hellenistic theatre, a necropolis, and ruined villas dating from Greek and Punic times. The excavations are ongoing, in dilatory Sicilian style, and should culminate in the restoration of the theatre, which

Map on page 186

BELOW: Eraclea Minoa at sunset.

Sciacca's Carnivale at the beginning of Lent involves the entire town in parades and competitions.

currently has inadequate covering "protecting" the delicate sandstone structure.

Further along the coast, is **Sciacca** ❾, a working fishing port with a large Arab population. The town was evangelised by San Calógero and prospered in Arab times thanks to its location, midway between Mazara and Agrigento. In the 16th century, Sciacca was torn apart by two warring families, the Norman Perollo and the Catalan Luna, and suffered a gradual decline until the revival of the port and spa, aided by an injection of Mafia funds and close links with North Africa. Sciacca lacks spectacular architecture but exhilarating sea views and an engaging ensemble of tawny, weather-beaten buildings justify a visit.

Corso Vittorio Emanuele, the main street, has sumptuous *palazzi* from all periods, including a Moorish mansion converted into a jeweller's, one of many which used to belong to the landed gentry. The loveliest civic building there is the Renaissance **Palazzo Steripinto**, with a crenellated facade of diamond-shaped design, a rusticated style borrowed from Neapolitan architecture.

Piazza Scandaliato, the bustling centre of both the town and the Corso, presents a scenic balcony for drinking in the views over an *aperitivo*. On summer evenings the square belongs to Tunisian hawkers flogging exotic clothes, leather goods or brightly painted Sciacca ceramics. The **Palazzo Comunale** (town hall) incorporates an Arab tower while, at the end of the piazza, the **Duomo** presents a confused image, with Arab-Norman apses buried in a baroque facade. From Piazza Scandaliato, steps lead down the port and numerous fish restaurants. After the slightly oppressive hinterland, visitors tend to appreciate this forthright, living town, noted for its sandy beaches and spa waters, and for seafood platters and aubergine spaghetti at a rough portside bar.

Sciacca's churches embrace all periods and styles. **San Calógero** and **San Domenico** are sober baroque works while the **Convento di San Francesco** combines clean lines with Moorish cloisters. **Chiesa del Carmine** is a Norman abbey with a Gothic rose window and a half-hearted baroque restoration. Facing it is a sculpted medieval gate and the Gothic portal of **Santa Margherita**. To the east, the ruined Romanesque **San Nicolò** church contrasts with **Santa Maria della Giummare**, a Catalan-Gothic church with crenellated Norman towers and a baroque interior. Just within the Aragonese walls is **Badia Grande**, an impressive 14th-century abbey.

Castello Bentivegna (Tues–Sat 10am–noon, 4–6pm), also called the "enchanted castle", is a folly in stone created by a peasant sculptor. Set among almond and olive groves just outside Sciacca, this forest of statues is the work of one man. In 1946, after great personal tragedy, Filippo Bentivegna returned from the United States and bought a patch of land in his native town. Using the rocks at the foot of Monte Kronio as his material, he sculpted 3,000 primitive heads of devils, politicians and knights. Not content with his work above ground, the sculptor then set about carving heads from olive wood and creating frescoed caverns in the mountain.

Sciacca is one of the oldest spas in Italy, known since prehistoric times and praised by Pliny. Mud baths and volcanic vapours are available at the **Terme Selinuntine**, an aloof Art Nouveau estab-

BELOW: some of Sciacca's eclectic architecture.

lishment that attracts well-heeled Italians with promises of cures for rheumatic and respiratory conditions. Just north, the **San Calógero** ❿ spa on Monte Kronio harnesses the powers of a "mini" volcano, bubbling hot springs and vapour-drenched grottoes used as saunas. The galleries, seats and water channels were hollowed out in ancient times by the Sicani or, according to the myth-makers, by Daedalus.

The rugged western hinterland

From Sciacca, a circular route and winding road leads 20 km (12 miles) inland to the mysterious mountain village of **Caltabellotta** ⓫, the highlight of this rural route, with its cluster of towers, churches and grey roofs. The village is spectacular, whether seen through spring blossom or swathed in mist. On the highest level, below the hulk of the ruined castle, is the Norman **Chiesa Madre** with its original portal and pointed arches fully restored for the year 2000. On the level underneath is the lopsided Piazza Umberto and the handsome **Chiesa del Carmine**, which has also been recently restored. Below stretch shadowy mountain views from the spacious Belvedere and the white Chiesa San Agostino. On the edge of the village lies **San Pellegrino**, a monastery with stupendous views of a mountainside studded with necropoli.

Northwest of Caltabellotta, but linked by circuitous country roads, is **Sambuca di Sicilia** ⓬, an historic Arab-Norman town with a popular lake and facilities for watersports and barbecues. Amateur archaeologists are drawn to neighbouring **Monte Adranone**, where the remains of a Greek colony have recently come to light, as well as huts and burial chambers from an Iron Age village. Further west still is **Santa Margherita di Bélice** ⓭, Lampedusa country,

Map on page 186

*Sciacca's name comes from the Latin and Arabic words for water (*aqua *and* xacca*), reflecting the town's origins as a Phoenician spa and Roman naval base.*

BELOW: Filippo Bentivegna's heads carved from lava.

bordering Palermo and Trápani provinces. However, in recent times it has become better known as the epicentre of the earthquake zone. Between here and the coast lies **Menfi**, another earthquake-damaged town, and a centre for the province's winemaking.

Pelágie Islands

The Pelágie Islands are generally reached by ferry from Porto Empédocle near Agrigento (an 8-hour crossing) but there are also direct flights from Palermo to Lampedusa.

This scorching archipelago of three islands lies amid strong currents off the African coast, closer to Tunisia than the Sicilian mainland. Although there are pockets of agriculture, the islands are unnaturally barren due to wanton deforestation and the virtual disappearance of the native olive groves, juniper and carob plantations. Fifty years ago, much of this lunar landscape was farmland bounded by dry stone walls but today, the local economy rests on fishing, from sponge fishing to canning, supplemented by tourism in Lampedusa. However, the islanders have belatedly realised the error of their unecological ways and started small-scale reafforestation programmes on Lampedusa.

In terms of cultural heritage, there are no outstanding sites but the waters are translucent, and rich in marine life, while the rugged native character and cuisine are distinctly Tunisian. Highlights of a stay on this North African outpost of Sicily include Moorish *dammusi* houses in local stone, excellent *couscous* and fish, quiet coastal walks and, except for high summer in Lampedusa, peace and quiet. Although the islands turn in on themselves in winter, in summer they are extremely welcoming. However, a curious feature of the islands in summer is the virtually continuous breezes and chilly nights.

BELOW:
looking down
on Caltabellotta.

Thanks to its location, **Lampedusa ⑭** is known as "a gift from Africa to Europe" or, thanks to its recent popularity with illegal immigrants, "the back-

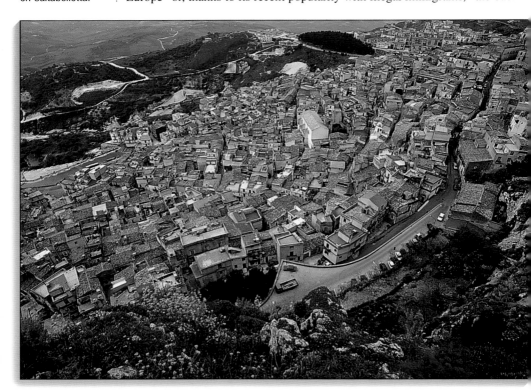

Map on page 186

door to Italy". The island was first settled by the Phoenicians and Greeks but was later owned by the Princes of Lampedusa. The family turned down a bid by Queen Victoria in favour of one by Ferdinand II of Bourbon in 1843. The Bourbons populated it with Sicilians but these have mostly been usurped by weather-beaten Tunisian fishermen, who live on the south coast. Sponge fishing is the mainstay of the island's economy, with a local cannery used to process a wide range of Mediterranean fish.

The Allies bombed Lampedusa in 1943 as a prelude to invading Sicily and the rest of Italy. Since then, the island's greatest claim to fame has been as a US radar base for bombing Libya. In 1986 a Libyan launch fired rockets on the island in retaliation for the American bombing of Tripoli. In fact, Gaddafi's missiles landed harmlessly in the sea but the Italian government was concerned enough to close the US base. In recent years, Lampedusa has been in the Italian headlines again, as boatloads of illegal immigrants (and the occasional drug-runner) are caught landing on the island's more remote beaches.

Lampedusa port contains a rabbit-warren of a casbah that reeks of spices, sardines, anchovies and goats. Indeed, the port is the best place for sampling such dishes as pasta with sardines, sweet and sour rabbit, or typical Sicilian candied fruit and spicy desserts. Buses from the port are infrequent and, despite the rocky roads, bicycles and mopeds are a popular way of exploring the interior. In the centre of the island is **Santuario di Porto Salvo**, a church in a lush garden draped in bougainvillaea and surrounded by grottos, once home to Saracen pirates. The white-steepled sanctuary contains a venerated statue of the Madonna, paraded every September. Other corners of the island that have escaped deforestation include the cove of **Cala Galera**, which has pockets of pine and Phoenician juniper. While the interior can be explored by bicycle, a boat trip is the best way of appreciating Lampedusa's secluded grottos, craggy inlets and sheer limestone cliffs.

Linosa 🅖, the island closest to Sicily, can be reached on a day trip from Lampedusa, and represents the tip of a vast submerged volcano, the last link in a volcanic chain that stretches to Vesuvius and beyond. The island, created as a result of a marine eruption, forms a rocky turtle shape indented by coves. The three visible volcanic cones may now be extinct but the beaches, still strewn with black boulders, can coat the unwary in ash and grit. Even so, in this cauldron of an island, most visitors congregate on the lavic beaches or quickly develop an interest in scuba-diving.

There is little to do on this lump of volcanic rock except rest, roast, swim, trek along dusty paths through vineyards or spot *dammusi*, pastel-coloured cubes with white window frames. These traditional Arab houses with domed roofs date back to designs created in Neolithic times by Tunisian settlers to the archipelago. The domed roofs are designed to keep the interior cool.

Lampione 🅖, an uninhabited reef, is scorched dry thanks to man's negligence. Its drama lies underwater: the translucent sea is unpolluted and rich in marine life, from sponge beds to hungry sharks. Sicilian pleasures are notoriously double-edged. ❑

Volcanic Linosa is far more fertile than Lampedusa, and produces carobs, whose leathery pods are made into animal fodder, fertiliser, or a chocolate substitute.

BELOW: looking up at Caltabellotta.

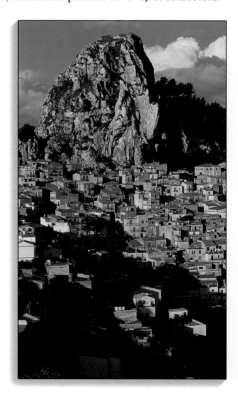

FESTIVALS SACRED AND PROFANE

Christianity and paganism, historical memory and folk tradition, all combine uninhibitedly in Sicily's frequent and fervent celebrations

Many Sicilian festivals mark a historical event with an overlay of religious worship. Palermo's feast of Santa Rosalia, for instance, celebrates the saint reputedly saving the city from plague in 1624 with a mixture of prayer and wild festivities. Other *feste*, although tied to the Christian calendar, have pagan elements lurking just beneath the surface. Thus *Carnivale* (literally "farewell to meat") marks the beginning of Lent and a period of abstinence, but is celebrated in many towns and cities with a licentious abandon that echoes the ancient Saturnalia.

Easter is the dominant Christian festival, but is celebrated in a variety of forms: processions of *tableux vivants* or holy relics, re-enactments of the Passion by chosen citizens, respects paid to the *Addolorata* (Our Lady of the Sorrows), and often more obscure rites besides. On Easter Sunday in Prizzi, for instance, the *Abballu de li diavoli* has devils in grotesque masks, led by Death himself, trying to prevent the Madonna meeting the resurrected Christ. It's a dramatic reworking of the Christian story, but also an unconscious echo of Lupercalia, a demonic pre-Christian festival.

▷ **TOURING TABLEAUX**
The Easter procession in Trápani tours the town for 20 hours non-stop, from early afternoon on Good Friday, through the night until Saturday morning.

△ **MYSTERY PLAYERS**
On Maundy Thursday in Marsala the *misteri* are re-enacted by citizens taking individual roles in different instalments of the Passion.

△ **BUN FIGHT**
In Agrigento for the feast of San Calógero special bread rolls are baked to be thrown to the crowds.

◁ **GREEK TRADITION**
Festivals are celebrated in the style of the Eastern Byzantine Church in Piana degli Albanesi, an enclave of Greek Orthodoxy.

▷ **MASKED MARCH**
Enna, Good Friday: 2,000 white-hooded members of the medieval fraternities process in total silence.

SECULAR CELEBRATIONS

Not all of Sicily's *feste* have a religious basis. Historical events, real or imagined, are commemorated with equal gusto throughout the island. In Adrano (top picture, far left), Piazza Armerina and elsewhere, the exploits of Roger II are recalled with medieval pageants involving a great deal of flag-waving, jousting and other pseudo-Norman jollity.

The *Festa della Castellana* in Cáccamo sees a procession of 500 costumed characters representing notables in the town's history.

The stars of Messina's annual procession (above) are two giants, Grifone and Mata, the mythical founders of the city, represented by ancient 8-metre (26-ft) mounted wooden figures.

The first signs of spring are excuse enough for a festival in many places, including Agrigento, where the *Sagra del Mandorlo in fiore* celebrates the blossoming of the almond trees in February.

△▽ **CAPITAL FUN**
Palermo's foremost festival is *U Fistinu*, six days of fireworks, processions and general mayhem in the name of ancient Santa Rosalia.

△ **SWEET MEMORIES**
Sugar statues are made to be eaten beside the graves of ancestors at *I Morti*, the bizarre Festival of the Dead celebrated on All Saints' Day in Palermo.

CALTANISSETTA PROVINCE

*As the heart of Sicily's Wild West, this dramatic, often
lawless landscape is a beguiling place for its craggy
scenery, traditional mores and Mafia lore*

Map
on page
198

The province is a place of subtle moods rather than specific sights: from the hill-top villages are spectacular views of mountain ridges and purple canyons, abandoned farms and ruined Norman castles. "This is ancient Sicily, the land of *latifundia* (feudal estates), sulphur mines, hunger and insecurity": the French writer Dominique Fernandez is not alone in relishing the Wild West feel of Caltanissetta. Given the sparsely-populated nature of the province, the visitor will often be alone with this harsh scenery.

Caltanissetta occupies a central position on a sulphur-bearing plain, its yellowish soil scarred with disused mines. Yet the province is far from uniform. There is a difference in character between the siege mentality of the bleak hilltop towns and the more accessible Greek flavour of Gela's coastal plains. This is a bitter province that feels betrayed by recent history: just as the sulphur mines brought hardship and a high mortality rate to the hinterland, so coastal industrialisation brought pollution but not prosperity, and mass emigration brought depopulation and despair. Although not the most poverty-stricken province, Caltanissetta is arguably the most aggrieved.

Caltanissetta ❶, the provincial capital, is a harsh summation of the region's struggle for survival. Its name reflects its cosmopolitan past: Arab conquerors added the prefix of *kalat*, Arabic for "castle", to the Greek name of Nissa. As befits an ancient bastion, it is a closed city, its defences raised against outsiders. Modern war damage means that medieval monuments are restricted to the outskirts, along with the original Greek settlements. Architecturally, the city is mostly 19th century, with only the occasional baroque monument to relieve the blandness.

Nonetheless, Caltanissetta is no mere market town but the agricultural heart of the Sicilian interior, with grain and cotton long grown in the countryside. As the historical hub of Sicilian mining operations, the city fell into decline in the 1960s with the collapse of the sulphur industry. Potassium and magnesium mining have now supplanted sulphur and the city has achieved modest prosperity. Still, life here has always been tough, even by Sicilian standards. Although the grinding poverty is no more, the city today is characterised by a wilful torpor verging on deadly passivity that even colours Caltanissetta's approach to crime.

Mafia lore

As the headquarters of the Criminal Justice magistrates courts, Caltanissetta is entrusted with trying the most controversial Mafia cases. Ironically, the province is itself tainted by Mafia association, while local citizens have arguably been the most reluctant to express the resurgence in civic values that charac-

PRECEDING PAGES:
on Castello
Manfredónico at
Mussomeli. **LEFT:**
Umberto I gazes
at Caltanissetta.
BELOW: San Cataldo
is noted for its
terracotta pottery.

terises Sicily in the new millennium. In 1992, despite public dismay, the town was entrusted with the investigation into the murder of Judge Falcone, his wife and bodyguards (*see page 81*). Much to the astonishment of American FBI agents cooperating on the case, Caltanissetta magistrates hoped to compete with the Mafia without access to a computer. Despite its presumed probity, the city's magistrates court remains Sicily's most understaffed and overworked. Cynics may say that this is intentional, giving *mafiosi* suspects a head start.

City sights

Caltanissetta's heart, in so far as it has one, lies in Piazza Garibaldi. There, the baroque **Duomo**, flanked by bell towers, overlooks the ugly neo-Romanesque church of San Sebastiano, the baroque Town Hall and a rusty bronze statue of Neptune. The cathedral interior is an engaging explosion of kitsch. In chapels to the right of the nave, saints in glittering glass cases compete for attention. A triumphal angel and cherubs adorn a gaudy glass and gold coffin, a Sicilian disguise for a rotting corpse.

Behind the Town Hall, Via Palazzo Paterno leads to the crumbling **Palazzo Moncada**. This was the home of the Moncada dynasty, the feudal rulers of the region from 1406 onwards. The baroque mansion is emblazoned with snarling lions posing as gargoyles. Emblematic of Sicily, the building was never finished and its leisurely "restoration programme" implies that it never will be.

Corso Umberto, the main street, is lined with dark, dilapidated buildings and scruffy bars. Oblivious to the rain, wizened men congregate outside to discuss politics or building permits. Inside, dry-tasting pastries are washed down with Amaro, a reminder that Caltanissetta is the main producer of this famous

A sign for AAST (Azienda Autonoma di Soggiorno e Turismo) directs you to a local tourist information office.

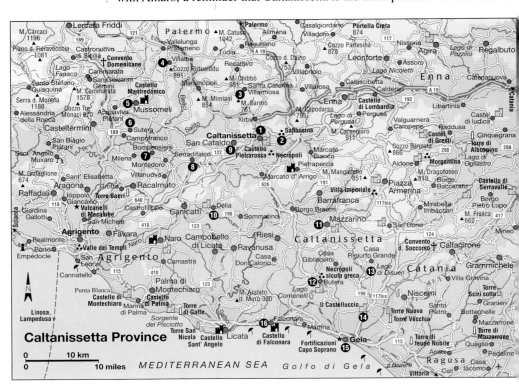

digestivo. The unwelcoming atmosphere is pervasive since the Nisseni, the surly locals, are suspicious of outsiders. The remaining sights are quickly dispensed with, unless you wish to stay and sample the local speciality: *stigliole*, stuffed kid's entrails. The **Museo Archeológico** (Mon–Sat 9.30am–1pm, 3–7pm), on Via Napoleone Colajanni, has prehistoric and Greek remains from local settlements, including rock tombs. Finest are the Attic vases, painted urns, a terracotta model of a temple and the earliest Bronze Age figures found in Sicily.

Map on page 198

Environs

Fortunately, the disappointing provincial capital is a stone's throw from several significant medieval or prehistoric sites which, although neglected, are worthy of more than cursory interest. **Santa Maria degli Angeli**, on the city's eastern outskirts, is a ruined Norman church with a richly carved Gothic porch. Virtually next door is the stump of **Pietrarossa Castle**, perched on a jagged spur. Frederick II sought refuge in this baronial fiefdom during his battle for supremacy with the Chiaramonte and Ventimiglia dynasties. However, the 1567 earthquake tossed the Norman-Arab castle into its present pitiful heap.

Five km (3 miles) south of Caltanissetta lie the Moorish ruins of **Gebel Habib** on Monte Gibil Gabel, meaning Mountain of the Dead in Arabic. (Take the San Cataldo to Pietraperzia road, direction Pietraperzia, for 2 km (1 mile), then follow signs for Gebel Habib.) This prehistoric site was also home to a Hellenised settlement, the original site of Nissa. Tumbledown fortifications remain, together with prehistoric and Greek tombs carved into the rock.

On the flanks of **Monte Sabbucina** lies a more impressive prehistoric necropolis, even if the best finds are now in Caltanissetta's Museo Archeológico. Take

The highlight of Easter Week in Caltanissetta is the Maundy Thursday procession of the Mysteries of the Passion, with sculptures borne by representatives of the ancient guilds. The mournful dirges of the cortège are a throwback to Arab and Greek culture.

BELOW: fountain in Caltanissetta's Piazza Garibaldi.

the old SS 122 road from Caltanissetta to Enna, leaving town through the barren Terra Pilata. The road crosses the Salso river at **Ponte Capodarso**, a delicate 16th-century Venetian bridge: 6 km (4 miles) along the Enna road, a scenic route is marked to the archaeological park of **Sabbucina ❷**. This Bronze Age settlement was later occupied by Hellenised Siculi (Sicel) tribes, who flourished here from the 6th to the 4th centuries BC. The Sicels lived within a square-towered fortress, parts of which survive. The remains include boundary walls, defensive towers, a sanctuary, two wells, the tracery of grid patterns and house foundations.

The wild west

A sweeping circular route west of Caltanissetta passes a series of shabby but atmospheric hill towns. Settlements were traditionally restricted to hill tops, whether castles or fortified towns, both for defensive purposes and as refuge from the malaria-infested plains. Moreover, in the interior, it was common practice for farm-workers to commute to the country from their home village. As for the fortresses, although feuding barons once inhabited these lofty strongholds, depopulation and desolation have turned many into virtual ghost towns. From such windswept eyries stretch views of ravines and deserted plains, sulphurous hills and abandoned mines.

Santa Caterina Villarmosa ❸, 20 km (12 miles) north of Caltanissetta along the SS 122 bis, is worth a cursory glance if you are interested in looking at lace and delicate embroidery, the town's main claim to fame. **Villalba ❹**, about 35 km (22 miles) west, just off the SS 121, is a notoriously down-at-heel Mafia haunt, once held by Don Calógero Vizzini, Genco Russo's legendary prede-

BELOW: the Castello Manfredónico at Mussomeli.

cessor. Vizzini was the main Mafia boss from 1942 until his death in 1954 and as mayor he ran this scruffy town like a private fiefdom. His tombstone in Villalba cemetery laments the death of a gentleman and praises his Robin Hood status as a defender of the weak.

Even before the rise of the Mafia, Villalba was doomed to be forever milked by absentee landlords, whose revenues from the production of wine and grain here provided them with a noble lifestyle in Palermo. Once a ducal hunting estate, Villalba is just one of the seemingly inaccessible settlements that characterise Caltanissetta. Along with other local Norman towns, it was a source of cheap labour for the feudal estate of Micciche, now known as **Regaleali**.

More than most surrounding market towns, **Mussomeli ❺**, 20 km (12 miles) south of Villalba, has suffered from Mafia mythology and emigration. Still, Mussomeli's loss has been Watford's gain, at least as far as gardeners, mechanics and restaurateurs are concerned. As for the Mafia, New York received some of Mussomeli's finest in the 1960s. Just east of town, on the Villalba road, stands **Castello Manfredónico**, named after Manfredi Chiaramonte, Frederick II's son, killed defending his kingdom against Charles of Anjou. Set on an impregnable crag, the lopsided castle blends into the rock. From the fortress are vertiginous views over the desolate valley below.

Mussomeli has always lived dangerously. This was the home town and political base of Don Genco Russo, the Mafia overlord from 1954 until the late 1960s. Mafia expert Clare Sterling describes him as a masterly political fixer despite being "a coarse, sly, half-illiterate ruffian loved by none". Known as Zi Peppi Jencu (Uncle Joe the Little Bull), he helped organise the Sicilian takeover of the American heroin cartel. During his trial in the 1960s, the Don presented

Map on page 198

The Regaleali estate, now owned by Count Tasca d'Almerita, ranks with Corvo and Donnafugata as Sicily's most famous wine producer.

BELOW: Mussomeli, a former Mafia stronghold.

Don Genco Russo, based in Mussomeli, was the Mafia's capo di tutti capi *after the death of Calógero Vizzini.*

a petition with 7,000 signatures from Mussomeli alone. The petition claimed the Don had "dedicated his life to our welfare, setting an example in probity and rectitude". According to Sterling, the trial's turning point came with the threatened publication of telegrams from 37 Christian Democrat deputies, one of them a Cabinet Minister, thanking the Mafia's *capo di tutti capi* for helping them get elected. Don Genco Russo was acquitted and died a natural death in Mussomeli in 1976.

The country road zigzags south for 13 km (8 miles) to **Sutera** ⑥, the first of several ragged towns set on rocky outcrops in old mining country around Caltanissetta. Beyond a series of acrobatic bends lies Sutera's shadow, **Bompensiere** ⑦. (From Sutera, follow the SS 189 south for 4 km (2 miles) before taking the rural road east towards Caltanissetta.) **Serradifalco** ⑧, 15 km (9 miles) east, is another neglected hill-top town, linked across a ridge to Villalba. **San Cataldo** ⑨, nestling in wooded hills to the east, was once the administrative heart of a great agricultural estate, but is today noted for its crafts, especially terracotta pots and wrought ironwork.

South to the coast

Sinuous upland roads link the craggy countryside with the Gela plains to the south. The higher peaks abound in mountainous vegetation but the wooded slopes soon give way to olives and almonds. The journey passes sleepy towns with populations reduced by emigration. They share a battered rural economy and dignified poverty. **Sommatino**, **Riesi** and **Niscemi** are typical of such spots, though the ruined castle at **Délia** ⑩ helps distinguish it from its neighbours.

From Caltanissetta, the SS 626 bridges the rugged hinterland and the coastal

BELOW: contours of Caltanissetta in spring.

plains towards Gela. **Mazzarino** ⓫ lies 10 km (6 miles) east of the main thoroughfare, reached along the SS 190. The town's modest reputation rests on Mafia lore and a ruined castle. Founded by the princes of Butera, the castle retains its original keep and some defensive walls. Ragged *palazzi* and a couple of undervalued churches add to the atmosphere of gentle nostalgia. Chiesa San Domenico contains a touching Madonna by Paladino while Chiesa dei Cappuccini houses an 18th-century marble tabernacle encrusted with ivory, ebony, coral and tortoiseshell.

In the 1960s this bedraggled country town hit the headlines as a Mafia stronghold run by a licentious abbot. Tales of the friars' orgiastic lifestyles were rife, gleefully embroidered by the press. Sensationalism aside, the good friars were far from blameless and admitted Mafia ties. The Mazzarino friars acted as messengers between the Mafia and their victims. At their trial in 1962, the friars were accused of extortion, intimidation and murder, as well as the creation and distribution of pornography. Under cross-examination, they admitted to writing some of the blackmail and ransom notes "but only because the mafiosi were illiterate and did not own a typewriter". Allegedly, verbal threats were delivered via the confessional.

Butera ⓬, a crumbling hill village perched on a chalky crest 18 km (11 miles) south, is the most attractive in the province. The fief prospered under Spanish rule, held by the Branciforte family, the Princes of Butera. Although currently closed, the battlemented 11th-century castle is fairly well preserved, with a powerful keep and mullioned windows. The Chiesa Madre has a Paladino Madonna and a Renaissance tryptich. Nearby, the Palazzo Comunale (Town Hall) has an intricate 14th-century portal and panoramic views over the Gela plains to the coast.

Butera was a former Sicani colony, heavily marked by the Hellenistic influence at Gela. Sanctuaries, funerary rites and fortifications in the region owe much to Greek influence. North of town, step tombs dating from the 8th century BC attest to this, their doors decorated with Greek spiral shapes. Just east of Butera as the crow flies is **Lago di Disueri** ⓭, a dam with a late Bronze Age necropolis on its rocky shores.

Southeast of Butera, on the SS 117 bis, the curious mound of **Il Castelluccio** ⓮ presents a dramatic break in the fertile Gela plains. This tumbledown castle keep, jutting out of fields of artichokes and wheat, was built by the warlike Frederick II. Nearby is a modern **war memorial**, a reminder that these fields witnessed the Allied landing in Sicily in 1943 (*see page 54*). Il Castelluccio overlooks the fertile **Gela plain**, rich in grain, wine and olives as well as artichokes and oranges, lemons and cotton. This land of plenty was once an open invitation to the Greeks, the first and most welcome wave of settlers. **Gela** ⓯ is often called the only truly creative Greek colony. It was renowned for its entrepreneurial spirit, inspired military architecture and artistic excellence. It became a Doric colony in 688 BC, settled by Greeks from Rhodes and Crete. However, the indigenous Sicani tribe transmuted the superior Greek culture into a unique shape. Exquisite coins, terracotta figurines,

Map on page 198

They had skirted sheer precipices which no sage and broom could temper. Never a tree, never a drop of water; just sun and dust.

— DI LAMPEDUSA
THE LEOPARD

BELOW: the Chiesa Madre, Mazzarino.

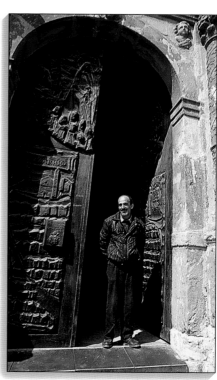

TIP

Sicily's most depressing towns often have excellent cuisine. If you're marooned on the Gela riviera, at least sample macaroni with aubergines or *stigghuilata 'mpanata*, focaccia-style bread stuffed with vegetables, meat or fish – a meal naturally accompanied by aristocratic Regaleali wines.

sculpted walls, and flourishing agriculture remain a testament to these times.

From here, Hellenistic influence spread to the rest of Sicily. Yet Gela was sacked by the Carthaginians in 405 BC, a year after Agrigento's fall, and was eventually razed by the Tyrant of Agrigento in 282 BC, who deported the entire population. The latest devastation was in 1943 when the Allies liberated Sicily and, in the process, bombed Gela to smithereens. Arguably, industrialisation has been the ultimate desecration, the Sicilian environment sacrificed to the northern Italian economy. The city is hideous and only those with a passion for Greek archaeology will brave the polluted outskirts.

Unlike the hill towns of the interior, Gela has no tradition of aristocratic rule. As a result, it has no castles or noble *palazzi*, nothing between its glorious Greek heritage and today's grim sprawl. Still, it is worth sifting through the industrial debris to reach the ancient city. Occupying the western slopes of Gela, the main archaeological site presents a strange contrasting scene. The walls built by Timoleon, the good Tyrant of Siracusa, are set amongst mimosa, eucalyptus and pines; just beyond the sand dunes are futuristic domes and glittering pipes.

The **Archaeological Museum** (daily 9am–1pm, 3–8pm), on Corso Vittorio Emanuele, is built over the ancient acropolis in the Molino a Vento quarter in the east of town, with recently excavated sections open to inspection. The museum displays painted Attic vases, coins, Ionic capitals and terracotta sarcophagi. Gela terracotta was renowned throughout Magna Graecia, prized for its painted designs and the delicacy of the figurative work. The star piece is a noble terracotta horse's head from the 6th century BC, part of a temple pediment. **Parco della Rimembranza**, close by, is a park with a single Doric column, the remains of a temple to Athena. From here, there are views over

BELOW: the keep of Butera castle.

the Gela plain, embracing the long horizon of the African sea, marred by the industrial mass on the beach below.

The **Capo Soprano fortifications** (9am–1 hour before sunset), dating from the same period, are Gela's chief glory. Situated at the western end of town, off Via Manzoni, these romantic walls were covered by sand dunes until 1948. Running parallel with the sea, the battlemented ramparts were rebuilt by Timoleon after the Carthaginians razed the city. The thick walls are topped with angle towers and sentry posts, with the remains of barracks inside the northern sections. Also in the Capo Soprano quarter are **Greek baths**, the only ones to have survived in Sicily, dating from the 4th century BC.

Golfo di Gela

From here, you can visit the moonscape of the Gela coast, travelling northwest to Agrigento or east to Ragusa and Siracusa. West of Gela, the sandy shore is littered with pillboxes, relics of Gela's most recent invasion. **Falconara** ⑯, to the west, is a small resort with two appealing beaches, Manfria and Roccazzelle. The stretches of golden sands beckon invitingly. **Castello di Falconara**, the local castle, is set in lush grounds overlooking the sea. Built in sandy-coloured stone, the feudal castle has crenellations and a 14th-century keep. This atmospheric spot is used by Palermitan aristocrats as their summer residence.

If the oil-laden winds are blowing the wrong way, take the SS 117 bus north across the plains, passing eucalyptus and cork plantations en route to Piazza Armerina and Roman Sicily (*see page 215*). These are Virgil's celebrated **Campi Geloi**, the plains in which the poet Aeschylus supposedly met his fate (*see page 27*). Archaeologists are still searching for the great tragedian's tomb. ❏

Map on page 198

The ancient walls at Capo Soprano are unique: the earlier, lower parts are meticulously dressed sandstone blocks. As stone was scarce, the later upper sections were built with crudely made bricks of sun-dried clay. Though fragile, they have been preserved by drifting sand.

BELOW: Castello di Falconara, in a superb location.

ENNA PROVINCE

This elevated inland province possesses the island's greatest Roman villa and a succession of blustery hill towns and strategic castles, as well as a reputation for spirituality

To Ovid, Enna was "where Nature decks herself in all her varied hues, where the ground is beauteous, carpeted with flowers of many tints". Enna is still strewn with narcissi in spring but is otherwise a poetic, aloof province with its head in the clouds. In this mythological land, the cult of Demeter (Ceres) has lasted for over 2,000 years, offering a satisfying explanation for the changing seasons. As the "navel of Sicily", Enna indulges in introspection. This desolate, sun-parched centre of Sicily is the only province with no outlet to the sea. Di Lampedusa likened the landscape to "a sea suddenly petrified at the instant when a change of wind had flung the waves into a frenzy". Yet there is much to proclaim, from the Roman Villa at Piazza Armerina, one of the wonders of the ancient world, to a hinterland studded with hill-top towns and Norman castles.

Enna ❶, known as Sicily's navel for its central position, is considered a sacred city thanks to the cult of Demeter and the myth of Persephone. Apart from clashes with Siracusa, Enna was prosperous and relatively independent during Greek rule. Under the Romans, Enna merely worshipped the old fertility goddesses under the new names of Ceres and Proserpine. Enna became the anonymous breadbasket of Rome, despite several great slave revolts. The Arabs also cultivated the region, planting cotton, cane and pistachio nuts, and building solid fortifications. The city's formidable castle owes more to Norman rule. Under the Bourbons, a cruel regime of "hangings and holidays" caused resentment and confirmed Enna's rebellious reputation.

Despite Persephone's gift of spring, Enna always feels cloaked in winter, shrouded in mist or blown by wintry gusts. According to writer Vincent Cronin, Enna's citizens are as "remote, grey and ethereal as the city they inhabit". Yet, whatever the climate, the ancient cult of fertility cannot be crushed: Enna province remains agricultural, producing corn, olives, cheese, nuts and wine.

City in the clouds

Enna's sights are fairly compact, but when the mist falls, expect to cling to the city walls between churches. Tradition has it that the newly restored **cathedral** (daily 9am–1pm, 4–7pm) was begun by Eleanor of Aragon but a fire in 1446 swept away most of the treasures. Nonetheless, the cathedral is a fascinating romp through Enna's mystical past. The elaborately carved white pulpit is encrusted with cherubs and rests on a Graeco-Roman base removed from a temple to Demeter, as does the marble stoup nearby. The quaint portico is matched by Gothic transepts and apses while the wrought-iron sacristy gate once graced a Moorish harem in the Castello di Lombardia. The beloved statue of the **Black Madonna** is stored

PRECEDING PAGES: sunrise seen from Enna, with distant Etna on the right. **LEFT:** Castello di Lombardia. **BELOW:** vegetables for sale outside Enna Cathedral.

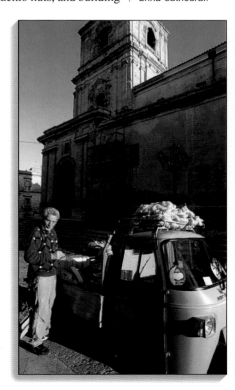

The octagonal Torre di Federico II was once one of Enna's linked system of watchtowers. Now it stands alone in the Giardino Pubblico.

within two sets of doors in a side chapel. On Good Friday, citizens sew *ex-voto* offerings on the Madonna's gold dress and parade her through the town.

Enna's esoteric past makes it susceptible to pagan magic. The black basalt base of the capitals incorporate sculptures of Hades and demonic symbols in an attempt to crush evil forces by fair means or foul. The adjoining **Museo Alessi** (Tues–Sun 9am–1pm, 4–7pm) displays the contents of the cathedral's treasury, including the prized Madonna's Crown, a sacred 17th-century diadem studded with diamonds.

Along bustling **Via Roma** are a string of dignified mansions and churches, such as the Catalan-Gothic Palazzo Pollicarini and the baroque Chiesa San Benedetto. Via Roma is pedestrianised for the evening passeggiata and contains a good pasticceria as well as cosy restaurants. At the bottom are sweeping views from the *belvedere* and **Torre di Federico II**, a tumbledown octagonal tower built by Frederick II. The tower is linked by secret passageways to **Castello di Lombardia** (daily 9am–1pm, 3–5pm) at the top of the hill, at the

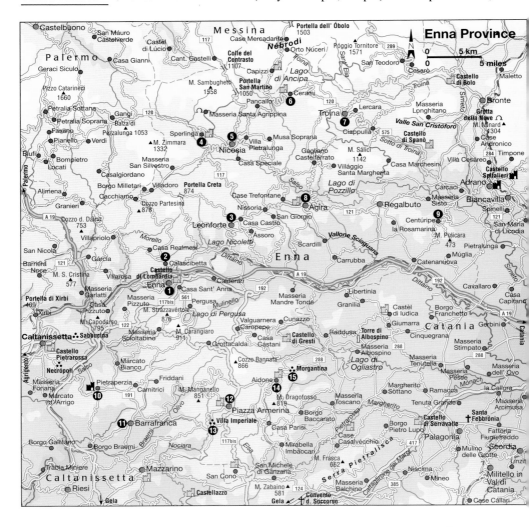

other end of Via Roma. As one of the largest medieval castles in Sicily, this imposing fortress began as a draughty Byzantine keep but acquired towers with each wave of invaders, from the Normans to the Swabians. A series of three courtyards leads to the majestic eyrie of **Torre Pisano**, the tallest of the castle's six surviving towers, which commands views over the whole of Sicily.

Just beyond the castle looms **Rocca di Cerere**, also known as the Temple of Demeter, a name full of misleading promise. The reality is a sole rock and rural views but no sign of a temple. Legend has it that Demeter's daughter Persephone was abducted by Hades and swept off to the shores of **Lake Pergusa**, and thence to the Underworld. Her mother's pleading won Persephone's freedom for part of the year, time to sow and spin the cycle of fertility. Hades' cavern is still on the south bank of the lake but his chariot and black horses are now hi tech Formula One cars. The lake, 9 km (5½ miles) south of Enna, is nowadays the focus of summer sailing competitions, and encircled by a racing track and restaurants, a sacrilegious end to Persephone's memory and the mythical meadows of pure narcissi.

Balcony over Sicily

This circuitous route explores the castle-studded landscape north of Enna. Facing the city is **Calascibetta ❷**, a decrepit but atmospheric hill village built by the Arabs while besieging Enna in 951. The Saracen stronghold was eventually taken by Count Roger but retains its intimate Moorish design. Rust-coloured buildings cling to the slopes and the Chiesa Madre is perched on top of a blustery cliff. From here, the SS 121 winds north to **Leonforte ❸**, a 17th-century Branciforte fiefdom best known for its colourful Good Friday procession and the **Granfonte**, a magnificent fountain. Set on the edge of town, the graceful arched fountain fills troughs from 24 spouts. As the writer Paul Duncan says: "Its construction (in golden-coloured stone to match the surrounding cornfields) was an act of isolated benevolence at a time when feudal dependents were more likely to be given a kick in the teeth than fresh running water." This testament to feudal largesse is watched over by the Branciforte: on the hill above, their tumbledown family seat and funerary chapel remain. The princely ghosts may still see their fountain appreciated by thirsty donkeys.

Sperlinga ❹, north of Leonforte on the SS 117, may well be Sicily's most intriguing castle (daily 9am–1pm, 2pm–sunset), with battlemented towers and bastions that reach to the bottom of the cliff. Above ground, the village is a string of modest cottages; below the castle, the rock is riddled with chambers, a secret underground city. Dating from 1082, the Norman castle became a Bourbon prison and was donated to the town by Baron Nicosia, its feudal owner, in 1973. After the bloody Sicilian Vespers in 1282, Sperlinga became the Angevins' last stand. The castle was besieged but the French forces within held out for over a year, aided by trap doors that deposited invaders in underground pits. The only access is still via a staircase hewn out of the rock. Steep, switchback paths climb to the summit, festooned with

Map on page 210

TIP

Enna has a number of good, family-run restaurants, which produce grilled vegetables, hearty soups, sausages on fennel seed, stuffed lamb or meatballs (*polpettone*).

BELOW: Enna's view of Calascibetta.

The Catalan porticos encircling San Nicolò in Nicosia have many headless statues, decapitated in the 1967 earthquake – an example of Sicilian restoration at its slowest.

BELOW: the imposing Granfonte at Leonforte.

warning notices. (A wall collapsed in 1999 but the castle has reopened.) From the crenellations stretch sweeping views over oak woods, olive groves and pasture. The rocky slopes of the village are also pitted with caves, some of which have been inhabited since Sicani times. The cave dwellings were occupied by Sperlinga's poorest peasants and their livestock until the 1980s. Even today, many cottages open into chambers used as store rooms or wine cellars.

Nicosia ❺, 8 km (5 miles) southeast of Sperlinga, is set on four hills and ringed by rocky spurs. It has been a Greek city, Byzantine bishopric, Arab fort and Norman citadel. In the Middle Ages, it was riven by religious rivalry between Roman Catholic newcomers from the north and the indigenous population who, in Byzantine tradition, followed the Greek Orthodox rite. After pitched battles, the matter was settled in favour of the natives: the 14th-century **San Nicolò** triumphed as the city cathedral, with its lacey Catalan-Gothic campanile rooted in a gracious Moorish tower. From the cathedral, which dominates the town, Salita Salamone climbs to **San Salvatore**, a Romanesque church that would look at home in Burgundy. From the delicate portico is a view over the rooftops to Santa Maria Maggiore on the facing hill. Below are buildings made of yellow and grey local stone. On the next square down is **Palazzo Salamone**, the seat of Nicosia's most illustrious family.

Piazza Garibaldi, the main square, is dotted with dingy bars and *circoli*, working men's clubs. Bandy-legged old men sit and chat in *gallo-italico*, a Lombard dialect stemming from northern settlers and shared with Aidone, Piazza Armerina and Sperlinga. Half the adult population emigrated between 1950 and 1970 and Nicosia has been further isolated by the route of the new motorway. Leading off Piazza Garibaldi are myriad *viccoli*, crooked alleys

climbing Nicosia's hills. From here, the steep **Via Salamone** winds above the cathedral, passing dilapidated palazzi and convents encrusted with garlands or gargoyles. At the top is **Santa Maria Maggiore**, wedged between boulders. After an 18th-century earthquake, the Norman church was rebuilt in baroque style. This elegant shadow faces a montage of bells that fell down in the last earthquake. From the terrace, the tumbledown castle is visible, overgrown with cacti and thistles on a rocky spur. *Cardi* (fried thistles) are a rustic delicacy but the **Trattoria La Pace** in Via della Pace believes in heartier fare.

The SS 120, a meandering mountain road, leads 20 km (12 miles) northeast to **Cerami ❻**, a jagged village dominated by a ruined castle. The wooded countryside is interspersed with orchards and lolling cattle. Just north of the SS 120 is the scenic **Lago di Ancipa**, a lake set in a lush wilderness. East of Nicosia are windswept views across the bleak Nébrodi mountains, their wrinkled blue-brown slopes and undulating wheatfields shimmering in the heat.

Further along the SS 120 lies **Troina ❼**, the loftiest town in Sicily, which occupies an Arab-Norman stronghold on a solitary ridge. This citadel has declined into an austere hill town with a nest of churches crammed into winding medieval alleys. Tall, draughty convents look out over scruffy terraces and the makeshift houses of returning emigrants. The churches are suitably grand, as befits the first Norman diocese in Sicily. The Norman **Chiesa Matrice** has a fortified bell tower, nave, crypt, tower and solid external walls.

In this citadel Count Roger and wife were besieged by Saracens in 1064. The couple escaped by classic Norman cunning: while their enemies were lulled into a drunken stupor, the Normans scurried along secret vaulted passages that burrow deep under the ruined castle. Inside, the fusty church has been revamped in baroque style, complete with flaking gold leaf and late Byzantine art. However, in the treasury Roger's ruby ring remains as a memento. Outside, an arched walk slopes under the bell tower and returns to the atmospheric Norman stronghold. The terraces are scarred with jagged bits of castle and chapel. On the *belvedere*, Troina's youth gather to enjoy rugged windswept views over the distant blue-grey hills.

Agira ❽, a tortuous 30 km (19 miles) south of Troina, is set on a hillside surmounted by a Saracen castle. The slopes once housed a Siculi settlement but are now given over to olives, grapes and almonds. These hills saw heavy fighting during the Sicilian campaign in 1943, hence the Canadian war cemetery on the town outskirts. Though not striking, the churches contain precious works of art. **Santa Maria Maggiore**, in the shadow of the castle, has a 15th-century triptych and sculpted Norman capitals, while **Santa Maria di Gesù** contains a painted crucifix by Fra Umile da Petralia. Laden down by a 16th-century facade, the Gothic **San Salvatore** has a treasury containing a bejewelled medieval mitre.

Further east, past **Lago di Pozzillo**, an artificial lake, a minor road leads off the SS 121 through orange and olive groves to **Centúripe ❾**. The name supposedly comes from the Latin for steep slopes, justifying the town's tag as "balcony of Sicily" and its magnificent valley views to Catania and Etna. Cicero

Map on page 210

Map on page 210

TIP

The hill towns are the place to sample an Enna speciality – *castrato*, charcoal-grilled castrated ram.

BELOW: the crooked alleys of Nicosia.

Peppers and prickly pears for sale in the hill town of Agira.

described this Hellenised Siculi settlement as the richest city in Sicily, thanks to its fertile soil, sulphur and salt mines. Classical statues, terracottas and vases are visible in the **Museo Archeológico** (Mon–Fri 9am–1pm). On the outskirts, further finds have been made at Castello di Corradino, the site of a cliff-top Roman mausoleum. At the foot of Monte Calvario are the ruins of a Greek villa and, in the Bagni valley, the remains of Roman baths. From here, the A19 motorway leads back to Enna.

Ancient Rome in the southern hills

The territory south of Enna has its fair share of shabby hill towns but the countryside is also home to several Greek settlements and Roman outposts, notably the magnificent Roman villa at Piazza Armerina. Southwest of Enna are a couple of isolated hill towns on the Caltanissetta border. **Pietraperzia** ❿, a market town stacked up on the slopes south of Caltanissetta, lives off the land but once provided a living for the Barresi dynasty. As major landowners in Caltanissetta and Enna provinces, they placed a fortified palazzo at the heart of their battered fiefdom.

Barrafranca ⓫ lies 10 km (6 miles) to the southeast of Enna, set on a spur in the Erei mountains. This Roman outpost and Norman fief was swallowed up by the Branciforte feudal estates in 1530. The baroque **Chiesa Madre** has fine paintings while the hamlet of Bastia overlooks Byzantine ruins. Otherwise, pleasures lie in the sampling of local produce, including olives, almonds and grapes. The town is pitted with caves, used as wine cellars. This backwater bursts into life at Easter, with a colourful procession of giants and an exuberant Christian pantomime.

BELOW: taking it easy in Nicosia.

Further east is **Piazza Armerina** ⑫ and the Roman Villa at Casale, Sicily's greatest wonder of the Roman world. As a town, Piazza Armerina is sorely neglected in favour of its Roman star. Yet though it is upstaged, Piazza Armerina is not overawed and has a faded elegance all of its own. Although the closure of the sulphur mines has cast a pall over the local economy, the town sees its salvation in tourism. (Even so, if time is short, head straight for the villa.)

In town, a series of flights of steps and alleys leads to the baroque **cathedral**, crowning the terraced hill. Theatrical staircases also accentuate the spacious *belvedere* and the Duomo's baroque facade. A Catalan-Gothic *campanile* with blind arcading remains from the original church and sets the tone for the lavish interior. Bordering the cathedral is **Palazzo Trigona**, a sober counterpoint to the baroque flights of fancy.

The hill-top quarter radiates from Piazza Duomo and Piazza Garibaldi. In keeping with 13th-century urban design, this is in fishbone formation, with tiny alleys fanning out delicately along the contours of the slopes. Beside Palazzo Trigona, Via Floresta leads to the picturesque Aragonese **castle**. Further south, the steep Via Castellina nudges the city walls and an old watchtower. A stroll down the steep Via Monte, the medieval main street, reveals an evocative slice of history, passing *palazzi* dating from Norman and Aragonese times.

Turnings right lead past turreted mansions to **San Martino**, a 15th-century church. A 1-km (half-mile) stroll north from the compact hillside quarter reaches **Sant'Andrea**, an unadorned but delightful Norman priory with a frescoed interior designed in a Coptic cross plan.

Imperial glory

Nestling among oak and hazel woods, the **Villa Imperiale** (Roman Villa) ⑬ lies 5 km (3 miles) southwest of town at **Casale**. A route signposted for Villa Romana cuts through the tumbledown side of town and hugs the foot of the hill emerging into open countryside, with flashes of olives and forsythia. The excellent hunting in these forests was the bait that drew the villa's original owners. The villa probably first belonged to Diocletian's co-emperor Marcus Aurelius Maximianus (Maximian) between 286 and 305, and then passed to later emperors. It was occupied throughout the Arab period but destroyed by the Norman King William in 1160.

The villa's fluid, impressionistic mosaics may have inspired the Normans in their designs for Palermo's Palazzo dei Normanni. In splendour, the only rivals are Hadrian's Villa at Tivoli or Diocletian's palace at Split. But Sicily's mosaics better reflect the flux of Roman politics, with the emergence of separate Eastern and Western Empires. One theory is that after Diocletian realised that the Roman world was too vast to be ruled by one mind and retired to Split, so Maximian withdrew to contemplation in Sicily.

Whether hunting lodge or country mansion, the villa disappeared under a landslide for 700 years. After a hoard of treasure was found in 1950, the villa was seriously excavated. Much remains to be unearthed in the hazelnut orchards, from the slave

TIP

If you intend to stay overnight in Piazza Armerina, it pays to plan ahead: there are only three hotels in the town – and one of those is closed for restoration. A fourth is situated outside the town, close to the Roman Villa. See Travel Tips for details.

BELOW: Agira's war memorial.

quarters to the water system. Yet a Sicilian muddle caused excavations to be abandoned in 1985 and has delayed the restoration of mosaics that suffered flood damage in 1991, and vandalism in 1998. Many were discoloured and some superficially damaged, including those in the Great Hall. If this were Venice, there would be a public outcry; since this is Sicily, manpower and funding focus on security, discouraging looters and fellow custodians from indulging in night raids. On top of everything, plastic roofing turns the site into a sauna in summer. However, the authorities have finally been galvanised into action, with a decision to place the site under regional protection in the year 2000, and a coherent plan to restore the villa in line with international curating standards.

To avoid the crowds and the heat, it is worth arriving early or late (open daily 8am–7.30pm). The vaulting may be lost and the frescoes faded but the villa's magic lies in the 50 rooms covered in Roman-African mosaics. Their vitality, expressive power and free-ranging content set them apart from models in Tunisia or Antioch. The stylisation of these mosaics is undercut by humour, realism, sensuality and subtlety. Above all, the visual energy of the mosaics shines through.

A triumphal arch leads to an **atrium Ⓐ** surrounded by a portico, then crashes down to earth in the male **latrines Ⓑ**, in a composition of a Persian ass, ram and pouncing leopard. Despite the savagery of the scene, the latrines look more civilised than many modern ones. The villa's centrepiece is the **courtyard Ⓒ**, with peristyle, pool and statue. The mosaics depict whimsical animals' heads, from a fierce bear and tiger to a horse with a stunted nose. The design has a symmetry, pairing domestic and wild or male and female animals; a butch ram thus sits beside a female deer. The **Circus Hall Ⓓ** illustrates chaotic races at the Circus Maximus. Nearby is the small **latrine Ⓔ**, with bidets for women, and the

The Roman Villa was recently classified as a UNESCO World Heritage Site: "As the mainstay of the rural economy of the Western Roman Empire, the villa symbolises the Roman exploitation of the countryside and is one of the most sumptuous examples of its type."

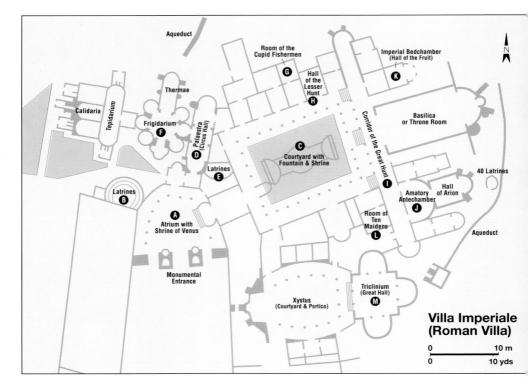

Villa Imperiale (Roman Villa)

Map on page 216

complex of thermal baths. In the octagonal **frigidarium** ❻, vestibules and plunge baths are adorned with tritons, centaurs and marine monsters, while in the anointment room next door, a man is massaged and perfumed by his naked servant.

The **Room of the Cupid Fishermen** ❼ depicts a naked mermaid clasping a dolphin in the presence of fishermen with bare buttocks or chests. Nearby is the **Hall of the Lesser Hunt** ❽, with a frenetic deer hunt, the snaring of a wild boar, and a toast to a successful day's sport. To the Romans, hunting meant food, sport and sensuality, adventure and pleasure, preferably all at once. Surrounding the main courtyard is the **Corridor of the Great Hunt** ❾, a gloriously animated work meant to be appreciated while walking. In this swirling mass of movement, chariots, lions, cheetahs, rhinos and huge swans merge in lovely autumnal colours. A mosaic sea separates Africa and Europe, echoing the division of the Roman Empire. Africa is personified by a tiger, elephant and a phoenix fleeing a burning house. The exotic, bare-breasted Queen of Sheba is being ogled by a tiger as well as by heterosexual Romans.

Sport and erotica are often neatly entwined. The **amatory antechamber** ❿, part of the Empress's suite, features Cupid fishermen netting a fine catch. The **Imperial bedchamber** ⓚ is decorated with figs, grapes and pomegranites, snatching at Greek fertility symbols. The **Room of Ten Maidens** ⓛ presents prancing girl gymnasts in costumes that prove conclusively that the bikini was not invented by Coco Chanel in the 1950s.

Nearby, the **Triclinium** ⓜ (Great Hall) is the villa's masterpiece, a flowing mythological pageant based on the Labours of Hercules. It is a symphony of pathos and poetic vision worthy of Michelangelo: the gods are threatened by chaos and decay; tortured giants writhe in agony; and a mighty nude Hercules

Aphrodite is dead: the ideal goddess of beauty has been superseded by this plurality of particular girls, portrayed on a pavement where the feet of huntsmen can trample them.

— VINCENT CRONIN
ON THE "BIKINI GIRLS"

BELOW: an antelope on a leash in the Corridor of the Great Hunt.

The Imperial Villa's plastic-roofed pavilions are due for reconstruction, to make viewing the mosaics more comfortable.

BELOW: three of the Ten Maidens.

is glorified. Passion is present in Cerberus, the three-headed dog; and in the fierce Hydra, which has a woman's face but snake-encrusted hair.

All the scenes normally excluded from Christian art lie here. The villa depicts a kaleidoscope of everyday life, highlighting intimate pleasures such as child's play and youthful dancing, massage and lovemaking. A timeless quality also infuses the mosaics' undisguised eroticism: the female nudes may have odd-shaped breasts but they dance in pagan abandon. The more accomplished male nudes are studies in virility, heightened by the use of chiaroscuro and three-dimensionality. Roman paganism worshipped heroism and masculine valour, a vitality crushed by cool Christian art. Roman gods are only too mortal. For all their energy and realism, they lack the sacred dimension of Greek or Christian art. Emperor Constantine, the last Roman proprietor of the villa, only became a Christian on his death bed. In essence, this villa remains a temple of paganism.

Greek influence

When you are sated with Roman sights, consider picnicking in the surrounding pine and eucalyptus woods. Alternatively, **Aidone** ⓮, 10 km (6 miles) northeast of Piazza Armerina, represents a window on the Greek world. The centre has a ruined castle and a clutch of austere churches enlivened by elaborate arches, warm brickwork and honey-coloured stone. San Domenico is noted for its diamond-point design on the facade. The **Museo Archeológico** (daily 9am–1.30pm, 3–7.30pm), set in a 17th-century monastery in the upper part of the village, is an introduction to the rural site of Morgantina, perhaps the most "legible" site in antiquity.

Morgantina ⓯ (9am–1 hour before sunset), just 5 km (3 miles) east, occu-

Map
on page
210

pies a rural paradise worthy of Persephone, its slopes covered in calendula, pines or olives and framed by grey-blue hills. This ancient Siculi settlement was Hellenised by a Chalcidian colony in the 6th century BC and survived for 500 years. After Morgantina fell to the Romans in 211 BC, the Greek population was sold into slavery and the farmlands given to Spanish mercenaries as a reward for subduing the city.

The remains are not aesthetically beautiful, like Piazza Armerina, but are supremely clear, an exposition of a Classical city in stone. The site reveals a civic and sacred centre bounded by a commercial district in the east and a residential quarter in the west. **Cittadella**, the hill site of the prehistoric city, is pitted with chamber tombs. Visible Hellenistic sections include: the *macellum* (covered market), designed like a shopping mall; a schoolroom complete with benches; a gymnasium with an athletic track; the *bouleuterion* (town hall); and boutiques, a granary and a theatre with good acoustics. Several of the noble **villas** contain the earliest known mosaics in the Western Mediterranean, including a floor inscription saying welcome (*euexei*). Theatrical steps lead to the **agora**, complete with aqueducts and fountain. Nearby is a temple with a *bothros*, a round well-altar used for sacrifices. The sanctuaries to the Chthonic gods show that the city's focal point was a devotion to the cult of Demeter and Persephone.

This is a reminder that mystical Enna marked the crossroads of Trinacria, ancient Sicily's three provinces. According to one historian, Enna is the hub of a giant geomantic chart, lying on ley lines spanning the island. This network of sacred spots supposedly provides the key to the region's occult power. From here, return to earth in bustling Catania Province (*see page 269*) or remain in the clouds in lofty Caltanissetta Province (*see page 197*). ❏

Morgantina was the centre of an uprising against the Greeks, led by the Sicel Ducetius. The revolt was quelled in around 450 BC, marking the end of native resistance to Greek rule.

BELOW: the Queen of Sheba appears in the Corridor of the Great Hunt.

RAGUSA PROVINCE

Ragusa favours subtlety over drama: rolling countryside framed by dry-stone walls gives way to Classical sites beside sandy beaches, or cave settlements close to the heart of baroque towns

Map on page 224

Discreet wellbeing is the keynote to the region. Novelist Gesualdo Bufalino proudly described his province as "*un ísola nell'ísola*", an island within an island. Historically, this was home to a cave-dwelling population who for millennia felt more secure clustering in grottoes or ravines. The tradition survived until recently, with caves in Ragusa, Módica and Scicli inhabited until the 1980s. It is perhaps not accidental that this earthy, community-minded province is almost a crime-free haven, surviving beyond the Mafia's reptilian gaze. Here the typical conditions for Sicilian crime are absent: a spirit of enterprise was established by Greek settlers; the feudal estates were administered better than most elsewhere and broken up earlier.

Thanks to favourable social conditions, the gap between rich and poor is narrower, especially in the country, where new agricultural approaches have not destroyed rural traditions. Unlike much of Sicily, there is a civilised balance between ancient *cultura contadina* (peasant culture) and the creativity of the *borghesia*, even if Ragusa and Módica sit smugly within a noble tradition. Class distinctions aside, the Ragusani are a hospitable people, more open than those in the mountainous interior. The provincial economy thrives on wine-growing, cattle-breeding and cheese making as well as market gardening, hot-house flowers and genetically modified tomatoes. Although Ragusa hoped to grow rich on asphalt and oil, the latter discovered in the 1960s, agriculture has brought more lasting prosperity. Still, given the underground nature of the people, it is fitting that the earth should become a source of wealth. Mines have produced asphalt that has paved the streets of Berlin, Paris, London and Glasgow. The excavations unearthed ancient quarries and Christian catacombs.

Yet industry and tourism have reached the province relatively late, with the result that, unlike other provinces, Ragusa has not concreted its coast with factories or tourist villages, even if greenhouses often blight the sand dunes. Instead, the province has cultivated an image for low-key tourism, profiting from its role as an "off the beaten track" destination. Culturally, however, there is much to enjoy, from cave settlements to Classical sites, the baroque charms of Ragusa and Módica and unspoilt beaches.

PRECEDING PAGES: across the valley to Ragusa Ibla. **LEFT:** the town's medieval rooftops. **BELOW:** detail on Ragusa's Duomo.

Capital rivalry

Ragusa was a Norman stronghold that became a fief of the Cabrera dynasty. However, the 1693 earthquake devastated the province and reduced Ragusa to rubble. The merchant class responded by building Ragusa Alta, the new city on the hill. But the aristocracy refused to desert their charred homes so recreated Ragusa Bassa (Ibla) on the original valley site. The towns only merged in 1926 and the rivalry remains. While Ragusa Ibla remains an enchanting, timeless pocket of Sicily, **Ragusa Alta ❶** is a bland city, saved only by baroque mansions, churches and bustling restaurants. The urban design is a mess: baroque opulence interlaid with Fascistic monumentality and a modern sector riven by gorges.

San Giovanni, the theatrical baroque cathedral, has an ornate facade and soaring *campanile*. Its sense of sweeping movement is echoed by the bustle of the surrounding bars and veterans' clubs in what is an exceptionally clubby city. Nearby, baroque mansions have wrought-iron balconies with sculpted cornices. One such is **Palazzo Bertini** on Corso Italia, with its sculpted masks representing "the three powers": a peasant, nobleman and merchant, a fair introduction to Ragusa's class concerns.

On Corso Vittorio Veneto is the crumbling **Palazzo Zacco**: a gap-toothed monster sticks out his tongue, mocking the church of San Vito opposite. Just south is a gorge crisscrossed by three bridges, one of which was built by a friar who tired of the daily uphill slog to his parish. The **Museo Archeológico** (daily 9am–1pm, 3–6.30pm) on Ponte Nuovo, one of the bridges, is rich in finds from Camarina and Siculi necropoli elsewhere in the province. Exhibits include tombs, Greek vases, Byzantine mosaics and a reconstruction of a potter's workshop. On the far side of the chasm is densely packed Ibla, now easily reached along the scenic new ring road, faced in subtle local stone.

In **Ragusa Ibla ❷**, the baroque city recreated on a medieval street plan, an old-world intimacy prevails. Snapshots of Ibla capture secret shrines, family crests and baroque fountains. Shrines lurk in alleys and facades, representing a need for reassurance as well as an expression of faith and a superstitious belief

Ragusa province is noted for its scented honey and robust cheeses, among the best in Sicily. Ricotta, mozzarella, provola and cacciocavallo are the main cheeses to sample, either in savoury or sweet dishes.

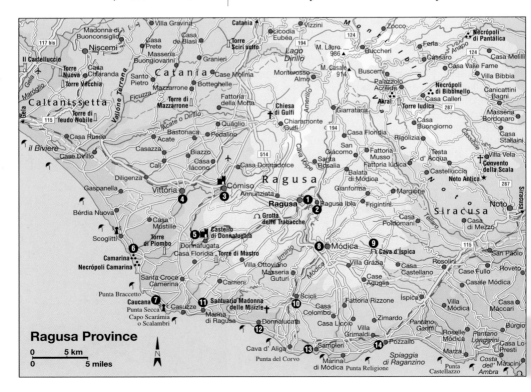

Ragusa Province

0   5 km
0   5 miles

Map on page 224

in future miracles. Ibla is also oriel windows and showy staircases, tawny-coloured stone mansions and filigree balconies hung with washing, dark court-yards popular with ambling dogs, secret arches and yellowing palm trees.

Gentrification has reversed the neglect of Ibla in recent years. The crumbling mansions are finally being restored and cherished by young, middle-class couples who have tired of the bland modern city. The easier access has helped open Ibla up to citizens from the upper town without losing Ibla's sense of separateness or leisurely pace of life. Where once Ibla was deserted in the evening, this pedestrianised quarter is now the focus for Ragusa's admittedly low-key nightlife. A number of lively bars have taken over historic palaces, with tasteful bohemian conversions coexisting with the clubby, patrician side of town.

Santa Maria delle Scale, framed by parched hills, represents the gateway to Ibla. This Gothic church was remodelled after the 1693 earthquake. A medieval portal remains, as does the Catalan-Gothic nave, complete with Renaissance ornamentation and arches adorned with beasts and flowers. From this balcony over Old Ragusa, 250 steps zigzag down to Ibla, offering a commanding view over isolated farms and the blue-tinged cupola of the cathedral below. **Palazzo della Cancelleria**, a baroque chancery, sits astride the winding staircase that links new and old Ragusa. The adjoining covered passageway, golden mansions and crumbling church make a quaint *chiaroscuro* introduction to Ibla. Next door, **Chiesa dell'Idria** is a chapel owned by the Cosentini, one of Ibla's leading families. Given the narrowness of the alleys, it takes time to gain a perspective on the robust bell tower and majolica-encrusted dome. Crushed between the church steps and Corso Mazzini is **Palazzo Cosentini**, an ancestral home adjoining the family chapel above. The sculpted balconies are a melange of bare-breasted sirens and monsters with flaring nostrils. Leering faces proffer scorpions or serpents instead of tongues, a warning not to gossip. On Piazza della Repubblica, the next square down, stands **Chiesa del Purgatorio**, a dramatic baroque church surmounting an elegant staircase. The bell tower is built on Byzantine city walls, visible from the steps of Salita dell'Orologio.

After the cosy claustrophobia so far, the spacious **Piazza Duomo** below comes as a shock. The square is lined with palm trees, baroque mansions and aristocratic clubs. The far end of the square is dominated by Gagliardi's **San Giorgio**, a masterpiece of Sicilian baroque. As the city centrepiece, this wedding cake cathedral was patronised by the nobility (St George was considered the unofficial patron saint of the Sicilian aristocracy). The sandstone church occupies a raised terrace and tricks one's eyes up from its convex centre, seemingly writhing with statues, in a crescendo to the balconied *campanile*, topped by a blue neoclassical dome that is a city landmark. Its smaller imitator, also by Gagliardi, is **San Giuseppe**, which gains in subtlety what it lacks in theatricality.

Adjoining Piazza Duomo is the arched **Palazzo Arezzo** belonging to Baron Vincenzo Arezzo, whose family has had a stake in Ragusa for centuries. The facade is adorned with sculpted hedgehogs, the family crest. The Arezzi still own much of the province, from

Giardino Ibleo is the focal point of the Ibla Buskers' Festival each October, when performers from all around the world are offered free hospitality in return for entertainment.

BELOW: Giardino Ibleo, the park of three churches.

Polizia Municipale are a town's local police force, mainly concerned with directing traffic and parking offences. The Carabinieri and Polizia Statale are far more serious.

BELOW: St George slays the dragon on Portale San Giorgio.

farmland to villas and a castle. Given their credo of enlightened paternalism, the family has endowed local hospitals, parks and churches. Ibla's nobles have always immortalised themselves in stone, linking grand baroque mansions to a graceful family chapel and even a chic gentlemen's club. Nearby is the **Circolo di Conversazione** (ring for admission), a literary salon founded by local noblemen and the indefatigable Vincenzo Arezzo. The *Belle Epoque* interior contains an allegorical *trompe l'oeil* ceiling but no conversation. Inspirational busts of Michelangelo, Galileo, Dante and Bellini represent art, science, poetry and music. But the art of aristocratic conversation is dead in sleepy Ibla: taciturn old fogeys gaze on frescoed nymphs or ponder news reviews over a cold coffee.

The adjoining **Palazzo Donnafugata** was the nobles' private theatre, gallery and reading club until opened to a slightly wider membership. Sadly, the sculpted marble staircase, sumptuous salons and gallery adorned with old masters are only visible during private banquets. Most symbolic is the heavily shuttered loggia on the *piano nobile*, an example of a *gelosia*, a secret spot from which to view visitors.

Behind the cathedral is **Palazzo la Rocca**, an austere baroque mansion transformed into the welcoming provincial tourist office, the sole city palace to which entry can be guaranteed. The facade is enlivened by bizarre balconies, depicting 18th-century aristocratic entertainment: a lute player and cherub blowing a hunting horn vie with gawky, naked lovers clinging to each other in gauche poses. The alleys in the shadow of the cathedral are what Italians readily term *suggestivo* (atmospheric). This, the heart of the ancient Jewish ghetto and artisan quarter, is slowly being restored and repopulated with younger residents and craft shops. In Largo Camerina, however, a traditional cabinetmaker survives, creating tables from olive, carob, cherry, cyprus and orange wood. More typical of the reinvigorated quarter is Al Portale, a fashionable bar carved out of former stables, close to Portale San Giorgio, or L'Antica Drogheria, on Corso XXV Aprile, a superior delicatessen selling Iblean honey and herbs, cheeses, salami and biscuits.

Giardino Ibleo, an appealing landscaped park, is set on a spur at the eastern end of Ibla. In spring, the statues, palm trees and pool are complemented by daffodils, broom and irises. Around the grounds are three ruined churches, victims of the 1693 earthquake. The multicoloured majolica dome of **San Domenico** overlooks Gothic **San Giacomo**, built on the site of a pagan temple, and **Chiesa dei Cappuccini**, a baroque monastic church. On the far side of the gardens is Portale San Giorgio, a Catalan-Gothic doorway depicting St George and the dragon. Carved in soft local stone, this is all that remains of the original church. From this uncharacteristically lush corner of old Ibla, both grizzled locals and young lovers take time to look out over terraces and dry stone walls to a valley embedded with ancient Siculi tombs.

Yet, despite its noble veneer, parts of Ibla are exceptionally poor. Within view of the heart of town are outlying quarters riddled with blind alleys, abandoned hovels and rock dwellings, side by side with remains of medieval, Byzantine and even pre-Christian

Ragusa. Set below the jagged landscape of modern Ragusa, the ancient Siculi tombs now tend to be used as storerooms, wine cellars or even garages. The valley floor is cut by a river that fed several mills until the 1980s; the scene is one of whitewashed cottages, steep steps, pots of geraniums, and peppers dried on walls Arab-style. The occasional impressive church, such as San Sebastiano, raises the tone of this ramshackle quarter. But more typical is the mill race, the air of lived-in scruffiness and the smell of woodsmoke. The elderly locals are being encouraged to move, but the last to flee will be Ibla's grandmothers, for whom lace making remains an engrossing winter pastime.

West of Ragusa

From Ragusa, the rural hinterland unfolds. On higher ground, olives, almonds and carobs abound but in well-irrigated areas greenhouse cultivation is gaining ground. Where there is enough water, on the coast or in river canyons, dwarf palms, holm oaks, plane trees, Aleppo pines and lentisks flourish. But on the plains, the view is of dust-coloured farmhouses, low dry-stone walls, endless fields, rugged limestone plains beaten to the colour of sandstone.

A dramatic descent from the Iblean hills leads across a vast plain to **Cómiso ❸**, a muddled medieval and baroque town, that had the misfortune to become a controversial NATO military base in the 1980s. Peace protests were the price residents paid for housing the last Cruise missiles located on European soil. As a bonus, 7,000 American soldiers subsidised the local economy until the final removal of the missiles in 1991. Since then, most of those employed by the former base have been taken on by the capacious Sicilian civil service, leaving part of the base as temporary housing for Albanian refugees. However, there are long-term plans to

Map on page 224

Legend has it that water from the Fonte di Diana in Cómiso will not mix with wine when poured by unchaste hands.

BELOW: retail opportunities, Ibla.

TIP

Around Vittória there are several wine trails, to put you on the right track for Cerasuolo di Vittória and Nero d'Avola wines and producers. Although the trails aren't yet signposted, a wine route map can be picked up from the local tourist office.

BELOW: Cómiso's Fonte di Diana is built over a Roman spring.

transform the base into a new airport to boost tourism in southeastern Sicily.

Ruled by the Aragonese Naselli dynasty from the 15th to the 18th centuries, Cómiso still has a feudal castle. The **Castello** retains its original Gothic portal and octagonal tower, converted from a Byzantine baptistry, but the rest was remodelled in the 16th century. Although shattered by the 1693 earthquake, fragments of Classical Cómiso survive: Piazza di Munícipio contains a **Fountain to Diana**, whose waters once gushed into the Roman baths. **Santa Maria delle Grazie**, a monastic chapel, offers the town's most gruesome sight: mummified bodies of monks and benefactors stacked in horrific poses.

Vittória ❹, further west, is a wealthy, wine-producing centre on the slopes of the Iblean hills. The city was founded in 1607 by Vittória Colonna, the daughter of a Spanish viceroy and wife of the Count of Módica. Since aristocratic power in parliament was closely linked to the size of the feudal estates, Vittória tried to make the town as populous as possible. Today, this neat city remains wealthy rather than healthy: under the surface lurks a crime and drugs problem, proof of the Mafia's toehold in the province, a fear confirmed by a big Mafia massacre here in 1999. Giuseppe Fava, a Sicilian journalist murdered by the Mafia, once dismissed Vittória as "a city built by those without the time, money, imagination or background to make anywhere better."

Even so, the elegant **Piazza del Pópolo** contains the baroque church of Madonna delle Grazie. Amid the bland modernity are bourgeois mansions with grand courtyards. From the city gardens are views across the fertile valley to the sea. Deforestation has made way for market gardening, with flowers and peaches added to the traditional crops of olive oil and wine. From here, it is a reasonable coastal drive northwest to Agrigento.

Map on page 224

South of Ragusa

Castello di Donnafugata ❺ (Tues–Sun 9am–1pm) lies 20 km (12 miles) southwest of the provincial capital. Set in a carob and palm plantation, this modern Moorish pastiche feels authentically Sicilian. The castle dates from 1648 but was redesigned as a full-blown *Ottocento* fantasy by Corrado Arezzo, Baron of Donnafugata, in the 19th century, and remained in the family until the 1970s. Arezzo, a prominent politician and campaigner for Sicilian independence, created Donnafugata as his whimsical refuge from revolutionary politics.

The exterior is a Venetian palace transplanted by magic carpet to *The Arabian Nights*. The crenellated facade, inspired by an austere Arab desert fort, is softened by an arcaded Moorish balcony. Below the arched windows opens an amazing loggia in Venetian-Gothic style. The Arab inspiration is not wholly fake: in the 10th century an Arab village named Ayn as Jayat (Fountain of Health) occupied the site, and the palace was inspired by La Ziza in Palermo (*see page 129*). The finest rooms are naturally on the *piano nobile* and include a smoking room, picture gallery, billiards room, winter garden and a salon for conversation. The frescoed music room illustrates the noble pastimes of painting, *bel canto* and piano recitals as well as tombola and chess.

Although sumptuous, the palace is coated in charming Sicilian neglect. In the atmospheric *salone degli specchi* (room of mirrors), floating drapes, faded gilt, inlaid tables and dusty chandeliers conspire to create an atmosphere straight out of *The Leopard*. During World War II, the Luftwaffe commandeered the pavilion, along with the rest of the castle. However, the troops respected Donnafugata so all the baron's quirky touches remain, from the cute well and the children's maze to the artificial grotto and the silly seat that squirts out water. The only damage done was to "the friar's joke", in which an unsuspecting visitor was embraced by a mechanical friar as he entered the house. Not surprisingly, a Nazi officer disliked the joke and shot the friar to smithereens.

The ancient Greek site of **Camarina** ❻ lies on the coast just 12 km (7 miles) west of Donnafugata. Founded in 598 BC, two centuries after Siracusa (the ferocity of the local Siculi tribes was a deterrent to earlier settlement), this sophisticated piece of urban planning covered three hills at the mouth of the Ippari river. The city of perfect parallel lines was destroyed by the Romans in AD 258. The **Antiquarium** (daily 9am–one hour before sunset) marks the centre of the site, an array of dispersed city walls, a tower, tombstones and sarcophagi. The foundations of a **Temple to Athena** lie beside the museum. Nearby, the **House of the Altar** has rooms radiating from a central courtyard with a battered mosaic floor. Other Hellenistic dwellings include a merchant's house, confirmed by the presence of scales and measuring devices. At the foot of the cliffs is the chic Kamerina Club Med, French hedonism only a stone's throw away.

At **Punta Secca**, the headland just south of Camarina, the Roman port of **Caucana** ❼ is slowly being excavated. The port was partly preserved by sand, as at Gela (*see page 203*) further down the coast. The lush site is lovely but inscrutable, a puzzle com-

The Castello di Donnafugata, a 19th-century palace built on the site of an Arab village, combines Venetian Gothic with Moorish whimsy.

BELOW: Piazza del Pópolo, Vittória.

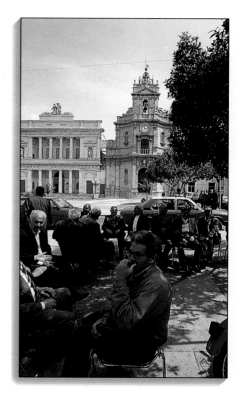

TIP

Cakes are a local art
form in Módica,
especially chocolate
pastries and *cubbaita*,
an Arab sweet made
from almonds, honey
and sesame seeds.
Try them at **L'Antica
Dolceria Bonajuto**, on
Corso Umberto, one of
the most distinguished
cake shops in Sicily.

pounded by the discovery of Hellenistic amphora, Roman coins and Jewish candelabra. Amid the rubble, the clearest find is a Byzantine church with a colourful mosaic of a goat.

Southeast of Ragusa

Beyond farmsteads and stone walls are two high road bridges and a sudden glimpse of a grey-brown town buried in a deep valley. **Módica ❽**, the former county capital, is perched on a ridge that spills down into the valley; the upper reaches were pitted with caves that were inhabited until recently but are now largely abandoned to prickly pears. At first sight, the setting is more prepossessing than the town but Módica repays exploration, from its mysterious alleys and mouthwatering food to its illustrious history as the most powerful fiefdom in Sicily. The prosperous Arab citadel of Mudiqah became a fief of the Chiaramonte family in 1296 and merged into the county of Módica. After succumbing to Spanish influence, it passed from the Caprera viceroys to the Henriquez, Spanish absentee landlords. Around town are the family crests of the three dynasties: respectively, mountains, a goat and two castles. Módica's charm lies in the complexity of the multi-layered town, with its tiers of sumptuous churches and shabby palaces stacked up on the hill.

Perched precariously on a slope, **San Giorgio** (daily 9am–noon, 4–8pm) makes a bold entrance against a backdrop of rocky terraces. This noble church surmounts a flight of 250 steps. The writer Vincent Cronin said: "After such a meandering introduction, which arouses our hopes to the highest pitch, all but the greatest building would appear to fail." But Gagliardi's masterpiece does not disappoint: its imagination, movement and magic encapsulate Sicilian

BELOW: the remains
of the ancient
port of Camarina
overlook Club
Med windsurfers.

baroque.This frothy concoction of flowing lines and curvy ornament seems barely rooted to the spot. The vision is one of rococo splendour, shadowy recesses and a soaring belfry silhouetted against the sky. San Giorgio's rival is the opulent **Duomo di San Pietro**, reached via a theatrical staircase along which tiers of apostles welcome visitors much like latter-day party greeters.

After such spectacle, other churches play walk-on parts. However, in the neighbouring Vicolo Grimaldi is the frescoed Byzantine chapel of **San Nicolò Inferiore**, under the baroque church of the same name. The well-maintained chapel was built in a grotto, in keeping with Ragusa's cave-dwelling heritage, and retains traces of frescoes. Just around the corner, **Cripta del Convento di San Domenico** (key and guide from the tourist office on Via Grimaldi) is a mysterious retreat in the poorly restored convent, now the town hall. The medieval crypt was unearthed during renovations in 1972: in different periods of its history it was used as a burial chamber for the Dominicans and as a torture chamber linked to the Inquisition.

Museo Campailla (Mon–Fri 9am–noon) is one of the most bizarre minor museums in the province: an early syphilis clinic founded by Tommaso Campailla, a 17th-century local doctor and philosopher, and used until the early 20th century. The cure, a refinement on 8th-century Arab practice, involved placing the patients in hot mercury chambers, heated by hot coals to produce a sauna-like effect, and subjecting sufferers to vaporous infusions. The eerie original chambers are still visible, surreally interconnected with rooms where city council workers go about their normal business.

From Módica, it is a short drive south to baroque Scicli and the coast or southeast to the Ispica canyon and Siracusa province. **Cava d'Ispica** ❾ (daily

Map on page 224

Although once known as "the Venice of the South", Módica suffered a disastrous flood in 1902 and as a result all its rivers were diverted and canals covered over.

BELOW: chromatic shades of Módica.

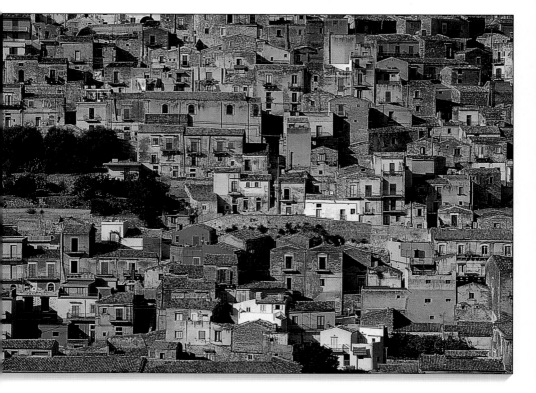

Rosario Gagliardi's masterpiece, San Giorgio in Módica, was begun in 1738. The 250-step stairway that leads to the church was not completed until 1818.

BELOW: Cava d'Ispica has been inhabited since prehistoric times.

9am–6.30pm) is an 11-km (7-mile) limestone gorge whose ghostly galleries and caves have been inhabited almost continuously since prehistoric times. The southern end of the narrow valley is overlooked by the **Castello**, a rock shaped like a castle. Below is a lush valley floor overgrown with oleanders, prickly pear, lentisk and carobs. The better tombs lie in the northern end of the gorge, close to the entrance to the site. The honeycomb of galleries conceal native Siculi "oven" tombs, Greek necropoli and early Christian tombs. Highlights include the **Larderia**, the most complete set of early Christian catacombs in southeastern Sicily, and the **Grotta di Santa Maria**, a rock chapel that was inhabited until the 1950s. Sadly, a lack of funds for maintenance means that sections of the site are off limits. Il Noce Antico (tel: 0932-906846) is a pleasant rustic *trattoria* with tables overlooking the archaeological site.

Southwest of the canyons is **Scicli ❿**, a neglected baroque gem in mothballs. The road from Ispica reveals vistas of a grotto-encrusted hillside opening onto San Matteo, the medieval settlement on the slopes, and the baroque heart of Scicli below. Scicli's fusty city churches and fantastic baroque mansions feel out of place in this sleepy market town. The ochre-coloured facades are decorated with sirens, monsters and fauns, part of the cavalcade of Christian and mythological creatures inspired by designs on Greek temples or Romanesque cathedrals. The baroque centre has been partly renovated in recent years and the predominantly elderly population has been leavened with new arrivals, young craftspeople, from carpenters to workers in forged iron. Still, much of the battered, inward-looking atmosphere remains, and there are, as yet, no hotels in town.

Piazza Italia, the main square, opens with the baroque **Chiesa Sant'Ignazio**. Its gilded interior holds a painting of an historic battle for Scicli between the

Turks and Christians in 1091. The successful intercession of a bellicose Madonna supposedly brought victory, an event celebrated in Scicli's city festival and in the number of churches dedicated to the Virgin. Just north, on Via Mormino Penna, the best-preserved baroque street, stands **San Giovanni**, with its well-restored concave-convex facade. Unlike much Sicilian baroque architecture, a dazzling exterior is matched by an equally impressive interior: the exuberantly stuccoed surface has a gaudy emerald and turquoise Moorish design. The church was previously the preserve of cloistered nuns, who had permission to sit in balconied splendour to watch processions on feast days.

Just south, **Palazzo Beneventano** has beautiful balconies, with fantastic corbels representing mythical beasts, Moors and ghoulish human masks. Almost as splendid is nearby **Palazzo Fava**, a riot of galloping griffons and horses ridden by cherubs. Just east, at the foot of the rock, loom the majestic cupola and domed apses of **Santa Maria la Nova**, signalling the start of Scicli's intriguing medieval quarter, dotted with modest houses, alleys and steps overflowing with pot plants.

Overlooking the town is a ruined castle and the newly-restored **Chiesa San Matteo**, on the site of the original Siculi settlement. The attractive new path that winds to the top has won favour as the locals' chosen summer stroll. From here, secret passageways, dating from Saracen sieges, are said to lead out of town. The hill is pitted with that which were inhabited until the 1980s. They still serve a purpose as wine cellars, garages and storerooms for farm produce.

Beside the seaside

Ragusa province has some of Sicily's best beaches. Less than 10 km (6 miles) from Scicli, the coastal landscape spans sand dunes, marshes, eye-catching rocky beaches, and shingle strands dotted with heather. Delightful sandy beaches await around the archaeological site of **Camarina**, with a secluded rocky beach on **Punta Braccetto**, the headland beyond. Heading eastwards, **Marina di Ragusa ⑪**, lined with fish restaurants, contains the only managed beaches, equipped for windsurfing and other water sports. In summer, this winter ghost town turns into a bustling resort, with 10,000 villas let to outsiders. Just east is the wooded coastal nature reserve of **Fiume Irmínio**, with the broad sandy beaches of **Donnalucata ⑫** beyond, a stretch of coast rapidly being swamped by greenhouses.

A 7-km (4-mile) coastal drive leads east to the rocky headland of **Punta del Corvo**, and on to coastline that is further south than Tunisia. **Sampieri ⑬** stands out for its self-consciously quaint atmosphere, a prettified fishing village popular with Ragusani out for a family romp in the sand dunes. Further along the coast, at the port of **Pozzallo ⑭**, the industrial complex is too close to the beach for comfort, although the beaches are perfectly acceptable further east, towards Siracusa province. Still, Pozzallo is a pleasant enough place to stay for a lunch of salted tuna or sardines, both caught and processed in the port. From here, escape on a day trip to Malta by ferry, or visit the baroque masterpiece of Noto. ❑

Map on page 224

C'era una volta in Sicilia *(Once upon a time in Sicily)*, was filmed in Scicli and Noto in late 1999. *The film, starring Michele Placido and directed by Fabio Conversi, depicts the arrival of Garibaldi's troops in Sicily.*

BELOW: grotesque cherubs adorn Palazzo Beneventano.

SIRACUSA CITY

Alluring, civilised, soporific Siracusa is less dynamic than Catania, less sultry than Palermo, yet somehow steals most visitors' hearts as the capital of sheer indulgence

Map on page 236

Cicero called it the loveliest city in the world: the island of Ortygia, separated from the mainland by a narrow channel. Its name resounds as Syracuse in academic circles abroad. This living essay on lingering nostalgia prides itself on discerning tourism, as sophisticated as the city itself. Siracusa is the summation of Sicilian splendour, with an emphasis on Greek heritage. The lack of Arab influence is often cited as an explanation for the city's low profile in terms of Mafia ties. It is oddly fitting that dozy Siracusa should be home to the International Institute of Criminal Science.

The cultivated city supposedly witnessed the birth of comedy in its Greek theatre. Today Siracusa boasts the only school of Classical drama outside Athens. Apart from tales of Artemis and Apollo, Siracusa gave the world architectural beauty with a baroque heart: Ortygia's facades are framed by wrought-iron balconies as free as billowing sails. As Sicily's greatest seafaring power, Siracusa indulges an affinity with the sea that pervades city myths and art. Siracusa's sensual sculpture of Venus emerging from the breeze-swept sea embodies this cult of water. Perhaps daunted by such a glorious past, today's citizens have a reputation for being lackadaisical dreamers and apathetic underachievers: local lore has it that even the leaders of the criminal classes have to be drawn from the neighbouring province of Catania.

LEFT: statuary around the Fonte Aretusa, Ortygia. **BELOW:** a Greek vase in the Museo Archeológico.

Classical glory

The city was founded in 733 BC, a year after Naxos, by Corinthian settlers who maintained links with Sparta. Although it was ruled by a succession of cruel but occasionally benevolent Tyrants, Siracusa rose to become the supreme Mediterranean power of its age under Dionysius the Elder. The decisive battle was Siracusa's defeat of Athens at sea in 415 BC.

During a despotic 38-year rule, Dionysius personified Sicilian tyranny. He was a demagogue, a megalomaniac, a military strategist, a monumental builder, an inspired engineer and an execrable tragedian. As the most powerful figure of his day, Dionysius presided over Siracusa's golden age, with the grandest public works in the Western world, surpassing Athens in power and prestige.

After the sun set on ancient Greece, Siracusa became a Roman province and was supposedly evangelised by St Peter and St Paul on their way to Rome. Certainly, the city catacombs are the finest outside the capital. Siracusa became the capital of Byzantium, albeit briefly, in the 7th century and produced several popes and patriarchs of Constantinople. After being sacked by the Arabs in AD 878 and the Normans in 1085, the city sank into oblivion but quietly prospered under Spanish rule.

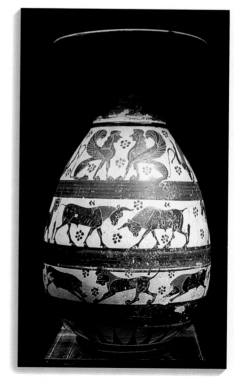

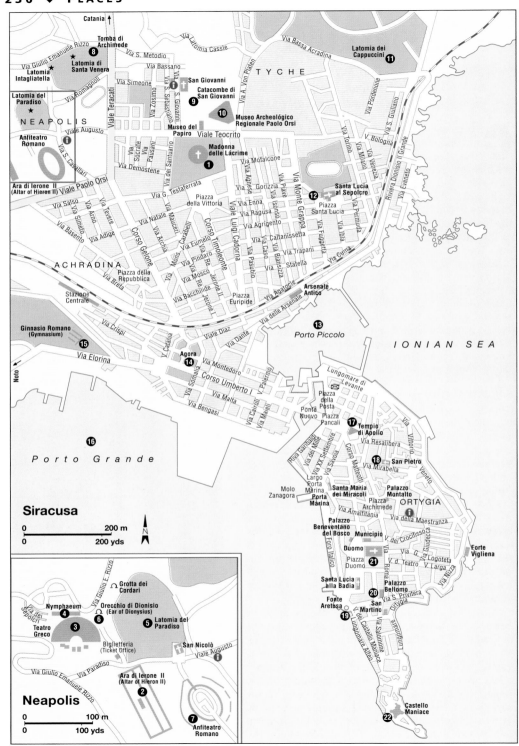

Catania ↑

Tomba di
Archimede

Via Giulio Emanuele Rizzo
8

Latomia di
Santa Venera

Via Giulio Emanuele Rizzo
Latomia
Intagliatella

Latomia del
Paradiso

NEAPOLIS

Anfiteatro
Romano

Ara di Ierone II
(Altar of Hieron II)

Viale Paolo Orsi

Viale Teracati

Via Romagnoli

Via Zosimo

Via S. Sebastiano

Via S. Metodio

Via Bassano

Via Simeone

Via Latomia Cassle

Via Bassa Acradina

TYCHE

Latomia dei
Cappuccini
11

Via A. Von Platen

Via S. Giuliano

San Giovanni

Catacombe di
San Giovanni
9

10

Museo Archeológico
Regionale Paolo Orsi

Museo del
Papiro

Viale Teocrito

Via Torino

V. Bologna

Via Milano

Via Veneto

Riviera Dionisio II Grande

Madonna
delle Lácrime
1

Via Socrate

Via Pausani

Via dei Santuario

Via Demostene

Via G. Testaferrata

Via Mofalcone

Via Agnese

Via Gorizia

Via Plave

Via Monte Grappa

Santa Lucia
al Sepolcro
12

Piazza
Santa Lucia

Via Permuda

Via Eleneto

Piazza
della Vittoria

Via Enna

Via Ragusa

Via Sonso

Via Agrigento

Via Paso

Via Blanisza

Via Fuggeta

Via Ibla

Corso Gelone

Via Natale

Via Archia

Via Maukeri

Corso Timoleonte

Viale Luigi Cadorna

Via Caso

Via Trapani

Via Cuma

Via Salso

Via Tevere

Via Simeto

Via Arno

Via Adige

Via Baseato

Mons. Carabelli

Via Eumelo

Via Pindaro

Via Mosco

Via Bacchilide

Via Re. Jetone II.

Jetone II.

Jetone I.

ACHRADINA

Via Breta

Piazza della
Repubblica

Piazza
Euripide

Via Anstocle

Statella

Via delle Arsenale

Arsenale
Antico

Stazione
Centrale

Via Crispi

Viale Diaz

Via Dante

Porto Piccolo
13

IONIAN SEA

Ginnasio Romano
(Gymnasium)
15

Via Elorina

V. Catania

Agora
14

Via Montedoro

Via Palermo

Corso Umberto I

Via Malta

Via Cairoli

Via Maleli

Via Bengasi

Via Somalia

Lungomare di
Levante

Piazza
della
Posta

Ponte
Nuovo

Piazza
Pancali

Tempio
di Apollo
17

Via Vittorio

Via Resalibera

Riva Garibaldi

Corso XX Settembre

Via Savoia

Corso Matteotti

Via Mirabella

18

San Pietro

Noto ↓

16

Porto   Grande

Molo
Zanagora

Largo
Porta
Marina

Porta
Marina

Santa Maria
dei Miracoli

Piazza
Archimede

Via Amalfitania

ORTYGIA

Via della Maestranza

Palazzo
Beneventano
del Bosco

Municipio

Duomo

Piazza
Duomo
21

Santa Lucia
alla Badia

20

Palazzo
Bellomo

San
Martino

Forte
Aretusa
19

V. dei Crocifisso

Via G. Logoteta

Via Larga

Foro Italico

V. d. Teatro

Via Roma

Via Nizza

Forte
Vigliena

Palazzo
Montalto

Via S. Privitera

Via Giudecca

Ortygia

Via Salamone

Via Castello Maniace

Lungomare Alfeo

Lungomare Alfeo

Castello
Maniace
22

Siracusa

0 ——— 200 m
0 ——— 200 yds

N

Grotta dei
Cordari

Orecchio di Dionisio
(Ear of Dionysius)

Nymphaeum
4

Via del Sepolcri

Via Giulio E. Rizzo

6

5

Latomia del
Paradiso

Teatro
Greco

3

Biglietteria
(Ticket Office)

San Nicolò

Viale Augusto

Via Giulio Emanuele Rizzo

Via Paradiso

Ara di Ierone II
(Altar of Hieron II)

2

Neapolis

0 ——— 100 m
0 ——— 100 yds

7

Anfiteatro
Romano

City sectors

Siracusa is a diffuse, segmented city whose ancient Greek divisions still resonate deeply with residents. **Ortygia**, the cultural island at the heart of the Greek city, remains true to its vocation: despite a grand baroque and Catalan carapace, this beguiling backwater feels intimate, informal and quietly cultured. This is where the locals choose to while away the long summer evenings. By contrast, **Tyche**, the northern quarter on the mainland, can feel like the city of the dead: studded with ancient catacombs, Tyche lay beyond the bounds of Roman Syracuse and thus remains a testament to the impact of early Christianity. **Achradina**, bordering Ortygia, remains the classic commercial quarter, while **Neapolis**, to the north, though no longer "new", still embodies the ancient Greeks' notion of public and sacred space, from theatres to sanctuaries.

While Tyche and Achradina suffered bomb damage in 1943, much of Siracusa is unscathed, and continues to slumber through natural and man-made disasters, from an earthquake in 1991 to a sluggish economy and slothful public administration in more recent years. Both as a useful landmark and as an antidote to Classical beauty, the ugly modern church of **Madonna delle Lácrime ❶** signals the way to the archaeological zones of Neapolis and Tyche. Visible from most of the city, this popular pilgrimage centre commemorates a modern miracle: in 1953 a statue of Mary reputedly cried and the spot became a shrine in the shape of a giant teardrop (daily 6am–12.30pm, 4–7pm).

To the west lies Neapolis, the ancient quarter also synonymous with its sprawling archaeological park (daily, 9am–one hour before sunset) containing rough-hewn quarries, grandiose theatres and tombs. Although set among shady fir trees and olive groves, the site is still sweltering in summer. Still, avoiding the boisterous coach parties and tawdry stalls selling painted papyrus scrolls, independent visitors can quickly melt into the spacious Greek ruins.

A stroll to the Greek theatre passes the rubble of **Ara di Ierone (Hieron II's Altar) ❷**, a sacrificial altar once decorated by imposing *telamones* (giants). Surrounded by trees, the vast **Teatro Greco ❸** seats 15,000 and is often called the masterpiece of ancient Greece. This astonishing accomplishment dates from 474 BC although much was altered in the 3rd century BC. The *cavea* (horseshoe of tiered seats) is divided into two by a *diazoma* (corridor), and vertically cut into nine blocks of seats bearing inscriptions to deities and dignitaries. A satisfying climb to the top provides striking views over modern Siracusa and the sea. On the terrace is a **nymphaeum ❹**, a complex of waterfall, springs and grotto that once contained statues and niches for votive offerings.

In the Roman era, the theatre became an amphitheatre, with water dammed and diverted to flood the orchestra for mock naval battles or gladiatorial combat. But among the Greeks, it was a stage that witnessed the first performances of all Aeschylus' tragedies. The theatrical tradition is maintained today, in alternate (even-numbered) years, with the dramas of Sophocles and Euripides played on a stage once viewed by such notables as Plato and Archimedes.

Although partially closed, **Via dei Sepolcri**, the

Map on page 236

ACTRESS Grazia Visconti loves playing tragedy in the Teatro Greco. She explains: "The sacredness of the site fills the actors with a sense of grandeur and destiny." She even practises singing in the vaulted chamber known as the Ear of Dionysius.

BELOW: the Ear of Dionysius, Neapolis.

path of tombs, offers glimpses of tombs and carved niches at the upper level, while the lower level leads down to the *latomie*, giant quarries used as prisons in Classical times. A wooded path slopes behind the back of the Greek theatre to a secret rocky arch and the lush **Latomia del Paradiso** ❺. These ancient quarries were once vaulted but are now open to the sun, bursting with olive and citrus groves or overgrown with cacti and ferns.

Here too is the cavernous **Orecchio di Dionisio (Ear of Dionysius)** ❻, named by Caravaggio after its resemblance to an upside-down earlobe. The poetic painter fancied that this echoing, dank, weirdly shaped cave was used by Dionysius to eavesdrop on his prisoners. The adjoining **Grotta dei Cordari** (currently sealed) is scored with chisel marks because it was here that rope makers stretched out their damp strands and tested their ropes for stress. A tunnel links Latomia del Paradiso with **Latomia Intagliatella** and a rocky arch leads on to **Latomia di Santa Venera**, lemon-scented quarries pitted with votive niches.

It is hard to imagine that these lush gardens were once torture chambers. After Siracusa's decisive victory over Athens, the prisoners of war were lowered by crane into these pits. There was no need to mount guard: keeping captives alive involved no more than lowering a slave's half-rations and a drop of water. After 10 gruelling weeks, the non-Athenians who had survived were hauled out and sold as slaves. The Athenians were left to suffer before being branded with the mark of the Siracusan horse and also sold as slaves.

A separate entrance (but the same ticket) leads to the **Anfiteatro Romano** ❼, the Roman amphitheatre ringed by trees but drowned by traffic noise. While this tumbledown affair is not comparable with the amphitheatre at Nîmes, the site has charm. A path of stone sarcophagi leads to the theatre, complete with

Allegedly, some of the Athenians held captive in the quarries in 415 BC were released when they were able to recite passages from Euripides, a poet admired above all others in Siracusa.

BELOW: the glorious Greek theatre of ancient Siracusa.

rectangular animal pits and the base of an Augustan arch. Between the Greek theatre and Roman amphitheatre is **San Nicolò**, a Romanesque church concealing a Roman cistern. A circuit along **Via Giulio Emanuele Rizzo** reveals a cross-section of the Classical city, including an aqueduct, the tomb-studded Via dei Sepolcri and rear views of Neapolis.

Map on page 236

Further uphill lie the **Grotticelli Necropolis**, a warren of Hellenistic and Byzantine tombs, including the supposed **Tomba di Archimede** (Tomb of Archimedes) ❽, framed by a dignified Roman portico. The Romans insisted that Archimedes' death was accidental, despite his creation of diabolical death traps used against them during the city siege. This quarter forms part of ancient Tyche, characterised by labyrinthine catacombs that often follow the course of Greek aqueducts. The **Catacombe di San Giovanni** (San Giovanni Catacombs) ❾ (9am–1pm, 2–5pm; closed Tues) provide entry to the persecuted world of the early Christians. Escorted by a friar, visitors view early Christian sarcophagi, a 4th-century drawing of St Peter and a mosaic depicting Original Sin. The network of galleries open into space-creating rotundas. On the walls are primitive frescoes and arcane symbols, with a mysterious fish-headed boat or dead dove bound by an *alpha* and *omega*. A secret Christian code? A pagan transmigration of souls? Academics disagree.

In the wild garden outside is the shell of **San Giovanni Evangelista**, with its rose window and sculpted door often masked by monastic underwear drying in the sun. This modest church was Siracusa's first cathedral and is dedicated to St Marcian, the city's earliest bishop. Crooked steps lead down to **Cripta di San Marziano** and more catacombs. Light filters in on faded frescoes of Santa Lucia, sculpted cornices and an altar supposedly used by St Paul. Amid Greek lettering and crosses are primitive depictions of a phoenix and a bull.

BELOW: devout theatre-goers.

Drawing and writing on papyrus is a Siracusan speciality. Artists will create a papyrus parchment to your design.

Probably the finest archaeological collection in Sicily lies in the **Museo Archeológico Regionale Paolo Orsi** ❿ (daily 9am–1.30pm; and 3.30–6.30pm in high season) on the neighbouring Viale Teocrito, fittingly built over a quarry and pagan necropolis. In succession, the well-organised museum reveals the prehistoric, Classical and regional sections from Siracusa and its colonies, ending with finds at Gela and Agrigento. In the prehistory section, the stars are reconstructed necropoli, earthenware pots from Pantalica, and depictions of Cyclops and dwarf elephants.

In the Classical sections, the tone is set by two strikingly different works: the "immodest modesty" of the headless Venus Landolina and an Archaic sculpture of a seated fertility goddess suckling her twins, found in Megara Hyblaea. Elsewhere, the collection bursts with beauty and horror: lion's head gargoyles, Aztec-like masks, a Winged Victory, a terracotta frieze of grinning gorgons; a Medusa with her tongue lolling out. Away from the horrors, smoothly virile marble torsos of *kouroi* (heroic youths) await. Beauty, both pure and sensual, lingers in the Roman sarcophagus of a couple called Valerius and Adelphia or in fragments of friezes from Selinunte and Siracusa.

Around the corner, the **Museo del Papiro** (daily, 9am–2pm) displays collections of papyrus parchment and presents Egyptian paper making techniques. Studios throughout the city offer to reproduce anything in papyrus, from old masters to holiday snapshots.

BELOW: meeting beside the Fonte Aretusa, Ortygia.

Off the adjoining Via Von Platen are the **Vigna Cassia Catacombs**, galleries of burial chambers and frescoed chambers, which lead to **Latomia dei Cappuccini** ⓫, the most picturesque quarries. Set on the coast, these huge honeycombed pits are matched by sculptural vegetation, but currently they can only

be viewed from Via Acradina above. From the adjoining Piazza Cappuccini are stirring views of the rocky shore. Further south are a series of (closed) catacombs surrounding **Santa Lucia al Sepolcro** ⓬, a Byzantine church founded by San Zosimo, the first Greek Bishop of Siracusa, and dedicated to St Lucy, the city's beloved patron saint.

On the **Porto Piccolo** ⓭ are the scant remains of the city's ancient **arsenal** and rough-hewn boathouses. Nearby stands the Byzantine bathhouse where legend has it that Emperor Constans II was assassinated with a soap dish in AD 668. On **Piazzale del Foro Siracusa**, just behind the port, is the so-called **Forum**, actually the **Agora** ⓮ of Achradina. This was the commercial centre of the Greek city but sadly suffered bombing by both the Allies and the Luftwaffe in 1943.

Further west lies the **Ginnasio Romano** (Roman Gymnasium) ⓯, a theatre and shrine occupying a picturesquely flooded spot. Although its origins are obscure, the shrine was conceivably dedicated to Oriental deities. The raised portico is well-preserved and shimmers obligingly. Nearby, the **Porto Grande** ⓰, where Dionysius defeated the Athenian navy in 415 BC, is now an industrial and mercantile port.

Ortygia

A stroll across **Ponte Nuovo** leads past prettily moored boats and pastel-coloured Venetian *palazzi* to the **Darsena**, the inner docks. On the far side is atmospheric Ortygia, with views of a tumbledown bridge and grand *palazzi* lining Riva Garibaldi. Rivalled only by Ragusa as the capital of aimless wandering, this partly pedestrianised island is the place for leisurely lunches, sum-

In the summer of 1999 the facades of Piazza Duomo were draped in Fascist insignia and alleys teemed with Mussolini's intimidating Brownshirts. The Sicilian director Giuseppe Tornatore had chosen Ortygia as the setting for Malena, his spirited romance set in Fascist times.

BELOW:
mending nets in
the Porto Piccolo.

Think-Tank Man

The idea of Archimedes leaping from his bath with a cry of "Eureka!" is, alas, untrue. While testing a gold cup suspected of being a mere alloy, Archimedes realised that the water displaced by an object was equal to the object's weight, not its volume. The object either floats or sinks so *Eureka* (Greek for "I have found it"): Archimedes had the principle of specific gravity and the basis of hydrostatics.

Archimedes, born in 287 BC, worked for Hieron, the Tyrant of Siracusa. While watching the Tyrant's builders and marine engineers at work, he devised theories worth a "Eureka!" each. His greatest discovery was the formulae for the areas and volumes of spheres, cylinders and other shapes, which anticipated the theories of integration by 1,800 years.

Archimedes was not a mere theoretician. He was intensely practical in an age when Siracusa was the most inventive place on earth. Dionysius's think-tank devised the

long-range catapult which saved Siracusa from the Carthaginian fleet. Archimedes built on this tradition with the Archimedean screw, still used for raising water, and with siege engines that did sterling service against the Romans. Polybius says the Romans "failed to reckon with the ability of Archimedes, nor did they foresee that, in some cases, the genius of one man is more effective than any number of hands."

"Eureka" apart, Archimedes is often quoted as saying "Give me a place to stand and I will move the world," implying that he understood the principles of leverage. It is unlikely that he anticipated the laser beam by arranging magnifying glasses to set fire to the Roman fleet at long range. But he did produce a hydraulic serpent contraption that enabled one man to operate a ship's pumps.

He also played a part in the construction of Hieron's remarkable 4,000-ton ship. Enough timber to build 60 conventional ships was brought from Mount Etna for the hull, which was then covered with sheet lead. The ship had three decks, one of which had a mosaic floor depicting *The Iliad*. The upper deck had a gymnasium, a lush garden with shady walks and a temple to Venus paved with Sicilian agate. The state cabin had a timepiece, a marble bath, and 10 horses in stalls on either side.

Yet this was no pleasure craft. It carried a long-range catapult, a device fitted to the masts that swung out over an attacking vessel and disgorged a huge rock, and also had a "cannon" that fired 18-ft (5.5-metre) arrows. Archimedes designed a system of screws for launching the vessel. It was then loaded with corn, 10,000 jars of Sicilian salt fish and 500 tonnes of wool and despatched to Ptolemy in Egypt as a gift.

Keen to exploit Archimedes' genius, the Roman commander Marcellus wanted him taken alive when the Romans occupied Siracusa. But a Roman soldier came across an old codger apparently doodling in sand. Archimedes was dabbling in his latest brainwave and protested sharply when the soldier unknowingly stepped on his drawing. The soldier drew his sword and casually killed one of the greatest men in the world. ❑

LEFT: a bronze statue of the great inventor.

mer promenades and sleepy ruminations amid a crumbling cityscape. Despite EU funds recently earmarked for the restoration of Ortygia, the city's bureaucratic lethargy and lobbying by vested interest groups mean that most projects remain stalled: the citizens grumble while the dilapidated palaces gradually collapse. Nonetheless, after the flight of families to the faceless suburbs in the 1960s, the city's creeping gentrification is attracting back a more enlightened generation, particularly young professionals in search of urban charm.

Graced with two natural harbours, fresh springs and the blessing of the Delphic oracle, this seductive island was dedicated to the huntress Artemis, with the chief temple known as "the couch of Artemis". In Christian times, the goddess fused with Santa Lucia, the city's patron saint, and her cult is still venerated in city festivals.

Heralding the entrance to Ortygia lurks the **Tempio di Apollo** (Temple of Apollo) ⓱ in the middle of an unprepossessing square. Now sunken and dishevelled, it is the oldest city temple, built in 565 BC and discovered by chance in 1862. This Archaic-Doric temple was dedicated to Artemis (Diana) as well as her brother Apollo, whose name is legible on the steps of the base. The squat temple has accrued Byzantine and Norman remains.

San Pietro ⓲, just southeast, was supposedly founded by St Peter before being converted into a Byzantine basilica. The 8th-century apses and blind arcading are incorporated into a 15th-century shell. Just west, Via XX Settembre contains tracts of the massive **Greek walls**. Dionysius was an indefatigable builder, and this immense wall, 5 km (3 miles) in length and built in 20 days by 60,000 men on double overtime, is still visible in other parts of the city.

From here, it is a short stroll to **Piazza Archimede**, the grandiose centre of Ortygia. This baroque stage set, adorned by a well-restored fountain, is framed by dignified mansions. The atmosphere is sustained by the mysterious **Via Maestranza**, the heart of the old guilds quarter, graced with Spanish palaces. Amid the sombre courtyards and swirling sculpture, local *pasticcerie* literally represent the icing on the cake.

Any turning to the west returns one to the sea, where **Porta Marina** presents the heart of the Catalan-Gothic quarter, centred on **Santa Maria dei Miracoli**, a finely sculpted 15th-century church. Just beyond is a graceful Catalan-Gothic archway and the remains of the city's medieval walls. Via Gemmellaro, one of the Moorish alleys off the piazza, hides some of Ortygia's best *trattorie*, including Archimede, the place for seafood and a surfeit of antipasti.

Heading south leads to **Fonte Aretusa** ⓳, a freshwater spring that is the symbol of Siracusa. Legend has it that the nymph Arethusa was pursued by Alpheus, a river god. As she reached the sea, Artemis kindly transformed her into a fountain and she reached Ortygia safely. There Alpheus pulled her under the waves and "mingled his waters with hers". Whether this was rape or the reuniting of lovers, Siracusani disagree. After a 17th-century earthquake, the spring is supposed to be mingled with sea water.

In any case, upside-down ducks and clumps of reedy papyrus plants make a romantic love nest. At night, the fountain sees a parade of Siracusa's youth, accompanied by flirtation, exposed thighs and the

Map on page 236

BELOW: Siracusa's fish market.

revving of ice-cream splattered mopeds. These flirtations continue on the harbour-side café terraces.

Just inland, on Via Cappodieci is **Palazzo Bellomo** ⓴ (daily, 9am–2pm), the loveliest Catalan-Gothic mansion in Ortygia and the city's compact art gallery. Inside, an elegant courtyard leads to the intimate and newly reorganised **Galleria Regionale**, housing Caravaggio's masterpiece, the *Burial of St Lucy*, and Antonello da Messina's *Annunciation*. Other highlights include 14th- to 18th-century works, from Byzantine icons to Catalan and Spanish paintings, Sicilian jewellery and Renaissance tombs.

From here, a flight of steps leads to the **Duomo** ㉑ (8am–noon, 4–7pm), a temple to Athena masquerading as a Christian cathedral. Classical columns bulge through the external walls in Via Minerva, a sign that the temple has only been encased in a church since the 7th century. Before then, the temple was a beacon to sailors, with ivory doors and a gold facade surmounted by the goddess Athena bearing a glinting bronze shield. It is humbling to think that Dionysius himself worshipped at this temple.

Yet the exterior conjures up a Spanish spell: a baroque facade with dramatic *chiaroscuro* effects, including an inside porch boasting twisted barley-stick columns. Yet the cool, striking interior betrays its Greek origins. The worn but lovely fluted Doric columns belong to the Temple to Athena (Minerva). Notwithstanding a Greek soul, the temple also glorifies later conquerors. A Norman baptismal font rests on bronze lions; above is a medieval wood-panelled ceiling; a baroque choir and Byzantine apses strike new notes; only the Arab presence is missing. The apses were slightly damaged in the 1991 earthquake but the Greek sandstone fluted columns survived.

Freshly baked bread in decorative shapes.

BELOW: Siracusa's baroque Duomo, inside and out.

Sea strolls

At night or siesta time, the atmospheric Porto Piccolo is quiet except for the crashing of waves. Locals warn lone travellers against exploring the port at night, yet with care it is worth risking the occasional *scippatore* (bag-snatcher) for the rough-and-ready restaurants, crumbling *palazzi* and sea views. Moreover, since Ortygia has become the focus of city nightlife, from cosy bars and pubs to pizza parlours and *birrerie* (beer halls), the evening bustle is an increasing guarantee of safety. The western shore, especially the strip between Porta Marina and Fontana Aretusa, offers a summer parade of fashion victims in search of food and company. This pool marks the traditional start of gentle *passeggiate* or bracing sea walks.

Nearby, short cruises around the headland are available on the *Selene*, departing from Molo Zanagora off Largo Porta Marina. The island's dilapidated eastern shore, partly built on the old Spanish bastions, is equally intriguing, with **Lungomare di Levante** offering facades of battered mansions and warehouses. Even so, the former Jewish ghetto around Via Giudecca may feel sightly ominous at night, particularly the dark alleys behind Via Nizza. However, the adjoining promontory of Forte Vigliena has been enlivened by a summer bathing platform and a couple of bars.

Set on the southernmost tip of Ortygia, the fortified hulk of **Castello Maniace ㉒** dominates the point and once served as protector of Syracusa's two shores. Still an army barracks, the troops played an important role in the "Sicilian Vespers" operation, the anti-Mafia campaigns of the early 1990s. (The soldiers were drawn from outside the province of Siracusa to try to prevent any collusion with local criminals.) This Swabian fortress retained its

Map on page 236

Siracusa's most atmospheric restaurants are in the back streets of Ortygia. Specialities include seafood, particularly swordfish and shrimps, stuffed artichokes and stimpirata di coniglio, a rabbit and vegetable flan.

BELOW: Ortygia looks out on a stormy sea.

Map on page 236

The city has two tourist offices: one in Ortygia (Via Maestranza 33, tel: 0931 65201), the other close to Neapolis (Via San Sebastiano 43, tel: 0931-481232).

BELOW: imposing Castello Eurialo, built by Dionysius I. **RIGHT:** Ortygia balconies.

military purpose until 2001, when the newly restored castle was converted into an exhibition centre and the adjoining barracks dismantled. Previously, visitors who peered too long at the Gothic doorway were discouraged by nonchalant soldiers waving automatic weapons. Beyond, **Lungomare d'Ortygia** offers safer, windswept views over the rocky shore.

Great escapes

Close to the city are sandy beaches and two unique spots, a Greek castle and a dreamy riverscape of papyrus plantations. Further afield, south of Siracusa, off the SS 115 to Noto, lie popular beaches at the small resorts of **Arenella**, **Ognina** and **Fontane Bianche**. Although Siracusa's beaches tend to be full of golden bodies rather than golden sands, a more atmospheric swimming spot is 20 km (12 miles) north of Siracusa: **Brúcoli**, a rocky beach set around a Spanish castle, enjoys views of Etna on clear days.

In ancient **Epipolae**, 8 km (5 miles) northwest of Siracusa is **Castello Eurialo** (daily, 9am–one hour before sunset; follow signs to Belvedere). The fort represented the fifth component of the Greek *pentapolis* and was the most magnificent of Greek military outposts. Designed by Dionysius, the castle protected Siracusa's most exposed flank, the conjunction of the northern and southern city walls. Apart from amazingly solid masonry and moats hewn out of the rock, the castle boasted labyrinthine passageways and a keep surrounded by five towers. As a final security measure, the sole entrance was concealed by a patchwork of walls. When Dionysius was in residence, he would not allow his wives into his bed without first being searched. According to legend, his bed was surrounded by a moat, and his wives reached it across a little wooden drawbridge, which he then drew up.

Just south of the city, 5 km (3 miles) along the road for Canicattini Bagni, is **Fonte Ciane**, a picturesque spot close to the ruined Temple of Olympian Zeus. Ciane is a mythical river dedicated to a nymph who was transformed into a spring after trying to thwart the rape of Persephone by Hades. Canoes, easily rented from the tiny riverside marina from March onwards, are the best way to explore the relaxing Ciane and Anapo rivers, framed by canopies of lush foliage. (Unless you are lucky enough to encounter the only boatman with the right keys, expect to have to haul the canoe over a weir.) The Ciane weaves its way through groves of papyrus with tendrils as delicate as cobwebs. The origins of this wild plant are obscure: it was either imported from Egypt or native to Siracusa. Either way, its habitat is endangered but it flourishes in this idyllic backwater.

Although the river banks are now too overgrown to permit a trip all the way to Fonte Aretusa in Siracusa, the Ciane is a fitting place in which to contemplate the passing of Greek Siracusa. Not that the passage of time feels great in this Sicilian backwater. As the writer Vincent Cronin said: "The spirit of Archimedes, Gelon and Dionysius are more real to the people of Siracusa than of any citizens since the Greek period." Since then, the greatest city of the Classical age has slumbered. ❑

SIRACUSA PROVINCE

Outside Siracusa city, this harmonious southeastern province offers a cross-section of Sicily: a blend of baroque, Classical and prehistoric sites

Map on page 252

The Greeks colonised this area two centuries after settling the rest of eastern Sicily. Since then, Siracusa has rested on its laurels, parading its Greek heart and Levantine soul with the effortless superiority of a born aristocrat. Economically, however, the province has fallen behind its more entrepreneurial neighbours, Catania and Ragusa. Siracusa short-sightedly destroyed a sizeable stretch of coast in the 1950s in the rush for petrochemical riches. It is now paying the price for short-term gain in the form of polluted beaches, antiquated industries, an ill-equipped workforce, and lack of tourist facilities. Nonetheless, this corner of Sicily has an elegance and grace unmatched by other provinces. Most visitors can turn a blind eye to the bubbling crisis and simply relish Siracusa's traditional sense of *discreto benessere*, discreet wellbeing.

PRECEDING PAGES: papyrus on the River Ciane. **LEFT:** part of the doorway of San Sebastiano in Ferla. **BELOW:** the theatrical staircase of San Nicolò Cathedral, Noto.

The province has been shaped by the cataclysm of the 1693 earthquake. Although all Norman castles were razed, the region responded with some of the greatest baroque architecture in Sicily, notably in Noto. The journey south from **Siracusa** ❶ provides a fair introduction to the provincial landscape, from low-slung farms to lemon groves, from sandy beaches to a more rugged hinterland. The terrain spans limestone escarpments and rocky gorges, the flat coastal strip and, just inland, gentle farming country dotted with olive and almond groves. The market town of **Avola** gives way to a greater baroque setting, stacked up on a hill.

Noto ❷ is the finest baroque town in Sicily, both blatantly theatrical and deeply rational. Visitors praise its proportion, symmetry, spaciousness and innate sense of spectacle. Sicilians simply call it "a garden of stone". Yet much is crumbling in the garden and most museums and interiors are closed for eternal "restoration". Luckily, on this open-air stage, Noto's chief pleasures are on permanent display.

After Noto Antica was destroyed in the 1693 earthquake, Prince Landolina instigated its rebuilding, planting the new Noto on the flanks of a distant hill. The city was composed around three parallel axes running horizontally across the hillside, with three squares to create interest, each enlivened by a scenic church as a backdrop. The whole design is clothed in warm, golden limestone, with monumental flights of steps to enchant with tricks of perspective. The realisation of this ambitious plan was the work of Gagliardi and Sinatra, gifted local architects who also worked in Ragusa province.

This century, this cool cityscape has been ill-served by politicians, heavy traffic, neglect and acts of God. Despite the beauteous architecture, the glowing limestone buildings are inherently fragile and susceptible to erosion and pollution. Since recent minor earthquakes, much has theoretically been under restoration, aided

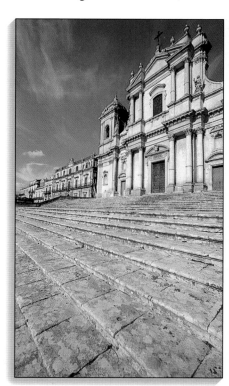

by UNESCO and EU funds. But the finest churches still remain shored up or swathed in scaffolding, and the great baroque palaces are closed to the public.

Noto council's controversial notion of restoration was to convert the finer mansions, such as Palazzo Trigona, into conference centres. More imaginatively, the vast monastery of San Tommaso has been transformed into a sinister prison. But the city faced its greatest crisis in 1996, when the cupola and roof of the Cathedral of San Nicolò collapsed after a heavy thunderstorm. Despite the availability of funds, the restoration work was only finally authorised in late 1999.

Urban theatre

The monumental **Porta Reale** leads to **Corso Vittorio Emanuele**, a stately thoroughfare broken by three equally monumental squares. At the western end, **Piazza XVI Maggio** is graced by gardens of palms, monkey puzzle trees and a fountain of Hercules taken from Noto Antica. Behind these shady gardens lies **San Domenico**, a curvilinear Gagliardi church influenced by Roman and Spanish baroque. Facing it is the ornately gilded **Teatro Emanuele**. Also surveying the spacious square is **Collegio dei Gesuiti**, a typical casualty of neglect and earthquake damage. Now propped up by scaffolding, this fragile wreck was a conservatoire until the rumblings of the 1989 earthquake drowned the baroque music within. Just south, on the western end of Via Ducezio, stands the **Carmine**, created by Gagliardi's assistant, Vincenzo Sinatra, from its concave facade to a doorway guarded by two *putti* (cherubs), the symbol of the Carmelite order. The elaborate white interior, studded with stuccowork, is at odds with Noto's emphasis on minimalist baroque interiors.

The Corso sweeps onwards to **Piazza Municipio**, Noto's stage set. The

In summer, Noto is strangely quiet. Visitors have the place to themselves as the city is abandoned by its residents for the seaside resorts of Noto Marina or Lido di Avola.

BELOW: the baroque splendour of Palazzo Villadorata.

golden grace of the buildings matches the majestic proportions of the design; the set is framed by amber hills, a natural note intruding on man-made scenery. On the square, **Palazzo Ducezio**, the elegant town hall, borrows from French architecture with more than a nod to Versailles. Opposite is **San Nicolò**, the once splendid cathedral, now clad in canvas. The scaffolding was removed in 1999, revealing a theatrical staircase and facade but the cupola, the roof and the cool pastel interior still await completion.

In one sense, the city of Noto is a facade for disappointing interiors: only the town hall atrium, with its lavish marble floors, shimmers softly. The adjoining **Palazzo Vescovile** makes a mundane showing, an episcopal palace resembling functional stables. The neighbouring baroque facade of **Palazzo Landolina** should herald the triumphant progress to Piazza Municipio but is currently under wraps.

Instead, **Palazzo Villadorata**, in Via Nicolaci, which leads north from Piazza Municipio, is Noto's pride and joy. Also known as Palazzo Nicolaci after its noble owners, this baroque jewel has been restored to its former glory. Don Nicolaci, a patron of the arts, donated a wing of the palace to the city library.

Around the windows are friezes of mythical monsters, a snarling parade of griffons, sphinxes, sirens, centaurs and cherubs. Arabesques climb the walls, clashing with crested cornices and billowing wrought-iron balconies. The sloped courtyard was designed for carriages and includes an access ramp so that the prince could ride directly into the *piano nobile*.

Palazzo Villadorata plays a starring role in the city drama but secondary characters should not be overlooked, especially convents and churches. Via Giovanni XXIII, behind San Nicolò, reveals subtle details as niches for statues, sculpted cornices and bulging "goose-breast" balconies.

The spacious lower town was only for the clergy and the aristocracy. Above the grandiose public face of Noto rises the *popolare* district, clustered around the hilly Piazza Mazzini. The **Crocifisso**, a domed Gagliardi church that dominates Piazza Mazzini, has a portal flanked by Romanesque lions rescued from Noto Antica. When the church reopens, visitors will also be able to appreciate the interior, with its Francesco Laurana *Madonna*, an incongruously serene sculpture amid the frenzy of baroque. The **Giardino Pubblico** at the eastern end of the Corso Vittorio Emanuele is a peaceful end to any visit to Noto. The ancient weeping fig trees form a verdant roof over the park.

Noto Antica ❸ nestles in the foothills of the Iblei mountains, the phoenix that never rose from the ashes. It was a complex city full of Classical, Romanesque and baroque churches, convents and mansions. All this was buried under rubble in the 1693 earthquake. An eyewitness recorded the quake as "so horrible that the soil undulated like the waves of a stormy sea, and the mountains danced as if drunk," and the city collapsed in one terrible moment killing more than a thousand people. The fallen masonry represents one of Sicily's three capitals in Arab times; each controlled a third of the island. Today, a ruined castle, bastions, tombs and crumbling homes are all that remain.

Map on page 252

TIP

Noto may look good enough to eat but restaurants and bars are scarce in this baroque confection. Worth trying: **Mandolfiore**, a chic *pasticceria* and *gelateria* on Piazza del Carmine.

BELOW: the Fontana d'Ercole, Noto.

TIP

To sample the catch of Marzamemi fishermen try **Adelfio** (Via Marzemini 7), a shop selling the finest local produce, especially tuna and anchovies in every form. Choose your own lobster or mullet from the tanks at **L'Acquario** (Via Jonio 1), one of the most atmospheric restaurants in Sicily.

BELOW: Noto's San Nicolò Cathedral, now domeless.

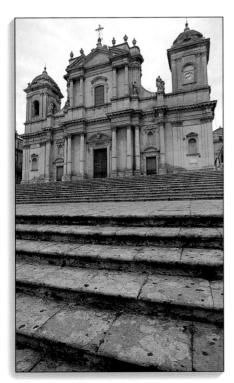

The southern coast

Southeast of Noto lies **Eloro** ❹, a Classical site on the unpolluted coastline that stretches south to Capo Pássero. Now in ruins, the Siracusan city of Elorus (open 9am–one hour before sunset) was founded at the end of the 6th century BC. Well-preserved turreted walls survive, as do porticos, a pair of gateways, the agora and a Sanctuary of Demeter. Just outside the site stands the **Colonna della Pizzuta**, a curious Hellenistic funeral column that looks like a chimney stack. In the neighbouring hamlet of **Caddeddi**, a villa from the same period has been unearthed, along with mosaics depicting hunting scenes. Beside this wild site are rocky and sandy beaches that tend to be deserted, but the most appealing beaches await in Vendicari, 6 km (4 miles) south.

The journey south to the deserted **Vendícari wetlands** passes citrus and almond groves. The Vendícari salt marshes, now a nature reserve, are popular with nesting and migrating birds. However, most Siracusani are sun-worshippers rather than ornithologists, even if the beaches are exposed to blustery sea breezes. For those simply in search of an invigorating walk, Vendícari has much to offer: the reserve embraces a sweeping crescent of sand and marshes, with medieval water channels cut to reach the salt pans. The site also includes battered medieval fortifications, a Swabian tower and abandoned tuna-processing sheds. A marked trail leads through the salt marshes but the rangers also conduct botanical walks (in Italian only).

Further down the coast lies **Marzamemi** ❺, the most appealing fishing village in the province. As a former feudal domain, the village retains a crumbling noble palace, adorned with the Villadorata family crest. Despite its recent elevation to small-time summer resort, at heart Marzamemi remains a working fishing village, complete with lobster pots and the obligatory fishing nets drying in the sun. *Cernia* (grouper) is a highly prized Mediterranean fish but mullet, mussels and tuna are also on local menus.

In summer, Sicilians from Catania and Siracusa flock south to **Pachino** ❻ and the sandy beaches around Capo Pássero. The pillboxes littering this stretch of coast are a testament to troubled times. In July 1943 the Allied invasion of Sicily took place on these shores. While General Patton and the American forces landed near Gela, General Montgomery and the British 8th Army landed between Pachino and Pozzallo. Giuseppe Tornatore's film *Malena* includes a dramatic re-enactment of the landing on Pachino's beaches. Nowadays, Pachino is a quiet wine-producing centre with a faded baroque heart. The hinterland is devoted to market gardening but the coast is rapidly developing attractive resort amenities, unpretentious and often family-run.

Beyond is **Capo Pássero** ❼, the southernmost tip of the province, and home to several low-key seaside resorts. Until recently, these were villages dependent on tuna fishing and processing. Today, only one tuna fishery remains, run by Don Bruno di Belmonte. Nearby, Scandinavian visitors collapse on beaches after a surfeit of full-bodied red Pachino wine and locally grown strawberries. More energetic visitors can row to the islet off **Portopalo**.

Map on page 252

North of Siracusa

Swimming is not advisable on the northern stretch of coast, except at **Brúcoli**, just north of **Augusta**. As the coastline with Europe's highest concentration of chemical effluents, this area is an ecological disaster. Petrochemical plants based around Augusta have destroyed 48 km (30 miles) of beach. At night, this stretch of coast has a savage beauty of its own, with its glittering towers, gargantuan oil tanks and livid smokestacks. But for the moment, the Greek tragedy has placed **Thapsos** out of bounds.

The Classical site on **Penisola Magnisi** is too close to the belching fumes to be acceptable. Acrid fumes also threaten to engulf the important site of **Megara Hyblaea ❽**, one of the earliest Greek cities in Sicily, founded in 728 BC. Cypresses shield it in poetic desolation but industrial blight is tangible. A wall and a group of sarcophagi front the ramparts of a Hellenistic fortress. Beyond are the foundations of an Archaic city, as yet unexplored.

As a smaller mirror image of Siracusa, **Augusta ❾** once had charm and prestige. However, while its islet setting, double harbour and faded baroque centre remain, so does rampant industrialisation. Cement works and petrochemical plants blight views of the park, Castello and quaint causeway. Augusta's good restaurants provide scant compensation.

The ancient interior

The rocky, wild, sparsely populated hinterland is one of Siracusa's charms. The parched slopes and odd mounds conceal several significant Classical sites. The desolate countryside has an austere appeal matched by the dusty baroque country towns along the route. This is Sicily with its roots laid bare, a prehistoric and

There is some hope on the polluted horizon around Augusta: serious clean-up operations are being run by the ecological group Mare Nostrum, which welcomes help from local factory workers.

BELOW: making tracks on Capo Pássero.

Among the Greek ruins at Akrai are reliefs cut directly into the rock face. This one shows heroes banqueting.

BELOW: the pre-historic Necrópoli di Pantálica.

Siculi land that predates Siracusa city by centuries. The rocky tableland is home to **Pantálica**, the region's foremost prehistoric site. The drive to Pantálica skirts the bleached white or pale green Iblean hills before reaching the lush **Anapo Valley**. Dedicated hikers with a full day to spend in Pantálica will choose the northern entrance, reached via Palazzolo and Ferla. However, for more convenient access and less walking, choose the southern route via **Sortino**, following signs for Pantálica Sud. This rural drive passes country villas, citrus groves and goatherds negotiating dry stone walls.

Despite their importance, the **Necrópoli di Pantálica** ❿ (daily 9am–sunset) are off the beaten track. However, Siracusani have long been drawn to the lush gorges, a verdant paradise remote from the barren image of the Iblean hills. Apart from the loveliness of this sprawling site, Pantálica offers a slice of Sicily's earliest history: this Siculi necropolis contains rock tombs dating from the 13th to the 8th century BC. As the largest Bronze and Iron Age cemetery in Sicily, it contains over 5,000 tombs carved into the sheer cliffs of a limestone plateau, not to mention cave dwellings. Although Pantálica's history is shrouded in mystery, tradition claims it as Hybla, the capital of the Siculi king who allowed Greek colonists to occupy Megara Hyblaea. Certainly, some of these gaping holes are 3,000 years old.

The tombs lie at the end of a gorge carved by the Anapo river and studded with citrus trees and wild flowers, acanthus and prickly pears. In this secret garden lie tiered rows of tombs, a honeycomb-pitted surface of jagged rectangular openings cut into the pale rock. Mule tracks and marked paths follow the Anapo river towards a disused railway line, with easier paths marked "A", and more challenging ones marked "B". Walkers are rewarded with discreet picnic

Map on page 252

spots, as well as views of sheer rockfaces and deep ravines. Apart from the tombs and dwellings, there remains a Byzantine rock chapel, and early Christian frescoes. It is hard to return to the windswept plateau, leaving behind this sacred chasm bursting with snapdragons, asphodel and daisies.

A country drive leads southwest to **Palazzolo Acréide ⓫**, a sleepy town with an air of surprise that outsiders should stray so far. The baroque centre displays several theatrical set pieces, whose charms are only diminished by the air of abandon. The town's rough-hewn charms are apparent in **Palazzo Zocco** on Via Umberto, with its chaotic baroque ornamentation. **Chiesa Annunziata**, an early baroque church, has a portal guarded by Spanish barley-shape columns. However, many of the town's rewards are low-key: the occasional gargoyle, carved doorpost or billowing balcony.

A road signposted for Teatro Greco leads to the Classical city of **Akrai ⓬**, a Greek site set on high windy moorland. The attractive walled park (daily 9am–1pm, 3–7pm) encloses a Greek theatre, quarries and temples founded in 664 BC by Siracusa. The confusing site contains stone carvings, votive niches, commemorative plaques, a necropolis, catacombs and the remains of a Temple to Aphrodite. The most impressive views are of the deep quarries framed by dry stone walls, firs, bay trees and wild olives. The lovely site suffers from poor management, with temples and sculptures arbitrarily locked. The **Santoni** (Holy Ones) is a series of 12 crudely carved sculptures, made in honour of the goddess Cybele, the Magna Mater whose esoteric cult originated in Asia. These precious finds lie a few fields away but require a custodian's presence.

Leading out of town, the **Strada Panoramica** lives up to its name, offering views across the Greek settlements towards Ragusa province. ❑

"Here is Sicily of the Stone Age, intent on nothing higher than the taking of food and the burial of the dead."
– VINCENT CRONIN ON PANTÁLICA

BELOW: the mobile vegetable store visits Palazzolo Acréide.

PUGNACIOUS PUPPETS AND COLOURFUL CARTS

Flamboyant manifestations of Sicilian folklore, boisterous puppets and garish carts portray the island's history in brash primary colours

The travelling puppet show has provided entertainment in Sicily for centuries, telling tales of saints, bandits or heroes, but most commonly the Paladins, the knights of Charlemagne's court, and their battles against the Saracens.

The Christians traditionally strut on the left of the stage, the turbaned, baggy-trousered Saracens on the right. The audience knows all the characters – the knights Orlando and Rinaldo, the beautiful Angelica and the wicked traitor Gano di Magonza – and identifies with them as characters in a familiar soap opera. Feelings run high, especially in the noisy battle scenes.

The puppets are up to 1.5 metres (5 ft) tall and exquisitely attired. Metal wires move their hands and a thicker bar turns their heads. A great puppeteer is judged by his skill in directing the battle, and by his sophisticated sound effects – thundering, stamping feet and a running commentary in an archaic dialect.

WHEELED WONDERS

The brilliant yellows, reds and blues of the puppet theatre also adorn Sicily's sculpted carts, where every inch is painted with bold images. The artists raid motifs from their multiracial heritage: Arab adornment and arabesques; chivalric legends and Biblical epics; the Crusades and the Napoleonic wars. The few carts that survive today are found in tourist areas, but come into their own on feast days and at funerals.

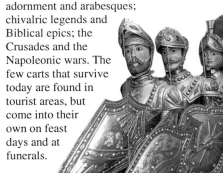

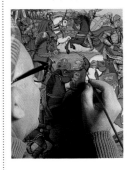

△ **WAR ON WHEELS**
The side panels on a cart in Palermo depict scenes from *Orlando Furioso* – the same bloodthirsty drama that is traditionally enacted by puppets.

△ **ACTION PAINTING**
Wars between Crusaders and Saracens are still a popular theme for cart-painting: here an artist incorporates a self-portrait into the battlefield action.

△ **MAKING A HERO**
Puppets are carved from beech, olive or lemon wood and their limbs joined with metal links before armour is fitted.

◁ **KNIGHT DRESS**
Four Paladin knights in immaculate bronze armour on display in the Museo Internazionale delle Marionette, Palermo.

EXHILARATING POTTERY

Traditional Sicilian ceramics display the same vivacity and vibrant use of colour as the island's puppets and carts.

Thanks to the inexhaustible deposits of clay surrounding the town, Caltagirone had a reputation for pottery even before the Arabs introduced local craftsmen to the glazed polychromatic colours – particularly blues, greens and yellows – that have become typical of Sicilian ceramics. As well as functional items such as vases, bowls and jugs, Caltagirone craftsmen also produce decorative tiles, medallions and figurines in the same lively colours.

Santo Stéfano di Camastra is the second great ceramics centre on the island. On the Messina–Palermo road, the small town seems overwhelmed with its pottery: tiers of dishes, tureens and bowls line both sides of the road. The traditional style here has a rustic look and feel, often featuring fish designs. The other local speciality is tiles decorated with smiling suns and saints.

△ HEAVY FIGHTING
Puppets from Acireale are taller and heavier than their Palermo counterparts. Here an Acireale Orlando battles with a giant.

◁ MORTAL COMBAT
Puppet battles are not just between Christians and infidels: the knights also slay dragons, crocodiles and other monsters.

△ FANCY WOODWORK
A painted cart in Monreale, now a tourist attraction, displays a finely carved backboard as well as the traditional vivid panels.

CATANIA CITY

*As Sicily's second city, Catania is a bold baroque affair,
a vibrant and volcanic eruption of black lava-stone,
and the natural springboard to Mount Etna*

Map on page 262

Palermo

Catania

C atania is a city of contradictions: brash, belligerent and beleagured yet also vibrant, cultured and resilient, forged on Etna's slopes. It is a commercial success, has a dynamic arts scene and is a showcase of Sicilian baroque. Catania should be comfortable but is deeply uneasy, understandable for a city living in Etna's shadow. The edgy tone is captured by Etna, glittering red on a menacing Catanese night. The approach to Catania along the *circonvallazione* (ring road) reveals the extent of nature's wrath. Recent volcano flows are visible between the grim tenements or piled like slag heaps by the roadside.

The Catanesi have long had a reputation for being sharp operators with a flair for commerce and industry. The city has produced many of the island's best engineers and entrepreneurs – as well as many of the most active Mafia leaders. In the 1960s, Catania won plaudits as "the Milan of the South" but several decades later chaotic city politics and corruption in both cities gave the slogan a hollow echo. Catania's high crime rate even earned it the label of "little Chicago", despite the fact that most citizens had no contact with the Mafia. Nonetheless, various city administrations were compromised by their presumed criminal links. According to reports from *pentiti* (Mafia turncoats), Cosa Nostra had also switched key operations from Palermo to Catania by the 1980s.

LEFT: eel seller in Catania market.
BELOW: Porta Ujeda, leading into Piazza del Duomo.

Under the volcano

This ancient Siculi settlement was colonised by settlers from Naxos in 729 BC. As an ally of Athens, Catania incurred the wrath of Siracusa and citizens were sold into slavery in 403 BC. By contrast, the Roman conquest brought prosperity, particularly under Augustan rule. But in AD 253 St Agata, the city's beloved patron saint, suffered martyrdom by being rolled in hot coals and having her breasts cut off. At her February festival she is tastelessly commemorated by breast-shaped jellies and cakes.

Sant'Agata's statue is still used to ward off impending lava flows, with mixed success. The 1669 eruption struck the city centre while 12,000 people were attending Mass and the 1693 earthquake killed two-thirds of the population. Even in 1983 an eruption caused widespread panic. The city's fears of becoming a latter-day Pompeii are based on hard facts.

Under Spanish rule, Catania was "a city of gentlemen, merchants and masons", dominated by landowners like Prince Biscari. While the architecture is less ebullient than in Noto or Siracusa, this is still trailblazing baroque, with spacious streets and sinuous churches. However, as Sicily's commercial powerhouse, modern Catania stands accused of selling its soul to property speculation and neglecting its baroque heritage. Until recently, the city centre was undervalued

*The house where
Vincenzo Bellini was
born in 1801 is
now the Museo
Belliniano, housing
the composer's death
mask as well as
original scores,
photographs and
other memorabilia.*

and dilapidated, the province of students and the poor, at least after nightfall. But after years of lethargic city administration, political change is in the air.

Catania has improved dramatically under the leadership of Enzo Bianco, the popular city mayor. In recent years, the city has acquired investment for economic expansion as well as European Union funding for inner-city regeneration schemes. The cathedral has been restored and the reorganisation of the main classical sites is under way; the port area is also being relandscaped. Culturally, there has been an explosion of artistic activities, including large-scale open-air events, and the best nightlife in Sicily, with the creation of new bars, restaurants and clubs in the historic centre. This is also an energetic university city with an active arts scene, including good drama, classical music, a September jazz festival and myriad pop-rock spectaculars in summer. The crumbling city backstreets may still have a relatively high incidence of petty crime but the city is no longer considered to be in the clutches of the Mafia.

City sights

Visually, Catania seems the most homogeneous Sicilian city. From 1730 it was stamped with the vision of one man, Giovanni Vaccarini, an architect influenced by grand Roman baroque. His work has a sculptural quality allied to a native vigour. Billowing balconies, sweeping S-curves and a taste for *chiaroscuro* are intermixed. Until your eyes adjust, the colour of the volcanic stone seems oppressive, but the clever chromatic effects are a tribute to Vaccarini's skill.

Piazza del Duomo ❶ is the baroque centrepiece, a dignified composition on a grand scale. The buildings in the square make use of flat facades, restrained decoration, elegant windows and huge pilasters. The ensemble seems

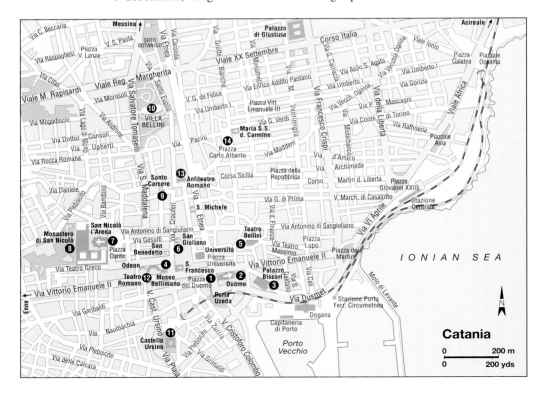

harmonious, despite being designed by several architects. In the centre is the city symbol, **Fontane dell'Elefante**, Vaccarini's fountain: an ancient black volcanic elephant is surmounted by an Egyptian obelisk taken from the Roman circus.

The newly restored **Duomo** ❷ (daily 8am–noon, 4–7pm) was begun by Count Roger in 1092 and rebuilt by Vaccarini after the earthquake. It is a magnificently confused summation of Catanese history: Roman theatres were raided to adorn the lugubrious baroque facade with granite columns. The interior conceals vaulted subterranean Roman baths, a Romanesque basilica lies under the nave, and Roman and Byzantine columns line the transepts. St Agata's chapel, a gaudy shrine of multicoloured marble, has recently been restored, as have the tombs of the 14th-century Spanish rulers of Sicily. More controversially, these were moved to the nave, including Queen Constance's graceful tomb and the Roman sarcophagus containing the ashes of other Aragonese royals.

Just east is **Palazzo Biscari** ❸, in Via Museo Biscari, the most accomplished baroque mansion in Catania. It is still partly owned by the Moncada family, the Biscari descendants, but the public can attend concerts in the *salone della musica*, a rococo wonder, with a grand staircase, minstrel's gallery and allegorical ceiling. Via Dusmet offers the best view of the facade, with its frolicking cherubs, caryatids and grinning monsters.

Via Crociferi, just west of the Duomo, is arguably Catania's most charming street, with its succession of baroque churches and noble *palazzi*. Created on top of a lava flow in the 17th century, this pedestrianised street is often bustling with students hurrying to lectures. At the southern end of the street, opposite the newly restored church of **San Francesco**, is **Museo Belliniano** ❹ (Mon–Fri 9am–1pm), its shabby baroque facade concealing a museum of musical memorabilia and original scores of the composer's work.

The father of *bel canto* is buried in Catania Cathedral but is also commemorated in the well-restored **Teatro Bellini** ❺, which opened in 1890 with his opera *Norma*. North along Via Crociferi stands Vaccarini's **Chiesa San Giuliano** ❻, distinguished by its graceful loggia. From here, the end of the pedestrian zone, Via Sangiuliano leads to the crescent of **Piazza Dante**, the focus of a dilapidated but intriguing area.

San Nicolò l'Arena ❼ (daily 10am–noon) resembles a grim religious factory rather than a church. As the largest church in Sicily, this unfinished, desolate 16th-century work was conceived on a vast scale. It has an eerie, amputated look, with truncated stumps of columns framing the door like rotten teeth. Inside is a Hollywood-esque folly, Sicily's first classical staircase. After a long period of closure, the church has been restored, including the vast sundial, although the cupola is still under scaffolding. The adjoining **Monastero di San Nicolò** ❽ (variable opening) is a mammoth Benedictine monastery now housing Catania University's Faculty of Arts. Brydone, an 18th-century visitor, was awed by "a facade almost equal to that of Versailles". Long-term archaeological excavations are under way in the entrance courtyard, but beyond lie the charming former cloisters, complete with a battered garden and a curiously decorated folly.

North of this neglected baroque square is **Chiesa**

Map
on page
262

TIP

Catania is best explored on foot and by public transport, so if you arrive by car, leave it in the central multistorey car park, Parcheggio Bellini/ Borsellino, close to the market.

BELOW: an Egyptian obelisk surmounts Vaccarini's Elephant Fountain.

Catania's best beaches are to the south of the city, on the Golfo di Catania.

BELOW: pigeons find a baroque perch in the Giardino Bellini.

di Santo Carcere ❾, also known as **Sant'Agata al Carcere** (Tues–Sat 4–7pm). According to legend, and supported by graffiti on these Roman walls, it was here that St Agata was held captive before her martyrdom. Although the site was converted into a fortified church in the 12th century, the 3rd-century crypt remains. More impressive is the Romanesque portal moved from the cathedral after the 1693 earthquake. Sculpted with griffons and glowering beasts, the door conjures up suitable horrors for a Roman prison, the church's original function.

The grandiose **Via Etnea**, the main city thoroughfare, runs parallel to Via Crociferi and climaxes in a stunning view of Mount Etna. Busy throughout the day, the street is particularly popular at night when the Catanesi indulge in the evening *passeggiata*, a parade past chic shops selling jewellery, shoes, fruit sorbets and nougat ice cream. The most elegant section of the street lies between Piazza Duomo and **Villa Bellini** ❿. This delightful and well-kept public park represents a retreat from Catania's constant bustle. One part is named *labirinto* after the maze of paths, all leading to aviaries and an Oriental bandstand. Between the fig trees, palms and playing children are snowcapped or smouldering views of Etna.

To the south of Via Etnea is **Castello Ursino** ⓫ (Tues–Sun 9am–6pm), a newly restored Swabian castle built on a steep bastion. It commands a view of what was once the harbour: the moat was filled in by the lava flow of 1669, which also left the castle marooned inland, and deposited a large lump of lava outside the walls. Now an art museum and exhibition space, it was the Aragonese seat of government in the 13th century and became a palace under the Spanish viceroys. The courtyard displays a cavalcade of Sicilian history, featuring fine Hellenistic and Roman sculpture. The **Museo Civico**, housed on the upper floors, contains a wide-ranging art gallery, with space for temporary exhibitions elsewhere in the castle.

Classical Catania

The city's ancient remains are unlike the spacious marble theatres or golden sandstone temples found elsewhere in Sicily. Instead Catania offers cramped, low-lying monuments in sombre black lava stone. Yet if you are prepared to traipse down unpromising alleys, the rewards are worthwhile. While most Classical remains enjoy splendid isolation, Catania's are fully integrated in the urban fabric, generally in dilapidated parts of town, where every second turning reveals the odd Roman column, tomb or hypocaust.

Teatro Romano ⓬, also called Teatro Greco, off 266 Via Vittorio Emanuele (daily 8am–1 hour before sunset), was built on the site of a Greek theatre but has Roman underground passages and *cavea* as well as some of the *scena* and *orchestr*a. The original marble facing was plundered by the Normans to embellish the cathedral. Next door is the semicircular **Odeon**, used for oratory and rehearsals. The building materials were chosen for their contrasts: volcanic stone, red brickwork and marble facing. It was first excavated in the 18th century when demolition of encroaching buildings began. The intimate site is still hemmed in by a medieval and baroque quarter.

In Piazza Stesicoro, off Via Etnea, lies the

Anfiteatro Romano (closed though visible), the battered remains of the largest amphitheatre in Sicily, dating back to the 2nd or 3rd century AD. This was where St Agata supposedly met her doom and where earthquake ruins were dumped in 1693. Ancient **necropoli** stretch north and east of this site and are visible in many spots, including below the Rinascente store in Via Etnea.

Markets and meeting places

Just south of the Duomo, sandwiched between the cathedral quarter and the port, is **La Pescheria**, the noisy morning fish market. On slabs of marble lie sea bream and swordfish, mussels and sea urchins, squirming eels and lobsters. The area is centred on **Porta Uzeda**, the monumental baroque city gate connecting the port with the public city. Beyond the adjoining park of Villa Pacini, the colourful portside area encircling Via Dusmet is given over to fishermen, traders and the sporadic attentions of *scippi* (bag-snatchers). Not far away is **Le Ciminiere**, the hanger-like home to Catania's most dynamic arts and entertainment complex. Set on the seafront between the port and the station, this former sulphur refinery still retains its trademark chimneys.

A visit to the scruffy but appealing **Fera o Luni** market (daily except Sun) on **Piazza Carlo Alberto** creates an appetite for Catania's varied cuisine, including *pasta alla norma,* named after Bellini's opera. Framed by two churches, and hemmed in by backstreets, the rectangular square is a sea of bright awnings; below lie displays of lemons, garlic and herbs, with clothes, household goods and leatherware on the far side. Browsers will be drawn to the Sunday antiques market here, which sells everything from junk to Sicilian ceramics, handcrafts and country-style furniture. ❏

Map on page 262

TIP

Find refreshment in summer at *chioschi* (kiosks), which serve fruit syrups drunk with *seltz* (soda water) and sometimes salt. The usual one is *seltz e limone con/senza sale*, a soda water and crushed lemon concoction with or without salt.

BELOW: taking the air in Piazza del Duomo.

CATANIA PROVINCE

*Although the province embraces coastal Catania,
with its quaint fishing villages, its gaping heart
is the volcanic hinterland of Mount Etna*

Map
on page
270

Like Californians living on the San Andreas Fault, Sicilians are waiting for "the big one", the earthquake or eruption that will reverberate down the centuries. Until then, however, they are happy living the good life, picking nature's riches from the trees. Over 20 percent of Sicilians live on the flanks of the volcano. Farmers are drawn by the fertile soil while wealthy city residents have constructed villas for the views, cool summer climate and winter skiing on the slopes. Unlike Sicilian earthquakes, Etna's eruptions destroy property but are rarely life-threatening. Moreover, within 20 years, volcanic ash is ideal for producing sun-drenched fruit, wine and aubergines. But there is always an acknowledgement of the volcano's prior claim: "Etna has taken back my orchard," cried a farmer in 1992, as the river of lava swept past his fruit trees.

However, coastal Catania turns away from the volcanic hinterland, with its atavistic spirit and peasant culture. This is commercial Sicily, profiting from its entrepreneurial roots as a Greek trading colony. From Catania, the economic ripples reach the rest of the province, as do the effects of a healthy public administration allied to the native entrepreneurial spirit. To dub it Silicon Valley, as the locals do, is something of an overstatement, but the province is thriving, in Sicilian terms at least. Catania University's noted engineering faculty provides the impetus for the microelectronics and telecommunications industries.

As far as tourism is concerned, there is considerable investment in hotels, thanks partly to the increasing popularity of Etna's natural wonderland. As a result, Catania has budding resorts and significant commercial centres while exercising strict control over the Etna national park and curbing rampant building elsewhere. Etnaland, Sicily's first theme park worthy of the name, is planned for Fiumefreddo in the next couple of years, complete with miniature volcanoes and simulations of eruptions. As for urban planning, in late 1999 the province belatedly woke up to the fact that a section of the coastline had been sullied by building speculation: a lackadaisical enforcement of planning regulations had allowed the Simeto Valley nature reserve to be covered in illegal, makeshift housing. But the authorities stunned the locals with their efficiency in demolishing the site in a matter of days, thus setting the tone for more law-abiding practice in future.

PRECEDING PAGES: bold ceramics from Caltagirone. **LEFT:** Caltagirone's dramatic Scalazza. **BELOW:** glamour at the grocery store, Acireale.

Coast of Cyclops

Heading north from **Catania ❶** is a welcome release: sea breezes sweep away images of Catania's scruffy outskirts. The province hugs the Ionian Coast towards Taormina, and the Coast of Cyclops, named after the Homeric myth, presents a spectacular seascape. The

A fishing boat in Aci Trezza decorated in traditional style with designs supposed to bring luck to the fisherman.

Isole Ciclopi are jagged lumps jutting out of the sea just off the coast at Aci Trezza. Legend has it that these basalt rocks were flung at the fleeing Odysseus by an enraged, blinded Cyclops. The scenic rocks are now used as an oceanography station by Catania University. In summer, the coastal restaurants are full and flotillas of fishing craft double up as pleasure boats, but essentially the character of the local fishing villages remains unchanged: the daily markets display catches of anchovies and sardines, octopus and small fry for fish soup.

Aci Castello ②, on the Riviera dei Ciclopi near Catania, is memorable for its dramatic castle perched on a rocky crag overlooking the sea. The crenellated Norman fortress is well preserved despite frequent eruptions and a fierce attack by the Aragonese. A charming garden of local plants has recently been created on the roof terrace. From the castle, locals potter on the rocks or wander down to one of several fish restaurants along this gnarled coast.

Aci Trezza ③, a fishing village hoping to become a resort, is celebrated for its connection with Verga, the Catania-born writer, and his novel inspired by this

Map on page 270

seafaring community. *I Malavoglia* (*Under the Medlar Tree*, 1881) depicts the benighted lives of a fishing family with humour, perception and an intuitive sympathy. Visconti's *La Terra Trema*, inspired by Verga's novel, was filmed on the same spot. Verga was a master of such lines as: "Unfortunately the boy was conscientiously built, as they still make them at Aci Trezza." More tellingly, he feared the sea: "Property at sea is writ on water."

Close to the harbour awaits the **Casa del Nespolo** (daily 9.30–11.30am, 4.30–7pm), a tiny new fishing museum linked to Verga's novel. A new Verga trail begins in Aci Castello castle, with a costumed staging of sections of his work, followed by a guided visit to the Verga museum in Aci Trezza, and even a literary boat trip in the bay before an inevitable fish dinner in Trattoria Verga overlooking Aci Trezza harbour.

Acireale ❹ is proud of its royal appellation and stands aloof, both from the over-commercialised resorts and the rural hinterland. As Akis, the Greek settlement fared badly in the face of eruptions and earthquakes. However, thanks to the ravages of Etna and the talent of local craftsmen, the town is predominantly baroque. Compared with most coastal resorts, even Acireale's modern blocks of flats are respectable and unshoddy. As a proper living town rather than a satellite or ugly resort, the city is admired for its sense of balance, quality of life and sulphur spas, and shows little sign of searching for tourism. Upper-crust families still cultivate a distance, indulging in *noblesse oblige* charity work and membership of exclusive clubs. This snobbish, elitist image helps make Acireale a place for status-seeking Catanese to get married. Only during carnival are social differences put aside, as the town becomes a lively outdoor pleasure dome. Acireale advertises itself as having *il piu bello carnevale della Sicilia*, the best carnival in Sicily. This is borne out by the illuminations, the inventiveness of the floats and the enthusiasm of the crowds. Stalls sell masks, shoddy toys, feathered costumes, nougat, nuts and mushroom pastries.

The **Duomo** occupies centre stage, its 17th-century grandeur tampered with this century. However, the peeling vaulted interior is original enough, with *trompe l'oeil* decoration and stucco in musty browns and yellows. The inlaid marble floor contains an appealing 1848 Meridian Line. The **Palazzo Comunale** represents the first flowering of Catanese baroque, with its elegant, graceful facade and delicate wrought-iron balconies. French writer Dominique Fernandez considers this town hall a masterpiece, "full of imagination and rustic ingenuity". On the same square, set among the city cafes and grand churches, stands the restored white baroque vision of **Santi Pietro e Paolo**. In Piazza Vigo further down is **San Sebastiano**, such an exuberant baroque feast that the riot of cherubs and fancy carving on the facade threatens to spill into opera.

In the compact historic centre, the grandiose baroque buildings are gathered around Piazza Duomo, typifying the curious contrast between the spacious public squares and the small-scale design of the town beyond the grand *piazze*. Yet the tiny, dark alleys yield rewards in the form of pastry shops and ice-cream

Giovanni Verga (1840–1922), one of the key exponents of Italian literary realism, sought fame and fortune outside Sicily but eventually returned to his home province to live out his last years in solitude.

BELOW: pleasure-craft in Aci Trezza harbour.

*Acireale is credited
with inventing
sorbets, aided by a
profitable monopoly
on snow held by the
local archbishop
until modern times.*

parlours. Castorino, a cafe in Corso Savoia, is famed for its ice cream, pastries, cassata and *pasta reale*, decorated marzipan concoctions.

Acireale is surrounded by citrus groves, a source of wealth that continues to sustain the local land-owning class. From the town's public gardens stretches a fine view over the Coast of Cyclops, with the rocky shore riven by coves. Just below Acireale is the quaint fishing hamlet of **Santa Maria la Scala**, with its lava-stone shore, beached boats, watchtower and handful of simple trattorie. **Santa Venera**, a spa to the south of town, exploits the healing properties of Etna's radioactive waters. Sulphurous lava mud baths have been beneficial for rheumatism and skin conditions since Roman times.

Fiumefreddo di Sicilia ❺, north of Giarre-Riposto, is named after a cooling river that flows through thick clumps of papyrus. This feudal town has a tumbledown Phoenician tower and two castellated mansions. **Castello dello Schiavi**, the stranger of the two villas, has sculpted stone slaves leaning over an 18th-century parapet. Until the creation of the Etnaland theme park, the town's chief attractions are clear: coastal views and clean beaches. Fiumefreddo is a calming interlude before the volcanic hinterland. Alternatively, it is a springboard to chic Taormina (*see page 287*).

South from Catania

BELOW: the port
of Santa Maria
la Scala, near
Acireale.

The southwest of the province is occupied by **Piana di Catania**, a dullish plain that comes a poor second to Etna's attractions. The plain was reputedly the abode of the mythological cannibal Laestrygones. Until the 19th century it was better known as a malaria bed and, as a result, there are few farmhouses. Still, the orchards, citrus groves and pasture now make the plain a touch more

cheerful. **Militello in Val di Catania** ❻ is the only significant centre, with its medieval quarter, ruined castle and baroque churches. Even so, it is a place best visited by accident not design. By contrast, a couple of towns in the hilly southern interior have considerable charm, especially Caltagirone.

Grammichele ❼, approached via the SS 417 from Catania, is a bizarre baroque town, a champion of bold town planning after the 1693 earthquake. Within a hexagonal design, roads radiate from the central square like the spokes of a wheel. The Chiesa Madre and town hall personify the city's cool baroque image and clean geometric design. However, the clinical effect is mocked by the shabby, down-at-heel population.

Caltagirone ❽, further south along the SS 417, is a charming city covering three hills. The name derives from the Arabic words for castle and cave but its history is more ancient. It was settled by the Greeks but the mood is dramatic baroque. Like Acireale and Noto, hilly Caltagirone feels like a grand theatre, with spacious squares and majestic mansions. Most churches seem truly monumental and contain grand works of art, yet Caltagirone is best known as the capital of Sicilian ceramics.

The upper town is surprisingly grand for this part of Sicily, with the finest and most imposing public buildings clustered around **Piazza Municipio**. The **Corte Capitaniale** is a dignified mansion decorated by school of Gagini sculptures while the remodelled Norman cathedral is essentially true baroque. The **Museo Civico** (Tues–Fri 9am–1pm), situated on Via Roma below the cathedral, was once a fearsome Bourbon prison, and retains its barbaric, spike-studded metal doors. There is a museum inside with of Greek and Roman finds and prized Renaissance ceramics.

Map on page 270

A jug and vases from the 17th century; similar designs and colours are still used in Caltagirone today.

BELOW: pensioners gather at their club.

*Caltagirone's **Mostra dei Pupi Siciliani**, (daily 10am–1pm, 3.30–7pm; Via Roma 65; tel: 0933-54085) is both a puppet show and a museum displaying the differences between Palermitan and Catanese puppetry.*

Caltagirone is renowned for its decorative majolica. Signs of the industry are everywhere: ceramic designs occupy tiles, niches, ledges, and even parapets. Ceramic flowers even grace a bridge, **Ponte San Francesco.** The lovely formal gardens below Piazza Umberto are home to the **Museo della Cerámica** (daily 9am–6.30pm) housing a collection of Sicilian ceramics from prehistoric times to the present. Also in the gardens is the **Teatrino**, a majolica-decorated folly with ballustraded terraces. The star is the **Scalazza**, the staircase linking the old and new sections of the city. Each of the 142 steps is decorated in vivid majolica tiles depicting mythological scenes. In July, a colourful festival, "the tapestry of fire", takes place on the steps. Every year, this ingenious carpet of light is reinvented in different designs. The carpet consists of 5,000 tiny oil lamps on the steps; these are covered by delicate paper cylinders called *coppi.*

Etna environs

Etna is the gaping chasm where the heart of Catania province should be. The volcano munches Messina too, with new lava mouths opening all the time. Locals joke that not even the Mafia can close Etna's myriad mouths. *Mongibello,* the Sicilian name for Etna, comes from the Arabic word for mountain. Locally, Etna is known as *"a muntagna"* (the mountain). The volcano is addressed as "she", even though the word is masculine. Place names are symbolic: Linguaglossa is a corruption of *lingua grossa,* referring to the fat tongue of lava that engulfed the village. The native Siculi worshipped Etna long before the arrival of the Greeks. Adranus, their God of Fire, was believed to inhabit the turbulent depths of the volcano. To the Greeks, Etna was Hephaistos' forge, moulding black magic from incandescent lava.

BELOW: the bizarre gorge of Gola dell'Alcántara.

To present-day Sicilians, Etna is still an atavistic god. As Pino Torrisi, a carpenter, says: "You must never speak badly of Etna. She was here 200 million years ago, and we are guests on her slopes; we are nothing against her will." The sense of appeasing the mountain gods still survives in Zafferana Etnea, a hiking village and ski resort that found itself in the path of the 1992 volcanic eruption. Before abandoning his farmhouse to the volcano, Giuseppe Fichera left bread, cheese and wine to satisfy "the tired and hungry mountain". Even gods of destruction need food and rest.

The circular journey around the volcano is a game of light and shade. From the Ionian coast to the fertile Etna foothills is a feast of glistening citrus and olive groves, orchards and nut plantations. But clinging to Etna's flanks are dark volcanic villages and ruined Norman castles. It is a strange trail from green slopes to the moonscape above. From Taormina, a scenic railway runs to Randazzo, travelling along the valley floor, crossing a bridge made of lava blocks and even disappearing inside a lava cutting. But to appreciate Etna's grandeur, drive around the base or follow a similar route on the Circumetnea railway.

Leave the coast at Fiumefreddo, near Taormina, for a foray into the Alcántara Valley, starting with **Gola dell'Alcántara ❾**, a delightful gorge discovered in the 1950s when a Taormina film director was so enchanted with the prospect of a secret gorge that he had a tortuous path built down to the river. He was the first of many to capture Alcántara on film. Seen from above, the view is of wooded crags descending to a weirdly pitted river canyon. The bed is rocky, the remains of a prehistoric lava flow that created the peninsula of Capo Schisò. The canyon was created not by erosion but by the splintering collision of volcanic magma and cooling water. The impact threw up lavic prisms in monstrous shapes: these warped black basalt boulders resemble a cross-section of a fossil.

A lift leads down to the grey-green river. In summer, low water levels make the initial section accessible to visitors in waders or swim suits. The athletic can clamber to caves but a waterfall with a sheer drop is a barrier to further exploration of the gorge. Beyond are dangerous whirlpools and fast-flowing currents in ever-narrowing tracts, deceptive rapids that have occasionally claimed lives in recent years.

Francavilla di Sicilia ❿, just west along the SS 185, is set in a fertile valley of citrus plantations and prickly pears. Founded by King Roger, Francavilla prospered under Spanish rule. Roger's **ruined castle** occupies a lone mound in the valley and once guarded the route to Randazzo. The other Norman relic is the hermitage of **La Badiazza**, perched atop a rocky platform and victim of the 1693 earthquake. The **Chiesa Madre** has a Gagini Madonna, matched by the sculpted Gagini fountain in Piazza San Paolo. The **Matrice Vecchia** has a Renaissance door with a vine-leaf motif. The finest sight is the **Convento dei Cappuccini**, a 16th-century monastery on a lovely hillock, protected by Spanish sentry boxes and marble parapets. Inside is a profusion of *intarsia* work and carving, the handiwork of 17th-century monks.

Castiglione di Sicilia ⓫, set on Etna's northern flanks just south of Francavilla, is also a stop on the scenic Circumetnea railway. Perched on a crag, this ancient bastion possesses Greek ramparts but is better known as a Norman fiefdom. Narrow medieval alleys wind to the crumbling lava-stone church of San Pietro and the grander Maria della Catena. The **Norman castle** dominates the valley, with its jagged lookout tower, walls and roofs. This rocky citadel compels respect, as do the ominous views of rubble and volcanic debris trailing from Etna's summit.

Linguaglossa ⓬, another stop on the scenic rail route, 18 km (11 miles) southeast of Castiglione, is an unsophisticated ski resort and workaday walking and logging centre. The baroque **Chiesa Madre** pays tribute to the forests, with 18th-century choir stalls and a coffered ceiling, while the village's lava-stone pavements attest to its proximity to Etna. Although not prepossessing, the village makes an acceptable hiking base. Treks lead through pine forests to **Grotta del Gelo**, a lava-stone cave with weird light effects.

West of Castiglione lies **Randazzo** ⓭, the most atmospheric and coherent medieval town on the northern slopes of Etna, and the one closest to the craters. Originally settled by Greeks fleeing from Naxos, it reached its apogee under the Normans. During Swabian rule, Randazzo was a summer court and retreat from the heat of Messina. It remains a

Map on page 270

TIP

The Circumetnea, in existence since 1894, is the single-track rail route around Etna, a leisurely journey from Catania, taking in Paternò, Adrano, Bronte, Maletto and Randazzo, returning to the coast at Giarre-Riposto. The trip takes about 5 hours. For more information, tel: 095-374842.

BELOW: a vineyard near Linguaglossa.

*Pistachio nuts grow
abundantly in the
volcanic soil on the
terraced slopes
around Bronte.*

self-contained market town, with crenellated churches and sturdy 14th-century walls. For a town in the jaws of Etna, Randazzo has survived magnificently. The 1981 eruption threatened to engulf the walls and blocked surrounding vineyards, roads and railway lines, leaving the lava flow visible today. But human beings are to blame for any damage to the medieval core: Allied bombing in 1943 destroyed much of the Nazis' last stronghold in Sicily, including the fortress and finest *palazzi*.

Until the 16th century, a competition for supremacy fuelled the three rival communities. Each parish church took its turn as cathedral for a three-year term: the Latins were centred on the church of Santa Maria, the Greeks had San Nicolò and the Lombards San Martino. The churches were fiercely battlemented and ostentatious. Ultimately, the Catholics triumphed and Santa Maria is now the cathedral.

Porta San Martino, one of two surviving city gates, marks the entrance to the walled medieval town. The elegant Piazza San Martino is the heart of the shell-damaged Lombard quarter, set against the city walls. Appropriately, **Chiesa San Martino** has a 13th-century banded lava and limestone Lombard bell tower matched by an early baroque facade in grey and white stone. Virtually next door is the **Castello-Carcere**, a medieval castle and Bourbon prison due to become the city archeological museum. Beside the lava-stone windows is an inscription to Philip II and bullet holes that attest to the Nazi defeat in August 1943.

Via Umberto contains symbols of Randazzo's past role as a royal city, including the **Palazzo Reale**, the severe Swabian summer palace now demoted to a minimarket. Yet surprising signs of wealth remain in the chic jewellery shops, occasionally daubed with anti-Mafia slogans. Via Umberto ends in spacious

BELOW:
Randazzo, on Etna's
northern slopes.

Map
on page
270

Piazza Municipio, the bustling heart of Randazzo. Competing offices of the political parties remain a legacy of ancient rivalries. A giant outdoor chessboard is a chance to settle old scores. The square is dominated by **Palazzo Comunale**, the well-restored town hall. Leave the crowds by turning down **Via degli Archi**, a quaint arcaded alley, to Piazza San Nicolò and the Greek quarter. In one corner is Santa Maria della Volta, a 14th-century shell of a bombed church. In the centre of the square is the impressive Greek **San Nicolò**, with its original 14th-century apses and huge early baroque lava-stone facade and tapering campanile. Inside the church are several Gagini sculptures, including, appropriately, a St Nicholas.

At the end of Corso Umberto is **Santa Maria**, the Latin church, well sited opposite the smartest bar in town. It is an elegant grey lava stone church in Norman-Swabian design, with Norman apses and walls and side portals in Catalan-Gothic style. The odd interior contrasts Satanic-looking black columns and altar with a pure Gagini font and a 15th-century view of the town.

Admiral's estate

Between Randazzo and Bronte extends a wooded, volcanic landscape south to **Maletto ⑭**, noted for its wine and strawberries. Maletto marks the highest point on the Circumetnea line and offers views of recent lava flows. From Maletto, take a right fork to Admiral Nelson's castle at Maniace or continue south to Bronte. Following signs to Castello di Nelson leads to **Abbazia di Maniace ⑮** (daily 9am–1pm), one and the same. Set in a wooded hollow, the fortified abbey was founded by Count Roger, with the chapel commemorating a Saracen defeat in 1040. With Norman help, the Byzantine commander Maniakes routed the Arabs and regained Sicily for Constantinople. But the estate is better known as the fiefdom of Admiral Horatio Nelson, Duke of Bronte.

The title and estates were presented to Nelson by Ferdinand IV in gratitude for the Admiral's part in crushing the 1799 rebellion in Naples. Nelson's descendant, Viscount Bridport, only relinquished his Sicilian seat in 1981, when the 12,500-hectare (30,000-acre) estate was broken up and the orchards, nut plantations and dairy farms sold. Nevertheless, Nelson memorabilia remains, from paintings of sea battles to the Admiral's port decanter.

Inside the castle compound, the best part of the Benedictine abbey owes nothing to Nelson. The late Norman chapel has an original wooden ceiling, doorway and statuary. The original castle is unrecognisable, thanks to the 1693 earthquake and heavy anglicisation. It resembles a gracious Wiltshire manor from outside, an image confirmed by the genteel English cemetery. Even the gardens are home to neat hedges as well as cypresses and palms.

Between Maletto and Bronte are subtle shifts in scenery. Walnut and chestnut groves on the higher hills are dotted with jagged volcanic clumps, including the lava flow of 1823. Around Bronte, the slopes are covered with small nut trees, a reminder that 80 percent of Italy's pistachio crop comes from these well-tended terraces.

As Duke of Bronte, Nelson never visited his vast Sicilian estate, despite wistful dreams of retiring here with Emma Hamilton. The closest he got was in Emma's nickname for him, "My Lord Thunder", a reference to Bronte, the mythical giant who forged thunderbolts for Jupiter.

BELOW: Randazzo's largest church, Santa Maria.

The Norman castle in Adrano was built of black volcanic rock by Roger I. Once a Bourbon prison, it now houses a museum of Greek and Bronze Age artefacts.

BELOW: Adrano's convent church of Santa Lucia.

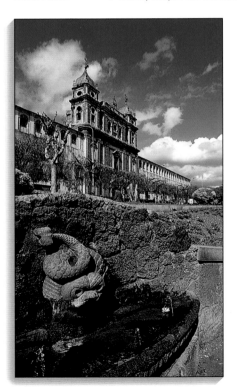

Bronte ⑯, founded in 1520 by Charles V, is an ill-planned town sandwiched between two lava flows on the western slopes of Mount Etna. As the administrative centre for the 24 hamlets of the Dukedom of Bronte, the town flourished but its present status is one of mere market town, noted for nuts. Bronte is resolutely shabby, its dingy charm residing in the neglected late Renaissance churches with crenellated towers. It is indeed a pious town: even urchins cross themselves when passing one of the many churches. In Piazza Pio IX the **Chiesa Madre** has a fine mosaic ceiling while **Chiesa San Sebastiano** opposite has faded frescoes and Greek-style columns.

South of Bronte, the prosperous air of solid chalets on the alpine plains gives way to ramshackle dwellings and rough scrubland. The pistachio plantations cede to scruffy, cacti-strewn slopes, with lumps of lava interspersed with white lava-coated trees. The makeshift mood reflects a region devastated by the 1985 eruption: everything built in haste but, given Etna's whims, with no time to repent at leisure.

Adrano ⑰, set on Etna's southwestern slopes, is a shabby market town with mythical roots. On the outskirts are the remains of a grander past: the Greek city of Adranon was founded by Dionysius I in the 4th century BC. In antiquity, the city was celebrated for its sanctuary to Adranus, the Sicel god of fire. Still today, during the bizarre August festival, a child dressed as an angel "flies" along a cord linking the old city powers: the castle, town hall and a statue of the god of fire himself. So far, Adranus has kept his city safe from fiery Etna.

Its battered charm lies in the busy **Piazza Umberto**. Like Randazzo, political associations and social welfare clubs are clustered around the main square. Here, too, is the austere **Norman castle**, sitting on its squat Saracen base. This powerful bastion was rebuilt by Roger I in the 11th century and remodelled by the Aragonese. The interior, once a Bourbon prison, houses a museum (daily 8.30am–noon) with minor Greek sculptures and Sicel ceramics. On the floor above is Queen Adelaide's chapel, a mysterious room decorated with purplish lava stone capitals by Roger's third wife.

Beside the castle, the **Chiesa Madre** is a Norman church disfigured by clumsy restoration. The dilapidated interior displays a luridly coloured polyptych and dusty missals. The heavy basalt columns conceivably came from the Greek Temple to Adranon that once occupied the site. Plutarch records a dramatic eve of battle appeal to the gods: in response, a bronze statue of Adranus suddenly quivered into life. A final twinge of nostalgia for ancient Adranon is evoked by the **Greek city walls**, lying at the end of Via Buglio.

Biancavilla ⑱, built on a basalt escarpment 5 km (3 miles) south of Adrano, was founded by Albanian refugees in 1480. Some of the 1991 influx of latter-day Albanians were resettled here but swiftly transfered to Palermo province, and then to wealthier Northern Italy. The sole Albanian link is the Madonna of the Alms, an icon brought over by the first refugees, and visible in the comically grandiose **Chiesa Madre**.

If Biancavilla is today best known for its prickly pears, **Paternò** ⑲, halfway between Biancavilla and

Catania, is famous for its oranges, the juiciest in Sicily. The town is of baroque inspiration but the **Norman castle** on a hilly volcanic site is more striking. The severity of the 14th-century lava-stone keep is echoed by the Great Hall and frescoed chapel. Frederick II died here while journeying to his favourite fortress of Enna (*see page 210*). Nearby is **Chiesa Madre**, a Norman church with a Gothic facelift, and the ruined Gothic **San Francesco**. More recently, the Nazis used this hill as an observation post and drew heavy Allied fire, leading to the death of 4,000 people. Known as Rocca Normanna, the castle quarter now enjoys happier associations: in summer, visitors can attend concerts, sample the local stuffed aubergines, or simply drool over terraces glistening with orange groves.

Nicolosi, east of Paternò, is both a charmless ski resort and the southern gateway to Etna's terraced wine and walking country. Lying east of the wooded Monti Rossi twin craters, the town was wiped out by the 1669 eruption. Today it marks the start of bracing treks to about 200 spent cones and prehistoric craters, and affords a fine view of Etna's active central crater and numerous secondary ones. (The helpful headquarters of Etna National Park, on Via Etnea, can advise on hiking routes.)

Just east, along the road to **Trecastagni ❷⓪**, the lava beds of 1886 and 1910 are visible. Once a medieval fiefdom, Trecastagni is noted for the **Chiesa Madre**, a Renaissance church probably designed by Antonello Gagini, as good an architect as he was a sculptor. Nearby, the 15th-century Chiesa del Bianco has a quaint, low bell tower while the Lombard-Romanesque Sant'Antonio di Padova has 17th-century lava-stone cloisters. Yet more appealing than the sights is the chance to appreciate traditional Etna craftsmanship: these lava-stone streets contain workshops dedicated to producing Sicilian carts and wrought

Map on page 270

It is worth sampling local produce in the villages. Sicilian pastries, roast lamb or sausages seasoned with fennel are typical fare, followed by luscious chestnut or citrus blossom honey, conserved peaches and fresh grapes, or crunchy, fruity nougat and delicious sorbets

BELOW: almond trees on Etna's fertile slopes.

TIP

Although respectable red wine is produced on Etna's slopes, it is wise to avoid Fuoco di Etna, an explosive but evil-tasting liqueur, especially before climbing Etna.

ironwork, basket weaving and painted ceramics, as well as traditional Etna carving in lava stone or gnarled olive wood. Nor are Trecastagni's almond biscuits, sorbets and red wines to be sniffed at.

Ascending Etna

Circling the volcano is intriguing and safe but an ascent requires caution. Depending on the season and Etna's mood, the menu may include a mere mass of clinker, a spent cone, a smoking cone, or even a seething lava front (*fronte lavica*). When it works, it is wonderful, with suphurous vapours, heat coursing through the soles of your shoes, and sightings of spitting fireballs. But if conditions are misty, you might as well be in a hotel room breakfasting on bad eggs or rotting cabbage.

An organised group trip is the sensible, relatively inexpensive way of experiencing Etna, but for sheer adventure, a private alpine guide is recommended. Without a guide, suitably clad explorers can clamber about at their own risk up to a certain altitude, currently 3,000 metres (9,850 ft). Even so, it is essential to get advice on routes and weather conditions from the refuge personnel. In fact, unless you are extremely fit and appropriately dressed, the best way to make an ascent of Etna is to purchase a cable-car ticket that also includes a guided drive and walk to the summit. (These trips, available to individuals or groups, are accompanied by guides who often speak basic English, French and German.) At the cable-car summit, just outside the bar, suitable footwear and warm clothing can be hired. From here, reinforced minibuses take passengers to the correct departure point from that to begin an ascent to the chosen destination, a route and goal which changes according to the group and the level of volcanic activity. At

BELOW:
the scorched
Silveri crater.

Map on page 270

this stage, the guides might gently try to deter the elderly and infirm from walking the final stage, but it is entirely an individual decision.

Once driving in the volcanic foothills or national park, follow signs for Etna Sud, the main southern access point, reached via **Zafferana Etnea** ㉑. Set on Etna's eastern slopes, this unprepossessing mountain resort hit the national headlines for a month in 1992 when Etna threatened to engulf the village. The resort had barely recovered from the 1984 earthquake and a minor eruption in 1986, when the baroque **Chiesa Madre** became the focus of fervent prayers as the local vineyards and citrus groves were swallowed up. The path of the 1992 eruption has finally been landscaped into a strange cross between a garden memorial and a tourist attraction, signposted "*Colata Lavica 1992*", Lava Flow 1992. Since Zafferana is only 500 metres (1,650 ft) from the crater on Monte Serra Calvarina, landslides and further eruptive activity are still common.

From here, a road leads to the **Sapienza** base camp and an ascent of Etna. As one climbs the scenic **Casa Cantoniera** road, citrus groves and wooded slopes give way to a wasteland of lava flows, bare slabs of brown rubble half-covered by snow. Even in deepest winter, snow is unevenly distributed, because of heat generated by the volcano. Recent volcanic debris is strewn around in folds of hardened lava, a desert of bluish clinker; occasionally, Etna violets and broom struggle for survival.

Route to the top

The base camp of **Rifugio Sapienza** ㉒, situated at 1,800 metres (5,900 ft), includes a refuge and hostel run by the Italian Alpine Club. Like much on Mount Etna, the centre lives dangerously, and has been rebuilt after an eruption

Zafferana Etnea's autumn festival, Ottobrata, began as a celebration of the local produce but now the autumn harvest of nuts, mushrooms, honey and wine is also enjoyed as a pleasant weekend outing for middle-class Catanese.

BELOW: the cable car from Rifugio Sapienza.

Map
on page
270

*Glowing on the top
and then repeating
its shape, as though
reflected, in a wisp
of grey smoke, with
the whole horizon
behind radiant with
pink light, fading
gently into a grey
pastel sky. Nothing I
have ever seen in Art
or Nature was quite
so revolting.*

– EVELYN WAUGH
ON ETNA

BELOW: Valle del
Bove, a chasm now
filled with lava.

recorded on a plaque as 9 April 1983, an event depicted in lurid technicolor inside. Before shunning the lava-stone souvenirs and taking the cable car to the top, glance at the spent cone just in front of the refuge, one of many extinct cones nearby. A winter **cable car** trip may be made in the company of skiers comparing eyewitness accounts of Etna's most recent devastation. En route are grim views of a burnt-out cable car destroyed in the 1983 eruption, along with ruined access roads, the wreckage of a ski lift and the original mountain refuge, buried by lava in 1971. At the summit, hardy visitors set off by minibus, leaving the less adventurous to simply admire the snowcapped views, usually best in the morning or at sunset, before sloping off to the mountain bar and videos of the volcano in action.

Torre del Filósofo, Empedocles' so-called observation post, wrecked in a past eruption, currently marks the highest point one can go with a guide, close to the southeast crater. Daring skiers peer into any active cone at their own risk. Empedocles did not live to tell the tale: the Greek philosopher allegedly leapt into the main crater in 433 BC in a vain attempt to prove that the gases would support his body weight. The charitable interpretation is that it was also a quest for divine consciousness in death. But, as his sandal was found on the edge, perhaps he merely slipped.

The view from the top will depend on volcanic activity and weather conditions, particularly the prevailing winds: it is vital to avoid the gases and volcanic matter emitted from active craters. Blue smoke indicates the presence of magma while a *corona*, a halo of sulphurous vapour, is a rare event. At most, you may see an active crater belching out sulphurous fumes or exploding *bombe*, molten "bombs", or the bottom of the misty cone bubbling with incandescent lava. In periods of intense seismic activity, the volcano spits out molten rock or fireballs, a dramatic sight, especially at night, but the guides have to judge a safe distance from which to view the phenomenon.

On the summit, the guides' current favourite gimmick is to let visitors watch a demonstration of the forging of black Etna ashtrays from molten lava, a feat involving long tongs like those used in the making of Murano glass in Venice. In exceptional circumstances, visitors may be shown a lava front some distance away from the volcano. Usually bathed in mist and emitting a stench of sulphur, the lava front sounds like the clinking of china cups or the hissing of some chained animal.

The descent of Etna may not be an anticlimax if you can visit a lava front, but visitors are strongly discouraged to do this without a guide or local help. In the most recent eruptions, **Valle del Bove ㉓**, best seen from **Milo**, has formed a lava front, hence its eerie, barren surface, devoid of vegetation. This former gaping chasm acted as a natural reservoir for the lava, thus sparing the valley towns. However, it was partly filled by lava in 1986 and 1992, and again in the dramatic eruption of early 2000. Today the volcanic dykes are barely visible under new lava. However, for most people, the descent by cable car will simply mean a return to the tacky bars and lurid shops selling lava-stone ashtrays. ❏

Etna's wrath

When Sicily's famous volcano erupts, the results are always unpredictable. As a local resident, Giovanni Giuffrida, says: "Lava is like a mole, it takes cover, burrows and reappears where you are not ready to catch it." In terms of duration, an eruption can last 10 minutes or 10 years (like the outburst of 1614).

Over centuries, the Catania coastline has receded or advanced in response to Etna's major lava flows. Even the 1908 earthquake, which razed Messina and claimed over 60,000 victims, did not change the coastline. But lava flows from Etna have often redrawn the map, most recently in 1978/79 when lava spilled into the sea, and reached the chapel doors at Fornazzo, a village near Giarre on the coast. A miraculous intervention was claimed after the molten lava was halted by a statue of the Madonna.

Historically, two of the most catastrophic eruptions occurred in 1381 and 1669, with lava flows that engulfed Catania and destroyed Nicolosi. In modern times, lava came close to Trecastagni in 1886 and 1910, while significant eruptions demolished the villages of Gerro and Mascali in the 1920s, and in 1923 narrowly missed Castiglione and Linguaglossa. Randazzo was narrowly spared by an eruption in 1981, which reached the town walls and destroyed surrounding property and vineyards, with repercussions as far east as the Alcántara gorge near Taormina.

The route to Etna Sud, the southern access point, passes lava flows dating from 1984, which destroyed the previous road. Beyond, closer to the volcanic heart, the 1983 eruption destroyed most of the Rifugio Sapienza and neighbouring property, ski lifts and roads. The barren patches south of Bronte, destroyed after an eruption in 1985, are a reminder that no vegetation grows on a fresh volcanic site for almost 20 years.

During the 1992 eruption, the biggest in recent years, the Americans were called in to save the resort of Zafferana Etnea, on Etna's eastern slopes. A US Navy and Marine task force, armed with the world's largest helicopters, set up base in Sapienza. The huge choppers made forays to the mouth of the crater, dropping blocks of concrete into the seething river of lava and stemming the flow.

The southeastern crater has been responsible for virtually all the eruptions since 1997, including the activity that began in February 1999 and continued into 2000. For much of the time, the glittering red cone was visible from Catania during the day, while tourists in Taormina could see nightly firebombs shooting out from a secondary cone. Volcanic ash reached the coast at Giarre-Riposto, coating the town in impenetrable dust, shattering car windscreens and damaging fruit trees.

Then, dramatically, in February 2000 the southeastern crater split into two, with fireballs and eruptive matter being tossed into the air to a height of 600 metres (2,000 ft), a nightly firework show visible from all over the province. The eruption continued for some time after the initial explosion, and any lasting effects it is likely to have on surrounding Catania remain to be seen. ❑

RIGHT: firebombs shoot high into the night sky.

STUDIO DI PITTURA
CARLO SILIGATO

Map
on page
288

TAORMINA

As Sicily's foremost international resort, Taormina was
popular before the war as a "fashionable loafing
place", a languorous image it maintains today

Taormina is Sicily's most dramatic resort, a stirring place celebrated by poets from Classical times onwards. Goethe waxed lyrical about the majestic setting: "Straight ahead one sees the long ridge of Etna, to the left the coastline as far as Catania or even Siracusa, and the whole panorama is capped by the huge, fuming, fiery mountain, the look of which, tempered by distance and atmosphere, is, however, more friendly than forbidding." D. H. Lawrence was equally enamoured, calling Taormina "the dawn-coast of Europe".

Yet this elemental site has been domesticated into a safe, sophisticated, unSicilian pocket. A century of tourism has toned down the subversive native spirit, effaced poverty and displaced undesirables. French visitors liken Taormina to a Sicilian St Tropez, stylish but unreal. Still, after Sicily's chaotic major cities, or the wariness of some of the islands' remote mountain villages, who wants reality? May, September and October are the loveliest months in Taormina, when the city enjoys a semblance of solitude combined with the pleasures of a mild climate.

The terraced town was once a wintering place for frustrated northerners and gay exiles. Today, this safe haven appeals to romantic couples of both sexes, sedate shoppers and the cultured middle classes. As a resort, Cefalù, near Palermo, is Taormina's only serious rival. But Taormina is the only Sicilian resort with top-quality hotels and an enlightened, if rampantly commercial, approach to tourism.

Local gossip has it that the town is uncontaminated by corruption because even the Mafia likes a crime-free holiday haunt. Yet despite designer glamour and the hordes of blasé cruise-liner passengers, the site's majesty is not manufactured. Nor is the heady decadence and timeless charm. Taormina may now have its first Internet cafe, but the locals prefer to pass the time of day chatting from an ancient balcony overlooking the sea.

The town is largely closed to traffic, so parking is expensive and inconvenient, with access strictly controlled and places limited. As the local slopes are steep, the hotels scattered around several locations, and the "courtesy buses" unreliable, many visitors will need to use taxis to reach their hotels or to go out on the town. Fleecing tourists is a local art so establish the taxi fare before setting out: there are fixed rates for many journeys but you'll need to find this from your hotel, and insist that the driver knows you know.

Illustrious past

Taormina started as a Siculi settlement at the foot of Monte Tauro. It was an outpost of Naxos (*see page 309*) until the Greeks fled the first colony for

PRECEDING PAGES:
the Greek Theatre.
LEFT: a picture gallery in an ancient building on Via Teatro Greco.
BELOW: locally-grown fruit for sale.

A gate tower has stood on this site, now Piazza IX Aprile, as part of the town's defences since the 6th century. It was rebuilt in the 12th century, and the clock added in the 17th, since when it has been known as Torre dell'Orologio.

Taoromenion in 403 BC. Under the Romans, the city acquired a garrison and the new name of Tauromenium. The town also prospered in medieval times and became the capital of Byzantine Sicily in the 9th century. It was the last Byzantine stronghold to fall to the Arabs, destroyed in 902. But it was rebuilt almost immediately, and captured in 1078 by the Norman Count Roger d'Altavilla, under whom it enjoyed a long period of prosperity. Aristocratic leanings later drew Taormina into the Aragonese camp and support for the Spanish, with the Catalan legacy reflected in the town's array of richly decorated *palazzi*.

Taormina's *raison d'être* is the **Teatro Greco ❶** (daily 9am–5.30pm), a setting that is pure drama, with the *cavea* (horseshoe of tiered seats) hewn out of the hillside. In Greek theatres, sea and sky were the natural backdrop; the Romans preferred proscenium arches. Where the Greeks worshiped nature, the Romans tried to improve on it. The Hellenistic theatre was built under Hieron in the 3rd century BC and enlarged by the Romans in AD 2. Like Tindari's Greek theatre, Taormina's was turned into an arena for gladiatorial combat. Roman theatrical conventions caused the view to be obscured by arches. By adding a double portico and colonnades behind the stage, they showed insensitivity to the natural setting.

Romantics side with the Olympian gods in seeing Roman grandiosity as no match for the timeless character of Greek art. However, Roman erudition is evidenced in the well-preserved *scena* (the construction behind the stage that served as a backdrop and also storage area). But in the 19th century, the granite columns and Corinthian capitals were wrongly repositioned on the site. Still, Greek purists are delighted to see the Roman *scena* crumble, the better to appreciate the Greek atmosphere.

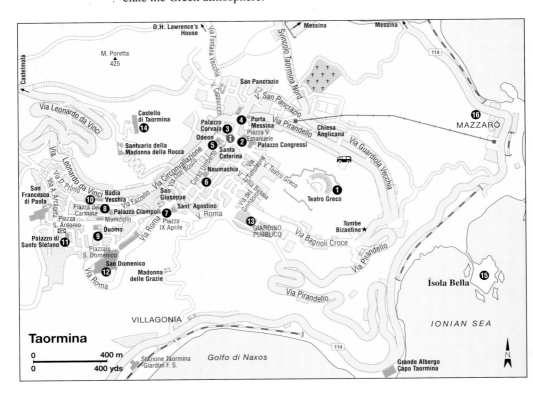

Taormina

Not that cats sunning themselves on the ruins distinguish between Greek marble and pinkish Roman brickwork. In high season, the theatre is best explored early in the morning or near closing time, to avoid the crowds. Views from the terraces above the *cavea* and *parascenia* (wings) reveal a perfect fusion of the elements. The writer Vincent Cronin likened the theatre to a seagull suspended between sky and sea. The scene is shrouded in mystery by a smouldering volcano or snowcapped peak. Citrus groves carpet the slopes while the cliff face is a tangle of cacti and orchids. Below stretches a craggy coastline and the romantic islet of Isola Bella.

The theatre is still used today, not for performances of Classical plays, as at Siracusa, but as the venue for an international arts festival, Taormina Arte, which presents drama, cinema, ballet and music every July and August (tickets and information from the tourist office).

Piazza Vittorio Emanuele ② lies beyond, a noisy market square built over the Roman forum. Bordering the piazza is **Palazzo Corvaja ③** an historic mansion where the Sicilian Parliament met in 1411. Now a tourist office and exhibition centre, this eclectic building incorporates a crenellated Saracenic tower, a secluded courtyard, sculpted parapet, and Catalan-Gothic decorative details around the doorway and windows.

On the far side of the square stands the medieval gate of **Porta Messina ④** and, through the arch, the tiny church of **San Pancrazio**, built over a Temple to Isis. Nearby is the **Odeon ⑤**, or Teatrino Romano, a Roman concert auditorium partly hidden by the charming church of Santa Caterina.

Corso Umberto, the pedestrianised main street, is a feast for shopaholics. The 15th-century *palazzi* have been converted into craft shops, boutiques and bars.

Map on page 288

TIP

When choosing your hotel, it is worth paying extra to have a room overlooking Mount Etna, particularly when it is in an eruptive phase. **San Domenico Palace** and **Grande Albergo Capo Taormina** are two that provide magnificent views of the volcano.

BELOW: traditional puppets for sale.

TIP

The map of Taormina available free from the tourist office contains a series of well-presented walks (in various languages), ranging from gentle archaeological strolls to challenging hikes around Monte Tauro.

Luxury food emporia display bottled peppers, candied fruit, marzipan animals and fresh kumquats. Majolica tiles, leather goods and traditional puppets vie with elaborate cut-glass chandeliers and reproductions of Classical statuary. Just off the Corso lies the **Naumachia** ❻, a hybrid construction second only to the Greek theatre in importance. Originally a vaulted cistern connected to the city baths, it evolved into a Hellenic *nymphaeum* and Roman gymnasium. The atmospheric arched buttress walls remain, propping up the Corso. For lunch, the restaurant terraces of the adjoining Via Naumachia beckon, with Gambero Rosso arguably the best.

Halfway down the Corso, **Piazza IX Aprile** ❼ offers glittering views of Etna and close-ups of preening poseurs at chic cafés. **Sant'Agostino**, the forbidding 15th-century church on the square, has been converted into a cosy library. The city churches feel more like social than spiritual centres: **San Giuseppe**'s rococo interior overflows after a Sunday service; after much hand-shaking, the congregation spills into the cafés, disdaining the outstretched palm of the odd blind beggar outside.

The Corso continues beyond the Porta di Mezzo, a clock tower marking the city's medieval quarter. Steps lead to the Catalan-Gothic **Palazzo Ciampoli** ❽, now Hotel Palazzo Vecchio. After admiring its Aragonese battlemented facade and mullioned windows, call in for a sweet Sicilian pastry at Bar Saint Honoré before climbing Via Venezia, a charming alley by the Corso, or strolling down to the cathedral.

Piazza del Duomo is a central meeting place. At sunset, or at the first sign of spring sun, kids fetch their footballs, the *jeunesse dorée* pose, and Taormina's perma-tanned lounge lizards, not a dying breed, search for foreign prey. Matrons

BELOW:
Piazza del Duomo.

still swan around in weighty furs: in Taormina, the fur coat parade lasts until May. The **Duomo** ❾ itself (daily, 8am–noon, 3.30–6.30pm) draws crowds to its winter cycle of classical concerts. The crenellated stone facade has a severity that survived Renaissance remodelling but is softened by the baroque fountain on the square, which sports sea horses, cherubs and a podgy female centaur. This weird mythological creature is the city symbol, confirmed by a stone centaur unearthed on the Greek site.

Opposite the fountain, steps lead to Piazza del Carmine and the **Badia Vecchia** ❿, a battlemented 15th-century abbey (summer daily 9am–1pm, 4–7pm; winter Mon–Fri 9am–1pm, 4–6pm, Sat 9am–1pm). Although over-restored, the abbey still has Trecento flourishes, Gothic arched windows, fret-work and friezes. Set on a lower level, **Palazzo di Santo Stefano** ⓫ is a gracious ducal palace and Taormina's loveliest medieval building. Highlights are the Norman-Gothic windows, delicate lava stone cornices, and the lacy frieze of *intarsia* work (decorative wood inlay), a Saracenic legacy.

From here, Via del Ghetto winds down to **San Domenico** ⓬, a 15th-century monastery converted into a *de luxe* hotel. During the war, it was Marshal Kessel-ring's headquarters and suffered bomb damage, although the cells and cloisters were spared. The cells are now distinctly unspartan bedrooms.

English connection

It is a short stroll to the **Giardino Pubblico** ⓭, a lush park bequeathed to the town by an eccentric Englishwoman in the 1920s. Florence Trevelyan adorned her hanging gardens with pagoda-style follies and observation towers for bird-spotting (she was a keen amateur ornithologist). The tiered gardens are linked

Map on page 288

In summer, there's a combined cable-car and bus service (Funibus) to beaches around Taormina, including Mazzarò, Giardini Naxos and Letojanni (see Messina Province, page 297).

BELOW: Taormina and Castelmola, high above.

Map on page 288

The sun designs seen on modern ceramics can be traced back to the late Greek period.

BELOW:
cable cars from the city to Mazzarò.

by mosaic paths and wind past caged peacocks and tropical plants, from spiky cacti and lilies to dull English hedges.

St George's Anglican Church also dates from Trevelyan's time. Her contemporary, D. H. Lawrence, lived for a few years in a villa in Via Fontana Vecchia, part of which has been renamed Via David Herbert Lawrence. When King George V visited, Lawrence was the only British resident to ignore him. Undeterred, the King called on the writer and helped water his garden. In Taormina, the sickly Lawrence chose to live a solitary life, writing of sensuality. His former home is still a private house, marked by a plaque: "D. H. Lawrence, English author, lived here 1920–1923".

Also on the north side of town, perched on Monte Tauro, is a tumbledown medieval **castello** ⓮. It can be reached by a half-hour ascent up a steep, winding path that passes by the clifftop **Santuario della Madonna della Rocca**. It is a strenuous climb, which should not be attempted in the middle of a summer's day, but the panoramas from the top are worth the effort.

Via Leonardo da Vinci climbs circuitously from Taormina to **Castelmola**, a hamlet perched on a limestone peak (there is a bus service). From this natural balcony over the sea, there is a sense of what Taormina used to be. Out of season it is home to old craftsmen and part-time potters, but in summer it resembles a tourist trap, with trinket shops and bars. Caffe San Giorgio is the place for celebrity autographs, a reminder of (separate) visits by Churchill and Kesselring. Once Churchill's local, it is now devoted to hearty German drinkers downing beer or local almond wine.

Below Taormina, sheer cliffs drop to the tempting islet of **Isola Bella** ⓯. From Via Pirandello, a cable car (*funivia*) links the city to the pebbled beach at **Mazzarò** ⓰. Nearby are entrances to underwater caves, where scuba divers spot shrimps, red starfish, perch, scorpion fish and sea urchins. If you prefer your fish on a plate, leave the sea for the grey and pink cliffs above Taormina. For details of beaches close to Taormina, see Messina Province chapter (*see page 297*).

Chic living

As Sicily's glitziest resort, Taormina is sophisticated fun, from the summer cultural season to the Sunday posers. The chic crowd wears Valentino ties and Armani suits; even dogs are clad in little coats. The backdrop is equally vivid: balconies hung with geraniums and bougainvillea; inner courtyards with sculpted cornices, grape-carved motifs, and miniature lemon trees.

Taormina by night is a fitting farewell. The Catalan-Gothic facades are illuminated and the squares tinged pink in the moonlight. From the belvedere, Etna's fiery cone glitters before dissolving into the sea, stars and smoky peaks. The locals say a prayer in Chiesa Santa Caterina before picking up a pastry for dinner. Strollers slip into a fashionable restaurant in the aptly named Vicolo Stretto (narrow alley). Solitary walkers climb Salita Ibrahim to the Carmine, a tranquil monastic spot with a tower and wild garden behind. Dreamers take Via Caruso to the Badia Vecchia and bay views, a reminder that Taormina, like Vancouver, is a setting in search of a city. ❏

Foreign Vices

When Harold Acton pronounced Sicily "a polite synonym for Sodom", he was really referring to Taormina. The camp city was founded during a period of Greek decadence and has always lived down to its debauched reputation. In this, it has been helped by its theatrical foreign residents. From the Belle Epoque to Edwardian times, Taormina was, along with Capri, the quintessential homosexual haunt.

The gay resort was first publicised by a trio of Germans: a poet, a painter and a photographer. Goethe pronounced Taormina a "patch of paradise on earth" in 1787. Otto Geleng, a landscape artist, settled there nearly a century later. The Prussian's paintings of the scenery drew gasps when they were shown in Paris salons. Although married to a Sicilian, he was a believer in the dictum of girls for procreation, boys for pleasure.

His younger friend, Wilhelm von Gloeden, arrived in 1880 and stayed until his death 50 years later. The exiled blond baron photographed nude Sicilian shepherd boys whose beauty elevated them to the status of Greek gods. His lithe peasants, draped in panther skins or photographed against sunsets, soon entranced jaded Berliner high society.

Oscar Wilde often helped in the compositions, crowning the boy models with laurels or posing with pan pipes. Von Gloeden swooned over Wilde, declaring the poet "beautiful as a Greek god". Wilde returned the compliment, at least artistically, but preferred his "marvellous boys" as companions.

A later voluptuary with showbiz connections was the Bavarian Gayelord Hauser, the Hollywood dietician to the stars. In the 1940s, Gloria Vanderbilt, Marlene Dietrich, Rita Hayworth and Joan Crawford danced until dawn at his parties. But while most of Taormina's male population ogled the screen goddesses, Hauser was more enamoured of the local gods.

Truman Capote and Tennessee Williams were regular guests at the wild parties at Villa Hauser. Both worked in Taormina before alcohol and drugs wreaked havoc with their writing. Capote accused Williams of "hiring boys for the afternoon" but both were often picked up drunk in bars on the Corso. Drunk or sober, Williams singularly failed to live up to his "lone wolf" reputation in Taormina.

Somerset Maugham and Anatole France were familiar figures on the Taormina scene, indulging in "the Disneyland of sin". Inspired by gossip about gay Taormina, the poet Jean Cocteau also came to see "the boys with almond eyes".

All this was seemingly at odds with Taormina's air of twee Edwardian gentility, not to mention the mores of the English expatriate community. Douglas Sladen's book on *fin de siècle* Sicily confessed: "Nobody goes about naked, as might be imagined from the photographs." Thus reassured or disappointed, the British turned Taormina into a cosy seaside resort. When showing Evelyn Waugh around Taormina in the 1950s, a downcast Harold Acton pointed out a placard inscribed "Nice Cuppa Tea" and complained that Taormina was now "quite as respectable as Bournemouth". ❏

RIGHT: a shepherd boy poses for von Gloeden.

MESSINA PROVINCE

Messina stands astride two worlds: an outward-looking coast with popular resorts turns its back on the seemingly remote, mountainous hinterland

Messina's official slogan is *"Monte e Mare"*, a promise of oceans and mountains through the gateway to Sicily. Certainly, Messina delivers rugged ranges and contrasting coastlines. The Tyrrhenian coast is one of rocky inlets, saltwater lakes, sand dunes and dry gravel-beds; citrus groves are fringed by myrtle, broom and prickly pear. The Ionian is a gentler but equally exotic coastline with sandy shores and similarly bland resorts. Both coasts offer Classical sites, stumpy castles, seafood dishes and an enticing hinterland.

Coastal refinement is set against a backdrop of ancient mountain culture, with lifestyles that are aeons apart. The raggedy hinterland is the place for Moorish churches and for those on the trail of Madonnas by Antonello Gagini, Sicily's greatest sculptor. The wooded hillsides abound in bizarre festivals and wrinkled peasants on slow-moving mules. After this, Taormina (*see page 287*) comes as a shock, an international oasis. But the coastal glitz of Taormina is grafted on to self-contained rural Sicily.

Messina, which thrived for centuries as a seafaring power, was a Phoenician-Punic colony settled by the Greeks in 730 BC. Although it flowered as a Norman stronghold and crusader port, Messina bears a distinct Greek imprint. This stretch of coast is awash with Greek-inspired myths: sailors north of Messina were wary of the twin demons of Charybdis, the whirlpool, and Scylla, the six-headed sea monster. It took an 18th-century scientist to demystify the whirlpools as the meeting of clashing currents. Although diverted after the 1908 earthquake, strange counterflows still exist, colourfully known as *bastardi*. Messina's decline set in with the outbreak of plague in 1743, followed by earthquakes and, in the 1800s, by a naval bombardment and cholera epidemic.

But the greatest calamity was the 1908 earthquake, which killed 84,000 people in 30 seconds. The shore sank by half a metre and the reverberations were felt in Malta a day later. In 1943, Messina represented the Nazis' last stand: the city was devastated and 5,000 people died during Allied bombing. Such disasters have engendered a salvage mentality: every recoverable stone has been reused or recreated.

The ensuing fresh start favoured economic enterprise. Today, the province has pockets of industry at Messina and Milazzo, with oil, tyres, terracotta and cement replacing the dependence on fruit production. Tourism is important and hotels abound, partly thanks to the well-organised Mafia infrastructure. However, the province's long-term prosperity depends on better communications, symbolised by the building of a suspension bridge over the Straits to the mainland. As yet, the benighted bridge is only a gleam in the regional government's eye. The cynical Sicilian view

PRECEDING PAGES: Messina harbour with the mainland of Italy beyond. **LEFT:** looking over Messina. **BELOW:** the dome of the Tempio del Cristo Re.

is that it will never be built because it would lead to the loss of several thousand jobs in the ferry industry. However, after years of procrastination, the long overdue Messina-Palermo motorway is operational, with the final two sections probably completed by 2002.

Messina city

The wide boulevards, grid system, imposing public buildings and matter-of-factness make **Messina**  the most American-looking Sicilian city. While not instantly appealing, Messina's apparent blandness conceals a handful of sunken treasures and lively cafes. As a touring base, however, Taormina or a Tyrrhenean coastal resort are infinitely preferable.

The port's protectress is the Madonnina, the tall statue built on ancient harbour walls. Curved around the sickle-shaped harbour is the neglected Cittadella, the remains of the 16th-century Spanish bastion. At the Maritime Station, trains are dismantled, devoured by the cavernous ferry and shipped over the Straits. The harbour welcomes grey NATO warships docked in deep water and long-prowed feluccas in pursuit of swordfish. Ever present are the boats of the Guardia di Finanza, the efficient fraud squad on the trail of drug smugglers. Despite the bustle, the overwhelming feeling is one of space and sweeping views; the townward side of the harbour has no walls. Unlike Palermo, Messina does not turn its back on the sea.

The **Duomo** (daily 9.30am–7.30pm) symbolises the stubbornness of the natives: this Norman cathedral has survived medieval fires, earthquakes and wartime American firebombing. It is set on a lower level than the surrounding streets that were redeveloped after the earthquake. The sculpted main portal

In Classical times Messina was called Zankle, after its sickle-shaped harbour, the name also reputedly referring to the sickle with which Zeus castrated his father.

BELOW: the performing clock on the Duomo's campanile.

Messina Province

TYRRHENIAN SEA

and much of the Gothic facade are original, including the vivid farming scenes. The designer pink and grey interior impresses with its pleasing proportions. Restored treasures include a painted wooden ceiling, 14th-century mosaics in the semi-circular apses, glittering Renaissance altars and a Gagini statue of St John. The high altar boasts an extravagant Madonna, a vision of Sicilian literalism adorned with a silver crown and Byzantine gold background.

The **Orion fountain**, outside the cathedral, is a Renaissance masterpiece by Giovanni Montorsoli, a pupil of Michelangelo. It is a tribute to Orion, a mythical city founder, and also a celebration of water, from the Tiber to the Nile. This riot of cherubs and watery figures is overshadowed by a free-standing Flemish belfry. The old campanile contains an astronomical clock from Alsace. Its most spectacular performance is at midday: religious and mythological scenes are played out to the accompaniment of a cock crowing and a lion roaring.

Piazza Antonello, the next square north, houses a cluster of Art Nouveau public buildings leading to the vaulted Vittorio Emanuele gallery, an elegant Art Nouveau concoction. In a neighbouring square is the **Chiesa dei Catalani** (open for Sunday Mass only), a sunken Arab-Norman church with Byzantine echoes. Built on the site of a Temple to Neptune, this eclectic church has Norman arches, blind arcading, 13th-century portals and honeycomb apses. The facade features a star-shaped abstract design on the domes. Inside, the three naves have barrel and cross-vaulting, spindly capitals and a cupola resting on Byzantine plumes. The mellow stonework is often festooned with flowers: as Messina University chapel, it is much in demand for academic weddings.

The city churches are a wayward mixture of restoration and invention. However, **Santa Maria degli Alemann**i, a few blocks south of the cathedral, is an

Map on pages 298–299

The ferries into Messina from the mainland bring trains as well as cars and passengers.

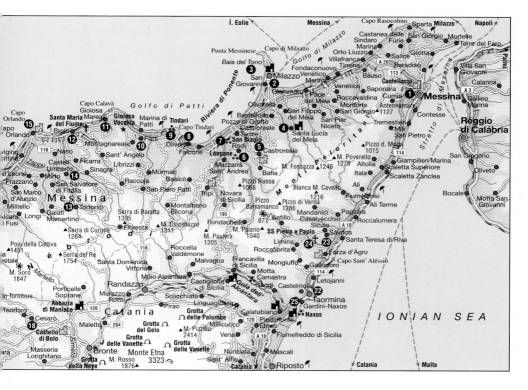

Antonello da Messina, born in the city around 1430, also worked in Naples and Venice, where he developed a startlingly "modern" technique. There are works by Antonello in Messina's Museo Regionale.

BELOW: open-air refreshments.

authentic roofless Gothic ruin, founded by the Order of Teutonic Knights. Behind it is the severe 17th-century **Sant'Elia** church, named after a patron saint who failed to save the city from the 1743 plague. Messina's magpie approach to architecture is illustrated by the neoclassical Town Hall, mock-Renaissance Chamber of Commerce, Fascistic Tribunal and Art Deco Prefecture. Contemporary churches can be Rhenish, Bavarian, Spanish or, like San Giuliano, a Byzantine pastiche. Even genuine relics are given a contemporary twist by an incongruous setting: San Francesco, a Gothic fortress of a church, overlooks a frothy ice-cream parlour.

In Piazza Unità is Montorsoli's Fountain of Neptune but the original Renaissance sculpture lies in the **Museo Regionale** (daily 9am–2pm), on Via della Libertà. The museum is noted for its works by artists connected to the city. Antonello da Messina is Sicily's master painter and southern Italy's greatest Renaissance artist. His moving St Gregory polyptich blends Flemish technique with Italian delicacy and a Sicilian sense of light. The best-preserved panel is the Virgin and Child. Caravaggio, an equally influential figure, worked in Messina and his theatricality imbues Sicilian art. His familiar dramatic poses and doomy shadows are here in *The Adoration of the Shepherds* and *The Raising of Lazarus*.

Messina by night

Writer Rodolfo de Mattei likens the city to "a sailing ship, low in the water, ready for a night cruise". Indeed, mercantile Messina looks romantic at night, its lights glittering along the harbour front. Summer strollers take a *passeggiata* from the seafront to the lively cafes on Piazza Cairoli. After dinner, underage lovers enjoy the scenic drive up Viale Umberto to the botanical gardens.

In summer, city life shifts to **Mortelle**, a youthful resort 10 km (6 miles) north of Messina. En route, the coastal road passes the Ganzirri lake, once famed for its mussel beds, now a popular place for dinner in summer, and **Torre del Faro**, the tip of the toe of Italy. This peninsula was once graced by a Temple of Neptune whose columns ended up in Messina Cathedral. Today's view is of gigantic pylons and power cables that supply Sicily with electricity.

Mortelle, just around the cape, offers sandy beaches, open-air films and pop concerts. However, for sophisticated international nightlife, the Messinesi prefer Taormina. This stretch of coast is devoted to popular summer tourism and fishing. As a result, the air is heavy with a peculiar combination of petrol fumes and grilled swordfish.

The Tyrrhenian Coast

From Messina to Milazzo and the coast, follow the SS 113, the old Roman road, for the best scenery. The first stretch climbs the Monti Peloritani, winding past pine groves, broom, oleanders and geraniums. But even from the motorway are dazzling glimpses of azure inlets through the pines. On the way out of town are views of three ruined forts and apricot-coloured churches in the hills. Just before the SS 113 passes under the motorway, take the rough road on the right to the **Badiazza** (always

Map on pages 298–299

open). This fortified Benedictine convent is set in an overgrown gully. Local lore has it that these 12th-century ruins were converted from a Byzantine granary. What is not in dispute is that the abbey was the meeting place of Eleanor of Anjou and her future husband, Frederick of Aragon.

The SS 113 allows panoramic views of pine forests and the Straits, particularly from Portella San Rizzo, the road leading along the crest of the Peloritani range to Monte Antennamare. The coastline from Messina to Palermo has been heavily fortified since Aragonese times. The headlands are still dotted with defensive towers built by the Spanish and exploited by the French. The Napoleonic forces boasted of being able to transmit a message to Naples in under two hours by lighting a string of fires in the coastal towers.

Tunnels thread through pine and olive groves to **Milazzo ❷**. The vision of this verdant peninsula is slightly marred by the presence of an oil refinery. Compensations lie in the welcoming breezes and dramatic castle, with views of the jagged green spit stretching towards the Aeolian Islands (Isole Eolie). This is the place to while away the time waiting for a ferry by sampling swordfish or *bottarga* (mullet roe).

Traces of ancient civilisations around Milazzo include a Bronze Age settlement north of the castle and a Greek necropolis in Piazza Roma. From the Norman era onwards the citadel of Milazzo was regularly besieged; the victors could hold sway over the Tyrrhenean Sea. The unprepossessing commercial centre lies at the foot of the castle, clustered around the isthmus, but the historic nucleus is the walled city. *Palazzi* with baroque balconies and elegant stonework embellish the lower town, particularly Via Umberto I. Here too, **Duomo Nuovo**, the new cathedral, is memorable for its Renaissance paintings in the apse. But

According to local tradition, Milazzo, known as Mylae in Classical times, was the site of Odysseus' shipwreck.

BELOW: Torre del Faro, the tip of Messina province.

On 20 July 1860 Giuseppe Garibaldi led his Redshirts against the Bourbon troops garrisoned in Milazzo castle. His victory freed Sicily from Spanish rule.

BELOW: Santa Maria di Pollina.
RIGHT: Milazzo crowned by its Norman citadel.

the most satisfying churches are the 15th-century San Giacomo and Chiesa del Carmine, a 16th-century Carmelite convent.

Salita San Francesco, a steep stairway, climbs through the Spanish quarter to the impressive medieval citadel, its flanks encrusted with churches. The 17th-century San Salvatore belonged to a Benedictine abbey whereas San Rocco represents an older, fortified church. San Francesco di Paola is a frescoed 15th-century shell with a baroque facelift. The cluttered interior contains a Madonna and Child by Gagini. Facing the castle is the **Chiesa del Rosario**, once a seat of the Spanish Inquisition. This Dominican church is studded with stucco, an oddly fluffy vision for the rigorous interrogators.

The **Castello** (Tues–Sun 10am–noon, 3–5pm), perched beside a rocky precipice, occupies the site of the Greek acropolis. Originally Arab-Norman, the citadel later fell into Hohenstaufen, Aragonese and Spanish hands. The castle was even a British base during the Napoleonic Wars. But its finest hour was in July 1860 when its seizure by Garibaldi's forces spelt the rout of the Royalists and the Republican conquest of Sicily. Garibaldi himself led the hand-to-hand combat against the Bourbons. The surviving fortress is of 13th-century Hohenstaufen dynastic design with Aragonese walls. A Gothic gateway leads to the keep and parliamentary Great Hall. Also within the castle walls, the Mannerist **Duomo Vecchio**, currently being restored, overlooks an open-air theatre.

Boat trips to the **Baia del Tono** ❸ visit reefs, coves and grottoes, including favoured swimming spots such as the Baia San Antonio or Baia la Renella. Near the Baia del Tono is **Grotta di Polifemo**, Polyphemus' cave, where Odysseus blinded the Cyclops. The 7-km (4-mile) boat trip around the peninsula from **Al Faro** (the lighthouse) to Baia del Tono affords views of Sicily's two

active volcanoes, Etna and Stromboli. Alternatively, a stroll along the Al Faro promontory from the lighthouse to Capo di Milazzo leads through lush vegetation to the cape. For the energetic, a climb to the heights of Monte Trinita is a chance for a lingering look over to the Aeolian Islands (*see page 313*).

Map on pages 298–299

Inland excursions

If the hinterland beckons, then **Santa Lucia del Mela** ❹, 20 km (12 miles) inland from Milazzo along a winding rural road, is a Saracen village with a Norman castle. It rose to prosperity in the 16th century as a trading post on the Lombard silk route. The churches are well endowed with works of art, thanks to the wealth generated by the local silver mine. The Norman **cathedral**, revamped in 1607, contains a Gothic portal and 16th-century treasures including an Antonello Gagini statuette of St Lucy. The church attached to the castle seminary contains a Gagini Madonna while the library has a collection of illuminated manuscripts. Garibaldi stayed in the monastery of San Francesco before he fought his decisive battle against the Bourbons the following day.

After following the SS 113 west from Milazzo, take the turning south signposted Castroreale for another foray into the hinterland. **Castroreale** ❺, a shabby upland village dominating the Micazzo valley was founded by the Siculi in the 8th century BC. Although the settlement flourished as a medieval barony, a ruined tower is all that remains of Frederick II's summer home. If trapped overnight in this medieval time warp, male visitors may consider staying or dining with the lonely abbot at the crumbling Collegio dei Redentori, a depopulated monastery. Many churches in the region were damaged by the 1978 earthquake, although they retain their original treasures.

The fertile coastal plain is rich in vineyards, olive plantations and orange groves, not to mention money-making spas. Bland **Castroreale Terme**, Castroreale's coastal counterpart, holds some appeal for enthusiasts of water cures. This noted spa centre faces the Aeolian archipelago and claims cures for liver congestion, gastritis, constipation and genital diseases, with treatments including mud baths and the drinking of sulphurous waters.

From here, an inland road leads to the archaeological site of **Longane** ❻ (10am–sunset), near **Rodi**. Set on the edge of the Peloritani mountains, this megalithic and Sikel settlement was razed by Messina in the 5th century BC. The remains of a turreted fort are visible and there are Bronze Age cavity tombs are found in the nearby necropolis. From Rodi, join the SS 185 as if returning to the coast. Just before Castroreale Terme lies the Roman site of **San Biagio** ❼, a Roman villa built in the first century (daily 9am–one hour before sunset). The baths feature a black and white mosaic of fishermen and dancing dolphins.

The SS 113 takes you westwards to **Oliveri** ❽ and a chance to exchange churches for seafood and excellent beaches. Between here and Cefalù is arguably the cleanest stretch of coastline on the island. Oliveri itself is a standard Sicilian resort with a Norman-Arab feudal castle and sandy beaches. On the seafront is a converted *tonnara*, the traditional tuna-processing plant,

*The hill-top village of **Roccavaldina** is worth a detour for its unique 16th-century herbalist's pharmacy. Amid painted pestles and mortars are 238 beautiful majolica jars, jugs and vases commissioned from Renaissance craftsmen and used to store medicines until the 19th century.*

BELOW: waiting for the ferry in Milazzo.

a reminder of life before tourism. Yet the tuna, aubergine and pasta dishes show that life post-tourism retains something of its original flavour.

Oliveri is on the **Golfo di Patti**, a wilder spot than the Gulf of Milazzo, stretching west to the rocky ridges of Capo Calavà. Its bays are framed by the moody Nébrodi mountains. The coastal road crosses *fiumare*, wide, dry torrent-beds, and overlooks World War II pill box defences. Dominating the headland is **Tindari** 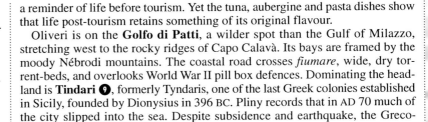, formerly Tyndaris, one of the last Greek colonies established in Sicily, founded by Dionysius in 396 BC. Pliny records that in AD 70 much of the city slipped into the sea. Despite subsidence and earthquake, the Greco-Roman city prospered until razed by the Arabs in 836.

The **archaeological park** (daily 9am–two hours before sunset), overrun by goats, is pleasingly wild. Italian visitors are more impressed by the sacred Black Madonna housed in the church bordering the park. The Greek city covers a Bronze Age site and has left its mark in impressive boundary walls and assorted public buildings. The Greco-Roman theatre cannot compare with Taormina's but enjoys a superb natural setting overhanging the bay. Classical drama, concerts and opera are now performed here in summer. A wide thoroughfare, one of three original *decumani,* links the theatre to the vaulted basilica. This Augustan basilica was once a grand entrance to the *agora,* a ceremonial space for meetings and festivals. Nearby are the remains of Roman baths, villas, workshops and taverns. One villa is adorned with geometrical mosaics while the thermal baths enclose mosaics of dolphins, bulls, warriors and the Trinacria, the symbol of Sicily. The on-site **antiquarium** displays sculptures, ceramics, a tragic mask and a bust of Augustus.

Santuario della Madonna Nera, built on to an old chapel, stands on the site of the acropolis. This glittering church is a contemporary effusion of kitsch beloved by Sicilians. It is revered all over Southern Italy as a shrine to a black-faced Byzantine icon with miraculous powers. The Madonna Nera bears the motto: *Nigra sum, sed hermosa* ("I am black, but beautiful"). Among other miracles, she is credited with causing the sea to withdraw to provide a magic mattress of sand to cushion a child's fall over the cliff. The sanctuary attracts many pilgrims, particularly on the Madonna's feast day, 8 September.

Below Cape Tindari is the **Oliveri lagoon**, one of Sicily's loveliest natural havens. Migratory birds, including grebes, coots and egrets, are drawn to the pale green saltwater pools and wide beaches of translucent grey pebbles. The lagoon's capricious sands are a sublime spot, yet also the place for a picnic of fresh bread and local *caciocavallo* cheese.

Patti ❿ is set on a low hill overlooking a cultivated plain. The medieval quarter, linking Via Ceraolo and the cathedral, has a quiet charm and several art-filled churches. San Nicolò and San Michele contain works by Gagini while the 15th-century Sant'Antonio Abate has Corinthian capitals supporting delicately rounded arches. The remodelled **cathedral** is home to remarkable treasures: a subtle Madonna by Antonello da Saliba and the Renaissance sarcophagus of Queen Adelasia, the wife of Roger I, complete

Ancient Tindaris was named after the legendary Spartan king Tindareus, step-father of Helen of Troy (her true father was the promiscuous god Zeus). The city's first citizens were refugees from Sparta after the long Peloponnesian War against Athens.

BELOW: Castoreale, Frederick II's summer retreat.

with the original Norman effigy. Traces of Norman rule also lie in the ruined tower, gateway and stretch of city walls.

Sadly, this historic hill town is ringed by a jagged necklace of new development. Even so, Patti has recently unearthed its greatest attraction, a **Roman villa** (daily 9am–one hour before sunset) at Marina di Patti. Its fate is indeed curious. This sumptuous late-Imperial villa was destroyed by an earthquake in AD 4 but restored and then occupied until Byzantine times. After centuries of oblivion, it was rediscovered during the construction of the motorway in 1973. The gracious rooms lead off a porticoed peristyle, looking incongruous beside the motorway flyover. The mosaics display geometric, animal, figurative and floral motifs, often of African inspiration. The stylised compositions and subtle chromatic range make for a satisfying whole. But like the finer villa in Piazza Armerina (*see page 215*), Patti suffers from periodic waterlogging and wilful neglect. After a surfeit of art and architecture, picnic among the poppies, as the Roman aristocracy did, or retreat to the beaches of **Marina di Patti**.

Seaside and mountains

From Patti to Capo d'Orlando are a cluster of bland resorts fighting a battle against coastal ribbon development and the Mafia, currently losing the former but winning the latter. From the sandy resort of **Gioiosa Marea** ⓫, one can walk up to the ghost town of **Gioiosa Vecchia**, abandoned after an 18th-century landslide. **Brolo** ⓬, just west, has a crenellated Saracen tower, crumbling city walls and several grand *palazzi*. But food is the real incentive: fish soups and squid dishes, as well as strong-tasting salami from the hills behind Brolo.

From Brolo, a rural foray inland visits Raccuja, Tortorici and Castell'Umberto,

Map on pages 298–299

The towns along this stretch of coast are traditional Mafia strongholds, but the clan's grip on the community has been weakening since 1992, when local businesses formed an association to resist payment of pizzo *(protection money).*

BELOW:
Oliveri lagoon,
seen from Tindari.

Santo Stéfano di Camastra is famous for its ceramics, and its streets are full of potteries and shops selling locally made ware.

a case of the journey being more pleasurable than the destination. Citrus groves give way to pine forests and steep ridges, with stunning views from the hill-top villages to the Aeolian Islands. This is the **Madonie** mountain range, parched in summer and dotted with ski resorts in winter (*see page 146*). From Brolo, a tortuous inland road leads to **Raccuja** via Sinagra. In winter, you can continue south along the SS 116 to the ski resort of **Floresta**. Heading back to the coast from Floresta, turn left off the SS 116 to visit a couple of villages before returning to the coast at Capo d'Orlando. **Tortorici** ⓭, the first significant village, is traditionally associated with Mafia activities but also possesses several fine churches and school of Gagini sculptures. About 10 km (6 miles) north along switchback roads is **Castell'Umberto** ⓮, a former feudal domain with a long Dominican tradition. Constant landslides persuaded the citizens to abandon the historic centre for a new home. Nonetheless, the *centro stórico* still has a whimsical, rustic charm, with its ruined castle and vine-hung churches.

Capo d'Orlando ⓯ is a windswept headland subject to sudden storms. Set on the edge of a fertile plain, the town is geared to tourism and citrus farming. There is little of interest in this sprawling resort save a sandy beach strewn with whale-shaped boulders or a climb to the ruined medieval castle and church perched on the cape.

Sant'Agata di Militello ⓰, the first significant seaside resort west of Capo d'Orlando, has been at the forefront of anti-Mafia campaigns in recent years. However, holidaymakers more readily associate the resort with summer promenades, its popular pebbled beach, and regular hydrofoils to the Aeolian Islands. Sant'Agata is dedicated to fun and seafood, with the local castle turned into a restaurant. Before travelling inland, try the swordfish or *granite* (sorbets).

BELOW: much of the Madonie is a nature reserve.

Monti Nébrodi

A rural drive through the wooded hinterland of the **Nébrodi** mountains (also known as the Caronie) takes you into remote, rugged hill-walking country. The rounded silhouettes of the Nébrodi offer vistas of rocky outcrops or rolling hills covered in oak and beech woods or rough pasture. Apart from grazing sheep, the terrain is home to falcons, hawks, eagles and wild fowl. Compared with the Madonie range, the Nébrodi are less accessible: transport within the range is necessarily slow since the lack of east-west roads often means retracing one's steps to the coast.

San Fratello , 18 km (11 miles) from the coast, is one of the most characteristic villages, particularly colourful during its famous demonic festival, the Easter Feast of the Jews (*Festa dei Giudei*), a shrieking costumed chase through the village. It is not so much anti-Semitic as Sicilian, hence a sacrifice of subtlety to spectacle. This Lombard colony, founded by Roger I, retains its distinctive Gallic dialect dating back to Norman times. This scenic mountain village has a Norman church and a 15th-century Franciscan monastery. The SS 289 road then snakes through rugged terrain to **Cesarò** ⑱, which stands in the shadow of the volcano's northwestern slopes. If the views of Etna prove too seductive, then explore the foothills of the volcano in the adjoining province of Catania. Alternatively, follow a winding route around the confines of the park to **Mistretta** (SS 120, then SS 117) or backtrack to Sant'Agata and the coast.

For those wishing to remain on the coast, the SS 113 leads west to **Santo Stéfano di Camastra** ⑲, one of Sicily's best centres of pottery production. The rows of vivid streetside wares make purchase a mere formality. About 8 km (5 miles) west of Santo Stéfano is **Halaesa** (daily 9am–1 hour before sunset), a Siculi settlement that flourished under the Greeks. Excavations are in progress Sicilian-style, bribery and political clout permitting. **Castel di Tusa** ⑳, which marks Messina's western provincial border, is noted for its ruined castle, rocky beach, and eclectic avant-garde hotel, the Atelier sul Mare (tel: 0921-334295). From here, leave Magna Graecia for Mafia country or Messina's lush Ionian coast.

From the coast, the enchanting SS 117 road leads 16 km (10 miles) inland across the Nébrodi range to **Mistretta** ㉑, a rust-coloured town commanding a ridge. The mellow stone town is noted for power rather than piety, despite its 22 churches. The Mistretta Mafia clan, led by Giovanni Tamburello, is adept at extortion. However, the jury at the 1992 trial failed to convict Tamburello, despite damning evidence by supergrass Antonino Calderone. With its ruined feudal castle, sculpted Chiesa Madre, red-tiled houses and cobbled streets, the town has a faded charm. Since it is not visibly wealthy, Mafia money must be stashed away elsewhere.

The Ionian Coast

This narrow coastal strip is characterised by a contrast between the barren slopes facing the shore and the wooded slopes facing inland; there are architectural contrasts too, between the baroque or modern coastal towns and the medieval settlements in the hilly

Map on pages 298–299

TIP

Before setting out to explore the Nébrodi mountains, it is worth consulting the main park office at Cesarò (tel: 095-696008), who can advise on hiking routes, pony trekking, rural accommodation and maps.

BELOW: the rural pace of life.

hinterland. From Messina, the motorway hugs the shore south to **Taormina** ㉒ (*see page 287*), hemmed in by mountains. The exotic coastal vegetation, ravaged by rampant development, is wilder further south. From the old coastal road south, tempting tracks explore the hinterland.

If you are travelling on the motorway, at **Santa Teresa di Riva** leave the coastal crowds for mountain air and curious hamlets. Despite the proximity of Taormina, this is timeless Sicily, as remote as anywhere on the island. The scenery is stark: skeletal peaks and brooding ravines; mountains gouged by winter torrents and scorched brown in summer. Such fierceness is softened by sweet-scented scrub and the curves of Moorish monasteries.

Just inland is the battered mountain village of **Sávoca** ㉓, best known for its macabre mummies, embalmed in a crypt by local monks. The monastery was in use until 1970 and awaits restoration by a Catholic mission. The catacombs of the **Cappuccino Convento** (daily; summer 9am–1pm, 4–7pm; winter 9am–1pm, 3–5pm) contain 32 ghoulish mummified corpses dating from the 17th century. At a time when corpses were thrown into the communal ditch, genteel mummification was a tradition among noble families. The bodies were drained, sprinkled with salt and left to dry for a year before being washed in vinegar, aired and then dressed in their original clothes. These gruesome, wizened faces and shrunken puppet-like forms are mummified abbots, lawyers, noblemen and priests. Others lie naked in caskets or as skulls squeezed into high niches.

After this macabre scene, leave the monastery for the evocative medieval village, a former Saracen stronghold. Sávoca's name derives from sambuca, the elder trees that still perfume the hills. A paved path climbs cacti-dotted terraces and olive groves to the village. The roads were repaved with the proceeds of *The Godfather*, filmed on location here. Coppola found his perfect setting in the dusty piazza, the windswept church, the shots of Etna smouldering in the distance, and the shimmer of the Ionian Sea below.

Equally atmospheric are the churches overgrown with prickly pear, the tumbledown dovecote, abandoned houses and the terraces slipping into the sea. The church of San Nicolò lost its choir in a landslide but kept its dignity while the Chiesa Madre retains the charm that caught Coppola's eye. This solitary church, on a narrow ridge overlooking the sea, was renovated with film money. The scruffy Bar Vitelli, immortalised in Michael Corleone's wedding banquet, comfortably hosts peasants and *borghesi*, united in their thirst for a cool *granita di limone* (lemon sorbet).

Casalvécchio Sículo, set above Sávoca, is a livelier but less complex village. Its Chiesa Madre has a gilded interior full of chanting crones. Nearby are windswept views over terraces. On the outskirts of the village, take the first turning left, a steep road signposted to **SS Pietro e Paolo** ㉔, a monastic church down in the Val d'Agro. Despite its desolate location on the bank of the dry Agro river, SS Pietro e Paolo is the most significant Norman church in Eastern Sicily. The twin-domed exterior is reminiscent of a Turkish mosque. A banded facade combines red brick, black lava, cool limestone and grey granite. Blind arcading and mosque-like decor complete

A number of the mummies in Sávoca's catacombs are daubed with green paint. This was not a 17th-century ritual but is the result of modern vandalism, and impossible to remove without damaging the corpses.

BELOW:
remains to be seen in the catacombs of the Cappuchin Convent, Sávoca.

the picture. A Greek inscription over the west portal names Gerard the Frank as the master builder, an imported craftsman who oversaw talented artisans. Restored in 1171, the church is a synthesis of Byzantine and Norman styles. Moorish roundness and decorative flourishes compete with Norman verticality and austerity. Yet the interior is a happy marriage between stylish Arab stalactites and solid Norman squinches.

Before ascending to Taormina, consider visiting neighbouring **Giardini-Naxos ㉕**, the first Greek colony in Sicily. It was founded (as Naxos) on an ancient lava flow by Euboeans in 735 BC and became a springboard for colonisation of Catania and the east coast. But after supporting Athens against Siracusa, the colony was destroyed by Dionysius in 403 BC. The archaeological site (daily 9am–1 hour before sunset) occupies the promontory of Capo Schiso (follow signs for "*scavi*"). A stretch of Greek lava-stone city walls remains but the elusive Temple of Aphrodite is still being excavated, as are some noble houses. The museum contains Greek, Roman and Byzantine exhibits, including a head of Silenus, god of fertility and wine.

The Greeks would bewail the great colony's degeneration into a downmarket pleasure beach. Lemon groves are giving way to ribbon development, for Giardini-Naxos is Sicily's fastest-growing resort. Still, for the young crowd there are compensations: cheap and cheerful *trattorie*, wide beaches fringed by volcanic rocks and a riotous nightlife that Silenus might have sympathised with. Moreover, unlike Catania province, this stretch of coast offers sandy, rocky or pebbled shores, with a wide variety of free and private beaches. **Letojanni**, a humble fishing village until the 1960s, is now a bustling resort with facilities for horse riding, water sports and sub-aqua photography. ❑

Map
on pages
298–299

← ⚏	bar Turrisi
← ⚏	bar Duomo
← ⚏	hotel Panorama di Sicilia
← ✕	bar trattoria 777
← ✕	Le Mimose PIZZERIA
← ✕	da Pippo
← ✕	La Campagnola
← ✕	PIZZERIA Valle dell' Etna
← ⚏	bar S. Giorgio

There's no shortage of tourist amenities in Giardini-Naxos, Sicily's fastest-growing resort.

BELOW: Capo Sant'Aléssio, near Taormina.

THE AEOLIAN ISLANDS

Although two of the Isole Eolie still have active volcanoes, the archipelago as a whole is characterised by a sleepy charm that is barely affected by the recent growth in tourism

Map on page 314

A rching out from the north coast of Sicily lies an underwater volcanic ridge 200 km (125 miles) long, from which rise the rocky islands of the Aeolian chain. Seven of them are inhabited today, as they have been since before the Bronze Age; there are fragments of Iron Age villages and Roman buildings to be seen, and Greek graves within the Spanish walls of Lípari's citadel.

The mineral-rich volcanic rocks of the Aeolians provided the basis of their early wealth: obsidian, a black, glass-like rock used to make cuting tools, was mined in Lípari and traded all over the Mediterranean more than 5,000 years ago, and pumice works are still active on the island. In the 17th century the woods of oak on the islands' fertile slopes were cleared to make terraced fields to grow grain and wine for export. Patterns of building still clearly show how houses were built on the rocky ridges each side of a valley, leaving the narrow flat *lenze* available for cultivation. Though agriculture and fishing are now only small-scale, many families grow most of their own vegetables, and harvest olives and capers for salting.

The decline in the traditional sources of income led to a dramatic drop in the islands' population, from over 20,000 in 1911, to around 12,000 in 1971. Many relocated in Australia in the 1950s and among the locals you will hear returned emigrés with a Queensland tang in their voices. There is even a Miss Eolie competition in Sydney. Now tourism is begining to develop, providing a major new source of income. But the strict controls on building and the relative remoteness of the islands ensures that even in high summer you can find an empty beach or a quiet house where you can watch the sunset accompanied only by the sound of cicadas in the olive trees.

There are ferries and hydrofoils to the Aeolians: the ferry is cheaper and provides better views of each island you pass. Their volcanic origins are immediately apparent. Each has at least one crater, and black rivers of rock among the lurid reds and yellows bear witness to past lava flows. Strómboli and Vulcano are still spectacularly active, though the last eruptions were in the 1880s.

PRECEDING PAGES: the ferry leaves Marina Lunga, Lípari. **LEFT:** the hydrofoil arrives at Marina Corta. **BELOW:** pumice and obsidian for sale to tourists, Lípari.

Lípari

The largest of the islands and home to half the Aeolian population, Lípari is the lively hub of the archipelago, and its mineral wealth and thermal waters led the fortunes of the whole region. As the boat approaches, the crowded roofs of old **Lípari Town ❶** come into view, dominated by the citadel set on a small hill, its massive Spanish walls enclosing the cathedral and the 17th-century bishop's palace.

Hydrofoils dock at **Marina Corta** on the southern side of the citadel, ferries just to the north at **Marina**

Swordfish are a favourite catch of Aeolian fishermen, and a regular part of the Aeolian diet.

Lunga. The two are linked by the main shopping street, Corso Vittorio Emanuele. The Tourist Information office (open Mon–Sat, Sep–Jun) is at the Marina Lunga end of the street, from where it is easy to find your bearings. The main sights are all within a short stroll of the harbour.

From the **citadel** (daily, 9am–7pm) you can look down on the whole town, a cool vantage point among the pines in the Archaeological Park. This also provides the best views of the other two main classical sites, the **Zona Archeologica** and the **Contrada Diana necropolis**, both to the west of Corso Vittorio, both now sadly neglected and overgrown. The maze of backstreets between Via Marte and Via Garibaldi are picturesque with some elegant stonework and lush potted plants decorating the tall facades.

The excavations opposite the **cathedral** provide a striking illustration of the layers of building on the site over 2,000 years up to Roman times, each culture stamping its authority by further development of the stronghold. This archaeological evidence is unique in Europe and has enabled the dating of other sites. The superb **Museo Eoliano** (daily 9am–2pm, 4–7pm), housed partly in the bishop's palace, contains a wealth of material from across the archipelago, including the oldest and most complete set of Greek theatrical masks in existence.

A good road rings Lípari, linking the eight main villages. A taxi tour frequently provides enthusiastic commentary and plenty of stops for photographs. **Cannetto** ❷, 4 km (2½ miles) north of Lípari Town, has a long pebble and black sand beach and a range of small bars and *trattorie*. About 1 km (½ mile) further you can take a winding path down to **Spiaggia della Papesca**, a sandy beach whitened by pumice dust. It is this dust that turns the sea an extraordinary turquoise all along to **Porticello** about 2 km (1 mile) to the north. Pumice is still

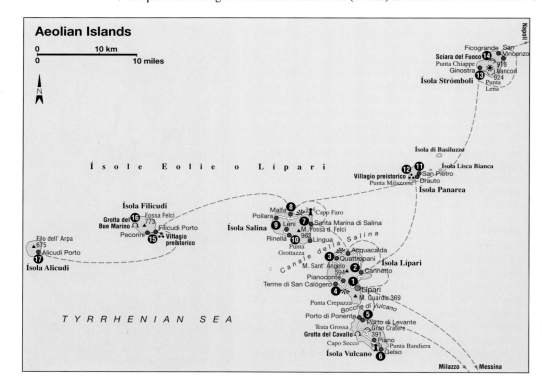

Aeolian Islands

0 ——— 10 km
0 ——— 10 miles

N

Ísole Eolie o Lípari

TYRRHENIAN SEA

Ísola Strómboli
Ficogrande San Vincenzo
Sciara del Fuoco ⑭
Punta Chiappe 918
Ginostra ✳ Vancori
924
Punta Lena ⑬

Ísola di Basiluzzo

Ísola Lisca Bianca
Villagio preistorico ⑫ ⑪ San Pietro
Punta Milazzese Drauto
Ísola Panarea

Ísola Filicudi
Grotta del ⑯ Fossa Felci
Bue Marino 773
Pecorini Filicudi Porto
⑮ Villagio preistorico

Malfa ⑧
Pollara Capo Faro
Leni ⑦ Santa Marina di Salina
Ísola Salina ⑨ M. Fossa d. Felci
Rinella ⑩ 962
Lingua Salina
Punta Grottazza Canale della
M. Sant' Angelo Acquacalda
594 Quattropani
Pianoconte ③ Ísola Lípari
Terme di San Calógero ② Cannetto
① Lípari
④ M. Guardia 369
Punta Crepazza Bocche di Vulcano
Porto di Ponente ⑤
Testa Grossa Porto di Levante
Grotta del Cavallo Gran Cratere
391
Capo Secco Piano
Punta Bandiera
Ísola Vulcano ⑥ Gelso

Filo dell' Arpa
675
Alicudi Porto ⑰
Ísola Alicudi

Napoli

Milazzo ◄ ► Messina

Map on page 314

quarried here, and sold for a wide range of products including building blocks, cosmetics and fertiliser. You can buy chunks and carvings from roadside stalls or pick up small pumice stones all along the beaches.

Continuing the circuit of the island for 2 km (1 mile) or so, you come to the northernmost village, **Acquacalda**. A few bars and a small *trattoria* along the stony beach look out to Salina across a narrow strait. From Acquacalda the road winds up past the **Puntazze** rocks, with wide views right across from Strómboli to Alicudi, and on through fields and green countryside for 5 km (3 miles) to **Quattropani ❸**. Here there is a pretty church and views across the fertile westerly side of the island. Another 6 km (4 miles) on, past several small hamlets, is **Pianoconte**, home to Lípari's largest vineyards and three restaurants. Just outside the village, down a narrow road towards the coast, are the thermal baths of **San Calógero ❹**. The modern spa hotel is closed, but you can explore the ancient site and splash yourself with the hot therapeutic waters that come out of the ground in a domed chamber dating from the Mycenean period. Back on the main road, the circular route winds back down another 4 km (2½ miles) to Lípari Town, passing **Quattrocchi** where the *belvedere* provides a resting place and views across to Vulcano.

Vulcano

Only 1 km (½ mile) from Lípari, across the Bocche di Vulcano, the steaming crater of Vulcano rises behind the its smaller cousin, **Vulcanello**, which erupted from the sea in 183 BC. As the boat arrives in **Porto di Levante ❺** you can smell the sulphur fumes and the lime green, yellow and red rocks add to the extraordinary experience. Porto di Levante's **beach** is popular despite the smell, and immediately to the south of it, behind a huge multi-coloured rock, are the famous mud baths (*fanghi*). The therapeutic qualities of the mud for the treatment of arthritis, rheumatism and skin disorders have been praised for centuries. After your mud bath you can wash off in the thermally heated sea, taking care to test the water, as some areas are scaldingly hot.

Ten minutes' walk across the isthmus is the beautiful curve of black sand at **Porto di Ponente** where in the evening there are westerly views to the sunset and the jagged forms of the rocks Pietralunga and Pietra Menalda off the coast. To the north the road leads to **Vulcanello** and about 2 km (1 mile) away on the northeastern extreme of the island to the **Valle dei Mostri** (Valley of the Monsters), a bizarre collection of natural sculptures created by lava and erosion that are particularly evocative in early morning or evening when shadows create the impression of wild beasts.

Any visit to Vulcano should include a climb to the active crater, **Gran Cratere** or **Fosse di Vulcano**. The ascent takes about an hour and, though it's hot and exposed, can be undertaken by anyone who's reasonably fit. Take water and wear stout shoes. The smell of sulphur intensifies as the path zigzags up the slope, over black sand and crusty volcanic rock, and past deep furrows cut by previous eruptions. At the top you are rewarded by the extraordinary unworldly sight of the massive bowl

TIP

If you take a bath in Vulcano's health-giving mud, limit it to a maximum of 20 minutes and take care not to get mud in your eyes as it stings badly. Jewellery and leather will be permanently stained by contact.

BELOW: steaming crater over Porto di levante, Vulcano.

of the crater, hissing and steaming and crusted with crystals of yellow and red. A walk round the crater takes about half an hour and there are excellent views of the other islands and the flat southern plain.

The crater and the views of the archipelago can also be seen from **Capo Grillo** about 10 km (6 miles) from Porto di Levante. The hamlet of **Gelso** ❻ on the south coast is named after the mulberries that are grown in the area. It is about 15 km (9 miles) from Porto di Levante but bus services are extremely limited. The easiest way to get there is to negotiate a boat trip with a local fisherman, ensuring enough time for lunch at one of Gelso's excellent *trattorie*.

Salina

In lush green contrast to Vulcano's sering colours, Salina's two peaks are thickly wooded with conifer, sweet chestnut and oak and the island's small towns and quiet beaches offer a peaceful relaxing stay. Boats arrive at **Santa Marina di Salina** ❼, halfway along the island's east coast. Here there is a small main street and a couple of bars and *trattorie* where you can watch the comings and goings on the quay. About 2 km (1 mile) along the rocky palm-lined coast lies **Lingua**, its tiny lighthouse marking the southern tip of the island, and behind it a lagoon previously used for salt extraction, which gave the island its name.

The main town, **Malfa** ❽, is 7 km (4 miles) from Santa Marina, its small harbour backed by a steep jumble of picturesque old boatsheds and crumbling fishermen's houses. In the town, and indeed all over the island, you will see signs advertising Malvasia, a sweet golden dessert wine made from sun-dried grapes and still produced by small growers on the island. Excellent local organic red wine can also be found. Bus services run from Malfa all over the island. Beware of missing the last bus back, for finding a taxi can be difficult.

From Malfa the road winds steeply for about 6 km (4 miles) to the small village of **Pollara** ❾ perched on one side of a half-submerged crater. There are two beautiful beaches reached by a small path 20 minutes' walk from the bus stop by the church. To the right is a tiny beach ringed with boathouses hacked into the cliff. To the left the path leads down to a black sandy beach backed by huge white cliffs. In the summer canoes and pedaloes can be hired for exploring the dozens of coves and inlets.

Between the two peaks, from which the ancient name for the island, Didyme (twin), derives, the road runs directly south through the **Val di Chiesa** past the **Santuario della Madonna del Terzito**. This convent and church have been the object of pilgrimages for many years and the first pages of the visitors' book make interesting reading. A party of young children, accompanied by their priest, have noted their pious thoughts on the visit: no mean feat when travel was by rowing boat. Behind the church is the path up to **Monte Fossa delle Felci**, the easterly peak, now a nature reserve. The ascent is shaded by mixed woodland and well signposted, culminating in a rocky scramble and fabulous views. Depending on the route you take, the walk is between four and six hours. The steep path down to Santa Marina is very slippery and

The gentle 1994 film Il Postino (The Postman), *which was nominated for a handful of Oscars, was shot entirely on location on Salina.*

BELOW: taking a sulphur bath in Vulcano.

has to be taken slowly. From Val di Chiesa the road descends steeply through the small village of **Leni** and twists 3 km (2 miles) down to **Rinella** ❿, a pretty fishing port where most of the ferries and hydrofoils make a second stop. There is a small beach below low cliffs in which you can see a row of caves now used for storage, but once used for isolating smallpox victims.

Map
on page
314

Panarea

The smallest inhabited island of the Aeolians, Panarea is also known locally as the island of flowers, its carefully tended villas awash with bougainvillea and hibiscus. Rather chic compared with its rugged neighbours, Panarea's tiny harbour fills up in the summer with a well-heeled crowd and a flotilla of elegant yachts. The three villages of **Ditella**, **San Pietro** and **Drauto** form a continuous huddle of pretty, neat houses and tiny lanes along the eastern coast. The ferries dock at **San Pietro** ⓫. From Drauto it is an easy 1-km (½-mile) walk past steps to the sandy beach to **Punta Milazzese**, a beautiful rocky headland where the remains of a **Villagio preistorico** (Bronze Age village) ⓬ can be seen. The artefacts found there in 1948 are on display in the museum in Lípari. Just past the headland is the tiny bay of **Cala Junco**, with excellent swimming. By boat it is also possible to see the caves and other tiny coves along the steep cliffs.

A steep signposted path leads from Cala Junco up into the high western side of the island, across the peak of **Punta del Corvo** and back down to San Pietro, a fairly stiff but enjoyable three-hour walk. To the north of Ditella, at **Calcara**, there's a fumarole where jets of gas and steam emerge from fissures in the rock, coating the surface with yellow, white and green minerals. In Neolithic times great pits were dug around the fumarole and filled with votive offerings of

The Aeolian Islands, blustery and storm-swept in winter, are named after Aeolus, the Greek god of the winds.

BELOW:
pretty Panarea.

TIP

You can hire walking
boots for a climb of
Strómboli's volcano
from the tour office
beside Bar Ingrid,
opposite the church
of San Vincenzo.

wheat to ensure good crops and appease the gods of the underworld. Below
Calcara is a stony beach. From San Pietro you can get a boat trip out to
Basiluzzo, now uninhabited though a Roman jetty lies submerged and scraps of
mosaic can be seen on its rocky heights, and to the tiny islets of **Datillo** and
Lisca Bianca, where the swimming is superb.

Strómboli

Even those who have never heard of the Aeolian Islands have heard of Strómboli. The climb to its crater, blasting rod hot rock into the sky, is an unforgettable
reminder of the power below the earth's crust. **Strómboli** town, officially made
up of three villages, but usually grouped together simply as Strómboli, is a
lively little place, busy with hikers of all shapes and sizes, and offering a good
range of restaurants and bars where you can sit to plan your ascent. For days of
relaxing, there are long flat beaches, black sand to the north of the jetty, stone
and shingly sand to the south. Tiny **Ginostra** ⓭ on the southwest side of the
island is accessible only by sea, and the ferry has to weigh anchor and wait
while passengers and assorted packages are brought out in small boats.

Boat trips are also possible to **Strombolicchio**, a tiny island of dramatic
coloured craggy rock topped with a lighthouse, and round to the base of **Sciara
del Fuoco** ⓮, the fiery slope where lava from the craters flows down to the sea.
This is particularly exciting at night when the explosions above and the glowing lava can be seen brightly against the dark sky.

The ascent to the summit and its four active craters is officially forbidden
without a guide, but you can book to join a group at a number of agencies in
the village. If you decide to risk climbing unaccompanied, it's not difficult to

BELOW: Strómboli's
cloud-capped
volcano.

Map on page 314

follow the well-worn main route, which is very clearly marked with painted tags on the rocks. But you should not attempt the climb if it is raining or there is heavy cloud on the summit. You will need to allow seven hours, and time your departure to allow you to get down before dark.

The craters erupt every 20 minutes or so with varying intensity, huge roars and booms echoing round the rocks with each cloud of rock, dust and gas thrown up. There are fabulous views of the distant islands of Filicudi and Alicudi and from the high ridge of **i Vancori** opposite, you can look down on the craters and across the whole archipelago.

Filicudi

Four hours by ferry from Lípari, or an hour on the speeding hydrofoil, Filicudi's smooth humped shape, reminiscent of a whale, lies quietly in the clear water. From **Filicudi Porto ⓯**, with its ugly modern buildings and hotel development, the island's rugged beauty can be explored along the narrow paths and tracks that cross the island. A boat trip gives views of the sheer northern side, the **Grotta del Bue Marino ⓰** a cave where Mediterranean monk seals used to live, and **Canna**, a natural obelisk towering 70 metres (230 ft) out of the sea.

The much-reduced population has left many houses empty and their ruins are being taken over by giant *fici d'India* (prickly pear cactus). On **Capo Graziano**, the tail of the island, less than 1 km (½ mile) along from the port, are the remains of the oldest settlement on the Aeolians, a Bronze Age village dating from the 18th century BC. The island is popular with divers due to the excellent quality of the water and the variety of marine life and there are a few restaurants, a bar and a couple of hotels (open only in summer).

Alicudi

At the western end of the chain, Alicudi is a near-perfect cone, scattered with hamlets and terraced fields right up up to its peak at **Filo dell'Arpa**, where the remains of the old settlements, secure from maurauding pirates, can be seen among the gorse and heather. The tiny 17th-century church of San Bartolo perches high above the sea looking down the steep slopes of Scorbio to the small plain of Bassina round the coast to the east. The island has no roads, and donkeys carry their burdens up the ancient stepped paths. The quiet lapping of the water on the rocky beaches and the sound of birdsong amongst the old olive trees are the only sounds to disturb the tranquillity.

All the 100 or so residents live on the eastern side of the island, in a scattered settlement around **Alicudi Porto ⓱**. For the energetic it is possible to circumnavigate the whole island on foot, a total distance of about 7 km (4 miles), but this entails a scramble in some places and two short swims around impassably steep sections. Allow six or seven hours and take water and a picnic. A boat trip round to see the twisted colourful strata and black lava flows offers a less strenuous option. There are two small shops and a hotel (summer only). Otherwise, although Alicudi has had mains electricity since 1991, this is Sicilian life as it was for centuries. ❏

Apart from Strómboli and Vulcano, the Aeolian volcanoes are now extinct, but tremors from seismic activity deep underground are still felt in this area. The last major rumble was in 1981, with its epicentre in the sea between Alicudi and Filicudi.

BELOW: a village donkey on Alicudi. **OVERLEAF:** sunset over Etna.

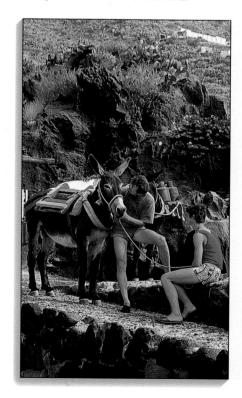

INSIGHT GUIDES

TRAVEL TIPS

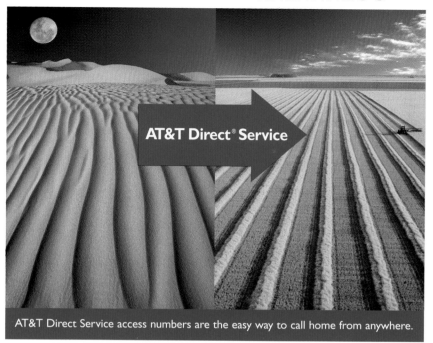

AT&T
direct
service

The best way to keep in touch when you're traveling overseas is with **AT&T Direct** Service. It's the easy way to call your loved ones back home from just about anywhere in the world. Just cut out the wallet card below and use it wherever your travels take you.

For a list of AT&T Access Numbers, cut out the attached wallet guide.

AT&T

Israel 1-800-94-94-949	Portugal ▲ 800-800-128
Italy ● 172-1011	Saudi Arabia ▲ 1-800-10
Jamaica ● 1-800-USA-ATT1	Singapore 800-0111-111
Japan ● ▲ 005-39-111	South Africa 0800-99-0123
Korea, Republic ● ...0072-911	Spain 900-99-00-11
Mexico ▽ ● ..01-800-288-2872	Sweden.............020-799-111
Netherlands ● ..0800-022-9111	Switzerland● ...0800-89-0011
Neth. Ant. ▲⊕001-800-USA-ATT1	Taiwan.............0080-10288-0
New Zealand ● 000-911	Thailand ❮.......001-999-111-11
Norway...............800-190-11	Turkey ● 00-800-12277
Panama 00-800-001-0109	U.A. Emirates ● 800-121
Philippines ● 105-11	U.K. 0800-89-0011
Poland ● ▲ ..00-800-111-1111	Venezuela 800-11-120

FOR EASY CALLING WORLDWIDE
1. Just dial the AT&T Access Number for the country you are calling from.
2. Dial the phone number you're calling. *3.* Dial your card number*

For access numbers not listed ask any operator for **AT&T Direct**® Service.
In the U.S. call 1-800-222-0300 for **AT&T Direct** Service information.
Visit our Web site at: **www.att.com/traveler**
Bold-faced countries permit country-to-country calling outside the U.S.

●	Public phones require coin or card deposit to place call.
✦	Public phones and select hotels.
▲	May not be available from every phone/payphone.
○	Collect calling only.
▽	Includes "Ladatel" public phones; if call does not complete, use 001-800-462-4240.
⊕	From St. Maarten or phones at Bobby's Marina, use 1-800-USA-ATT1.
❮	When calling from public phones, use phones marked Lenso.
*	AT&T Calling Card, AT&T Corporate, AT&T Universal, MasterCard®, Diners Club®, American Express®, or Discover® cards accepted.

When placing an international call *from* the U.S., dial 1-800-CALL ATT.
WW   © 6/00 AT&T

Israel 1-800-94-94-949	Portugal ▲ 800-800-128
Italy ● 172-1011	Saudi Arabia ▲ 1-800-10
Jamaica ● 1-800-USA-ATT1	Singapore 800-0111-111
Japan ● ▲ 005-39-111	South Africa 0800-99-0123
Korea, Republic ● ...0072-911	Spain 900-99-00-11
Mexico ▽ ● ..01-800-288-2872	Sweden.............020-799-111
Netherlands ● ..0800-022-9111	Switzerland● ...0800-89-0011
Neth. Ant. ▲⊕001-800-USA-ATT1	Taiwan.............0080-10288-0
New Zealand ● 000-911	Thailand ❮.......001-999-111-11
Norway...............800-190-11	Turkey ● 00-800-12277
Panama 00-800-001-0109	U.A. Emirates ● 800-121
Philippines ● 105-11	U.K. 0800-89-0011
Poland ● ▲ ..00-800-111-1111	Venezuela 800-11-120

FOR EASY CALLING WORLDWIDE
1. Just dial the AT&T Access Number for the country you are calling from.
2. Dial the phone number you're calling. *3.* Dial your card number*

For access numbers not listed ask any operator for **AT&T Direct**® Service.
In the U.S. call 1-800-222-0300 for **AT&T Direct** Service information.
Visit our Web site at: **www.att.com/traveler**
Bold-faced countries permit country-to-country calling outside the U.S.

●	Public phones require coin or card deposit to place call.
✦	Public phones and select hotels.
▲	May not be available from every phone/payphone.
○	Collect calling only.
▽	Includes "Ladatel" public phones; if call does not complete, use 001-800-462-4240.
⊕	From St. Maarten or phones at Bobby's Marina, use 1-800-USA-ATT1.
❮	When calling from public phones, use phones marked Lenso.
*	AT&T Calling Card, AT&T Corporate, AT&T Universal, MasterCard®, Diners Club®, American Express®, or Discover® cards accepted.

When placing an international call *from* the U.S., dial 1-800-CALL ATT.
WW   © 6/00 AT&T

CONTENTS

Getting Acquainted

The Place

Area: 25,700 sq. km (9,920 sq. miles).
Capital: Palermo.
Highest point: Mount Etna (3,323 metres/10,906 ft).
Population: 4,990,000.
Language: Italian.
Religion: Catholic.
Time zone: Central European Time, one hour ahead of Greenwich Mean Time. Summertime (one hour ahead) is from the beginning of March to the end of October
Currency: Lira.
Weights & measures: Metric.
Electricity: 220 volts AC (50 cycles), two- or three-pin plugs.
International dialling code: 39.

Climate

Sicily is deservedly renowned for its sunshine. The hottest months are July and August, when high temperatures are intensified by lack of rain and the cities empty as the population heads for the beaches.

Along the coasts winters are short and generally mild. The Etna ski resorts are usually open December to March. But from February onwards the coastal areas begin to bloom with spring flowers, the almond blossom is out, and

Sicily defies its parched image by turning spectacularly green. Temperatures remain comfortable into May or June, but the landscape begins to turn more brown.

Government

Sicily is an "autonomous region", Italy's first and still the one with the greatest degree of independence from central government. As such, it has its own parliament and many of its other institutions are separately organised.

The nine Sicilian *provincie* also have considerable independence, electing their own councils, as do the *comuni*, the towns and villages. In the past town councils were regularly dissolved on the grounds of corruption. During the 1993 political purges, over 20 percent of the island's local administrators were under investigation for possible Mafia links.

Deputati (Deputies or Parliamentarians) in the Sicilian Regional Assembly are highly paid, and their large monthly salaries excludes a massive sum for support staff and travel expenses. The politicians ensure political support by dubious means. In their wake come a legion of unnecessary postal workers, false invalids and incredibly young pensioners.

The influence of *clientelismo*, the granting of favours in return for support, is still enormously strong in political and economic life. A local politician can and does expect practical support from those he has helped, and such support readily becomes a pre-condition for help. The personal is political in a very special way in Sicily. The spread of *tangenti*, kickbacks for contracts,

although evidently not unique to Sicily, is widespread. In recent years, however, as a new generation of local administrators has succeeded the old guard, and a new electoral system has been introduced, the political situation has gradually improved.

Economy

Sicily suffers from its distance from the main European markets, and the difficulty of communications is compounded by poor rail and postal services. On paper, Sicily falls well below EU averages for income and productivity, and is still far more dependent on its traditional agricultural skills than the rest of Italy. But its poverty should not be exaggerated. The black economy ensures that such cities as Catania and Palermo may come near the bottom in national league tables of productivity but score highly on consumer spending.

In the main inland areas of the *latifundia* durum wheat (used for making pasta) is still the main crop. In the more fertile and lower lying areas, such as the Conca d'Oro, the slopes of Etna, around Catania, and the western part of Trápani province, intensive farming produces fruit, olives and wine. On the coast south of Ragusa around Comiso vast greenhouses stretch for miles across the plain.

Italy's largest fishing fleet sails out of Mazara del Vallo, but heads for international waters. Inshore fishing has declined in importance, although tuna (*tonno*) is still fished in the traditional manner in Trápani province, as is swordfish (*pesce spada*) off Messina. Processing and packaging of agricultural produce and fish is the base for much of Sicily's healthiest, though often small-scale, industry.

The results of industrialisation have been mixed. Some areas (Augusta, Gela, Termini Imerese and much of Catania) now have large industrial complexes which provide work and have injected considerable amounts of cash into the local economies. They have

Average Temperatures

	Jan	Feb	March	April	May	June
°C	12	10	14	18	21	24
°F	54	50	58	64	70	76

	July	Aug	Sept	Oct	Nov	Dec
°C	28	28	24	22	18	13
°F	85	85	76	72	64	55

Public Holidays

Banks and most shops are closed on the following public holidays:

1 January: New Year's Day (*Capodanno*)

6 January: Epiphany (*Befana*)

March–April (variable): Easter Monday (*Lunedì di Pasqua*)

25 April: Liberation Day

1 May: May Day (*Festa del Lavoro*)

15 August: August holiday (*Ferragosto*)

1 November: All Saints' Day (*Ognissanti*)

8 December: Feast of the Immaculate Conception

25 December: Christmas Day (*Natale*)

26 December: Boxing Day (*Santo Stefano*)

Note also that banks may close early the day before a public holiday. If the holiday falls on a Tuesday or a Thursday, many offices may also close on the preceding Monday or the following Friday. This is known as a "*ponte*", bridging the gap.

In addition to the above, most towns and villages have at least one annual holiday of their own (*feste del Santo Patrono*).

Planning the Trip

What to Bring

Sicilian summers (May to October) are hot and you will need light clothing. But remember that many churches and cathedrals will not allow bare legs (i.e. no short skirts, or shorts) or bare shoulders. In spring (April to May) and autumn (October to November) bring light clothes, but also a summer jacket or sweater for the evenings.

Between December and March, it is advisable to bring some warmer clothes since winter, particularly in the mountainous central areas, can be very cold. Hotels and houses tend to be less well heated than is usual in northern climates: indoors is sometimes chillier than out! Mount Etna is often snow-covered in winter, and its lava-based rock requires strong footwear at any time of year. (*See Ascending Etna, page 370*).

Casual wear is accepted in all but the grandest hotels and restaurants, but most Sicilians will dress smartly when dining out.

Entry Regulations

VISAS & PASSPORTS

For visits up to three months, no visas are required by visitors from EU countries, the US, Canada, Australia or New Zealand. A valid passport (or in the case of those from EU member countries, a valid identification card) is sufficient. Nationals of most other countries require a visa. This must be obtained in advance from an Italian Embassy or Consulate.

For a list of Consulates in Sicily and Embassies in Rome, *see Practical Tips page 329*.

---

also injected considerable amounts of pollution into the nearby coastal waters, and sometimes into the drinking water.

Unfortunately, much of the new industry is still dependent on subsidies in one form or another, and, situated far from the main markets in the north, this is unlikely to change.

One industry which continues to grow is tourism. This has become essential to the island's economy, fuelling much of the construction and service sector and bringing with it a typical pattern of seasonal work (and, unfortunately, seasonal unemployment).

Unemployment, under-employment, and continuing emigration are significant factors in the political, economic and social fabric. Emigration from the country to the cities continues, further fuelling Palermo's and Catania's population growth, building boom and social problems.

Difficult to measure, but undoubtedly important, is the black economy: not only the drug trade with its associated money laundering, but submerged money-generating activity in apparently legitimate businesses.

The island suffers from the entrenched privileges of the political system, and the notorious criminal underground that has supported and been supported by it.

Business Hours

Shops

Shops are generally open 9am–1pm and 4–7.30pm. Except in tourist resorts, shops are closed on Sundays. Food shops and petrol stations are also closed on Wednesday afternoons. In cities other shops are closed on Monday mornings.

Bars and restaurants are legally obliged to close one day a week: a notice indicates which day.

Office hours are normally 7.30am–12.30pm and 3.30–6.30pm. Public offices are frequently open to the public only in the mornings.

Banks

Banks are open Mon–Fri 8.30am–1.30pm. Some also open in the afternoon 2.30–4pm or 3–4.30pm.

You will need to have your passport or some other form of identification with you when changing money. Remember that changing money can be a slow operation. Allow plenty of time and ideally visit in the morning. You may sometimes be asked to leave handbags, cameras and metal objects such as keys in a secure locker at the entrance.

Not all banks will provide cash against a credit card, and a few of the smaller local banks may refuse to cash traveller's cheques in certain currencies.

CUSTOMS

Used personal effects may be imported and exported without formality.

The import of narcotics, weapons and pirated materials is forbidden (except to members of Cosa Nostra, of course!). Certain items (e.g. alcoholic drinks, tobacco, perfume) are limited as to the amount one may take in or out, and these amounts vary for those coming from the EU, other European countries or outside Europe. This can seem confusing, particularly since the amounts also vary depending on whether the goods were bought duty paid (i.e. in Italy) or duty-free (i.e. at a non-EU airport, or on a plane or boat from outside the EU).

For EU citizens: Provided goods obtained in the European Community are for your personal use there is no further tax to be paid.

For non-EU citizens: The duty-free allowances are 200 cigarettes, 50 cigars, or 3 lb (1,360 g) of tobacco; 1 US quart of alcoholic beverages and duty-free gifts worth up to $100.

If you plan to import or export large quantities of goods, or goods of exceptionally high value, contact the Italian Consulate and your own customs authorities beforehand to check on any special regulations which may apply.

The customs authorities are quite active in Sicily, partly to combat smuggling from North Africa, and partly because of the level of Mafia activity and the associated movements of goods and money. But this is very unlikely to affect the ordinary tourist.

For more information on UK import regulations, contact HM Customs and Excise, Dorset House, Stamford Street, London SE1 9PS, tel: 020 7928 0533, or your local Customs and Excise office.

Note that different regulations apply to all types of commercial import and export. For further information, contact the Italian Consulate in your own country or your own customs authorities.

Animal Quarantine

If you want to take a pet you need to have a vaccination certificate for rabies and an officially stamped document stating that the pet is healthy. This must be obtained no more than one month before you travel. For further information, contact the Italian Consulate in your country.

Health

EU residents are entitled to the same medical treatment as Italians. Visitors will need a form E111 before they go. This covers medical treatment and medicines, although you will have to pay a prescription charge and a percentage of the costs for medicines. Note that the E111 does not provide for repatriation in case of illness. If you wish to cover this, you will need to buy private insurance.

If you are not covered by a reciprocal scheme, you should ensure you have private health cover.

The International **Association for Medical Assistance to Travellers** (IAMAT) publishes for its members a directory of English-speaking doctors abroad. IAMAT offices:

Australia
575 Bourke Street, 12th Floor, Melbourne 3000.

Canada
1267 St Claire Ave,
W. Toronto, M6E 1B8.
Regal Road, Guelph,
Ontario N1K 1B5.

New Zealand
PO Box 5049,
Christchurch 5.

USA
417 Center Street,
Lewiston,
NY 14092.

If you are taking medicines on prescription, ensure that you have adequate supplies to cover the period of your trip. You should also take details of the prescription in case the medicines are lost.

If you need medical treatment while in Sicily, take form E111 to the **Unità Sanitaria Locale** (local health office), who will direct you to a doctor covered by the state system and supply you with the necessary paperwork.

In an emergency, you can go directly to a hospital or doctor, but you may have to pay for treatment. If so, ensure that you have receipts: you can then claim reimbursement in the UK. The same applies if you have private insurance.

In many areas in summer, there is a **Guardia Medica Turistica** (tourist emergency medical service) which functions 24 hours a day. Telephone numbers are available from hotels, chemists, tourist offices and local papers. The **Guardia Medica** or **Pronto Soccorso** (first aid) for the area are able to help in an emergency.

Lists of duty pharmacists are published in the daily papers (*Giornale di Sicilia* for Palermo and the west or *La Sicilia* for Catania and the east).

The general emergency number is **113**.

MOSQUITOES

There are a lot of mosquitoes in Sicily, as you will quickly discover if you leave your light on and the window open for any length of time. Slow-burning mosquito repellent rings can be bought cheaply and are effective, as are the small electrical devices which plug into a standard socket. Take and use mosquito repellent.

WATER SUPPLY

Tap water is safe to drink in most places, but Italians generally prefer to drink mineral water, and this will usually be offered in restaurants. In some places the water supply becomes erratic in summer.

In a few places, particularly in the south of the island, the ground water has become polluted by industrial effluents, and the water from village pumps may not be good to drink.

If in doubt, ask the locals. Water supplies marked *Non potabile* should not be used for drinking.

Photography

Sicilian summer light is extremely bright. You will need to make allowances for this, both in choosing film and in setting the camera. Film and most photographic equipment is expensive in Italy. Buy film before you travel.

For reasons of safety, do not leave cameras or photographic equipment visible in a car.

Flash photography and tripods are generally not allowed in museums. In churches, use discretion about photography, in particular about using a flash.

Getting There

BY AIR

Sicily has two main airports, at Palermo (Punta Raisi) and Catania (Fontanarossa). There is also a small airport at Trápani. Messina uses the Reggio di Calabria airport on the mainland across the Straits. Lampedusa and Pantellería, two of the smaller islands, may also be reached by air from Palermo or Trápani.

Useful Addresses

For tourist information outside Sicily:
Canada: Office Nationale Italien de Tourisme, 1 Place Ville Marie – Suite 1914, Montreal, Quebec, H3B 3M9, tel: 514 866 7667.
Ireland: Italian State Tourist Office, 47 Merrion Square, Dublin 2, tel: 01 766397.
UK: Italian State Tourist Board, 1 Princes Street, London W1R 8AY, tel: 020 7408 1254. (Also helpful: The Italian Institute, 39 Belgrave Square, London SW1, tel: 020 7235 1461.)
USA: Italian Government Tourist Office, 630 5th Avenue – Suite 1565, New York, N.Y. 10111, tel: 212 245 4822/3/4.

Alitalia is the main agent for flights to Sicily. The journey by scheduled flight from Britain, Ireland or Canada is usually via Milan, Rome or Naples. There are no direct flights from the Republic of Ireland to Sicily. Information can be obtained from Alitalia, from the national airlines or travel agencies.

There are direct charter flights from several UK airports (Gatwick–Palermo, Luton–Palermo) to Sicily. Information may be obtained from the **Air Travel Group**, 227 Shepherds Bush Road, London W6 7AS, tel: 020 7533 8888, or any travel agency.

For information on buses from Palermo and Catania airports to the city, *see Getting Around, page 333.* For Sicily airport and airline information, *see Practical Tips, page 328.*

BY CAR

Travelling to Sicily by car from the UK or Ireland is not cheap. Costs include petrol, motorway tolls, hotels en route and the ferry crossing to the island. If you wish to have the use of a car in Sicily, consider Fly-Drive options (flying and hiring a car). *See Getting Around, page 334* for information on car hire.

If you do decide to travel by car, you will need a current driving licence (with an Italian translation unless it is the standard EU licence) and valid insurance (green card). Additional insurance cover, which can include a get-you-home service, is offered by a number of organisations including the UK and US Automobile Associations.
Insurance in the UK
Europ-Assistance,
Sussex House, Perrymount Road, Haywards Heath,
West Sussex RH16 1DM
Tel: 020 8680 1234.
Insurance in the USA
Europ-Assistance Worldwide Services Inc.,
1133 15th Street, Suite 400, Washington DC 20005
Tel: 202 347 7113.
You must carry your driving

licence, car registration and insurance documents with you.

Routes to Sicily
The total journey from London to Palermo is around 2,650 km (1,660 miles). London to Milan is around 1,150 km (720 miles). From Milan to Villa San Giovanni is 1,300 km (810 miles) and Messina to Palermo is 200 km (130 miles). It is advisable to take several days for the journey. This allows you to visit places en route as well as making the entire trip more pleasant.

The usual route from France is via the Mont Blanc tunnel. But at the time of writing the tunnel is closed due to a big fire which seriously damaged the whole structure in 1998. Until it reopens, the quickest alternative remains the Gran S. Bernardo tunnel or, if you have time, the passes through the Alps. For updated information concerning the Mont Blanc tunnel, contact the **Azienda di Turismo in Aosta**, tel: 0165 33352.

From the north of Italy, take the Autostrada del Sole (A1), a motorway which starts in Milan, down to Villa San Giovanni. From there, ferries run approximately every 20 minutes across the Straits of Messina. The crossing takes about 30 minutes, but in the high season there may be long queues. It is not possible to book.

There are also ferries from Reggio di Calabria to Messina, but these are much less frequent.

Fuel is expensive in Italy, so it's advisable to fill up in France. The A1 is a toll motorway from Milan to Salerno (south of Naples). Pay either cash or with magnetic cards (Viacard) bought from ACI offices at the border or at motorway services. Large cars, campers, caravans and boats cost extra. The last stretch from Salerno is free.

BY RAIL

The journey from London by train takes approximately 42 hours, changing at Milan, Turin or Rome.

Sicily by Coach

It is not easy to reach Sicily from Northern Europe by coach as there are no direct services. But if you are already in Italy there are express coach services from Rome to Messina, Catania and Siracusa, with connections from Catania to Palermo. For information, enquire at travel agents in Italy.

There is no direct service to Sicily but there is normally one direct service from Calais to Milan and Rome a day, or you may travel via Paris, from which there are frequent services. The cost is about the same as flying.

Train timetables change twice a year, so for up-to-date information, contact British Rail European Enquiries, Victoria Station, London SW1, tel: 0990 848848, or the Italian tourist offices. In Italy, stations and travel agents have details of train times and can make reservations. There are also detailed timetables published commercially and available for a small fee from newsstands.

For those under 26, youth rail cards (Interrail and Eurail) give free use of the European rail system for a month, and may work out cheaper than the standard tickets. In Italy, there are also a number of special deals available: the *chilometrico*, which allows one or more persons to travel 3,000 km (1,864 miles). Enquire at stations or travel agents for details of current offers.

The advantages of travelling by train are the chance to see some of Europe's most beautiful landscapes en route and to make stops along the way. It is also a very sociable way to travel.

There is a daily *rapido* service between Rome and Palermo, Catania and Siracusa.

The crossing from Villa San Giovanni to Messina is an experience in itself: the train carriages are literally (and time-consumingly) shunted into the ferry, and then shunted off again at

Messina. If you arrive on an overnight train, your first view of Sicily from the ship's deck may be of early morning sunlight on the sea and the mountains.

BY SEA

If you wish to avoid the long drive or train ride through Italy, you can take advantage of the following ferries:
Genoa-Palermo: Grandi Navi Veloci (Gruppo Grimaldi, 20 hours).
Livorno-Palermo: Grandi Navi Veloci (19 hours).
Naples-Palermo: Tirrenia (11 hours).

There is also a ferry run by Siremar from Naples via the Aeolian islands to Milazzo. This is a good route for anyone arriving by train and heading for the Aeolian islands themselves.

Ferries may most easily be booked through your local travel agent, but booking is also possible direct through the Italian offices. For addresses in Sicily, *see Getting Around, page 332*. The following are the addresses in Northern Italy.

In Genoa
Grandi Navi Veloci
Via Fieschi 17. Tel: 010 589331.

In Naples
Tirrenia Staz. Marittima
Molo Angioino. Tel: 081 7201111.
Linee Lauro
Tel: 081 5513352/091 6111616.

Tirrenia gets booked up early. Cabins are available on all of the services, but in high season they must be booked well in advance.

Travelling this way can work out to be expensive but there is a considerable saving on petrol, motorway tolls and an overnight stop.

Arriving by boat in Palermo is certainly more relaxing than the trip down the length of Italy's boot. You also have the satisfaction of following in the footsteps of travellers in previous centuries. Arriving by boat from Naples on 2 April 1787, Goethe memorably described his first views from the deck of the ship: the city backlit,

Monte Pellegrino rising above it and the Conca d'Oro, green with spring in the afternoon sun.

Package Holidays

From the UK, Ireland or the USA, this is usually the easiest and most economical way to visit Sicily. It can be an advantage to travel with a company that has good local representation on the island. Most package holidays visit Taormina or Cefalù, the chicest resorts, but some travel companies are more adventurous.These are some of the UK companies now offering interesting packages to Sicily.

Italiatour, part of the Alitalia group, offers escorted tours, self catering, *agriturismo* holidays, fly-drive, and à la carte packages. Sold through selected travel agents or directly from Italiatour at:
9 Whyteleafe Business Village, Whyteleafe Hill, Whyteleafe, Surrey CR3 0AT,
Tel: 01883 621900
Fax: 01883 625222
E-mail: italiatour@dial.pipex.com
The Magic of Italy and **Italian Escapades**, both at:
227 Shepherd's Bush Road, London W6 7AS
Tel: 020 8748 7575
These companies can arrange fly-drive and individual holidays in addition to their standard packages. Magic of Italy provides civilised package holidays, with a good choice of accommodation and resort and the presence of an English-speaking courier or representative.

Many of the large British package holiday companies (CIT, Thomson, Cadogan, Rambler's Holidays, Saga) run holidays to Sicily. Two-centre holidays are increasingly popular, with a chance to stay in a major city, followed by a week at a coastal resort.

Prospect Music & Art Tours, based in London, also run fascinating history of art tours to Sicily. Contact them at:
454 Chiswick High Road, London W4 5TT.
Tel: 020 8995 2151/2163.

Practical Tips

RADIO & TELEVISION

There are dozens of private radio and TV stations, most of them awful. The commercial radio stations provide a mix of pop and phone-ins. The national radio stations (RAI) include news, current affairs and documentary-type programmes, and also, particularly on RAI 3, some classical music.

Reception of the BBC World Service is only possible in the short wave band and not usually good in Southern Italy.

National TV stations (which include RAI, with three channels, and seven others) broadcast some local news programmes. Occasionally a local travelogue or documentary makes it onto the local television stations. On the whole, however, the local television is bad to appalling.

If you have children, be aware that Italian private television sometimes, during the night, fills its schedules with pornographic films of a type that would be encoded or banned elsewhere.

NEWSPAPERS

The main Italian papers (*Corriere della Sera, La Repubblica*) publish southern editions, but the local dailies have a higher circulation in Sicily. They carry far more local information.

Particularly useful for the visitor are the sections covering current boat, train, air and bus timetables, together with daily information on duty chemists, petrol stations, etc. This is presented in a clear fashion

so visitors with a smattering of Italian should understand it. In addition, all the Sicilian papers provide details of musical and theatrical events.

Il Giornale di Sicilia, Palermo's morning paper, covers the western part of the island and provides a supplement for each of the western provinces. It offers the most complete practical listings (timetables, etc.).

La Sicilia, Catania's main paper, also has provincial supplements for Siracusa, Ragusa and Enna. Identified with right of centre politics, La Sicilia occasionally contains some interesting reporting, but is as unlikely to rock boats as Il Giornale.

La Gazzetta del Sud is not strictly a Sicilian paper: it is based in Messina and Reggio di Calabria. It is the highest circulation daily in Messina province and is somewhat less parochial than the purely island papers.

INTERNATIONAL NEWSPAPERS

British and other American and Northern European papers can be found in cities and in tourist resorts, generally one day after publication. The *International Herald Tribune* is also quite widely available. In less touristy areas, you may have difficulty finding non-Italian papers.

MAGAZINES

The following are Sicilian publications that may be interesting to visitors.

Sicilia Magazine – a glossy, highly illustrated magazine in Italian and English. It includes articles on art, culture and personalities. It is published in Catania four times a year.

Sicilia Illustrata – this glossy monthly covers Sicilian current affairs, politics and culture.

Kalos – this is a highly illustrated bi-monthly on art and history.

Sikelia – this is an academically oriented journal on Sicilian art, history and culture. It appears in black and white, and is published bi-monthly.

Sicilia Tempo – an economic and political monthly.

Post Offices are generally open Mon–Fri 8.30am–1.30pm. In Palermo, the main post office in Via Roma (near Piazza Domenico) is open 24 hours (full service from 8am–8pm). Stamps (*francobolli*) are also available from tobacconists (*tabacchi*).

The postal service is not renowned for its speed. If you need to send an urgent letter, send it by *Posta Prioritaria* (special stamps are available from any tobacconists and the mail should be posted in the blue pillar boxes).

In restaurants, a service charge is included in the bill unless the menu indicates otherwise. In hotels, provided good service has been given, leave about 10,000 lire a week in your room for the maids, and give about the same to the head waiter for the dining room staff. These tips are usually divided among the staff concerned.

Taxi drivers will expect around 10 percent of the fare, although 5 percent is acceptable on very short trips. Tips to local guides depend on their ability and the length of the trip: between L2,000 and L5,000 per person is normal. The driver will expect a similar tip.

In many small towns and villages, churches and other monuments may appear to be permanently closed for lunch: there is usually a custodian (or elderly "helper") nearby who will be pleased to open the door. A tip of around 2,000 lire per person and many *grazie* are then appropriate.

Telephones

Telephone boxes take phone cards, which you can buy at bars, newspaper kiosks and post offices; some telephone boxes still take 100, 200 and 500 lire coins, too. It is not uncommon to find telephone boxes out of order, particularly in the large cities. More reliable are the public telephones available in many bars and some other commercial premises.

Telephone directories are available at main offices of Telecom in cities and at Palermo and Catania airports. You can also make calls here. The call is metered and you pay at the desk when you have finished.

If making phone calls from a hotel, you will usually pay an additional charge which can be high. Cheaper rates apply to calls made between 6.30pm and 8am, on Saturday after 1pm and all day Sunday.

For calls within Italy, all telephone numbers must be preceded by the area code even if the call is made within the same district. Call 12 for directory assistance for all of Italy (L1000).

To make international calls, dial 00, then the appropriate country code (*see below*) followed by the number (omitting any initial 0).

International dialling codes:

Australia:	61
Canada and USA:	1
Ireland:	353
UK:	44

Telephone offices

In Palermo
Piazza Giulio Cesare: 24 hours.
Via P. Belmonte 92: 8am–8pm.
At the port: 8am–8pm.
At the airport: 8am–10pm.

In Catania
Via A. Longo: 24 hours.
Piazza Giovanni XXIII: 8am–8pm.
At the airport: 8am–8pm.

In a real emergency, send a telegram. This may be done from a post office, Telecom office, or by dialling 186 from a private phone. It is possible to have mail sent *poste restante* to main post offices. Letters should be marked *fermo posta*.

Airlines

PALERMO

Alitalia. To buy tickets, use a travel agency, or go to Alitalia's main office in Palermo, Via Mazzini 59, tel: 091 6019111. For information on national and international flights, tel: 1478 65643 toll-free, or from a portable telephone, tel: 06 65643. For international booking tel: 1478 65642.
Air France
Piazza V. Emanuele 48,
Monreale (Pa)
Tel: 091 6403283.
Air Malta
Via Catania 24, Palermo
Tel: 091 6255848/6255895.

CATANIA

For information on **Alitalia**: Via L. Rizzo 18, tel: 095 252111.

To buy tickets or for information on **Air France**, go to Corso Martiri della Libertà 184–186, tel: 095 532210. Open Mon–Fri 9am–12.30pm and 4–8pm, Sat 9am–12.30pm. Also at Fontanarossa airport, tel: 095 345921.

For tickets and information on British Airways, Lufthansa, Air Malta, Meridiana, Swissair, KLM, Air France and A. Eagles try a travel agency or go to Catania airport Biglietteria, tel: 095 345367 (open 24 hours).

For information on Qantas/TWA, Corso Martiri della Libertà 38, tel: 095 535054/534961. This is a private tour operator. Open Mon–Fri 8.30am–1pm and 3.30–7pm, Saturday 8.30am–noon.

Airports

Punta Raisi

Palermo Airport
Tel: 091 591698.
This is the Tourist Information office, open Mon–Sat 8am–noon, Sun 8am–8pm.
Flight information
Internal arrivals
Tel: 091 7020486
Internal departures
Tel: 091 7020302
International arrivals
Tel: 091 7020400
International departures
Tel: 091 7020301.

Fontanarossa

Catania Airport
Tel: 095 7306277/095 7306288.

Messina

(Reggio di Calabria airport on the mainland: connection via hydrofoil from Messina)
Tel: 0965 320287.

Tourist Information

Most tourist offices in Sicily have some staff who speak English, French or German. Availability of these staff varies however, as does their ability.

Many have a wealth of information on their province, including detailed brochures, maps and books. Again, however, there is considerable variation in their enthusiasm for sharing this with the visitor. The best are excellent; the worst appear to see their function as preventing disturbances to the daily newspaper reading and coffee drinking.

If writing for information, be prepared for a long wait: the postal service is not speedy.

The provincial tourist offices are now all called **AAPIT** (Azienda Autonoma Provinciale per l'Incremento Turistico), and are often abbreviated to APT. The local offices are usually called Azienda Autonoma di Soggiorno e Turismo

(AAST). In small places they are sometimes called Pro Loco, and may have restricted opening hours.

PALERMO PROVINCE

Palermo City
The regional tourist office covers the whole of Sicily although it is not open to the general public. The address is:
Via Emanuele Notarbartolo 9
Tel: 091 6968031/091 6968091
E-mail: sicily@www.sicily.infcom.it
Website: www.sicily.infcom.it
    Palermo Province and city are covered by:
AAPIT, Piazza Castelnuovo 34
Tel: 091 6058111
E-mail: aapit@gestelnet.it
Website: www.aapit.pa.it
Open Mon– Fri 8am–8pm, Sat 8am–2pm.
    Information offices are also at the airport (tel: 091 6165916) and the station (tel: 091 6165914).
    The local tourist office for Palermo itself is illogically situated a 40-minute walk outside the city centre:
Azienda Autonoma di Turismo, Palermo e Monreale, Villa Igiea,

Salita Belmonte 43
Tel: 091 6398011.
Open Mon–Fri 8am–2pm, also Thurs 3–6.30pm.

Cefalù
ASST, Via Amendola 2
Tel: 0921 421050/421458.
Well-informed and helpful, with plenty of documentation. Staff speak either English or French. Open Mon–Fri 8am–2pm and 4–7pm, Sat 8am–2pm.

Ustica
c/o **Ass. Turistica Pro Loco**
Piazza V. Longo
Tel: 091 8449190.

TRAPANI PROVINCE

Trâpani City
AAPIT
Piazza San Francesco D'Assisi 27
Tel: 0923 545511
E-mail: apttp@mail.cinet.it
Website: http://www.cinet.it/apt
An active well-informed office, with plenty of documentation and enthusiastic, helpful staff. Open Mon and Wed 8am–2pm and 3–6pm, Tues, Thurs, Fri and Sat

8am–2pm. There is also an **Information Office** at Piazza Saturno, tel: 0923 29000. Open Mon–Sat 8am–8pm, Sunday 8am–noon.

Erice
ASST
Via C. A. Pepoli 11
Tel: 0923 869388.
Open Mon–Sat 8am–2pm in summer.

Gibellina
Piazza XV/I/LXVIII
Tel: 0924 67877.
Open Mon–Sat 8am–8pm, Sunday 8am–noon.

Mazara del Vallo
Piazza S. Veneranda 2
Tel: 0923 941727.
Open Mon–Sat 8am–8pm, Sunday 8am–noon.

AGRIGENTO PROVINCE

Agrigento
Azienda Provinciale per il Turismo
Via Empedocle 73
Tel: 0922 20391.
Open Mon–Sat 8am–2pm.
AAPIT
Viale della Vittoria 255
Tel: 0922 401352/401354.
Open Mon, Wed, Thurs and Sat 8am–2pm; Tues and Fri 8am–2pm and 3.30–7.30pm.

Sciacca
Corso V. Emanuele, 84
Tel: 0925 21182.
Open Mon–Sat 8am–2pm and 4–6pm.

Embassies & Consulates

In Rome
Australian Embassy
Corso Trieste 25/c
Tel: 06 852721.
Open Mon–Thurs 9am–noon and 1.30–5pm, Fri 9am–noon.
Canadian Embassy
Via Zara 30
Tel: 06 445981. Open Mon–Fri 8.30am–12.30pm and 1.30–4pm.
Irish Embassy
Piazza Campitelli 3
Tel: 06 6979121.
Open Mon–Fri 10am–12.30pm and 3–4.30pm.
New Zealand Embassy
Via Zara 28
Tel: 06 4402928.
Open Mon–Fri 8.30am– 12.45pm and 1.45–5pm.
South African Embassy
Via Tanaro, 14–16

Tel: 06 8419794.
Open Mon–Fri 8.30am–noon.
UK Embassy
Via XX Settembre 80a
Tel: 06 4825441/4873324.
Open Mon–Fri 9.30am–1.30pm.
US Embassy
Via Vittorio Veneto 121
Tel: 06 46741.
Open Mon–Fri 8.30am–noon.

In Naples
UK Consulate
Via Crispi 122, Naples
Tel: 081 663511.
Open Mon–Fri 9am–12.30pm and 2–4.30pm.
US Consulate
Piazza della Repubblica
Tel: 081 5338111.
Open Mon–Fri 8am–noon (8–10am for visas).

CALTANISSETTA PROVINCE

AAPIT
Corso Vittorio Emanuele 109
Tel: 0934 530411.
Open Mon, Wed, Fri and Sat 8am–2pm and 4–7pm; Tues and Thur 8am–2pm.
Information office
Viale Conte Testasecca
Tel: 0934 21089.
Open Mon–Sat 8am–noon.

Police/Carabinieri: 113/112
Vigili del Fuoco (fire brigade and ambulance service): 115
ACI (Italian Automobile Club in case of breakdown): 116

ENNA PROVINCE

Enna

AAPIT, Via Roma 411, tel: 0935 528 288/800-221188. Open Mon, Tues, Thurs, Sat 9am–1pm and 4–7pm, Wed and Fri 9am–1pm and 3.30–6.30pm.
ASST, Piazza N. Colaianni 6, tel: 0935 500875. Open Mon–Sat 8am–2pm.

Piazza Armerina

AAPIT, Via Cavour, 15, tel: 0935 680201. Open Mon–Sat 8am–2pm. Aidone– Morgantina, tel: 0935 86777 (only during the summer)

RAGUSA PROVINCE

AAPIT, Via Capitano Bocchieri 33, Ragusa, tel: 0932 621421 (near the archaeological museum). Well-informed and helpful staff, most leaflets available only in Italian. Open Mon–Sat 8am–2pm.

SIRACUSA PROVINCE

AAPIT, Via San Sebastiano 43, Siracusa, tel: 0931 481232. Open Mon–Sat 8am–2pm.
ASST, Via Maestranza 33, Siracusa, tel: 0931 65201. Helpful and friendly staff and a wealth of information available. Not all staff speak English. Open Mon, Wed, Thurs and Sat 8.30am–2pm, Tues and Fri 8.30am–2pm and 4–7pm.

CATANIA PROVINCE

Azienda Provinciale per il Turismo, via Cimarosa 10, Catania, tel: 091 7306222;
e-mail: apt@apt-catania.com
website: www.apt-catania.com

AAPIT, Largo Paisiello 5, Catania, tel: 095 312124/310888.
There are also information offices at the airport (tel: 095 7306266) and the railway station (tel: 095 7306255).

MESSINA PROVINCE

Messina

AAPIT, Via Calabria 301, tel: 090 640221. Open Mon–Sat 9am–noon.

Taormina

Palazzo Corvaja, Piazza S. Caterina, tel: 0942 23243. Open Mon–Sat 8am–2pm and 4–7pm, Sun 9am–1pm.

Giardini Naxos

Via Tysandros 54, tel: 0942 51010. Open Mon–Sat 8am–2pm and 4–7pm.

AEOLIAN ISLANDS

Lípari

Azienda Autonoma di Turismo, Corso Vittorio Emanuele 202, tel: 090 9880095. Open Mon–Fri 8am–2pm and 4.30–7.30pm, Sat 8am–2pm. July–Aug: Mon–Sat 8am–2pm and 4–10.30pm.

Vulcano

Porto di Ponente, tel: 090 9852028. Open Jun–Oct only.

SECURITY & CRIME

The vast majority of tourists have pleasant, trouble-free holidays in Sicily. Although the Mafia has a strong hold on the island, it is highly unlikely that the average tourist will knowingly come into contact with them. The following information will ensure help in all unfortunate eventualities.

The main problem for tourists is petty crime: pick-pocketing and bag-snatching (by young criminals known as *scippatori* or *scippi*) together with theft from cars. Theft of all sorts is more likely in Palermo, Catania and the historic centre of Siracusa. Most tourist resorts require caution, but Taormina and Cefalù are normally extremely safe. You can greatly reduce the possibility of theft by taking some elementary precautions. Remember too, that very little violent theft occurs: the chances of being mugged are very much higher in London or New York.

Expect the police to have a casual attitude to petty crime and a slightly suspect attitude to a woman on her own. Expect, also, to have to prove who you are and where you are staying before even beginning to embark on your tale of woe. In the event of a serious crime, contact your country's consulate or embassy as well as the *Carabinieri*. Following that, try the Sicilian approach: summon the most influential Sicilian you know on the island and request advice. Having friends in the right places helps.

Anti-theft Precautions

Avoid looking like a tourist and do not wear your wealth ostentatiously: carry your camera out of sight, and do not wave money or wallets. If carrying a handbag, keep it on the side away from the road (one speciality is the motorbike snatch-and-drive). It is best to leave money and valuables in the hotel safe. It hardly needs saying that a wallet poking out of a back pocket is an easy target. You should keep a separate record of credit card and cheque numbers, just in case.

If you are robbed: Report it as soon as possible to the local police. You will need a copy of the declaration in order to claim on your insurance. Even more importantly, it is highly likely that part of your property will be returned, often very rapidly. There is apparently an unspoken agreement between police and thieves: provided documents and credit cards are returned and no violence is used, the police apply minimum effort to arresting those responsible. So although your camera, unused film, cash and traveller's cheques have gone for good, the thieves may call the police within hours to report the whereabouts of your passport, credit cards, exposed film and possibly even your empty wallet.

Possible Danger Zones
Palermo, Catania and Ortygia in Siracusa are the most likely places for *scippi*. Avoid the station areas of Palermo and Catania, and also the myriad unlit back streets of Palermo's historic centre after dark. La Kalsa in Palermo is fairly safe during the day, provided you take precautions, but should be avoided

Female Travellers

If you are blonde, expect attention: you will get it. Whatever your colouring, sexist though it may be, you will probably enjoy Sicily better if you think hard about your dress and behaviour, particularly if travelling alone.

Either dress down or very formally (as Italians do). Wear a wedding ring and refer to your husband as if he is travelling with you, but is at a conference at that moment. (The wedding ring alone may be viewed as a challenge.)

Reject offers of lifts or guides, and try to avoid sitting alone in parks or on beaches. This last may be impossible, so be ready to ward off the over-friendly. An alliance with a convenient family party may help.

Avoid city centres alone at night, especially side streets. Ask the hotel's advice on the safety of an area. Going out in the evening, consider a taxi to your destination.

You are unlikely to be in any danger, but the Sicilians' determined pursuit may begin to feel like a hunt with you as the quarry. If you do feel in real danger, appeal to other women, particularly those accompanied by men: if you successfully claim a man's protection, you will probably put yourself off-limits to both him and others.

by night. Also avoid the San Cristoforo area of Catania (behind the castle) at all times and be wary in the portside fish markets. In Siracusa, by all means visit the characteristic restaurants, but steer clear of the Via Nizza port area late at night unless there are plenty of people about. In Mazara del Vallo, explore the Moorish Casbah but ideally in company.

Car Crime
Never leave luggage or valuables visible in a car; in fact, if possible leave nothing visible in a car. Cars are best parked off the street (e.g. in a hotel car park, of which there are sadly very few). You must have all the car documents with you when driving, but carry them with you when you park: if you should be unlucky enough to have the car stolen, they will help you record the theft.

Particularly in Catania and Palermo, some *scippatori* specialise in what could be called mobile crime: stealing from "moving" cars. It works something like this: you are crawling in a traffic jam. Suddenly a motorbike swerves in front of you. You brake. A youth approaches the car, pulls open the door, grabs whatever is reachable, leaps on the back of the motorbike and is gone.

For the thief, the pickings are good: typically cameras or handbags placed beneath the driver's legs or seat. The moral: lock the car doors when driving. Particularly if the windows are open, which they will be if it is hot, keep valuables in the boot, rather than in the car.

Drugs
As you would expect from the world's Mafia headquarters, drugs are in plentiful supply on the streets, even in small towns and villages. Do not, however, be tempted to buy. Apart from the possible legal penalties (jail, fines, expulsion), you are touching the edge of a truly criminal world. You would probably prefer to have no deeper contact with it.

Getting Around

Maps

The Sicilian tourist offices can supply maps which may be adequate if you are staying in one place. If touring, you will certainly need a good map. The best Italian maps are those produced by the **Touring Club Italia** (TCI). Their map covers the whole of Sicily together with the islands. The scale is 1:200,000, 1 cm to 2 km.

In the UK, the TCI maps can be bought from **Stanfords Map Shop**, 12 Long Acre, Covent Garden, London WC2 (tel: 020 7836 1321). In Sicily, maps should be available from bookshops, and some garages.

Travel within Sicily

Hiring a car will certainly make travelling around easier. However, public transport is a reasonable alternative, particularly if time is not of the essence. By combining bus and train, you can reach most parts of Sicily quite easily, although you may occasionally find yourself waiting for some hours for a connection. If you are going to any of the smaller islands, a car may be a liability rather than an asset: the smallest islands have no roads to speak of. A car is better left behind, which means paying for a garage.

Bicycles are only selectively useful, unless you are a professional cyclist or a masochist. Much of Sicily is simply too mountainous and too hot to be comfortably visited by bike. Bikes can be hired in the places where the terrain suits them, such as the smaller islands and the flat parts of Trápani Province.

Hitchhiking tends to be slow. The risk of getting stranded in the middle of nowhere is high. Women are strongly advised to think six times before trying it, and then take the train.

The main Sicilian newspapers carry details about local flights, boats, train and bus schedules. This is by far the best way to get up-to-date and accurate details on all of these. For information on Sicilian newspapers, *see Media, page 327.*

By Air

From Palermo Airport (Punta Raisi) regular buses run to and from Palermo's main station, stopping at Piazza Ruggero Settimo in front of the Teatro Politeama. The buses are run by Ditta Prestia & Commandè, tel: 091 580457.

Timetables vary according to the season and are displayed at both the airport and the station. The first journey to the airport is at 5am, and the last at 10.45pm. From the airport, the first bus is at 7.30am, and the last around midnight. The journey takes about an hour. The last bus usually waits for the final flight of the day.

Getting out of Palermo airport by car: If you are not going into Palermo, then avoid it. It is not the easiest first experience of Sicilian driving. If you are going west, this is easy. Simply take the A29 direction Trápani. If you are going towards Cefalù or Catania, then take the A29 towards Palermo, but follow signs for the A19 and A20 for Catania, Enna, Messina. This will keep you on the ring road around Palermo (Viale della Regione Sicilia). It is wide, busy and slightly chaotic, but much easier than the centre of Palermo.

Catania Airport: Alibus runs from 5am to midnight to the train station (every 20 minutes). Tickets can be purchased from tobacconists.

Getting out of Catania airport by car: If you are heading for Siracusa, follow the signs to turn south as you leave the airport. If you are going towards Palermo, follow signs for the A19.

Taxis & City Buses

In cities, taxis may be hailed, telephoned or found at taxi ranks. There are additional charges for luggage, on Sundays and holidays, and a special supplement to or from the airport. **In Palermo:** Autoradio Taxi, tel: 091 513311/513198; Radio Taxi: 091 6825441 **In Catania:** Radio Taxi, tel: 095 333216/330966.

In Palermo, Catania and Messina, the city buses are frequent and are the easiest way to get around. Tickets must be bought before boarding the bus, from a bus company office (AMAT), tobacconists (*tabacchi*) or newspaper kiosks. Tickets are then "cancelled" on entering the bus.

If you are heading north towards Taormina and Messina, you have to cross Catania first. Follow the signs for Catania Centro and Catania Porto. These will take you along the seafront into Catania. Then follow the signs for the A18. If going to Giardini Naxos, leave the motorway at Taormina Sud. For Taormina itself, leave the motorway at the second Taormina junction, Taormina Nord.

Trápani, Lampedusa and Pantellería also have commercial airports. Most of the traffic from these three is within Sicily.

Trápani Birgi, tel: 0923 841130 for information. Flights from and to Rome. Open daily dawn–dusk.

Lampedusa, tel: 0922 970299. Flights from and to Palermo, Milan and Rome. Open daily 8am–4pm.

Pantellería, tel: 0923 911398. Flights from and to Palermo, Milan and Rome. Open daily 8am–4pm.

By Boat

Ferries (*traghetti*) and hydrofoils (*aliscafi*) are the main transport to Sicily's smaller islands. The frequency of service varies according to the season. In summer, boats and hydrofoils leave for the main destinations several times a day, but in winter some of the smaller islands are only visited once a week. If the weather is stormy, which it often is, islands may be cut off for days at a time.

Ferry prices tend to be low. Where more than one company runs ferries or hydrofoils on a particular route, they normally work in competition, not collaboration, i.e. your ticket will only be valid on the ships of the carrier from whom you bought it. This sometimes makes single tickets a better bet than return ones.

For the Aeolian islands: Ferries and hydrofoils run frequently from Milazzo (Messina Province), which is reached by train from Messina and Palermo, and by bus from Messina and from Catania airport.

In the summer, there are up to 11 hydrofoils a day to Lípari and Vulcano, and 6 a day to Salina. There are ferries directly to the other islands several times a week, but all of the islands can best be reached from Lípari. The ferry takes about 2 hours to Lípari and the hydrofoil about 30 minutes. Lípari or Vulcano make a good base from which to explore all of the islands.

There are also boats to the Aeolian Islands from Cefalù, Messina, Palermo and Naples.

For Ustica: In summer, ferries and hydrofoils run daily between Palermo and Ustica. In the low season, there are ferries only.

For the Egadi Islands and Pantellería: from Trápani, ferries and hydrofoils run several times a day – even in the low season – to Favignana, Lévanzo and Maréttimo (the Egadi Islands). The crossing to Favignana by ferry takes 45 minutes. To Pantellería (daily in the summer, Mon–Sat in the winter), the ferry takes about 5 hours. (Trápani can be reached by train or by bus from Palermo.)

Bikes are usually available for hire on Favignana. The island is relatively flat and a bike is a good way to get about.

For the Pelagie Islands (Linosa and Lampedusa): Ferries run once a day (in fact overnight) in summer from Porto Empedocle (Agrigento Province) to Lampedusa stopping at Linosa on the way. In winter, there are ferries six times a week. It is worth taking a cabin if one is available. The ferry carries cars, but in summer it can be booked up. In summer there is also a hydrofoil service between the two islands. Agrigento can be reached by train or by bus. A town bus runs about every 30 minutes from Agrigento to Porto Empedocle.

BOAT COMPANIES

Note that in some cases, these are agencies, rather than the boat companies themselves.

Milazzo
Siremar, Via dei Mille, tel: 090 9283242/980090 (Ferries and hydrofoils).
SNAV, Via L. Rizzo, 17 tel: 090 9284509/9287642 (Hydrofoils).
NGI, Via dei Mille, 26 tel: 090 9284091/981116 (Ferries).

Messina
SNAV, Cortina del Porto tel: 090 362114/364045.

Alicudi
Siremar: 090 9889795.

Filicudi
Siremar: 090 9889960.
Lípari
Siremar: 090 9811312.

Panarea:
Siremar: 090 983007.

Salina
Siremar: 090 9843004 (S. Marina); 090 9809170 (Rinella).

Stromboli
Siremar: 090 986016/9812880 (Ginostra).

Vulcano
Siremar: 090 9852149.

Trápani
Siremar, tel: 0923 27780. (Hydrofoils to the Egadi Islands).

Siremar, Via Amm. Staiti, tel: 0923 540515. (Ferries to the Egadi Islands).
Traghetti delle Isole, tel: 0923 22467. Tickets at **Egatour Viaggi**, Via Amm. Stoiti 23, tel: 0923 21754. (Ferries to the Egadi Islands and Pantellería).
Alivit Due, tel: 0923 24073. (Hydrofoils to the Egadi Islands).
Aliscafi SNAV, tel: 0923 27101. (Hydrofoils to Pantellería).

Favignana
Siremar, tel: 0923 921368. (Hydrofoils and ferries).

Levanzo
Siremar, tel: 0923 924003. (Ferries and hydrofoils).

Maréttimo
Siremar, tel: 0923 923144. (Ferries and hydrofoils).

Porto Empedocle
Siremar, tel: 0922 636683/ 636685.

Lampedusa
Siremar, tel: 0922 970003. (Ferries)

Linosa
Siremar, tel: 0922 972062. (Ferries)

Palermo
Grandi Traghetti, Via F. Crispi, tel: 091 587801.
Siremar, Via F. Crispi 120, tel: 091 6902555 (Ferries and hydrofoils).
SNAV (Ag.), Via P. Belmonte 51, tel: 091 586533. (Hydrofoils).
Tirrenia, Palazzina Stella Maris, Via F. Crispi, tel: 091 333300.

Ustica
Siremar, Piazza Vito Longo, tel: 091 8449002. (Ferries and hydrofoils.)
SNAV, Via S. Bartolomeo, tel: 091 8449077. (Hydrofoils)
For more information about companies operating services from Genoa, Livorno and Naples see Getting There, *page 326.*

By Bus

Fast buses link Sicily's main towns and are a good way of getting around the island, particularly the interior and the south. Buses are more reliable and quicker than trains but cost more. The main

Train Services

Sicily's train service is adequate provided you want to go where it does: primarily along the coast from Palermo to Messina, on to Catania and Siracusa. These two lines also offer wonderful scenery. Try to sit on the sea side of the carriage.

Agrigento, Siracusa, Trápani and Enna can all be reached by train, but it takes patience and time. If you want to explore the interior of the island, the south or west coasts, or to hop between smaller destinations, you may find you have to wait several hours for a connection, even if your train does arrive on time, and there are many places the train simply does not go near.

Italian railways have several types of train:

Rapido: fast, often on time; a supplement is usually payable and

you may have to book a seat in advance. Some *rapidi* have first-class seats only.

Espresso: a main line long-distance train that does not stop at every small station.

Diretto: a main line long-distance train which stops at some smaller stations. Timetabled to run more slowly than an *espresso* (although not necessarily much more so).

Locale: a local train, not long-distance. It tends to be slow and stops everywhere.

Train information and tickets can be obtained at stations or in most travel agents. If you want to reserve seats, couchettes or sleepers, this is often quicker and more efficient than going to the station (where there are often long queues). Call 147 888088 toll-free.

exception where the train is generally better is the Palermo-Messina route.

The following lists the most important and popular routes and the bus company which runs them.

From Palermo
SAIS, Via Balsamo, 16.
Tel: 091 6166028/6171141.
Buses go to Rome, Caltanissetta, Catania, Caltagirone, Enna, Piazza Armerina, Gela, Sciacca, Messina.
Cuffaro, Via P. Balsamo, 13.
Tel: 091 6161510.
Buses go to Agrigento, Favara, Racalmuto, Grotte, Castrofilippo, Comitini.
Interbus. Tel: 091 6167919.
Buses go to Siracusa.
Segesta. Tel: 091 6167919.
Buses go to Rome and Trápani.
Salemi, Piazza Marina.
Tel: 091 6175411.
Buses go to Castelvetrano (near Selinunte), Marsala, Mazara del Vallo and Salemi.

From Trápani
City buses and those for the rest of Trápani province leave from Piazza Umberto.
AST, Piazza Montalto.
Tel: 0923 21021.
For Palermo and Agrigento, buses start from Piazza Garibaldi.

From Agrigento
City buses leave from outside the station in Piazza Marconi. The main bus station for the rest of Sicily is in Piazza Roselli, near the Post Office. Main bus companies:
SAIS, Via Ragazzi del 199, 12.
Tel: 0922 595260.

S. Lumia, Via F. Crispi 87.
Tel: 0922 20414.

From Caltanissetta
Buses leave from Via Catania.
SAIS, Via Calabria.
Tel: 0934 592597.
Buses go to Palermo, Catania, Agrigento, Enna.

From Enna
SAIS, Viale Diaz.
Tel: 0935 500902.
Buses leave from Piazza Scelfo in the lower town and connect with Piazza Armerina, Catania, Palermo, Caltagirone.

From Ragusa
All buses stop outside the railway station. Destinations include Rome, Catania, Messina, Siracusa, Caltagirone and Piazza Armerina.

From Siracusa
AST, Piazza delle Poste.
Tel: 0931 462711.
Buses go to Lentini, Catania, Comiso, Ispica, Módica, Noto, Pachino, and Ragusa.
SAIS, Via Trieste 28.
Tel: 0931 66710.
Destinations include Catania, Noto, Pachino, Palermo and Taormina.

From Catania
The bus terminal is in front of the central station.
AST, Piazza Giovanni XXIII.
Tel: 095 347330.
Buses connect with Acireale, Etna Rifugio Sapienza, and Caltagirone.
SAIS, Via d'Amico, 18.
Tel: 095 536168.
Buses go to Messina, Taormina,

Enna, Agrigento, Caltanissetta, Palermo, Nicosia, Siracusa, Noto, Pachino.

From Messina
Giuntabus
Via Terranova 8, Milazzo
Tel: 090 673782.
SAIS
Piazza della Repubblica 6.
Tel: 090 771914.
Buses connect with Taormina, Catania, and Palermo.

By Car

Motorways: There are toll motorways between Messina, Catania and Siracusa and on the northern coast from Messina to Rocca di Caprileone (with the rest due to have been built years' ago). The quickest route from Messina to Palermo (although not the shortest on paper) is to take the motorway to Catania. The northern coastal road, while offering some beautiful scenery, has a slow, twisting, lorry-infested stretch between Rocca di Caprileone and Castelbuono.

Non-toll: The motorway from Catania to Palermo is toll-free, as are those from Palermo to Trápani and towards Mazara del Vallo in the west of the island. The motorways are well-surfaced and fast. They are rarely blocked with traffic. Several of them curve spectacularly high above the valleys on stilts. The curves are sometimes necessary to avoid marshy ground, but were sometimes a means to extract additional finance from government contracts. Many of the dead of Sicily's Mafia wars are assumed to

Hiring a Car

Car hire is readily available all over the island. International car hire companies are all represented, and have agents in most resorts. Cheaper rates may be on offer from some of the local companies, particularly in the low and off-peak season. Check exactly what is included in the hire agreement. It is often better value to arrange

and pay for car hire through a travel agent in your home country before you travel.

These are the major hire companies:

Hertz, tel: 199 112211 (from a mobile phone: 0248 233 662).
Avis, Via Principe di Scordia 28, Palermo, tel: 091 586940.

Maggiore/Budget, Via A. De Gasperi 179, Palermo: tel: 091 513172; Palermo Airport: 091 591681; reservations: 1478 67067.
Europcar, Palermo Airport, tel: 0270 399700/591688
Sicily by Car, Via V. Di Marco 4, Palermo, tel: 091 581045/ 328531.

Speed Limits

In towns: 50 kph (31 mph)
On ordinary roads outside towns: 90 kph (56 mph)
On motorways: 110 kph (68 mph) for small cars (up to 1100 cc); 120 kph (74 mph) for all other traffic.

be buried in the concrete of the stilts: these are victims of *lupara bianca* ("white deaths"), homicides where bodies were never discovered.

Other roads: *Strada Statale* are the main non-motorway roads. They are numbered and appear on maps and in addresses as SS 115 etc. SS roads are usually well-signposted and surfaced.

The surfacing of other Sicilian roads varies from excellent to appalling, sometimes within a few hundred metres. Road works sometimes cause entire sections of road to become impassable. There are several notorious roads that have been closed for over 10 years. Main roads and junctions are usually well signposted, but in the countryside signs are sometimes missing or misleading. A good map is useful.

See the Language section, (page 381) for some common road signs.

Seat belts are compulsory, but you will be astonished at how few Sicilians wear them. The cars with Sicilian number plates and belted passengers are usually hire cars. Motorcycle helmets are also compulsory. Fines are high for those the police choose to catch without.

Infants up to 9 months must occupy a baby seat. Children between 9 months and 4 years must be seated on the back passenger seat.

Driving in the cities

Nervous drivers are advised not to make the Palermo or Catania rush hours their first experience of driving in Sicily; they could be scarred for life. In addition, parking in both cities is difficult to find.

Palermo is best negotiated by reference to a number of main roads such as Via Roma, and Via Maqueda which are bisected by Corso Vittorio Emanuele. Quattro Canti is a clear central point as is the Teatro Politeama. The Politeama, Palazzo Reale (or dei Normanni) and the station are signposted on main roads into the city, albeit slightly erratically. You may find it easiest to head for one of these initially. Many of the small streets in the centre, although heavily used by traffic, are unsuitable for use by nervous drivers. Apart from the risk of getting lost, visitors find the narrowness of the streets and the disregard of one-way signs alarming, not to mention the sight of underage drivers.

Both main cities have ring roads, which are frequently packed with traffic, but much easier to negotiate than the cities themselves. If crossing the area, or travelling from Palermo airport to Cefalù, the ring road is the best route.

The driver and the pedestrian: Sicilian pedestrians believe they own the roads. Sicilian drivers allow them to continue in their belief. You need to become quickly acclimatised to chaotic street sense: pedestrians will walk out in front of you, or stand in the street and hold conversations. As a driver, you are expected to expect this.

Petrol stations are few and far between on the many small roads in the interior. Fill up in the towns. Petrol stations often close for lunch 1–5pm. On Sunday, a single petrol station in each area will be open: local newspapers list these. Around Palermo and Catania there are self-service petrol stations which can be used 24 hours a day. Lists appear in the local papers.

Parking in the larger towns and cities is difficult. *Rimozione forzata* means that cars will be towed away. Do not leave anything that is removable visible in the car. Leaving camera equipment or valuables in a parked car is highly risky. Radios are also at risk. Italians carry their car radios with them. Consider

doing the same. Car theft is less likely, but the car should be left in a guarded car park whenever possible.

In Palermo: There are car parks run by AMAT (Azienda Municializzata Autotrasporti) at Piazza Castelnuovo, Piazza Verdi, Piazza Marina, Piazzale Ungheria and Piazza Spinuzza. These car parks are not free and the tickets can be bought from any of the shops listed nearby the car parks. In the city centre car parks (such as the Teatro Politeama), it is not uncommon to leave the car keys with the official in charge, who will then move the car around in the course of the day. Use your judgment as to whether this is a safe move.

At archaeological sites: At most of the key archaeological sights (such as the Roman Villa at Piazza Armerina and the Greek temples at Selinunte), there are semi-official car parks where a fee is payable to the watchful attendant.

Elsewhere, at other sites, urchins may offer to "keep an eye on" your car. It is wise to accept and pay a small fee in the reasonable assurance that the vehicle will still be there, undamaged, on your return.

Organised Tours

One way to get to know more about the area where you are staying is to take one of the organised tours. Virtually every travel agency in the main tourist resorts organises tours with English, French, German or Scandinavian-speaking guides. These can be good value for money. In the high season, tours from Taormina usually include: Vulcano, Lípari, Siracusa, Agrigento, Palermo, Gole dell' Alcántara, Piazza Armerina, Enna, Etna and an Etna sunset. From Cefalù, tours include Palermo, Agrigento, Piazza Armerina, Gangi, Petralia Sottana and other destinations in the west of Sicily. Visit local tourist offices for information.

Where to Stay

Hotel Accommodation

Sicily has over 500 hotels of various grades. Outside the main resorts, hotel standards are generally not as high as in northern or central Italy. For reasons of comfort, quality and security, consider staying in accommodation a grade above the one you would normally choose.

Hotel categories: Hotels are classified according to a star rating system: 5-star, of which there are only three on the island, are *de luxe*; 4-star are first class and exceptionally comfortable; 3-star are comfortable and economical; 2-star are hotels with fairly basic accommodation; and 1-star hotels range from simple to frugal.

There are considerable differences in price and quality depending on the market, i.e. availability and demand in a particular region. This pushes prices in Ragusa, for example, where there is a shortage of hotel accommodation, much higher than in Palermo. Also expect to find a huge difference in quality between hotels of the same grade in "tourist" and "non-tourist" towns. Off the beaten track, hotels will be very basic but conceivably cost the same as in better resorts. There are also price differences between high and low season.

The provincial and local tourist boards issue up-to-date lists of hotels which include prices. Hotels are not allowed to charge more than the price written on the rate card – usually located on the inside of the door – for each room.

Note that some hotels are open only in the high season (approximately May to October).

When busy, hotels may insist on guests taking either half or full board (i.e. dinner or lunch and dinner). This policy is a feature of many Sicilian resorts. Conversely, in the low season, do ask prospective hotels if they are able to offer reduced rates. Outside certain cities and resorts, most will, certainly if you look or sound doubtful about staying. Request a *sconto* (discount) because it is *bassa stagione* (low season).

Payment: Most hotels listed in the three-, four- and five-star categories will accept the usual credit cards, and will also take payment by Eurocheque. Traveller's cheques are less common. It is advisable to check when booking. Sicilian society generally looks upon cash payment with particular favour. There are several hotel groups operating in Sicily which are represented in the UK:

Jolly Hotels, 90a High Street, Rickmansworth, Herts, tel: 0800 282729.

Tips for Touring Visitors

Sicily does not always have accommodation in the most obvious or appealing places. Where it does, the hotels tend to be quickly booked, so reserve well in advance in the high season. In the case of Taormina, Cefalù and Ragusa, accommodation should always be booked well in advance. Even if touring out of season, it is worth calling a day ahead to reserve rooms.

Since distances in Sicily are so great, it is possible for touring travellers to find themselves stranded with nowhere to stay. The following list of accommodation also suggests contingency hotels. (The comments below make it clear which resorts are positively recommended and which are merely there for contingency purposes.)

Remember that there is a gulf between urban and rural Sicily. In the mountainous hinterland, particularly in lower-grade hotels, advise the hotel if you expect to check in late at night. If you are female (even several women

together) and travelling off the beaten track, expect to be interrogated on the absence of a male companion by a mistrustful hotel-keeper. However, once you are accepted as "respectable", the atmosphere changes to friendly acceptance.

Hotel safety: In general, the higher grade hotels are in safer and more salubrious areas. But take particular care in choosing hotels in the old quarters of Catania and Palermo. Families or women travelling alone should choose a hotel on a main street or in a modern quarter. In general, parts of historic Palermo and Catania can be deserted or slightly intimidating at night, with a greater risk of *scippatori* (street thieves).

Hotel reference: For easy reference between Travel Tips and the Places section of the book, accommodation has been listed under provinces, in the order they appear in the Places section. The provincial capital is covered first, followed by towns/resorts in alphabetical order. The hotel listing below contains a flavour of each city/resort to help you select the ones most suitable to your needs.

Villas

Villas are a popular alternative to hotels in Cefalù, Taormina, Mondello, Castellammare del Golfo and the more salubrious coastal and mountain resorts. As an independent traveller, it is difficult to book villas on the spot since most are booked well in advance or have tie-ins with foreign agents. As a result, villa holidays tend to be booked as packages through travel agencies and holiday companies in your country of origin.

In the US contact:

Villas International
71 W. 23rd Street, New York, NY 10010; toll-free in US (800) 221 2260.

Families Abroad
194 Riverside Drive, New York, NY 10025, tel: (212) 787 2434.

Home Abroad
405 E. 56th Street, New York, NY 10022, tel: (212) 42 9165.

Palermo City

Visitors need to choose between staying in the bustling centre of Palermo (ideal for seeing the historic sites) or in the select resort of Mondello, just outside town.

In Palermo city, accommodation is reasonably priced and easier to find than in most parts of the island. It is, however, advisable to choose a higher grade hotel in Palermo than you might elsewhere. For safety's sake, choose a hotel on a main street (see Hotel Safety above).

There is a large concentration of hotels at the southern ends of Via Roma and Via Maqueda, between the station and Corso Vittorio Emanuele. Further along the Corso, the hotels are more expensive. The modern Viale della Libertà quarter, within walking distance of the historic centre, is a good choice from many points of view, offering safety, convenience and fashionable neighbourhood bars. There are a few very inexpensive places around La Kalsa, but this area is best avoided.

Centrale
Corso Vittorio Emanuele 327.
Tel: 091 336666.
Fax: 091 334881.
A 4-star hotel, restored in 1997; 63 rooms with a 30s charm near Quattro Canti old quarter. Breakfast (not included in price) is served on the terrace, which has a remarkable view over the old town roofs. **LLLL**

Excelsior Palace
Via Marchese Ugo 3.
Tel: 091 6256176.
Fax: 091 342139.
Extremely comfortable 4-star hotel. Refurbished in the original 19th-century style. Rooms vary considerably so you may wish to see the room before booking. A good location opposite a park in the chic part of Palermo. Friendly staff. Excellent restaurants. **LLLL**

Forte-Agip
Viale Regione Siciliana 2620
Tel. 091 552033.
Fax: 091 408198.
Large (105 bedrooms), modern 4-star hotel. **LLLL**

Politeama Palace Hotel
Piazza Ruggero Settimo 15.
Tel. 091 580733
Fax: 091 6111588.
A modern and comfortable 4-star hotel in the central area near Politeama Theatre. **LLLL**

Villa Iglea Grand Hotel
Salita Belmonte 43.
Tel: 091 543744.
Fax: 091 547654.
Originally a villa built by the Florio family (one of the great entrepreneurial and political families of the 19th century), this 5-star hotel has been carefully restored to its early 20th-century glory. From its position in Acquasanta on a cliff above the city and the bay, the view stretches across to the Conca d'Oro. Facilities include a piano bar and restaurants. **LLLL**

Cristal Palace Hotel
Via Roma 477/d.
Tel: 091 6112580.
Fax: 091 612589.
Modern 3-star hotel across the street from the Grande Albergo delle Palme. Centrally located for the historic quarter. Comfortable. Breakfast not included. **LLL**

Europa
Via Agrigento 3.
Tel/fax: 091 6256323.
Very pleasant, good value for money, quiet 3-star hotel. Located in a central area within walking distance of the old centre and the fashionable Art Nouveau street (Via Libertà). **LLL**

Mediterraneo
Via Rosolino Pilo 43.
Tel. 091 58344.
Fax: 091 581845.
Comfortable 3-star hotel very close to Teatro Massimo, the heart of the old town. **LLL**

Grand Hotel et des Palmes
Via Roma 398.
Tel: 091 583933.
Fax: 091 331545.
One of the oldest hotels in the city centre. Wagner completed Parsifal here in 1882. Slightly shabby grand Victorian style. The Art Nouveau lobby is much grander than the modern bedrooms. Even if you are not staying, at least come here for a pre-prandial cocktail. **LLL**

Jolly Hotel
Foro Italico 22.
Tel: 091 6165090.
Fax: 091 6161441.
A large, modern 4-star hotel with a garden and pool it borders the seafront and the ramshackle Kalsa quarter. Walking around the area at night is not advised. A shuttle takes guests into the modern centre at Teatro Politeama. Breakfast not included. **LLL**

Hotel Prices

Price categories are based on the rate per night for two people sharing a double or twin room. Expect to pay around two-thirds of this price for a single room:
LLLL = L200,000–L450,000
LLL = L140,000–L200,000
LL = L100,000–L135,000
L = L55,000–L95,000
Prices include breakfast except where noted.

Moderno
Via Roma 276, CAP 90133.
Tel: 091 588683.
Fax: 091 588683.
Centrally located, clean 2-star hotel. Good value. Breakfast not available. **LL**

Posta
Via Gagini 77.
Tel: 091 587338.
Fax: 091 587347.
Two-star. Centrally located and comfortable. **LL**

Tonic
Via Stabile 126.
Tel: 091 585560.
Fax: 091 581754.
Recently restored, very comfortable 2-star hotel, centrally located. Breakfast not available. **LL**

Albergo Orientale
Via Maqueda 26.
Tel: 091 6165727.
Basic 1-star hotel. Half of the rooms are en-suite. Former palazzo with marble courtyard and Plenty of atmosphere (but no breakfast). **L**

Letizia
Via Bottai 30.
Tel/fax: 091 589110.
Centrally located near Piazza

Marina, a very square with a remarkable garden. Breakfast not included. **L**

Palermo Mondello Lido
For families with young children or those seeking a hectic nightlife, Mondello makes a better summer base than Palermo city. It also offers a greater level of safety than the city centre. During the season, much of fashionable Palermo moves to the resort. Mondello's hotels are then popular so early reservation is advisable. The best hotels tend to have private beaches. Elsewhere, most beaches tend to be paying.

Mondello Palace
Viale Principe di Scalea, CAP 90151.
Tel: 091 450001.
Fax: 091 450657.
Modern, luxury 4-star hotel on the seafront. Private beach, pool, restaurant and bar. **LLL**

Splendid Hotel la Torre
Piano Gallo 11, CAP 90151.
Tel: 091 450222.
Fax: 091 450033.
Three-star concrete block, but built on the rocky point of the bay, at the far end of Mondello Lido. It is on the beach and has a pool and tennis courts. Many rooms overlook the sea or garden. **LLL**

Conchiglia d'Oro
Viale Cloe 9, CAP 90151.
Tel/fax: 091 450359.
Reasonable 3-star, cheaper off-peak. Breakfast not included. **LL**

Residence Villa Esperia
Via Margherita di Savoia 53, CAP 90153.
Tel/fax: 091 6840717.
Two-star. **LLL**

Palermo Province

Bagheria
As the first of Palermo's garden suburbs, Bagheria is bursting with dilapidated 18th-century villas, none of which has yet been turned into villa-hotels.

Zabara Park Hotel
on the SS 113 road, CAP 90011.
Tel: 091 907111.
Fax: 091 907411.
Out of town 3-star motel with swimming pool and tennis courts. Breakfast not included. **LLL**

Cefalù
Cefalù vies with Taormina as Sicily's most appealing resort. Safety, convenience and good infrastructure make it an ideal choice for families or elderly people. The beaches are closer and far better than at Taormina. Like Taormina, the resort feels perfectly safe and free from petty crime. There is a wide range of accommodation to suit all pockets. Visitors out of season would do well to avoid hotels located on the beach since the beaches tend not to be very clean in the low season.

Hotel Prices

Price categories are based on the rate per night for two people sharing a double or twin room. Expect to pay around two-thirds of this price for a single room:
LLLL = L200,000–L450,000
LLL = L140,000–L200,000
LL = L100,000–L135,000
L = L55,000–L95,000
Prices include breakfast except where noted.

Carlton Riviera
Località Capo Plaia, CAP 90015.
Tel: 0921 420304.
Fax: 0921 420264.
About 5 km (3 miles) west of Cefalù, a large modern 3-star hotel right on the cliffs. Tennis courts, swimming pool. Open April to 1 October. **LLLL**

Baia del Capitano
Località Mazzaforno, CAP 90015.
Tel: 0921 420005.
Fax: 0921 420163.
One of the more pleasant hotels. About 5 km (3 miles) west of Cefalù. Modern but well-built 3-star, set in an olive grove. Swimming pool, tennis courts and nearby beach. Breakfast not included. **LLL**

Kalura
Località Caldura, CAP 90015.
Tel: 0921 421354.
Fax: 0921 423122.
About 3 km (2 miles) east of Cefalù. Slightly shabby 3-star, but most rooms have a sea view; pleasant terrace. **LLL**

Le Sabbie d'Oro
Località S. Lucia, CAP 90015.
Tel: 0921 421565.
Fax: 0921 422213.
About 2 km (1½ miles) from Cefalù. Modern 3-star, not far from a sandy beach. Breakfast not included. **LLL**

Riva del Sole
Via Lungomare 25, CAP 90015.
Tel: 0921-421230.
Fax: 0921-421984.
In the town, but on the seafront. Large rooms, some with a view of the sea or the old town, and a good restaurant. Breakfast not included. **LL**

Tourist
Via Lungomare, CAP 90015.
Tel: 0921 421750.
Fax: 0921 421750.
A friendly three-star hotel with a reasonable restaurant but "ackaged" breakfasts. **LL**

Al Pescatore
Località Caldura, CAP 90015.
Tel/fax: 0921 421572.
Two-star comfort. **LL**

Castelbuono
Hotel Milocca
Contrada Piano Castagna, CAP 90013.
Tel: 091 671944.
Fax: 091 671437.
Pleasant, inexpensive 3-star hotel located in the middle of an oak wood within the Parco delle Madonie. A car is essential. Swimming pool. **LL**

Isola Delle Femmine
Creeping pollution makes this an undesirable location, but its lingering popularity with visitors remains.

Saracen Club
Via dei Saraceni 1, CAP 90040.
Tel: 091 8671423.
Fax: 091 8671371.
Three-star. **LL**

Hotel Eufemia
Via Nazionale 28, CAP 90040.
Tel: 091 867800.
Fax: 091 8678002.
Comfortable 3-star. Breakfast not included. **LL**

Monreale
This pleasant cathedral town makes a low-key alternative to accommodation in Palermo City itself.

Carrubella Park Hotel
Via Umberto 233, CAP 90046.
Tel: 091 6402188.
Fax: 091 6402189.
About 1 km (½ mile) from Monreale, 3-star hotel with wonderful views across the Conca d'Oro. Breakfast not included. **LL**

Il Ragno
Via Provinciale 85 (Località Giacalone), CAP 90040.
Tel: 091 419256.
In the countryside about 10 km (6 miles) from Monreale in the direction of S. Giuseppe Jato. A good option if you are travelling by car and wish to stay outside the Palermo conurbation. Breakfast not included. **L**

Montelepre
Once the haunt of the bandit Giuliano, this mountain village makes an unusual base within easy reach of Palermo. (A car is essential.)

Rose Garden
Via Circonvallazione 120, CAP 90040.
Tel: 091 8784360.
Fax: 091 8784192.
Two-star. Breakfast not included. **L**

Ustica
This lovely island off Palermo is extremely popular with swimmers and nature-lovers. It attracts a large number of German, Scandinavian and Sicilian visitors. Hotels tend to fill up fast but there are many opportunities to rent rooms: call in at the Pro Loco tourist office (Vito Longo) if the fishermen on the port haven't already made you an offer. Alternatively, book a room through

Agenzia Osteodes Travel Agency
Via Magazzino 5, CAP 90010.
Tel: 091 8449210.
Fax: 091 8449210.

Grotta Azzurra
Loc. San Ferlicchio.
Tel: 091 8449048.
Fax: 091 8449396.
Four-star. **LLLL**

Punta Spalmatore
Loc. Spalmatore.
Tel: 091 8449388.
Fax: 091 8449482.
A 3-star "village" with bungalows and rooms for rent. Open Jun–Sep with prices varying from moderate to expensive depending on the season. Minimum one week rent. For reservations and/or information throughout the year, call **Orizzonti Gestioni,**
Tel: 02 58396325.
Fax: 02 58396430.

Stella Marina
Via C. Colombo 33, CAP 90010.
Tel: 091 8449014.
Fax: 091 8449325.
Two-star. **L**

Ariston
Via della Vittoria 5-7, CAP 90010.
Tel: 091 8449042.
Fax: 091 8449335.
Two-star. Breakfast not included. **L**

Diana
Contrada San Paolo, CAP 90010.
Tel/fax: 091 8449109.
Two-star. Breakfast not included. **L**

Clelia
Via Magazzino 7, CAP 90010.
Tel: 091 8449039.
Located on the main square, Clelia is the oldest pensione in town. Wonderful fish restaurant. **L**

Locanda Castelli
Via S. Francesco 16.
Tel: 091 8449007.
One-star. Three apartments for two people. Minimum one week rent. **L**

Trápani Province

Trápani City
Crystal
Via S. Giovanni Bosco, 17, CAP 91100.
Tel: 0923 20000.
Fax: 0923 25555.
Four-star. Breakfast not included. **LLLL**

Astoria Park
Lungomare D. Alighieri, San Cusumano, CAP 91100.
Tel: 0923 562400.
Fax: 0923 567422.
Set 3 km (2 miles) along the seafront towards Erice, a comfortable 3-star hotel with restaurant, bar, tennis courts, pool,

private beach. Breakfast not included. **LLL**

Vittoria
Via Crispi 246, CAP 91100.
Tel: 0923 873044.
Fax: 0923 29870.
Central city location with some sea views from this 3-star hotel. Breakfast not included. **LLL**

Cavallino Bianco
Lungomare Dante Alighieri 5, CAP 91100.
Tel: 0923 21549/23902.
Fax: 0923 873002.
Three-star hotel by the sea, half the rooms with views. Breakfast not included. **LL**

Moderno
Via Tenente Genovese, 20, CAP 91100.
Tel: 0923 21247.
Fax: 0923 23348.
Two-star hotel with 21 rooms. Breakfast not included. **L**

Castellammare del Golfo
This charming fishing port and small resort is an ideal base for families or for independent travellers who want to be close to Palermo yet in a quieter, more manageable location. It also appeals to those wishing to swim in clean waters near the nature reserve of Lo Zíngaro. Consider renting a villa in Castellammare.

Al Madarig
Piazza Petrolo 7, CAP 91014.
Tel: 0924 33533.
Fax: 0924 33790.
Modern 3-star hotel overlooking the port. Breakfast not included. **LL**

Belvedere Oasi del Golfo
SS 187, km 37, CAP 91014.
Tel/fax: 0924 33330.
Breakfast not included. **L**

Castelvetrano
Castelvetrano is not an especially interesting town but its hotels are mostly on the beach and are handy for the Greek ruins of Selinunte. (See Selinunte for hotels too.)

Alceste
Via Alceste 21, CAP 91022.
Tel: 0924 46184.
Fax: 0924 46143.
3-star near the beach of Selinunte. Breakfast not included. **LL**

Triscina Mare
Via Uno, 233, località Triscina di
Selinunte, CAP 91022.
Tel: 0924 84082.
Fax: 0924 84546.
Two-star. Breakfast not included. **LL**
Lido Azzurro
Via Marco Polo 98.
Tel/fax: 0924 46256.
One-star. **L**

Erice
Erice is a perfect base and an
extremely attractive village. In
summer, its hilltop site makes it far
more comfortable than Trápani
itself. However, in high season
accommodation is in great demand
so early booking is highly
recommended.
Elimo
Via Vittorio Emanuele 75,
CAP 91016 .
Tel: 0923 869377.
Fax: 0923 869252.
A small 3-star hotel in the old town
with a pleasant restaurant, bar and
roof terrace. **LLLL**
La Pineta
Viale Nunzio Nasi, CAP 91016.
Tel: 0923 869783.
Fax: 0923 869786.
Three-star. Breakfast not included.
LLL
Moderno
Via Vittorio Emanuele 63, CAP
91016.
Tel: 0923 869300.
Fax: 0923 869139.
A 3-star hotel in the old town. It
feels fairly intimate and has a
terrace and a good restaurant. **LLL**
Ermione
Via Pineta Comunale 43.
Tel: 0923 869138.
Fax: 0923 869 587.
Set in a pine grove just outside the
walls of medieval Erice, this
unattractive-looking 2-star hotel has
large rooms, great views, a pool
and an average restaurant. **LL**
Edelweiss
Cortile Padre Vincenzo 5, CAP
91016.
Tel: 0923 869420.
Fax: 0923 869252.
This basic but quiet *pensione* has a
distinctly Alpine feel; 2-star with 13
rooms. **LL**

Marsala
Hotel President, Via Nino Bixio 1,
CAP 91025.
Tel: 0923 999333.
Fax: 0923 999115.
Three-star. Breakfast not included.
LLL
Hotel Cap 3000
Via Trápani 161, CAP 91025.
Tel: 0923 989055.
Fax: 0923 989634.
Comfortable 3-star hotel with an
uncovered pool. Breakfast not
included. **LL**
Acos Hotel
Via Mazara 14 (on the SS 115 road)
Tel: 0923 999166.
Fax: 0923 999132.
A rather bland 3-star motel.
Breakfast not included. **LL**
Villa Favorita
Via Favorita 27, CAP 91025.
Tel: 0923 989100.
Fax: 0923 980264.
Two-star comfort with large rooms.
LL
Albergo Garden
Via Gambini 36.
Tel: 0923 982320.
Fax: 0923 982320.
Two-star comfort. Some of the
rooms are en-suite. Credit cards not
accepted. **L**

Mazara del Vallo
Hopps Hotel
Via G. Hopps 29.
Tel: 0923 946133.
Fax: 0923 946075.
Relatively expensive 3-star, but
traditional service; recommended
for its hospitality and good cuisine;
pool and garden. **LL**

San Vito Lo Capo
This is an up and coming resort
near Castellammare with a Wild
West feel about it. But it is pleasant
and safe, a good choice for families
or those on a limited budget, even
though prices have risen recently
due to the increasing presence of
tourists during July and August. The
most popular hotels are around Via
Savoia and Via Mulino.
Hotel Capo San Vito
Via San Vito 1.
Tel: 0923 972284.
Fax: 0923 972559.

This large 3-star hotel is 10 km (6
miles) south of Capo San Vito and
situated on the beach. There is a
private beach for guests, gardens
and tennis courts. Breakfast not
included. **LLLL**
Panoramic Hotel
Via Cala Mancina 1, CAP 91010.
Tel: 0923 972511.
Two-star near the beach. **LLL**
(Cheaper off-season)
Egitarso
Via Lungomare 54, CAP 91010.
Tel: 0923 972111.
Fax: 0923 972062.
A 2-star hotel on the seafront.
Breakfast not included. **LLL**
Vecchio Mulino
Via Mulino 49.
Tel: 0923 972518.
A 2-star hotel with panoramic
terrace views and good restaurant.
Breakfast not included. **L**
Sabbia d'Oro
Via Santuario 49, CAP 91010.
Tel/fax: 0923 972508.
Very inexpensive 1-star hotel. **L**

Selinunte
Selinunte has a number of standard
beach hotels.
Paradise Beach
Contrada Belice di Mare.
Tel: 0924 46333.
Fax: 0924 46477.
Set beside the sea 6 km (4 miles)
from Marinella. An impressive hotel-
club with sports facilities, a pool
and tennis courts, 250 rooms.
Closed Nov–Feb. Breakfast not
included. **LLL**
Alceste
Via Alceste 23, Marinella.
Tel: 0924 46184.
Fax: 0924 46143.
A terrace, garden and solarium.
Breakfast not included. **LL**
Garzia Hotel
Via Antonio Pigafetta 6–8,
CAP 91022.
Tel. 0924 46024.
Fax: 0924 46196.
A 3-star hotel with 68 rooms.
Breakfast not included. **L**

Egadi Islands

In July and August accommodation
can be very hard to find: book well

in advance for this period. However, the ferries tend to be met by locals offering rooms.

Approdo di Ulisse
Località Calagrande, Favignana, CAP 91023.
Tel: 0923 922525.
Fax: 0923 921511.
Three-star hotel, the most comfotable in the Egadi. Breakfast not included. **LLLL**

Egadi
Via C. Colombo 17, Favignana.
Tel/fax: 0923 921232.
Two-star. Closed Oct–Apr. Breakfast not included. **L**

Albergo Bouganville
Via Cimabue 10, Favignana.
Tel: 0923 922033.
Fax: 0923 922197.
Quiet rooms. Two-star. Breakfast not included. **L**

Pensione dei Fenici
Via Calvario 18, Lévanzo, CAP 91010.
Tel/fax: 0923 924083.
Two-star. Breakfast not included. **L**

Paradiso
Via Lungomare 8, Lévanzo.
Tel: 0923 924080.
One-star. Breakfast not included. **L**

Pantellerla

This volcanic, mountainous island is not part of the Egadi archipelago. It is nearer Tunisia than Sicily, and can be reached by a daily hydrofoil from Trápani in summer. Holiday accommodation is limited, but there are villa rental possibilities.

Club Village Punta Fram
Località Punta Fram, CAP 91017.
Tel: 0923 918075.
Fax: 0923 918244.
Three star. Breakfast not included. **LLL**

Cossyra
Loc. Cuddie Rosse-Mursia.
Tel: 0923 911154.
Fax: 0923 911026.
About 3 km (2 miles) from Pantellería port, this 3-star hotel has pleasant grounds, a pool, tennis courts and a private beach. **LL**

Port'Hotel
Lungomare Borgo Italia 6, CAP 91017.
Tel: 0923 911299.

Fax: 0923 912203.
E-mail: porthotel@pantelleria.it
Three-star. Breakfast not included. **LL**

Miryam
Corso Umberto 1.
Tel: 0923 911374.
Fax: 0923 911777.
Two-star. No credit cards. Breakfast not included. **LL**

Hotel Prices

Price categories are based on the rate per night for two people sharing a double or twin room. Expect to pay around two-thirds of this price for a single room:
LLLL = L200,000–L450,000
LLL = L140,000–L200,000
LL = L100,000–L135,000
L = L55,000–L95,000
Prices include breakfast except where noted.

Agrigento City

Unlike the rest of the province, the city is well provided with good-quality hotels. This section also includes the Valley of the Temples.

Villa Athena
Località Templi, CAP 92100.
Tel: 0922 596288.
Fax: 0922 402180.
This moderately expensive but serene 4-star hotel overlooks the Temple of Concord offering lovely views of all the temples. Set in charming gardens with pool, it is the only hotel within the Valley of the Temples so it is worth making the most of the spot for lunch or dinner graced by serene views. Patchy service. **LLLL**

Albergo della Valle
Via dei Templi, CAP 92100.
Tel: 0922 26966.
Fax: 0922 26412.
Four-star comfort. Breakfast not included. **LLLL**

Colleverde
Passeggiata Archeologica, CAP 92100.
Tel: 0922 29555.
Fax: 0922 29012.
This 3-star hotel is set further up the slope from Villa Athena, at the

start of Strada Panoramica. Lovely views of the temples. Reasonable restaurant. **LLL**

Grand Hotel Dei Templi
Contrada Angeli (Villaggio Mosè, on the SS 115, 3 km/2 miles east of the ruins), CAP 92100.
Tel: 0922 606144.
Fax: 0922 606685.
This crisp 4-star hotel is a typical conference centre. Swimming pool, good restaurant. **LLL**

Tre Torri
Contrada Angeli (Villaggio Mosè), CAP 92100.
Tel: 0922 606733.
Fax: 0922 607839.
Large 3-star hotel just east of the temples. Restaurant, bar, pool. **LL**

Pirandello
Via Giovanni XXIII 5, CAP 92100.
Tel: 0922 595666.
Fax: 0922 402497.
Three-star comfort. **LL**

Villa Holiday
Via Grabrici 9, CAP 92100.
Tel: 0922 606332.
Two-star in the town of Agrigento. Breakfast not included. **L**

Agrigento Province

San Leone (Coast)

Dioscuri
Via Lungomare Falcone-Borsellino 1, CAP 92100.
Tel: 0922 406111.
Fax: 0922 411297.
Comfortable 4-star hotel; restaurant, bar and garden. **LLL**

Pirandello Mare
Via G. de Chirico 17, CAP 92100.
Tel: 0922 412333.
Fax: 0922 413693.
Unattractive but very comfortable 3-star hotel; restaurant and bar. Breakfast not included. **LL**

Akragas
Via Emporium 16 (between the sea and the town), CAP 92100.
Tel/fax: 0922 414082.
Two-star coastal hotel with restaurant and bar. Ideal location for families. Breakfast not included. **L**

Cammarata

Rio Platani
Via Scalo Ferroviario, Str. Agrigento-Palermo, CAP 92022.

Tel: 0922 909051.
Two-star. Breakfast not included. **L**

Canicatti
To Italians, Canicatti is rather like
Timbuktu – an emergency stop only.
Belvedere
Via Resistenza 22, CAP 92024.
Tel: 0922 851860.
Fax: 0922 851860.
Two-star. Breakfast not included. **L**

Licata
This historic but down-at-heel town
is a possible overnight stop if
Agrigento hotels are full.
Piccadilly
Via Panoramica, CAP 92027.
Tel: 0922 893626.
Fax: 0922 893626.
Three-star. **LL**
Baia d'Oro
Località Mallarella, CAP 92027.
Tel: 0922 774666.
Fax: 0922 897036.
Three-star. Breakfast not included. **L**
Al Faro
Via Dogana 6, CAP 92027.
Tel: 0922 773846.
Fax: 0922 773087.
Three-star. Breakfast not included.
L

Porte Empedocle
Not recommended as a base but
Porto Empedocle makes a sensible
overnight stop if you are catching a
ferry to the Pelagie Islands.
Dei Pini
SS 115, Loc. Vincenzella,
CAP 92014.
Tel: 0922 634844.
Fax: 0922 632895.
Four-star. Breakfast not included. **LL**
Tiziana Residence
Località Durueli, CAP 92014.
Tel: 0922 637202.
Fax: 0922 637363.
Three-star. Breakfast not included.
LL

Sciacca
Sciacca is a possible base in
Agrigento province. While it is rather
scruffy, it is popular with Italians
and Germans taking thermal cures
in this spa town.
Grande Hotel delle Terme
Viale delle Nuove Terme,

CAP 92019.
Tel: 0925 23133.
Fax: 0925 87002.
This 4-star hotel has a thermal
treatment centre. Breakfast not
included. **LLL**
Garden
Via Valverde 2, CAP 92019.
Tel: 0925 26299.
Fax: 0925 26299.
Three-star accommodation.
Breakfast not included. **L**
Paloma Bianca
Via Figuli 5, CAP 92019.
Tel: 0925 25130.
Two-star. Breakfast not included. **L**

Pelagie Islands

Lampedusa
Gattopardo di Lampedusa
Via Beta 6, Contrada Cala Creta.
Tel: 011 8124089.
Fax: 011 8178387.
(High season, tel: 0922 970051).
All-inclusive (daily boat trips and full
board, free cars as the place has
no access to the sea). Open
Jun–Oct. Minimum one week stay.
LLLL
Baia Turchese
Via Lido Azzurro, CAP 92010.
Tel: 0922 970455.
Fax: 0922 970098.
Three-star hotel, open summer only.
LLLL
Alba d'Amore
Via Favorolo 33, CAP 92010.
Tel: 0922 970272.
Fax: 0922 970786.
Comfortable 3-star. **LLL**
Martello
Salita Medusa 1, CAP 92010.
Tel: 0922 970025.

Fax: 0922 971696.
Three-star. **LL**
Lido Azzurro
Contrada Guitgia, Lampedusa,
CAP 92010.
Tel/fax: 0922 970225.
Three-star. **LL**

Linosa
Algusa
Via Alfieri, CAP 92010.
Tel: 0922 972052
Three-star. **LL**

Caltanissetta Province

The province has limited
accommodation and, while the
hinterland is lovely, Caltanissetta
city is dull and does not make a
good base for touring. For those
who wish to stay in the mountains,
go to Enna.

Caltanissetta
San Michele
Via Fasci Siciliani.
Tel: 0934 553750.
Fax: 0934 598791.
Four-star hotel with restaurant. **LLL**

Butera
Stella del Mediterraneo
SS 115, Località Falconara.
Tel: 0934 349004.
Three-star. Breakfast not included.
LL

Gela
Gela is a sensible stopping place
only if you have to do business
there. The town has a large oil
refinery and a high rate of petty
crime.
Hotel Sileno
Loc. Giardinelli, SS 117/1,
Via Venezia.
Tel: 0933 911144.
Fax: 0933 907236.
Three-star. **LL**
Sole
Via Mare 32, CAP 93012.
Tel: 0933 925292.
Two-star comfort. Breakfast not
included. **L**

Mazzarino
Hotel Alessi
Via Caltanissetta 20.

Tel: 0934 381549.
Fax: 0934 381549.
A basic 2-star hotel. **L**

Enna Province

Enna
Enna itself has very few hotels so reservations are advisable. Because of Enna's altitude, take warmer clothes and expect to find views from your hotel window swathed in mist.
Grande Albergo Sicilia
Piazza Colajanni 7, CAP 94100.
Tel: 0935 500850.
Fax: 0935 500488.
This is a centrally located, comfortable and reasonably efficient 3-star hotel. Some of the rooms have fine views. The daily car parking fee is quite high. Breakfast is not included. **LLL**
Demetra
SS 121 contrada Misericordia.
Tel: 0935 502300.
Fax: 0935 502166.
Three-star. Breakfast not included. **LL**

Enna Pergusa
Lakeside resort with good facilities, set around Lago di Pergusa, about 5 km (3 miles) from Enna.
Park Hotel La Giara
Via Nazionale 125, Villaggio Pergusa, CAP 94100.
Tel: 0935 541687.
Fax: 0935 541521.
Three-star. **LLL**
Riviera
Villaggio Pergusa 21, CAP 94100.
Tel/fax: 0935 541267.
Three-star. This option can be noisy at weekends and on festival days due to the hotel being located inside the *autodromo*. Breakfast not included. **LLL**
Garden
Villaggio Pergusa, Via Nazionale, CAP 94010.
Tel: 0935 541694.
Fax: 0935 541690.
Three-star. **LL**

Nicosia
This untouristy inland town is a refreshing base for exploring Enna's hilly interior.

Pineta
Loc. San Paolo 35/A, CAP 94014.
Tel/fax: 0935 647002.
Three-star. Breakfast not included. **LL**
Vigneta
Contrada San Basilico, Vigneta.
Tel: 0935 646074.
Three-star. Breakfast not included. **L**

Piazza Armerina
This appealing town makes a good stop for visitors wishing to see its famous Roman Villa.
Park Hotel Paradiso
Contrada Ramalda, CAP 94015.
Tel: 0935 680841.
Fax: 0935 683391.
Three-star comfort. Breakfast not included. **LLL**
Villa Romana
Via Alcide De Gasperi, 18.
Tel/fax: 0935 682911.
Three-star. Breakfast not included. **LL**
Hotel Mosaici da Battiato
Contrada Paratore, 11.
Tel/fax: 0935 685453.
Close to the Villa Romana. Breakfast not included. **L**

Troina
This quiet town makes a good alternative to Nicosia.
Costellazioni
Contrada S. Michele, CAP 94018.
Tel: 0935 653966.
Fax: 0935 653660.
Four-star. Breakfast not included. **LLLL**
La Cittadella dell'Oasi
Loc. S. Michele, CAP 94018.
Tel: 0935 653966.
Fax: 0935 653660.
Unpretentious 3-star comfort. **LL**

Ragusa Province

The province is easily accessible on day trips from Ragusa city. However, the sudden economic boom of modern Ragusa means that city accommodation is scarce. Tourism is so low-key that unless you are lucky enough to find a bed in Ragusa or the resort of Marina di Ragusa, you may need to be based in Siracusa. On the plus side, part

of the province's charm lies in its lack of tacky tourism and in its warmth towards foreign visitors.

Ragusa
Sadly, there are no hotels in Ragusa Ibla (the medieval "lower" town). The only hotels are in Ragusa Alta (the baroque and modern "high" town). Parking can be tricky and the town's sign-posting and one-way system is confusing. Existing hotels are fairly similar: standard, mid-range, patronised by the business community. Higher-quality hotels are currently under construction so enquire at the tourist office before booking.
Mediterraneo Palace
Via Roma 189, CAP 97100.
Tel: 0932 621944.
Fax: 0932 623799.
Central 4-star hotel. **LLL**
Terraqua
Via delle Sirene, 35.
Tel: 0932 615600.
An expensive 3-star hotel near the beach in Marina di Ragusa. **LLL**
Rafael
Corso Italia 40, CAP 97100.
Tel: 0932 654080.
Fax: 0932 653418.
Inexpensive 4-star hotel. **LL**
Montreal
Via San Giuseppe 8, CAP 97100.
Tel: 0932 621133.
This 3-star hotel is arguably the most pleasant in town but is not outstanding. It is centrally located in Ragusa Alta. **LL**
San Giovanni
Via Traspontino 3, CAP 97100.
Tel: 0932 621013.
Near the railway station. Three-star. Breakfast not included. **L**
Eremo della Giubiliana
Contrada Giubiliana, Km 9, CAP 97100.
Tel: 0932 669119.
Fax: 0932 623891.
Between Ragusa and Marina di Ragusa this fortified medieval hermitage, converted into one of Sicily's most delightful hotels, is both charming and austere. The private airfield offers day trips to Sicily's outlying islands or to Malta. **LLLL**

Módica

Módica is an appealing provincial town and makes an acceptable, if less convenient, alternative to Ragusa.

Bristol
Via Risorgimento 8b.
Tel: 0932 762890.
Three-star. **LL**

Motel di Módica
Corso Umberto 1.
Tel: 0932 941022.
Three-star. Breakfast not included. **L**

Siracusa City

Most hotels are sited in safe modern quarters. Compared with much of Sicily, the hotels are more "international" and efficient, if occasionally a little characterless. Bear in mind that most hotels tend to be some distance from the archaeological sites and the island of Ortygia. This means that public transport or a car will be required, and the same may be true if you are planning to eat out in one of Siracusa's many excellent restaurants.

Jolly Hotel
Corso Gelone 45, CAP 96100.
Tel: 0931 461111/64350.
Fax: 0931 461126.
This 4-star hotel is in the bland shopping district but as a mid-town base is most convenient for the sights. **LLLL**

Forte Agip
Viale Teracati 30, CAP 96100.
Tel: 0931 463232.
Fax: 0931 67115.
Four-star business hotel. Despite rising out of a petrol station, it is the most convenient hotel, close to the archaeological park. **LLLL**

Grand Hotel
Via Mazzini 12.
Tel: 0931 464600.
Fax: 0931 464611.
The most romantic beds in Ortygia, in an Art Nouveau-style hotel overlooking the Porto Grande. **LLLL**

Park Hotel
Via Filisto 80, Siracusa,
CAP 96100.
Tel: 0931 412233/32758.
Fax: 0931 38096.
Elegant 3-star hotel with fairly

expensive restaurant and pool. Set in the modern quarter to the east of the town; in a quiet residential area. Ample parking. **LLL**

Albergo Bella Vista
Via Diodoro Siculo 4, CAP 96100.
Tel: 0931 411437.
Fax: 0931 37927.
Three-star comfort. **LLL**

Domus Mariae
Via Vittoria Veneto 76.
Tel: 0931 24854.
Fax: 0931 24858.
A restored ancient building in the historic centre, this 3-star hotel is run by nuns, who offer a warm welcome and good service. **LLL**

Como
Piazza Stazione 10.
Tel: 0931 464055.
Fax: 0931 464056.
Three-star hotel conveniently located midway between the archaeological park and Ortygia. Good restaurant. **LL**

Gran Bretagna
Via Savoia 21, CAP 96100.
Tel: 0931 68765.
As the only cheap pensione on Ortygia, it is often full. No credit cards. **LL**

Siracusa Province

Augusta

This is an emergency overnight stop for those catching an early ferry the next day. In the vicinity there is the touristy resort village of Brucol.

Brucoli Village
Località Brucoli.
Tel: 0931 994401.
Three-star. **LL**

Villa dei Cesari
Località Monte Tauro.
Tel: 0931 983311.
LL

Noto

Club Eloro
Contrada Pizzuta, Noto Marina,
CAP 96017.
Tel: 0931 812244.
Fax: 0931- 812200.
Three-star hotel on the Noto coast.
LLLL

Stella
Via Francesco Maiore 44,
CAP 96017.

Tel: 0931 835695.
This inexpensive *pensione* is Noto's only hotel in the baroque town. It is often full, so book ahead. **L**

Portopalo di Capo Passero

Jonic
Via Vittorio Emanuele 19,
CAP 96010.
Tel: 0931 842732.
Fax: 0931-842615.
An inexpensive hotel in the southernmost resort. **LL**

El Condor
Via Vittorio Emanuele 38.
Tel: 0931 842016.
One-star basic hotel. Open mid-Jun–Sep. **L**

Catania City

It is advisable to choose accommodation in the smaller towns outside Catania, but if you intend to stay in the city, take a superior hotel in the centre. If you have a low budget Catania offers several alternatives but the risk is that the service may be a little poor.

Excelsior
Piazza G. Verga 39, CAP 95129.
Tel: 095 537071.
Fax: 095 537015.
Expensive but comfortable 4-star Art Deco hotel and restaurant. Open all year round. **LLLL**

Central Palace
Via Etnea 218, CAP 95131.
Tel: 095 325344.
Fax: 095 715 8939.
This convenient if old-fashioned 4-star hotel is situated on the main shopping street. **LLLL**

Jolly Trinacria
Piazza Trento 13, CAP 95129.
Tel: 095 316933.
Fax: 095 316832.
Business-like 4-star hotel in the city centre; no parking. Breakfast not included. **LLL**

Nettuno
Viale Ruggero di Lauria 121,
CAP 95126.
Tel: 095 7125252.
Fax: 095 498066.
Three-star with pool and restaurant.
LLL

Villa Dina
Via Caronda 129, CAP 95128.

Tel/fax: 095 447103.
Three-star. Breakfast not included. **LLL**

Villa Mater Sanctitatis
Via Bottego, 10 CAP 95125.
Tel: 095 580532.
Fax: 095 580032.
Comfortable and economic 2-star. **L**

San Domenico
Via Cifali 76/B, CAP 95123.
Tel: 095 438527.
A well-situated but modest 2-star hotel. Breakfast not included. **L**

Catania Province

Aci Castello and Aci Trezza
This stretch of coast north of Catania makes a good base, with Taormina and Catania close by. The good-quality hotels tend to have sea views of rocky bays and good restaurants.

Catania Sheraton
Via A da Messina 45, Cannizzaro, CAP 95020.
Tel: 095 271557.
Fax: 095 271380.
A luxurious and expensive 4-star hotel with a pool, suites and a renowned restaurant, Il Timo. **LLLL**

Baia Verde
Via Angelo Musco 8, CAP 95020.
Tel: 095 491522.
Fax: 095 494464.
Expensive 4-star hotel in Aci Castello-Cannizzaro. **LLLL**

President Park Hotel
Via Litteri 88, Aci Castello-Aci Trezza, CAP 95026.
Tel: 095 711 6111.
Fax: 095 277569.
Four-star. **LLLL**

I Faraglioni
Lungomare dei Ciclopi 115, Aci Trezza, CAP 95026.
Tel: 095 276744.
Fax: 095 276609.
Set in a fishing village, a 3-star hotel with its own private swimming platform and a good regional restaurant. **LLL**

I Malavoglia
Via Provinciale 3, Aci Trezza, CAP 95026.
Tel: 095 276711.
Fax: 095 276873.
Three-star comfort. Breakfast not included. **LL**

Eden Riviera
Via Litteri 57, Aci Trezza, CAP 95026
Tel: 095 277760.
Fax: 095 277761.
Three-star comfort. **LL**

Hotel Prices

Price categories are based on the rate per night for two people sharing a double or twin room. Expect to pay around two-thirds of this price for a single room:
LLLL = L200,000–L450,000
LLL = L140,000–L200,000
LL = L100,000–L135,000
L = L55,000–L95,000
Prices include breakfast except where noted.

Acireale
Aloha d'Oro
Via A. De Gasperi 10 (Strada Panoramica), Acireale CAP 95024.
Tel: 095 604344.
Fax: 095 606984.
Four-star hotel beside the sea with two pools (one with Jacuzzi) and one of the area's best restaurants. Highly recommended. Breakfast not included. **LLLL**

La Perla Ionica
Via Unni 110, Capomulini, CAP 95024.
Tel: 095 7661111.
Fax: 095 7662222.
E-mail: lpi@tau.it.
Website: www.tau.it/laperlaionica
Over 300 rooms, restaurants, bars, 2 pools, tennis, disco. **LLLL**

Santa Tecla
Loc. Santa Tecla,
Via Balestrate 100.
Tel: 095 7634015.
Fax: 095 607705.
Four-star. Panoramic view of the sea. Closed Nov–mid-Mar. **LLLL**

Orizzonte Acireale
Via C. Colombo.
Tel: 095 886006.
Fax: 095 7651607.
Comfortable 3-star. Breakfast not included. **LLL**

La Perla Ionica
Via Unni, 110, Capomulini, CAP 95024.
Tel: 095 7661111.
Fax: 095 7662222.

E-mail: lpi@tau.it
Website: www.tau.it/laperlaionica
300 rooms, plus suites and apartments; two pools, tennis, gym, solarium, 2 restaurants and piano bar. **LLLLL**

Alcántara
Il Vulcanetto
Via Vittorio Veneto 34,
Mojo Alcántara.
Tel: 0942 963042.
Fax: 0942 963042.
Two-star basic hotel, not far from the weird Alcántara gorge. **L**

Caltagirone
Grand Hotel Villa San Mauro
Via Porto Salvo 10.
Tel: 0933 26500.
Fax: 0933 313661.
This 3-star hotel is the best, with a pool, a couple of unexceptional restaurants and high prices. **LLL**

Castelmola
Villa Sonia
Via Porta Mola 9.
Tel: 0942 28082.
Fax: 0942 28083.
Two-star. **LL**

Panorama di Sicilia
Via A. De Gasperi 44.
Tel/fax: 0942 28027.
Two-star. **L**

Linguaglossa
On the northern slopes of Etna, along with hotels in Nicolosi, accommodation tends to be fully booked during the skiing season.

Happy Days
Via Mareneve 9.
Tel: 095 643484.
Small, 2-star, basic hotel. Open in winter only. Breakfast not included. **LL**

Nicolosi
If you plan to stay for winter sports, book early. There are mountain walks from Nicolosi, planned through the local tourist office, all year round.

Biancaneve
Via Etnea 163.
Tel: 095 911194.
Fax: 095 911194.
Three-star. pool and tennis courts. **LL**

Gemmellaro
Via Etnea 160.
Tel: 095-911060.
Fax: 095-911071.
Three-star. Breakfast not included.
LL
Monti Rossi
Via Etnea 177.
Tel: 095 7914393.
One-star. Open winter only.
Breakfast not included. **L**

Paternò
Sicilia
Via Vittorio Emanuele 391.
Tel: 095 853604.
Fax: 095 854742.
Two-star and often full; surly
management but the only hotel.
Breakfast not included. **L**

Hotel Prices

Price categories are based on
the rate per night for two people
sharing a double or twin room.
Expect to pay around two-thirds
of this price for a single room:
LLLL = L200,000–L450,000
LLL = L140,000–L200,000
LL = L100,000–L135,000
L = L55,000–L95,000
Prices include breakfast except
where noted.

Zafferana Etnea
On the southern slopes of Etna.
A very good base for skiing.
Airone
Via Cassone 67.
Tel: 095 7081819.
Fax: 095 7082142.
Three-star. Closed in November. **LL**
Del Bosco Emmaus
Via Cassone 75.
Tel: 095 7081888.
Fax: 095 7081791.
Two-star. No credit cards. Breakfast
not included. **L**
Primavera dell'Etna
Via Cassone 86.
Tel: 095 7082348.
Fax: 095 7081695.
Three-star. **L**
Villa Pina
Via dei Gerani 19.
Tel/Fax: 095 7081024.
Simple 1-star. **L**

Taormina

During the Taormina peak season
(Apr–May and Jul–Sep) many hotels
insist on a half-board arrangement.
Bristol Park
Via Bagnoli Croce 92.
Tel: 0942 23006.
Fax: 094224519.
Four-star hotel in a dramatic
location, with pool, private beach,
restaurant of some standing and
covered parking. Pleasant
atmosphere. **LLLL**
Excelsior
Via Toselli 8.
Tel: 0942 23975.
Fax: 0942 23978.
This 4-star hotel commands a
promontory and enjoys lovely
grounds and a spectacularly sited
pool. Good restaurants. Parking.
Off-season reductions. **LLLL**
Grande Albergo Monte Tauro
Via Madonna delle Grazie 3.
Tel: 0942 24402.
Fax: 0942 24403.
An ugly exterior conceals a good-
value 4-star hotel. Closed Nov–Mar.
LLLL
San Domenico Palace
Piazza San Domenico 5.
Tel: 0942 23701.
Fax: 0942 625506.
This beautiful former monastery is
now a 5-star hotel. There are
magnificent views from many rooms
and from the terrace towards Etna
and the sea. Along with Palermo's
Villa Igiea, it is the finest hotel in
Sicily. Fine restaurant. **LLLL**
Villa Paradiso
Via Roma 2.
Tel: 0942 23922.
Fax: 0942 625800.
Four-star. Fine views and private
beach. **LLLL**
Villa Belvedere
Via Croce Bagnoli 9.
Tel: 0942 23791.
Fax: 0942 625830.
E-mail: hotbelve@cjs.it.
Comfortable 3-star. **LLL**
Villa San Michele
Via Damiano Rossi 11.
Tel: 0942 24327.
Fax: 0942 24328.
Three-star. Bed and breakfast only.
LLL

Villa Kristina
Via Leonardo da Vinci 23.
Tel: 0942 28366.
Fax: 0942 28371.
Two-star. Can be rather noisy in the
height of the season, but is good
value for money. Closed Dec–Feb.
LLL
Palazzo Vecchio
Salita Ciampoli 9.
Tel: 0942 23033.
Fax: 0942 625104.
Charming if quaint medieval
mansion in the town centre. Sea
views. Two-star. Visa accepted only.
Closed Nov–21 Dec and 10
Jan–Feb. **LL**
Ariston
Via Bagnoli Croce 168.
Tel: 0942 23838.
Fax: 0942 21137.
Three-star. American Express not
accepted. **LL**
La Campanella
Via Circonvallazione 3.
Tel: 0942 23381.
Fax: 0942 625248.
Two-star. Pleasant but not suitable
for the disabled. No credit cards. **LL**
Corona
Via Roma 7.
Tel: 0942 23022.
Fax: 0942 23022.
Two-star. Bed and breakfast only.
No credit cards. **LL**
Svizzera
Via Pirandello 26.
Tel: 0942 23790.
Fax: 0942 625906.
One-star. Clean and well run. No
credit cards in the low season. **LL**
Villa Greta
Via Leonardo da Vinci 46.
Tel: 0942 24360.
Fax: 0942 24360.
Two-star. **LL**
Villa Schuler
Piazzetta Bastione 16.
Tel: 0942 23481.
Fax: 0942 23522.
An individual 2-star hotel with lots
of charm. Closed Dec–Feb. **LL**
Terra Rossa Apartments
Via Bongiovanni 12.
Tel: 0942 24536.
Fax: 0942 23188.
Fairly basic flats, situated between
Taormina and the beach.
Substantial discounts for one

week's rent. No credit cards. Breakfast not included, but apartments have kitchen. **LL**

Taormina Mazzarò
This is the beach-level area of Taormina, below the old town. A cable car connects the resort to the hill-town of Taormina. Its popularity is confirmed by a variety of lively restaurants and clubs which tend to be less expensive than those in Taormina. Nightlife is more frenetic.
Grande Albergo Capo Taormina
Via Nazionale 147.
Tel: 0942 572111.
This sleek 5-star hotel is perched above the beautiful bay of Mazzarò. Salt-water pool built into the cliff. All rooms have private terraces. Private beach. **LLLL**
Villa Sant'Andrea
Via Nazionale 137.
Tel: 0942 23125.
Fax: 0942 23838.
Four-star comfort near the sea. **LLLL**
Ranieri Principe
Via Nazionale 228.
Tel: 0942 23962.
Fax: 0942 24716.
Three-star accommodation. **LLL**
Baia Azzurra
Via Nazionale 240.
Tel: 0942 23249.
Fax: 0942 625499.
Three-star comfort. **LLL**
Villa Esperia
Via Nazionale 244.
Tel: 0942 23377.
Fax: 0942 21105.
Three-star. Bed and breakfast only. Closed Oct–Nov. **LL**
Villa Moschella
Via Nazionale 240.
Tel: 0942 23328.
Fax: 0942 23328.
One-star. Large garden; all rooms with sea views. Bed and breakfast only. Closed Nov–Easter. Visa only. **LL**

Messina Province

Messina
Jolly Hotel dello Stretto
Via Garibaldi 126.
Tel: 090 363860.
Fax: 090 5902526.
Well-organised 4-star. **LLLL**

Royal Palace Hotel
Via Tommaso Cannizzaro 224.
Tel: 090 6503.
Fax: 090 2921075.
A comfortable but unremarkable 4-star hotel. **LLLL**
Paradis
Via Consolare Pompea 441.
Tel: 090 310682.
Fax: 090 312043.
Modern hotel overlooking the strait. **LLL**
Excelsior
Via Maddalena 32.
Tel: 090 293 8721.
Fax: 090 293 8721.
Three-star. Breakfast not included. **LL**

Messina Lido Mortelle
Giardino delle Palme
Road SS 113.
Tel: 090 321017.
Fax: 090 321666.
Modern 3-star hotel near the beach, 1 km (½ mile) from the lake. **LLL**
Faro
Via Circuito 45.
Tel: 090 321762.
Fax: 090 326670.
Simple 2-star. Breakfast not included. **L**

Capo D'Orlando
La Tartaruga
Via Consolare Antica 70.
Tel: 0941 955012.
Fax: 0941 955056.
Three-star. Breakfast not included. **LL**
Il Mulino
Lungomare Andrea Doria 46.
Tel: 0941 902431.
Fax: 0941 911614.
Three-star. Breakfast not included. **LL**
Amato
Via Consolare Antica 150.
Tel: 0941 911476.
Fax: 0941 912734.
Three-star. **L**

Giardini-Naxos
A lively but downmarket resort, popular with families and young holidaymakers. Accommodation is cheaper in winter.
Helenia Yachting
Via Jannuzzo 41.

Tel: 0942 51737.
Fax: 0942 54310.
Fine but unexceptional 4-star. **LLLL**
Naxos Beach Hotel
Via Recanati 26.
Tel: 0942 6611.
Fax: 0942 51573.
Four-star. **LLLL**
Kalos
Via Calcide Eubea 29.
Tel/fax: 0942 52116.
Three-star. **LLL**
Arathena Rocks
Via Calcide Eubea 55.
Tel: 0942 51349.
Fax: 0942 51690.
Three-star. Recommended although a little off the beaten track. Closed Nov–Easter. Breakfast not included. **LL**
La Sirenetta
Via Naxos 177.
Tel: 0942 53637.
Fax: 0942 53637.
Two-star. Closed Nov–Feb. **L**

Gioiosa Marea
Capo Skino Park
Contrada Capo Skino.
Tel: 0941 301167.
Fax: 0941 301340.
Three-star. Jul–Aug minimum stay: one week full-board. Closed November. **LLL**

Letojanni
Antares
Loc. Poggio Mastropietro.
Tel: 0942 36477.
Fax: 0942 36095.
Three-star. Great views. Not suitable for disabled or older guests due to its position. **LLLL**
San Pietro
Via L. Rizzo.
Tel: 0942 36081.
Fax: 0942 37012.
Three-star comfort; with private beach. Closed Nov–Easter. **LL**
Da Peppe
Via L. Rizzo 346.
Tel: 0942 36159.
Fax: 0942 36843.
Two-star. **LL**

Milazzo
This is the port for the Aeolian Islands. Milazzo is not a particularly panoramic or interesting town, but it

is convenient for an overnight stop if you plan to cross to the islands.

Silvanetta
Via Acquaviole 1.
Tel: 090 9281633.
Fax: 090 9222787.
Three-star comfort. **LLL**

Riviera Lido
C. da Corrie, Via Panoramica.
Tel: 090 9283456.
Fax: 090 9287834.
Ask for a room with a sea view. **LLL**

Hotel Prices

Price categories are based on the rate per night for two people sharing a double or twin room. Expect to pay around two-thirds of this price for a single room:
LLLL = L200,000–L450,000
LLL = L140,000–L200,000
LL = L100,000–L135,000
L = L55,000–L95,000
Prices include breakfast except where noted.

Aeolian Islands

The islands have a number of *pensioni/locande* but you should expect to have full board – this is the custom on the Aeolians. Islanders keen to let rooms to tourists will greet each ferry.

Alicudi
Ericusa
Via Regina Elena.
Tel: 090 9889902.
Fax: 090 9889671.
Basic but fine accommodation. A restaurant is attached and half-board arrangement is usually possible. No credit cards. Closed Oct–May. **LL**

Filicudi
Hotel Phenicusa
Via Porto.
Tel: 0941 302501.
Fax: 0941 301188.
Three-star hotel open Jun–Sep. The rooms are a bit run down but those facing the sea have a superb view. Breakfast not included. **LL**

La Canna
Via Rosa, 43.

Tel: 090 9889956.
One-star. Located above the harbour, the best hotel in Filicudi. The rooms are cosy and stylish, all overlooking the sea. Reservation is recommended. Breakfast not included. **L**

Lípari
Hotel Villa Meligunis
Via Marte 7.
Tel: 090 9812426.
Fax: 090 9880149.
Four-star hotel near the sea and the centre of Lípari. **LLLL**

Carasco
Porto delle Genti.
Tel: 090 9811605.
Fax: 090 9811828.
Three-star hotel, the best on the island, with its own private rocky beach and excellent views. Good buffet lunches. Closed 15 Oct–Easter. **LLLL**

Gattopardo Park Hotel
Viale Diana.
Tel: 090 9811035.
Fax: 090 9880207.
Three-star hotel near the centre of Lípari. Open Mar–Oct. Breakfast not included. **LLL**

Giardino sul mare
Via Maddalena 65.
Tel: 090 9811004.
Fax: 090 9880150.
A 3-star hotel on the sea and not far from the centre of Lípari; swimming pool. **LLL**

Rocce Azzurre
Via Maddalena 69.
Tel: 090 9813248.
Fax: 090 9813247.
Three-star. Breakfast not included. **LLL**

Augustus
Via Ausonia 16.
Tel: 090 9811232.
Fax: 090 9812233.
Two-star. Breakfast not included. **LL**

La Filadelfia
Via F. Mancuso 2.
Tel: 090 9812485.
Fax: 090 9812486.
Two-star. **LL**

Poseidon
Via Ausonia 7.
Tel: 090 9812876.
Fax: 090 9880252.
Two-star. Breakfast not included. **LL**

Villa Diana
Via Diana, Tufo.
Tel: 090 9811403.
Basic but comfortable 2-star hotel, open Apr–Oct. Breakfast not included. **LL**

Albergo Casa Vittorio
Vico Sparviero 15.
Tel: 090 9811523.
Basic hotel set among 18th-century *palazzi* in a secluded part of the island. Three apartments with single bed are available. No credit cards. **LL**

Panarea
Cincotta
Via San Pietro.
Tel: 090 983014.
Fax: 090 983211.
Three-star with fine terraces and facilities. **LLLL**

Lisca Bianca
Via Lani 1.
Tel: 090 983004.
Fax: 090 983291.
Three-star. Large garden and balconies in each room. Closed Oct–Mar. **LLLL**

Hotel Hycesia
Via S. Pietro.
Tel: 090 983041.
Fax: 090 9281658
Two-star. **LLL**

Hotel Tesoriero
Via Lani-S. Pietro.
Tel: 090 983098.
Fax: 090 983144.
Two-star. **LL**

Salina
Hotel Bellavista
Via Risorgimento 8, S.Marina Salina.
Tel: 090 9843009.
Three-star hotel with verandas and views. Much cheaper off-peak. **LLLL**

Signum
Via Scalo 11b, Malfa.
Tel: 090 9844222.
Fax: 090 9844102.
Three-star hotel near very beautiful cliffs. Breakfast not included. **LLLL**

Mamma Santina
Via Sanità 40, S. Marina Salina.
Tel: 090 9843054.
Fax: 090 9843051.
Basic 1-star hotel in the centre of Salina. Breakfast not included. **LL**

Strómboli
La Sciara Residence
Via Soldato Cincotta.
Tel: 090 986121.
Fax: 090 986004.
A comfortable 3-star hotel, one of Stromboli's best, which is reflected in the price. Closed 20 Oct–May. **LLLL**
La Sirenetta
Via Marina 33.
Tel: 090 986025.
Fax: 090 986124.
Elegant 3-star with its own nightclub and pool. Closed Nov–Easter. Breakfast not included. **LLLL**
La Locanda del Barbablu
Via Vittorio Emanuele 19.
Tel: 090 986118.
Fax: 090 986323.
Small (5 rooms) and intimate, offering basic bed and breakfast. Exellent home-made food served on an enchanting terrace. **LLL**
Miramare
Via Nunziante 3.
Tel: 090 986047.
Fax: 090 986318.
Basic but smart. Closed 7 Oct–mid-Apr. **LL**
Locanda Villa Petrusa
Via Vittorio Emanuele 13.
Tel: 090 986045.
One-star hotel some distance from the port, with pleasant garden. Breakfast not included. **LL**
Pensione La Nassa
Via Fabio Filzi.
Tel: 090 986033.
Good clean rooms near the sea. No credit cards. **L**

Vulcano
Les Sables Noir
Loc. Porto Ponente.
Tel: 090 9850.
Fax: 090 9852454.
Luxury 4-star hotel near the black-sand beach. Closed Nov–Apr. **LLLL**
Arcipelago
Loc. Vulcanello.
Tel: 090 9852002.
Fax: 090 9852154.
Three-star. Seawater pool. Minimum stay 3 days. Closed Nov–Easter. Breakfast not included. **LLL**
Garden Vulcano
Loc. Porto Ponente.
Tel: 090 9852025.

Fax: 090 9852359.
Old-fashioned 3-star hotel in exotic gardens, owned by a retired sea-captain who has decorated the rooms with his "treasures". **LLL**
Orsa Maggiore
Loc. Porto Ponente.
Tel: 090 9852018.
Fax: 090 9852415.
Large, modern 2-star hotel. Closed 20 Oct–20 Apr. **LLL**

Rural Holidays

Agriturismo describes a holiday stay in the country, often on a working farm. It can offer an interesting alternative to a hotel-based holiday. It provides a real opportunity for contact with Sicilians and a traditional way of life. Most *agriturismo* locations are, naturally enough, in small villages or out in the country. Best booked before setting out.

Palermo Province
Villa Levante
Contrada Forbaudo, 3 miles (5 km) from Castelbuono.
Tel: 0921 671914.
Fax: 095 7462378.
Prices range from L20,000 to L55,000 per bed.
Tenuta Gangivecchio
Contrada Gangi Vecchio.
Tel: 0921 644804.
Fax: 0921 689191.
L100,000 full board.
Fattoria Manostalla
Contrada Manostalla,
90041 Balestrate.
Tel: 091 8787033.
E-mail: aefar@tin.it
Website: www.wel.it
Swimming pool. Double room: L100,000 breakfast included.

Agrigento Province
Fattoria Mosè
Via Pascal, 4 Contrada Mosè, 92100 Agrigento.
Tel/fax: 0922 606115.
Apartments with 2, 4 and 6 beds. L50,000 per person (no cooking facilities)
La Montagnola
Contrada Gorghi-Montagnola, 92019 S. Margherita Belice.

Tel: 0925 32021.
Fax: 0925 997007.

Siracusa Province
Noto
Azienda Agricola Roveto.
For information: Sig. Giuseppe Loreto, Via Adige 3, Siracusa.
Tel: 0931 66024.
Fax: 0931 36946.
Although this has no *agriturismo* there are flats to rent (minimum of 3 days for two people) inside a nature reserve.
Siracusa
SS 115, 4 km (2 miles) south of Siracusa, Azienda Agricola Rinaura.
Tel: 0931 721224.
No *agriturismo*. One-room flats in farmhouse. Open all year.
Villaggio le Grotte
Viale Lidi, Fontane Bianche.
Tel: 0931 790625.
Bungalows. Open Jul–Aug.

Catania Province
Randazzo
L'Antica Vigna,
Via Montelaguardia, 95036, località Montelaguardia.
Tel: 095 924003.
Fax: 095 923324.
Six rooms, 16 beds.
L60,000–70,000 double room, breakfast not included.
Azienda Agrituristica Fondo 23
Via S. Giuseppe La Rena Fondo 23.
Tel: 095 592521.
No *agriturismo*. Flats inside a 14th-century farmhouse. Open all year.
Giarre
Azienda Agricola Russo Tocca, Loc. Mascari.
Tel: 095 931259.
Fax: 095 7794765.
No *agriturismo*. Flats near the sea. Open all year.

Messina Province
Capo d'Orlando
Azienda Agricola F.P. Milio Loc. S. Gregorio.
Tel: 0941 955008/0336 924666.
Fax: 0941 955281.
English spoken.
Caronia
(Nébrodi Mountains)
Masseria Santa Mamma.
Tel: 091 6255710/0941 794046.

Advance booking in recommended. Only flats. Closed in winter when snowing.

Portopalo di Capo Passero
Villaggio Turistico Capo Passero
Via Tagliamenti 22-26.
Tel: 0931 842030.
Two-room apartments (without kitchens) available all year. Full *pensione* available.

Camping

There are more than 80 official campsites in Sicily, the majority on the coast. The sites are ranked from 1- to 4-star according to the facilities they offer: 1-star sites are basic, 4-star luxurious. Hot water may not always be available. Some sites cram in large numbers at the height of the season. Many sites will also provide sleeping bag space for those without tents.

Prices are generally reasonable and vary from L6,000 to L12,000 per night per person plus a contribution for all utilities that varies from L10,000 to L24,000 according to the standard of the site. Prices may vary greatly between the different provinces. Phone ahead whatever the season. In the summer, sites may be full – or closed – if trade is slack.

Camping rough is frowned upon, and is illegal in the national parks. In summer, beware of starting fires which can be dangerous and destructive.

The following is a small selection of campsites.

PALERMO PROVINCE

Palermo
Trinacria
Via Barcarello 26 (Sferracavallo).
Tel/fax: 091 530590.
Two-star. Open all year round.

Cefalù
Costa Ponente
Loc. Ogliastrello.
Tel: 0921-420085
Fax: 091 423122.
Three-star.

San Filippo
Loc. Ogliastrello.
Tel: 0921 420184.
Open Apr–Oct.

Termini Imerese
Himera
Stazione di Buonfornello.
Tel: 091 8140175
Fax: 091 8159206.
Two-star.

TRAPANI PROVINCE

Castellammare del Golfo
Baia di Guidaloca
Località Guidaloca.
Tel: 0924 541262.
Three-star.
Ciauli
Contrada Ciauli.
Tel: 0924 39042.
Open July and August only. Two-star.
Lu Baruni
Scopello.
Tel: 0924 39133.
Open all year. Three-star.
Nausica
Via Milano 24.
Tel: 0924 33030
Fax: 0924 35173.
Open summer only. Three-star.

Castelvetrano
Lido Hawai
Loc. Triscina.
Tel: 0924 84101. One-star.
Il Maggiolino
SS115, Località Marinella di Selinunte.
Tel: 0924 46132. One-star.

San Vito lo Capo
El Bahira
Loc. Salinella.
Tel: 0923 972577.
Office is at Via La Malfa 68 in Palermo (tel: 091 322696).
Open June to October. Four-star.
La Pineta
Via del Secco, 88.
Tel: 0923 972818
Fax: 0923 974070.
Three star.
La Fata
Via Piersanti Martarella 78.
Tel: 0923 972133.
Open all year. Three-star.

Soleado
Via del Secco 40.
Tel: 0923 972166
Fax: 0923 974051.
Two-star.

EGADI ISLANDS

Favignana
Egadi
Contrada Arena.
Tel: 0923 921555
Fax: 0923 539370.
Open all year. Three-star.
Miramare
Loc. Marasolo.
Tel: 0923 921330.
Bungalows available. Open all year. Four-star.

AGRIGENTO PROVINCE

Agrigento
Campeggio Internazionale
San Leone.
Tel: 0922 416121.
Open all year.
Nettuno
San Leone.
Tel: 0922 416268.
Open all year. Three-star.

Eraclea Minoa
Eraclea Minoa Village
Tel: 0922 847310.
Three-star. Open Apr–Sep. Campsite by the beach below the ruins of a Greek theatre. No hotels and few houses. In good weather, the remains of Minoa are visible in the sea.

Lampedusa (Pelagie Islands)
La Roccia
Loc. Cala Greca.
Tel: 0921 970055
Fax: 0921 933822.
Open all year. Two-star.
Lampedusa
Contrada Cala Francese.
Tel: 0822 970055. Two-star.

Menfi
Geser Club
Contrada Le Dune.
Tel: 0925 74666.
Open May–Nov. One-star.

La Palma
Contrada Lido Fiori.
Tel: 0925 72232.
Open all year. One-star.

SIRACUSA PROVINCE

Augusta
La Baia del Silenzio
Loc. Campolato.
Tel: 0931 981881.
Open all year.

Avola
Sabbia d'Oro
Contrada Chiusa di Carlo.
Tel: 0931 822415.
Open all year.

Melilli
Happy Holiday
SS.114, Contrada Campane.
Tel: 0931 950151.
Open all year.

Portopalo di Capo Passero
Campeggio Captain
Contrada Capo Isola delle Correnti.
Tel: 0931 842595.

Siracusa
Campeggio Fontane Bianche
Loc. Fontane Bianche.
Tel: 0931 790333.
Open 1 May–30 Sep.

CATANIA PROVINCE

Acireale
Al Yag
Strada Provinciale per Riposto Via
Altarello.
Tel: 095 7641763
Fax: 095 7641533.
Open Jun–Sep. Three-star.
Panorama
Via S. Caterina, 65.
Tel: 095 7634124.
Two-star. Open all year.

Calatabiano
San Marco
Via San Marco, 19.
Tel: 095 641181
Fax: 095 642635.
Open all year. Two-star. Bungalows
available.

Catania
Jonio
Via Villini a Mare 2.
Tel: 095 4911439
Fax: 095 492277.
Two-star. Open all year.
Europeo
Viale Kennedy 91.
Tel: 095 591026. Fax: 095 591911
Bungalows available. Two-star.
Open all year.

Linguaglossa
Clan dei Ragazzi
Contrada Golfo Monica,
Strada Mareneve.
Tel: 095 643611.
One-star. Open all year.

Mascali
La Zagara
Via Spiaggia 157.
Tel: 095 7700132.
Two-star. Bungalows available
(2 and 4 bed). Open May–Sep.
Mokambo
Via Spiaggia 211, località
Fondachello.
Tel: 095 934369
Fax: 095 938731.
Two-star. Bungalows available. Open
Apr–Sep.

Nicolosi
Etna
Via Goethe (Pineta Monti Rossi).
Tel: 095 914309.
Two-star. Open all year.

Riposto
Praiola
Loc. Carruba.
Tel: 095 964366
Fax: 095 7124546.
Two-star. Open Apr–Sep.

MESSINA PROVINCE

Forza d'Agro
Forza d'Agro Mare
Tel: 0942 751158.
Open July and August.

Capo d'Orlando
Camping S. Rosa
Via Trazzera Marina.
Tel: 0941 901723.
Open 15 Jul–15 Sep.

Youth Hostels

The youth hostels in Sicily have a
tendency to be closed when you
want them. The private hostel in
Siracusa is the most reliable and
generally the most pleasant.
Enna
Via Nazionale,
Lago di Pergusa,
just outside Enna.
No telephone. Unless you like
the Grand Prix, check that no
race is scheduled before arriving.
The race-track runs around the
lake, close to the youth hostel.
Siracusa
Albergo per la Gioventù,
Viale Epipoli 45, Siracusa
Tel: 093 711118
Fax: 093 377922.
Clean and relaxed, four beds per
room, breakfast and sometimes
other meals.
Nicolosi (Catania)
Ostello della Gioventà Etna,
Via della Quercia 5
Tel: 095 7914686.
Good location for excursions on
Etna volcano.
Aeolian Islands
Via Castello 17, Lípari
Tel: 090 9811540
Fax: 090 9811715.
Hostel card required. No
reservations in August. Lock out
9.30am–1pm and 3–6.30pm,
curfew midnight–1am.

Furnari
Camping Bazia
Contrada Bazia.
Tel: 0941 81006.
Open summer only.

Gioiosa Marea
Camping Gioiosa
Contrada Capo Calavà.
Tel: 0941 301523.
Open Apr–Sep.
Camping Residence Cicero
Via Cicero S. Giorgio.
Tel: 0941 39554.
Open summer only.
Camping Tirreno
Contrada Calavà.
Tel: 0941 301028.
Open summer only.

Oliveri
Camping Baia del Principe
Via Lungomare 11.
Tel: 0941 313817.
Open summer only.

Taormina
Camping S. Leo
Capo Taormina,
Via Nazionale.
Tel: 0942 24658.
All year.

Letojanni
Camping Euro Marmaruca
Via IV Novembre.
Tel: 0942 36676.
Camping Paradise International
SS 114.
Tel: 0942 36306.
Open Apr–Sep.

Tusa
Camping lo Scoglio
SS 113.
Tel: 0921 334345.
Open summer only.

AEOLIAN ISLANDS

Lípari
Camping Baia Unci
Via Marina Garibaldi Canneto.
Tel: 090 9811909
Fax: 090 9811715.
Two-star. Open Easter–end Oct.

Salina
Campeggio Tre Pini
Frazione Rinella-Leni.
Tel: 090 9809155.
One-star. Open May–Sep.

Vulcano
Camping Togo
Via Porto Levante.
Tel: 090 985 2303.
Open Apr–Sep.

Where to Eat

Restaurants & Bars

There are various types of places to eat and drink:

Bar/Caffè: all types of beverages; also, they usually serve sandwiches and snacks.
Locanda, Osteria, Rosticceria, Trattoria: offer simple local dishes.
Ristorante: offers more elaborate and expensive menus.
Pizzeria: serves pizza and sometimes pasta dishes.
Gelateria: ice-cream parlour.
Tavola Calda: serves hot, inexpensive food. Usually self-service. You may be expected to eat standing up at the counter.

Most restaurants display a menu outside, and some offer a *menù turistico*: a fixed-price three-course meal. This is usually uninspired but good value.

All bars and restaurants must by law issue a receipt (*ricevuta fiscale*). Depending on the local level of activity by the Guardia della Finanza, you may find this pressed upon you, or not. Take it with you when you leave: the restaurant (and you) are liable to a fine if you don't.

Restaurant Menus

The menu, please/*il menù, per favore*
The bill, please/*il conto, per favore*
Thank you, that was a very good meal/*Grazie. Abbiamo mangiato molto bene.*

Starters (Antipasti)
aubergine in tomato sauce/*melanzane alla parmigiana*
aubergine, olives and tomato/*caponata*

ham/*prosciutto*
mixed cold starters/*antipasti misti*
peppers in oil/*peperonata*
seafood salad/*insalata di mare*
stuffed tomatoes/*pomodori ripieni*

First Course (Il Primo)
clear soup/*il brodo*
light soup/*la minestrina*
mixed/green salad/*un'insalata mista/verde*
egg/*un uovo*
pasta dishes: including *pasta e fagioli* (pasta soup with beans); *pasta al forno* (baked, stuffed pasta); *penne*; *ravioli*; *rigatoni*; *spaghetti*; *tagliatelle*; *tortellini*; *cannelloni* and *vermicelli*.

Second Course (Il Secondo)
meat/*la carne*
fish/*il pesce*
What kind of fish do you have?/*Che pesce ha?*
anchovies/*le acciughe*
beef/*il manzo*
chicken/*il pollo*
chickens' liver/*i fegatini di pollo*
clams/*le vongole*
crab/*il granchio*
dried salted cod/*baccalà*
eel/*l'anguilla*
lamb/*l'agnello*
liver/*il fégato*
lobster/*l'aragosta*
mackerel/*lo sgombro*
meatballs/*le polpette*
meat slices (rolled and stuffed)/*gli involtini*
mullet/*il cefalo*
mussels/*le cozze*
octopus/*il polipo*
oysters/*le ostriche*
prawns/*i gamberi*
pork/*il maiale*
rabbit/*il coniglio*
red mullet/*la triglia*
salami/*salame* (including *mortadella*)
sardines/*le sarde*
sausage/*la salsiccia*
shrimps/*i gamberetti*
squid/*i calamari*
steak/*la bistecca*
swordfish/*il pesce spada*
tripe/*la trippa*
trout/*la trota*
tuna/*il tonno*
veal/*il vitello*

Vegetables
artichokes/*i carciofi*
asparagus/*gli asparagi*
aubergine (eggplant)/*le melanzane*
basil/*il basilico*
beans/*i fagioli*
courgettes/*gli zucchini*
fennel/*i finocchi*
garlic/*l'aglio*
green beans/*i fagiolini*
green vegetables/*la verdura*
mushrooms/*i funghi*
onion/*la cipolla*
peas/*i piselli*
peppers/*i peperoni*
potatoes/*le patate*
spinach/*gli spinaci*
tomato/*il pomodoro*
vegetables (side dishes)/*i contorni*

Fruit, Nuts, Cheese & Desserts
almonds/*le mandorle*
apple/*la mela*
cheese/*il formaggio*
cherries/*le ciliege*
figs/*i fichi*
fruit/*la frutta*
fruit salad/*la macedonia*
grapes/*l'uva*
ice cream/*il gelato*
macaroons/*amaretti*
medlar/*la nespola*
melon/*il melone*
Parmesan/*il parmigiano*
peach/*la pesca*
pear/*la pera*
persimmons/*i cachi*
pineapple/*l'ananas*
prickly pears/*i fichi d'india*
strawberries/*le fragole*
sweets/*i dolci*
tart or cake/*la torta*
watermelon/*il cocomero*

Palermo City

Palermo's top hotels also have renowned restaurants. In particular, consider dining at Villa Igiea, the Excelsior Palace and Albergo delle Palme. (*For details, see the Where to Stay listing for Palermo, page 337*).

Acanto Blu
Via Guardione 19.
Tel: 091 326258.
Reservations essential. No credit cards. Closed lunchtime, Sunday and September. **LL**

Antica Focacceria San Francesco
58 Via A. Paternostro.
Tel: 091 320264.
Not to everyone's taste but deserves a visit. It is quaint, hectic, always open, cheap, and rough and ready. The place for innards, *arancine, panini con la milza* (milt) and *panini con panelle.* **L**

Cafe Quattro Canti
Corso Vittorio Emanuele 315.
Good for snacks like *crostini*; eat in the tea room. **L**

Cappuccio
Via Villareale 20.
A *tavola calda*/bar selling snacks like stuffed sardines, quiches and salami. **L**

La Carbonella
Via delle Madonie 39,
Traversa Regione Siciliana.
Tel: 091 513161.
Out-of-centre location. Pizza in the evenings. An outside dining area. Closed Monday and August. **LL**

Charleston
Piazzale Ungheria 30.
Tel: 091 321366.
Top-quality Sicilian cuisine, arguably Sicily's best. Dress elegantly, especially in the evenings (no shorts). Reservations required. Closed Sunday. From 1 June to early October the restaurant moves to Mondello, inside the Stabilimento Balneare (a private beach)
Tel: 091 450171. **LLL**

Cucina Papoff
Via La Lumia 29/b.
Tel: 091 325355.
Refined yet imaginative Sicilian cuisine in an Art Nouveau setting. Friendly atmosphere. Try the *u maccu*, broad beans in fennel. Closed Sunday and August. **LL**

Gigi Mangia
Via Principe di Belmonte 104/d.
Tel: 091 587651.
Delicious vegetarian appetisers. Try *il colonnello va a favignana*, a pasta dish with tomatoes, herbs and *bottarga.* Closed Sunday. **LL**

Gourmand's
Viale della Libertà 37.
Tel: 091 323431.
Restaurant in sophisticated ultra-modern style. The dishes are light and delicate, including antipasti and *spada affumicato.* Smoked tuna

and swordfish are homemade specialities. Closed Sunday and August. **LLL**

Osteria da Ciccio
Via Firenze 6.
Tel: 091 329143.
Offers *peperoni* (peppers) and swordfish in garlic and herbs. Closed Sunday. **LL**

Da Peppino
Piazza Sferracavallo 78.
Tel: 091 532934.
Fish dishes only. Closed Thursday. **LL**

Pizzeria Bellini
Piazza Bellini.
A bustling *pizzeria* in a lovely location, suitable after a visit to La Martorana church. Marlon Brando praises it in the Bellini's autograph book. It is open until 2am in summer so makes an attractive spot from which to view the illuminated churches. **LL**

Roney's
Viale della Libertà 13.
Chic terrace bar for superior people-watching. Moderately priced snacks and light food, from *calamari fritti* and *arancine* to ice cream. **LL**

La Scuderia
Viale del Fante 9.
Tel: 091 520323.
Excellent Sicilian cuisine. Closed Sunday and for two weeks in August. **LLL**

Self Service
Piazza Politeama (near to the tourist office).
Inexpensive Sicilian food to eat on the premises or to take away. **L**

Shanghai
Vicolo dei Mezzani 34.
Tel: 091 589702.
Definitely not the smartest place in Palermo – the house is crumbling – but it's on everybody's list. The den

views the chaotic Vucciria market, from which the food is hauled up in wicker baskets. Food may be cooked in front of you. Also an outside dining area. No credit cards. Closed Sunday and February. **L**

Trattoria al Buco
Via Granatelli 33.
Tel: 091 323661.
Sound cuisine served in an attractive modern decor. Closed Monday. **LL**

Trattoria Stella (Hotel Patria)
Via Alloro 104.
Tel: 091 6161136.
This snug neighbourhood restaurant is in the courtyard of a ruined *palazzo*. Its hearty cuisine makes it popular with locals. Closed Monday and for 2 weeks in August. In summer open Monday, closed Sunday. **LL**

Santandrea
Piazza S. Andrea 4 (near Vucciria).
Tel: 091 334999.
Located in a tiny *piazza* in the old centre. Very fine traditional cuisine. Delicious *antipasti* and desserts. Good selection of local wines. **LL**

Lo Scalino del Cardinale
Via Bottai 18.
Tel: 091 331124.
Open only for dinner. **LLL**

Trattoria Primavera
Piazza Bologni 4.
Tel: 091 329408.
Located in the old centre close to la Cattedrale. Traditional cuisine, excellent *pasta con le sarde* and *pasta con i broccoli*. **LL**

Mondello

Mondello continues to be a fashionable summer dining place. Many *trattorie* have outdoor terraces and sea views.

Chamade-mare
Via Regina Elena 45/47.
Tel: 091 450512.
Great selection of appetisers and delicious pizzas. Terrace. Always open. **LL**

Charleston le Terrazze
Via Regina Elena.
Tel: 091 450171.
On the jetty off the bay. Summer residence of the Charleston, the famous Palermo restaurant. Quality and price match the city branch. Dress code enforced for dinner (no shorts). Closed Oct–May. **LLL**

Ristorante Totuccio
Via Torre 26/a.
Tel: 091 450151.
A restaurant/piano bar located on the first floor, with good shellfish and a wide selection of *antipasti*. Try the *zuppa di vongole* (clam soup). Pizza evenings only. Closed Wednesday and January. **LLL**

At the other end of the market, one can snack cheaply from the stalls. *Pasta alle sarde*, deep fried fish, whitebait, shrimps, vegetables, mussels are all available – and the sea view is free.

Palermo Province

With the exception of Palermo and Cefalù, the province's *ristoranti* are unexceptional. Try *locande*, *osterie* or *trattorie* instead. Many of these open and close as the mood takes them; many remain shut throughout the winter.

Monreale

With the advent of mass tourism, prices in Monreale have risen out of all proportion to the quality of the cuisine and service.

Ristorante la Botte
Contrada Lenzitti 20,
Circonvallazione Monreale.
Tel: 091 414051.
Out of the centre location. Closed August. **LL**

Riccardo III
C. da Grotte-Monreale.
Tel: 091 414237.
This interesting restaurant is situated inside an old stable with a fireplace. No credit cards. Open weekends only, closed August. **LL**

Pizzeria Peppino
Via Benedetto Civiletti 12.
Tel: 091 6407770.
Best pizza in Palermo. **L**

Osteria delle Lumache
Via San Castrense 50.
This is an unpretentious place for standard Sicilian fare. **L**
Alternatively try the *focacceria* (bakery) next door for typical snacks. But the best way to eat in Monreale is to go to a well-stocked grocery and have a *panino* made up to taste.

Cefalù

Eating out can be expensive at the height of the season. However, many of the *trattorie* on the seafront (Lungomare) do *antipasto al buffet*, self-service starters at low prices.

Vecchia Marina
Via Vittorio Emanuele 73.
Tel: 0921 420388.
Very fine and expensive cuisine. Try the *casareccie con gamberi e carciofi* (homemade pasta with prawns and artichokes). **LLL**

Hosteria del Duomo
Via del Seminario 5.
Tel: 0921 421838.
Lovely open-air location overlooking

Marsala Producers

Sicily's best-known wine (*see page 90*) is produced in and around Marsala. In the town itself are the cellars of Florio, Lombardo, Vito Curatolo Arini, Rallo, Pellegrino and C.S. Marsala, among others.

Florio (now owned by Martini) and Pellegrino lead the market in

terms of sales. Wine-tasting (including a film and a short guided tour of the cellars) is possible at the bigger producers (*stabilmenti*).

Marco De Bartoli
C/da Fornara Samperi 292, 91025 Marsala (TP). Tel: 0923 962093. (French spoken.)

Pellegrino, 39 Via Fante, Marsala. Tel: 0923 951177.
Stabilimento Florio, V. Vincenzo Florio 1. Tel: 0923 781111. The Florio cellars are particularly amenable to visits and offer an interesting and enjoyable tour of the cellars. (Closed Friday pm.) Their *Vergine* marsala is best.

the cathedral. Authentic *caponata* and *penne* and *carpaccio di pesce*, thin slices of raw fish in a light marinade. Closed Monday, except summer, and December. **LLL**

Kentia
Via Nicola Botta 15.
Tel: 0921 423801.
Renowned for its charm, cuisine and garden. Expensive but good. Sample the *scaloppine ai funghi* and *panzerotti di magro* (*cannelloni*). There is an inexpensive set Sicilian menu. Closed Monday, except summer, and for 3–4 weeks in November. **LLL**

Price Guide

Restaurants are graded according to the price of a three-course meal for one, with half a bottle of house wine:
LLL = from L60,000 upwards
LL = L35,000–L60,000
L = less than L35,000

Osterio Magno
Via Belvedere 4.
Tel: 0921 923348.
Restaurant and *pizzeria* (pizza served evenings only) with seafood specialities. Closed Tuesday, except summer, and several weeks in winter. **LLL**

Da Nino Alla Brace
Lungomare 11.
Tel: 0921 422582.
Recommended for French/Sicilian cuisine in a garden setting. Young locals also congregate here to eat pizzas (served only in the evenings). Exceptional fish. Closed Tuesday, except summer, and November. **LL**

Lo Scoglio Ubriaco
Via Corso Ortolani di Bordonaro 2.
Tel: 0921 423370.
A terrace overlooks the harbour, so you can watch the fishing boats while enjoying *spaghetti al cartoccio* (baked spaghetti). Closed Tuesday (except in summer) and two weeks in November. **LL**

Terrasini
Caffè del Duomo
Piazza Duomo.

This is the place for snacks, ice-creams and cakes. **L**

L'Orlando Furioso
Viale Rimembranze 1.
Tel: 091 8682553.
Good spaghetti with lobster and grilled fish. Outside dining area. Closed Tuesday, except summer. **LL**

Trattoria La Ruota
Via Lungomare.
Tel: 091 8685151.
Grilled fish is their speciality. Open all year. **LL**

Ustica Island
There are a few *trattorie* around the port, all about the same in standard and price. In the centre of the village:

Mamma Lia
Via S. Giacomo 1.
Tel: 091 8449594.
Very good fish. **LL**

Da Mario
Piazza Umberto I 21.
Tel: 091 8449505. **L**

Trápani Province

Trápani
Da Peppe
Via Spalti 50.
Tel: 0923 28246.
Tuna specialities from May to early July, fish dishes all year. Closed Saturday, except in summer. **LLL**

Taverna Paradiso
Lungomare Dante Alighieri 22.
Tel: 0923 22303.
Specialities: *neonata* (baby sardines), *spaghetti ai ricci di mare* (spaghetti with sea-urchin). **LLL**

Casablanca
Via San Francesco d'Assisi 69.
Specialises in couscous, crêpes and fish. **LL**

P & G Ristorante
Via Spalti 1 (by the Villa Margerita park and the station).
Tel: 0923 547701.
This casual seafood place serves *neonata* (baby sardines), *risotto marinara* (seafood risotto) and, on Fridays only, couscous. Closed Sunday and August. **LL**

Flowers
Via Cosenza, 53.
Tel: 0923 553395.
Good fish and desserts. **LL**

I Trabinis
Circolo Arcigola, Largo Porta Galli.
Tel: 0923 24462.
Reservations essential. No credit cards. Closed Wednesday and Christmas. **LL**

Trattoria Safina
Piazza Umberto I 35 (opposite the railway station).
Huge portions at low prices. **L**

Colicchia
corner of Via delle Belle Arti and Via Carosio .
Tel: 0923 547612.
The place for *granita* or ice cream in the summer. *Cannoli* available. Closed Monday, except summer. **L**

Erice
Erice's quaint streets are overflowing with bars and restaurants so visitors are spoilt for choice. See page 154 for more on Erice's many pastry shops.

Monte S. Giuliano
Vicolo S. Rocco 7.
Tel: 0923 869595.
Very good traditional Trapanese cuisine. Try the stuffed aubergines (*involtini di melanzana*). **LLL**

Al Ciclope
Viale Nasi 45.
Tel: 0923 869183.
Prices range from inexpensive to very expensive depending on choice of menu. Closed Tuesday, except summer. **LL**

Taverna di Re Aceste
Via Conte Pepoli.
Tel: 0923 869084.
Authentic tavern famous for couscous and its tasty pesto sauces. **LL**

Ulisse
Via Chiaramonte 45.
Tel: 0923 869333.
Closed Thursday. **LL**

La Pentolaccia
Via Guarnotta 17.
Tel: 0923 869099.
Inexpensive if you do not have fish. Good choice of local wines. **LL**

Marsala
Marsala abounds in lively seafood restaurants along the Lungomare.

Al Baglio Oneto
C. da Baronazzo Amafi 55.
Tel: 0923 996963.

Sarde a beccafico, couscous and *cassata Siciliana* are a must. Closed Tuesday, except summer. Closed November. **LLL**

Enzo e Nino
Via Favorita 26.
Tel: 0923 989180.
Fish and couscous specialities. **LL**

Il Delfino
Lungomare Mediterraneo 672.
Tel: 0923 999565.
Excellent seafood of all kinds. **LL**

Ristorante Marsa-Allah
Lungomare Boeo 50.
Tel: 0923 715234.
Seafood dishes and charcoal roasts. **LL**

Caffe Kalos
Piazza della Vittoria (outside Porta Nuova).
Pizza, antipasti; snacks of pastries and *arancini.* **L**

Mazara del Vallo

Ristorante del Pescatore
Via Castelvetrano 191.
Tel: 0923 947580.
Swordfish and spicy pasta dishes. Good ice-creams. Closed Monday. **LLL**

Ristorante Baby Luna
Lungomare Mazzini.
Tel: 0923 948622.
Fish specialities. Closed Monday and two weeks between October and Christmas. **LL**

Al Pesciolino
Lungomare S. Vito.
Tel: 0923 909286.
Seafood of all kinds. **LL**

Odeon
Corner of Via Crispi and Corso Umberto.
This bar is the place for breakfast or snacks. **L**

San Vito lo Capo

Alfredo
Contrada Valanga.
Tel: 0923 972366.
Good seafood. Closed Monday. **LLL**

Antica Trattoria Cusenza
Via Savoia 24.
Tel: 0923 972768.
Fish dishes. **LL**

Ristorante Riviera
Via Lungomare.
Tel: 0923 972480.
An unpretentious *trattoria* in a small

Caltanissetta Cookery Course

Regaleali, the noted wine producers near Vallelunga in Caltanissetta province, also run a traditional cookery school on their estate.

The short courses are led by the family chef. Guests stay on the estate, living with members of Conte Tasca d'Almerita's family. Courses are taught in English or

Italian but, if there is the demand, other languages may be considered.

For details, contact:
Anna Tasca Lanza,
Regaleali Cookery School,
Viale Principessa Giovanna 9,
90139 Palermo (Mondello), Sicily.
Tel: 091 450727
Fax: 091 542783.

but lively resort. Closed Monday, November and part of December. Open Monday from 15 June to 15 September. **LL**

Selinunte

Lido Azzurro
Via Marco Polo 51, Marinella di Selinunte.
Tel: 0924 46211.
Fresh fish dishes. Inexpensive set menu. Closed late Oct–late Feb. **LL**

Ristorante Pierrot
Via Marco Polo.
Old-established fish restaurant with good *antipasti di mare.* **LL**

Egadi Islands

Favignana

Egadi
Via Cristoforo Colombo 17, Porto.
Tel: 0923 921232.
Excellent restaurant renowned for its fish, including tuna. No credit cards. Closed Wednesday, except summer, and several weeks in the winter. **LLL**

El Pescador
Piazza Europa 38, Porto.
Tel: 0923 921035.
Run by a fishing family. The house speciality is spaghetti with fresh tuna and capers (*spaghetti della casa*). The restaurant can be relied on to take the pick of the fresh catch. Closed Wednesday, except summer, and several weeks in winter. **LLL**

Ristorante il Nautilus
Via Amendola 6, Porto.
Tel: 0923 921671.
Excellent *carpaccio di tonno* and *spaghetti con tonno e gamberi* (with tuna and prawns). Inexpensive set

menu includes spaghetti with shrimps, capers and tomatoes. No credit cards. Closed Tuesday, except summer. **LL**

Pantelleria

Zabib
Porto di Scauri.
Tel: 0923 916617.
Good restaurant, open only for dinner. **LLL**

La Nicchia
Contrada Scauri Bassa.
Tel: 0923 916343.
Speciality is couscous. Closed Wednesday and 15 Jan–15 Feb. **LL**

Gabbiano Azzurro
Riva al Mare.
Tel: 0923 911909.
Cheap and cheerful. Closed Friday. **L**

Agrigento City

Le Caprice
Strada Panoramica 51.
Tel: 0922 26469.
Sicilian specialities and sea views. One of Sicily's best restaurants. Amazing array of *antipasti* and shellfish; tasty swordfish, shrimps and mussels. Closed Friday and first half of July. **LLL**

Taverna Mosè
Contrada San Biagio, Mosè.
Tel: 0922 26778.
Situated 1 km (½ mile) along Caltanissetta road. Although overrated, the *pasta alla norma,* sole and *scaloppine alla pirandello* (scallops with fresh vegetables) are good and the terrace offers a cool retreat. An atmospheric spot with a view of the temples. Closed Monday and August. **LLL**

Kalos
Piazza S. Calogero.
Tel: 0922 26389.
Involtini di pesce spada (rolled and stuffed swordfish) is worth the visit. Closed Sunday. **LLL**

Villa Athena
Via Passeggiate Archeologiche 33.
Tel: 0922 596288.
This lovely hotel-restaurant scores highly on atmosphere and views across the Valley of the Temples. Service can be surly. Reservation advisable. **LLL**

La Corte degli Sfizzi
Via Atenea 4, Cortile Contarini.
Tel: 0922 595520.
A trendy and fairly inexpensive restaurant/*pizzeria*. Several set menus at differing prices. Pizza available at lunchtime. Closed Wednesday, except summer, and November. **LL**

Del Vigneto
Cavalieri Magazzeni 11.
Tel: 0922 414319.
Set outside town on the Gela road (follow the signs). Authentic cuisine in rustic setting, overlooking vineyards. Closed Tuesday and November. **LL**

Il Simposio
Piano Lo Presti 19.
Tel: 0922 25610.
Simple and inexpensive *trattoria*. Piano bar at weekends. Closed Monday. **L**

For a change, have a picnic in the temples. Provisions can be purchased from the *Alimentari* (grocery store) at Via Goeni 23, Piazza Moro.

Agrigento Province

Caltabellotta
Trattoria La Ferla
Via Colonnello Vita.
Tel: 0925 951444.
A lovely restaurant with authentic rural cuisine in a scenic village in the mountains. No credit cards. Closed Monday and for two weeks which vary every year. **LL**

Sciacca
The best fish restaurants are in the lower town, near the port, and are mostly inexpensive. Before leaving Sciacca do not forget to try the *Tabisca*, a traditional local pizza with onion and cheese.

Hostaria del Vicolo
10 Vicolo Sammaritano.
Tel: 0925 23071.
Unpretentious pasta and seafood. Closed Sunday and Monday evening, and 15–31 October. **LLL**

Miramare
Piazza Scandagliato 6.
Tel: 0925 26050.
Fish specials and pizzas, with fine sea views from the terrace. **LL**

Caltanissetta Province

Caltanissetta
The city is not a gastronomic centre.

Cortese
Viale Sicilia 158.
Tel: 0934 591686.
The restaurant offers Sicilian specialities at moderate prices. Visa only accepted. Closed Monday. **LL**

La Piscina
Via dei Fasci Siciliani.
Tel: 0934 558464.
Traditional cuisine in restaurant with swimming pool! Closed Monday. **LL**

Il Gattopardo
Via Pacini 20.
Tel: 0934 598384.
This is both a restaurant and *pizzeria* but is open for dinner only. No credit cards. Closed Monday and one week in August. **L**

Butera
Lido degli Angeli
Contrada Falconara (turn left after castle on the road from Licata).
Tel: 0934 349054.
Restaurant is always open. No credit cards. **LL**

Gela
Centrale Totò
Via Generale Cascino 39.
Tel: 0933 913104.
Simple regional cuisine. Useful if stuck in dreaded Gela. Visa only accepted. Closed Sunday. **LL**

Mazzarino
Alessi
Via Caltanissetta 20.
Tel: 0934 381549.

Restaurant and *pizzeria*. Pizza only for dinner. Always open. **LL**

Mussomeli
La Baracca
Via Dogliotti.
Tel: 0934 952190.
Sandwiches and drinks only. No credit cards. Closed Friday and two weeks in August. **L**

Enna Province

Enna
Restaurants in Enna city are far more authentic and welcoming than those around the lakeside resort of Lago Pergusa. From many of Pergusa's *pizzerie* you can watch the motor racing or boating.

Ariston
Via Roma 353.
Tel: 0935 26038.
An established restaurant serving regional dishes. Closed Sunday and two weeks in August. **LL**

Centrale
Via VI Dicembre 9 (off Via Roma).
Tel: 0935 500963.
This established restaurant offers particularly good vegetable pasta dishes at moderate prices. Outside dining area. Closed Saturday. **LL**

Demetra
Contrada Misericordia.
Tel: 0935 502300.
Specialities include pasta with pumpkin and radicchio, scallops with asparagus. Closed Sunday. **LL**

La Fontana
Via Volturno 6.
Tel: 0935 25465.
Simple family-run *trattoria*. **L**

La Griglia
Via Falantano 19.
A *caratteristica trattoria* with tasty *bruschetta* and *maccheroni alla norma* (with fennel). **L**

Price Guide

Restaurants are graded according to the price of a three-course meal for one, with half a bottle of house wine:
LLL = from L60,000 upwards
LL = L35,000–L60,000
L = less than L35,000

Hostaria Impero
Via Ree Pentite 17.
Tel: 0935 26018.
Pleasant back-street *trattoria*. No credit cards. Closed Sunday. **L**

San Gennaro
Via Belvedere Marconi 6.
Tel: 0935 24067.
Family-run restaurant serving hearty soups, stuffed lamb, grilled vegetables, etc. **LL**

Piazza Armerina

La Ruota di Pioni Fiorella
Contrada Paratore Casale (near Roman Villa, Casale).
Tel: 0935 680542.
A good *trattoria* specialising in homemade pasta. Try the delicious *maccheroni*, fresh tomato pasta and pickled aubergines. **LL**

La Tavernetta
Via Cavour 14 (near the Duomo).
Tel: 0935 685883.
This town *trattoria* serves a very tasty pasta with aubergine and wild herbs. Fish specialities are also recommended. No credit cards. Closed Sunday, call ahead. **LL**

Mosaici
Contrada Paratore 11.
Tel: 0935 685453.
Reservations essential in the summer. No credit cards. **L**

La Dolce Vita
Viale Gen. Muscarà 43.
Tel: 0935 684300.
Very inexpensive. Closed Friday. **L**

Price Guide

Restaurants are graded according to the price of a three-course meal for one, with half a bottle of house wine:
LLL = from L60,000 upwards
LL = L35,000–L60,000
L = less than L35,000

Ragusa Province

Ragusa

Fumia
Via dei Cappuccini 23.
Tel: 0932 621463.
No credit cards. Moderate prices.
Closed Monday. **LL**

Osteria del Braciere
Contrada San Giacomo Bellocozzo.
Tel: 0932 231224.
An authentic and inexpensive rural *trattoria* just north-east of Ragusa. No credit cards. Closed lunchtime, Monday and 15 Jul–15 Aug. **LL**

U Sarrucinu
Via Convento 97, Ibla.
Tel: 0932 246976.
Facing San Giorgio, serving rustic dishes in a vaulted cellar. Set menu available. Closed Wednesday. **LL**

Villa Fortugno
Four km (3 miles) along the Strada Provinciale to Marina di Ragusa.
Tel: 0932 667134.
Country house cuisine with Sicilian sausages and pork stews. Closed Monday and 10 days in August. **LLL**

Módica

Trattoria delle Torri
Via Nativo 30–32.
Tel: 0932 751286.
Located in Costa, the charming Arab quarter, this *trattoria* serves wonderful traditional fare. American Express only. Closed Monday and for a few weeks during the year. Reservations essential. **LLL**

Trattoria la Rusticana
Viale Medaglie d'Oro 34.
Tel: 0932 942950.
No credit cards. Closed Sunday Jul–Aug, Sunday evening Sep–Jun. **LL**

Siracusa City

The better restaurants are on the island of Ortygia, where Siracusani beat a retreat at night (*see Nightlife, page 373*).

Archimede
Via Gemellato 8.
Tel: 0931 69701.
Arguably the best or at least most authentic restaurant on Ortygia. Service is friendly; the food is varied but seafood predominates, with an array of subtle (and fishy) *antipasti*. Closed Sunday, except summer. **LL**

Capriccio
Contrada Canalicchio 2 km (1 mile) from the Greek Theatre, following the SS 124 road.
Tel: 0931 69885.
This boisterous restaurant, *pizzeria*

and piano bar is suited to convivial groups. Large choice of *antipasti*. Al fresco dining. Pizza served only for dinner. **L**

Darsena
Riva Garibaldi 6.
Tel: 0931 66104.
Overlooking the bridge and inner harbour, this bold, bright *trattoria* serves barely dead shrimps and fish. Closed Wednesday. **LL**

La Foglia
Via Capodieci 29,
Ortygia (close to the Fonte Aretusa).
Tel: 0931 66233.
Vegetarian soups, salads and fish dishes. Original 14th-century glasses and plates, hand-embroidered tablecloths. Closed Tuesday, except December and summer. **LL**

Fratelli Bandieri
Via Trieste 42.
Tel: 0931 65021.
Once Siracusa's best restaurant, it still serves an incredible range of dishes. No credit cards. Closed Monday. **L**

Porticciolo
Via Trento.
Tel: 0931 61914.
Near the market. Offers delicious mixed-fish grills or fresh lobster. Closed Monday and for 10 days in November. **LL**

Ristorante Minerva
Piazza Duomo 20.
Tel: 0931 69404.
This is conveniently placed for lunch after visiting the cathedral. No credit cards. Closed Monday. **LL**

Zsa
Via Romana 73.
Tel: 0931 22204.
Ortygia restaurant serving authentic Siracusan specialities – grilled swordfish, seafood risotto, *pasta c'angiovi* (with pine nuts, sultanas and anchovies), and local *bruschetta*. **LL**

La Scaletta
Largo Porto Marina 1.
Tel: 0931 24727.
In Ortygia, in a picturesque spot overlooking the sea. Rustic, quaint but crowded. It serves *cucina casalinga*, including spaghetti and seafood dishes. American Express only. **LL**

If you fancy a picnic in the archaeological zone, pick up provisions from **Gastronomia**, Via Teocrito 127.

Noto
Trattoria del Carmine
Via Ducezio 9.
Tel: 0931 838705.
Home cooking and local specialities in a baroque town not known for its cuisine. No credit cards. Closed Monday, except summer. **LL**
Neas
Via Rocco Pirri 30.
Tel: 0931 573538.
The speciality is seafood dishes. Mixed grilled fish is a must. Closed Monday. **LLL**

Catania City

Catania is renowned for its excellent and diverse restaurants. They display eastern Sicilian dishes, such as *agnello alla menta* (lamb with bacon, mint and garlic). It is best to book if dining in expensive restaurants.
**La Cantinaccia e le Sue
4 Stagioni**
Via Calatafimi 1/a.
Tel: 095 382009.
This upmarket but intimate restaurant is designed in rustic style. Cuisine is international and

Sicilian with pizza served in the evening. Closed Wednesday and August. **LLL**
Enzo
Via Malta 26.
Tel: 095 384884.
A welcoming and inexpensive *pizzeria*. Try the *porcina* pizza with sausage and mushrooms. **L**
Il Giardino d'Inverno
In summer: San Giovanni la Punta 10 km (6 miles) from Catania;
In winter: Via Asilo S Agata 34.
Tel: 095 532853.
This patrician villa is designed in Art Nouveau style. Dishes include *crêpes con spinaci* (spinach pancakes) and *trancio di salmone* (salmon in herbs). Pizza evenings only. Also elegant tearooms on the premises. Closed Monday. **LLL**
Hostaria la Zagara
SS 114 road in the Vaccarizzo area.
Tel: 095 295020.
Renowned for its mixed grills of meat or fresh fish. No credit cards. Closed Tuesday. **LL**
La Siciliana
Viale Marco Polo 52.
Tel: 095 376400.
Considered Catania's best restaurant. Not cheap, but worth it. Specialities include roast lamb, breaded cutlets, seafood, imaginative vegetable dishes and good Cerasuolo wine. Closed Sunday evening, Monday and one week in August. **LLL**

Spinella and **Savia**
Via Etnea.
Catania's best places for hot snacks, pastries and ice-cream. Both opposite the entrance to Villa Bellini. **L**
Cantine del Cugno Mezzano
Via Museo Biscari 8.
Tel: 095 7158710.
Wide selection of the best wines (not only Sicilian). Wine tasting and dining. Closed Monday. **LL**
Cortile Bellini
Via Landolina 46.
Tel: 095 316117.
Typical Sicilian cuisine at moderate prices. Closed Monday. **LL**

Catania Province

Catania Coast (North)
Barbarossa
Strada Provinciale,
Aci Castello, SS 114 road to Aci Castello.
Tel: 095 295539.
Seafood as well as stuffed pancakes and notable wines. Closed Monday. **LLL**
Holiday Club
Via dei Malavoglia 10,
Aci Trezza.
Tel: 095 277575.
Set in spacious grounds with fine sea views. Dishes include tasty risotto and seasonal vegetables such as asparagus, chicory (endive) and mushrooms. **LLL**

Buying Wine Direct

It is possible to visit the following wine growers and to buy directly from them. Most producers in Sicily make wines of varying qualities and prices – the best wines come from particularly favoured vineyards or tight selections of the best grapes. All those listed below produce good quality wines. Not all of these growers speak a foreign language, but where they do, it is noted. Do telephone beforehand.
Az. Agr. Vecchio Samperi, Marco De Bartoli, C/da Fornara Samperi 292, 91025 Marsala (TP). Tel: 0923 962093. Speaks French.

Cantine Piero Colosi, Via Militare Ritiro 23, 98152 Messina. Tel: 090 53852.
Carlo Hauner, Tamara Thorgevsky, Lingua di Salina, 98050 S. Marina Salina (ME). Tel: 090 9843392. Speaks English.
Casa Vin, Duca di Salaparuta, Livia Astuni, Via Nazionale SS 113, 90014 Casteldaccia (PA). Tel: 091 953988.
cos, Giusto Occhipinti, Piazza del Popolo 34, 97019 Vittoria (RG). Tel: 0932 864042. Speaks French.
Loc. Malfa, 98050 Isola di Salina (ME), especially for Malvasia.

Regaleali, Distributed by MD Distribuzione, Via Denti di Piraino 7, 90142 Palermo. Tel: 091 6371266; fax: 091 363198.
Tenuta di Donnafugata, Gabriella Anca Ralla, Loc. Marzaporro, 90030 Contessa Entellina (PA). Tel: 0923 999555. Speaks English.
Tenuta San Michele, Barone Scammacca, Barone Scammacca del Murgo, Via Bongiardo (CA). Tel: 095 953613.
Terre di Ginestra, Maurizio Miccichè, Piano Piraino, 90040 San Cipirello (PA). Tel: 091 8576767. English spoken.

Galatea
Via Livorno, 146a, Acitrezza.
Tel: 095 277913.
Elegant restaurant with a view over
the sea. Wide selection of fish and
desserts. Closed Monday. **LLL**

Selene
Via Mollica 24.
Tel: 095 494444.
Set on a rocky spur on the seafront
between Ognina and Aci Castello,
with excellent views from the
terrace. Delicacies include
spaghetti with clams or shrimps.
Closed Tuesday and August. **LLL**

Il Timo Ristorante
Sheraton Hotel,
Via A. da Messina 45,
95020 Cannizzaro (near Aci Castello)
Tel: 095 271557.
This luxurious spot is renowned for
its grilled swordfish and fishy
antipasti. **LLL**

Acireale
Nino Castorina
Corso Savoia 109 (closed Monday)
Corso Umberto 63 (closed Tuesday)
Not restaurants but the place for
ice cream, *pasta reale* (marzipan)
and pastries. **L**

Panoramico
Viale Ionico 12 Litoranea.
Tel: 095 885291.
A panoramic restaurant with a
pizzeria and a piano bar. Good
seafood. Closed Monday. **LLL**

La Brocca di Cinc'oru
Corso Savoia 49/a.
Tel: 095 607196.
Traditional cuisine at moderate
prices. Closed Sunday evening and
Monday. **LL**

Belpasso
La Cantina
Strada Provinciale Nicolosi-Belpasso
Tel: 095 912992.
A rustic restaurant and *pizzeria*
offering very different menus. The
stars are mushroom or asparagus
risotto. No credit cards. Closed
Monday and three weeks in
November. **LL**

Mount Etna
At Rifugio Sapienza there are
mediocre restaurants and snack
bars. The best of a poor choice is

La Cantoniera, which was
destroyed in the lava flow of 1982
and rebuilt.

Nicolosi
Etna
Via Etnea 93.
Tel: 095 911937.
Traditional Etna cuisine in a post-
modern restaurant and *pizzeria.*
Specialities include mushroom
risotto, *cinghiale alla griglia* (grilled
wild boar) and *insalata di funghi
crudi* (raw mushroom salad). Pizza
only in the evening. Closed Monday
and for 2–3 weeks in February or
March. **LL**

Al Bongustaio
Via Etnea 105/f.
A typical restaurant with tasty
homemade *antipasti,* many made
with mushrooms. **L**

Pedara
La Bussola
Piazza Don Bosco 10.
Tel: 095 780250.
Designed in heavy Spanish style,
the restaurant concentrates on Etna
dishes, from roasts to game and
mushroom delicacies. Also bar and
pizza in the evening. Closed
Monday. **LL**

Randazzo
Trattoria Veneziano
Via Romano 8.
Tel: 095 7991353.
A restaurant with tasty regional
dishes. Closed Monday. **LL**

Trecastagni
Al Mulino
Via Mulino al Vento 48.
Tel: 095 7806634.
Set in a grand villa overlooking an
old windmill. Specialities include
pasta with mushrooms and sausage
with herbs. Closed Monday. **LL**

Zafferana Etnea
Al Parco dei Principi
Via delle Ginestre 1.
Tel: 095 7081990.
Interesting regional cuisine, with
Etna produce. Closed Tuesday. **LL**

C'era una volta
Località Sarro.
Tel: 095 7083355.

Specialities include *pappardelle*
(pasta) with mushrooms. Closed
Wednesday. **LL**

Taormina

Taormina has a huge choice of
eating places to suit all pockets
and tastes, from international style
to regional specialities. However,
many hotels insist on half-board
arrangements so you may be
obliged to restrict restaurant
sampling to lunch. The hilltop
village of Castelmola offers
inexpensive alternatives to dining in
Taormina itself. At the foot of the
cliffs, the coastal area of Mazzarò
has lively and inexpensive *trattorie*
and lovely sea views.

In Taormina, try to avoid most
restaurants in Corso Umberto,
which cater to indiscriminate
tourists and tend to be bland and
expensive. In general, dining in
Taormina is more elegant and
select than eating out in Mazzarò or
Castelmola.

Les Bouganvilles
Hotel San Domenico, Piazza S.
Domenico 5.
Tel: 0942 23701.
If you have no budget to stick to
and feel like giving yourself a treat,
the restaurant of the Hotel San
Domenico is where you should head
for. Specialities include *pesce
spada* (swordfish) *alla messinese,
fragoline di bosco in gelato
all'arancia* (wild strawberries with
orange ice-cream). **LLL**

L'Angolo
Via Damiano Rosso 17.
Tel: 0942 625202.
Pizzeria near the cathedral. Closed
Wednesday and January. **LLL**

Gambero Rosso
Via Naumachia 11.
Tel: 0942 23011.
This is family-run, welcoming, with
good Sicilian cuisine. **LL**

Il Giardino
Via Bagnoli Croci 84 (near the park
gates).
Tel: 0942 23453.
Very friendly, family-run restaurant,
With a little gentle persuasion, the
cook will play his guitar and sing
Sicilian folk songs. **LL**

Granduca
Corso Umberto 170/172.
Tel: 0942 24420.
This chic, old-fashioned and rather grand restaurant offers lovely views over the bay. The price covers the view as much as the food. **LLL**

Da Lorenzo
Via Roma 4.
Tel: 0942 23480.
Prohibitive prices but a glorious setting. Closed Wednesday and 15 days in December. **LLL**

Oasi Due
Via Apollo Arcageta 9.
Tel: 0942 24771.
The food is exceptional and inexpensive. **L**

Porta Messina
Largo Giove Serapide 4.
Tel: 0942 23205.
Specilities include *tuma fritta* (fried local cheese) and meat. Good and inexpensive. Closed Wednesday. **L**

Mazzarò

Reach the coast by a cable car (*funivia*) from Taormina.

La Conchiglia
Piazzale Funivia (near the cable car)
Tel: 0942 24739.
Inexpensive, serves very good pizza at weekends in the low season and all week summer. Closed Tuesday and for 15–20 days in October or November. **LL**

Da Giorgio
Vico Sant' Andrea 7.
Tel: 0942 625502.
On the beach of Isola Bella. Excellent for fish. **LL**

Oliviero
Via Nazionale 137.
Tel: 0942 23125.
At Mazzarò beach. Excellent restaurant. Also has a piano bar. **LL**

Il Gabbiano
Via Nazionale 115.
Tel: 0942 625128.
Try the *risotto alla marinara*. Closed Tuesday. **LLL**

Messina Province

Messina

Most of the better restaurants lie along Viale San Martino and in or around Via Santa Cecilia. For fish dishes it is best to leave the town

centre and go to the Ganzirri lake district.

Donna Giovanna
Via Risorgimento 16.
Tel: 090 718503.
Traditional Sicilian cuisine; always crowded. **LL**

No. 1
Via Risorgimento 192.
Tel: 090 717411.
Inexpensive and good pizzas. Evenings only. Closed Tuesday and Jun–Aug. **L**

Opera Prima
Via Laudamo 28.
Tel: 090 345111.
Specialities include vegetables and sweets. Closed Monday. **LLL**

Hostaria da Bacco
Via Cernaia 15.
Tel: 090 771420.
Good range of seafood. Closed Sunday. **LL**

Gambero Rosso
Via Consolare Pompea.
Tel: 090 393873.
Good and inexpensive fish. Closed Tuesday. **LL**

Price Guide

Restaurants are graded according to the price of a three-course meal for one, with half a bottle of house wine:
LLL = from L60,000 upwards
LL = L35,000–L60,000
L = less than L35,000

Castelmola

In season, this tiny village above Taormina represents a boisterous alternative to the town – and the steep climb is one way of working up an appetite. The village specialises in inexpensive bars and *paninoteche* (sandwich places) which are popular with younger visitors, and with heavy-drinking German and Scandinavian visitors.

Ciccino's
Piazza Duomo.
Tel: 0942 28081.
A rustic *pizzeria* near the cathedral, excellent for thin pizza cooked in a wood-fired oven (*forno a legna*). **LL**

Il Maniero
Via Salita Castello.

Tel: 0942 28180.
In a tower that was once part of a castle. Quickly fills up, reservations essential. Closed Wednesday. **LLL**

Milazzo

Salamone a Mare
Strada Panoramica 36.
Tel: 090 9281233.
Specialities include *tagliolini agli scampi* (pasta with shrimps) and fish of all sorts. **LLL**

Aeolian Islands

Fish plays a starring role, particularly in *ghiotto* sauce, a blend of capers, oil, tomatoes, garlic and basil. Black rice is popular, coloured by *seppia* (cuttlefish ink). Octopus and swordfish are also popular.

Lípari

The various *trattorie* around the harbour are mostly open-air, good, and fairly expensive. The exorbitant local service charge will add 20 percent to the menu prices. The local "tourist menus" should be avoided.

Filippino
Piazza Municipio.
Tel: 090 9811002.
This is a favourite with the islanders themselves. It is pricey but good. Delicacies include fish risotto and complicated main courses. Reservation recommended. Closed Monday, except in summer, and November. **LLL**

Vulcano

Lanterna Blu
Via Lentía 58.
Tel: 090 9852178.
Locals flock to this restaurant for its tasty fish dishes. In winter call ahead for opening times. **LL**

Da Vincenzino
Via Porto Levante 25.
Tel: 090 9852016.
Open all year. Simple and inexpensive. **L**

Salina

The better bars and *trattorie* are in the Santa Marina area facing the shore of Lípari. Many dishes

contain the tasty local capers. Try Salina's excellent Malvasia wine.
Il Delfino
Piazza Marina Garibaldi 5.
Tel: 090 9843024.
Good seafood at low prices. **L**

Panarea
Restaurants are expensive in this wealthy island ghetto – wine and fish cost more in most places.
Hycesia
Via S. Pietro.
Tel: 090 983041.
Good fish dishes and regional desserts. Closed Nov–Mar. **LL**

Strómboli
The best restaurants are in Stromboli town (San Vincenzo) but there are also several good *trattorie* in Ginostra.
Locanda Barbablù
Via V. Emanuele 17–19.
Tel: 090 986118.
This restaurant is in the small but very pleasant garden of the same hotel. The food is cooked by the owner, who imaginatively combines Sicilian and Neapolitan recipes. Closed November and February. **LLL**
Villa Petrusa
Via Soldato Panettieri 4.
Tel: 090 986045.
This restaurant in the main street offers reasonable food. No credit cards. Closed Nov–mid-Mar. **LL**

Filicudi
La Canna
Via Rosa 43.
Tel: 090 9889956.
The restaurant is in a small hotel with panoramic views and good homemade local food. Closed 15–30 Nov. **LL**

Alicudi
Ericusa
Via Regina Elena.
Tel: 090 9889902.
This is the only place to stay on the island and offers a reasonable restaurant too. (This is best organised on a full-board arrangement.) No credit cards. Closed Oct–May. **LL**

Attractions

The opening hours of most monuments are:
Churches and cathedrals: 8.30am–noon and 4–7.30pm.
Archaeological sites: 9am–one hour before sunset.
Museums, galleries and monuments: 8.30am–2pm.

Most museums and archaeological sites close one day a week, usually on Monday.

Opening times vary according to the season and are usually shorter in winter, on Sundays and on holidays. Many archaeological sites base their closing time on sunset.

Most museums, galleries and archaeological sites charge a small amount for admission. Reductions are available for children, students and senior citizens on production of a valid form of identification.

In museums and archaeological sites, be prepared for the civil service homeward rush: the staff will begin shepherding visitors towards the exit, none too politely, about 20 minutes before closing. Many archaeological sites are guarded at night, so resist the temptation to climb the fence and watch the sunrise.

Churches, and sometimes museums, may appear permanently closed: there is almost always a *custode* (custodian) or *sacrestano* (sacristan) somewhere nearby with a key. Enquire in a bar or of passing locals. In the middle of the countryside, try knocking at the door of the nearest farm. It is usual to give a tip to the custodian.

By doing the same thing, you may sometimes obtain entrance on days when a building is officially closed to the public, or to places closed for restoration. The discouraging, and sometimes disgraceful, sign *"chiuso per restauri"* (closed for restoration) graces a distressingly large number of monuments. The Italian Government may be praised for its investment in the Sicilian cultural heritage, but the effect on the monument does not always equal Rome's investment, and the time between start and completion of work is exceptionally long.

Sadly, some of Palermo's most impressive buildings, including the churches, are rarely open to the public nowadays. Many are nevertheless still worth visiting just to see the exterior. Given that some of the city sights have unreliable opening times, visitors pressed for time may like to consider a guided tour of the city booked with the Palermo Tourist Office, Piazza Castelnuovo 35, tel: 091 583847. Ideally request Pilar Visconti, a highly recommended guide.

For information on the Vucciria Market, *see Shopping, page 378.*

CHURCHES

Casa Professa (also known as Il Gesù), Piazza Casa Professa. First Jesuits' church in Sicily. Lovely baroque building, recently reopened after restoration. Open daily 7–11.30am.
Cattedrale (Duomo), Corso Vittorio Emanuele. Norman Cathedral containing Royal tombs and a small museum. The cathedral is open daily 7am–7pm. Museum open 9am–noon and 4–5.30pm daily.
La Magione, Via Magione. Fine Cistercian foundation in a rather run-down area. Open daily 8–11.30am and 3–6.30pm. Also open for Sunday service.
La Martorana (Santa Maria dell'Ammiraglio). Dreamlike Arab-Norman church with Byzantine mosaics. Open daily 9.30am–1pm and 3.30–7pm. In winter, closes at 5.50pm and on Sunday afternoons.

Oratorio del Rosario di San Domenico, Via dei Bambinai 2, near Vucciria market. Grandiose baroque with wonderful stucco work by Serpotta. Open Mon–Fri 9am–1pm and 3–5.30pm; Sat 9.30am–12.30pm. See custodian at No. 16.

Oratorio di San Lorenzo, Via dell'Immacolatella 5 (left of San Francesco church). Another whimsical Serpotta gem. Open Mon–Sat 9am–noon.

Oratorio del Rosario di Santa Zita, Via Valverde 3. Serpotta's masterpiece. Contact the custodian. Open Tues–Fri 9am–1pm and 3–6pm, Sat 9am–1pm.

Sant' Agostino, Via Sant'Agostino. 13th-century, interior redecorated in 1671 by Serpotta. Beautiful rose window and portal. Open Mon–Sat 7am–noon, 4–5.30pm, Sun 7am–noon.

San Cataldo, Piazza Bellini. Key available from custodian of La Martorana. Open Mon–Fri 9am–3.30pm, Sat–Sun 9am–1pm.

San Domenico, Piazza San Domenico (near the Vucciria Market). Baroque monastic church. Open daily 9–11am.

San Francesco d'Assisi, Piazza di San Francesco d'Assisi. Gothic church with Renaissance arch. Open Mon–Sat 7am–noon, 4.30–6pm.

San Giovanni degli Eremiti (St John of the Hermits), Via dei Benedettini. Byzantine-style church with five domes set in a garden rich with exotic plants. Remains of a mosque visible in the church. Lovely cloisters. Open Mon–Sat 9am–6.30pm, Sun 9am–12.30pm.

San Giovanni dei Lebbrosi (St John of the Lepers), Via Cappello 38. Near Corso dei Mille. The oldest church in Palermo (1076). Open Mon–Sat 9.30–11am, 4–5pm. Also see **Ponte dell' Ammiraglio**, the Norman bridge (built 1113) in Corso dei Mille nearby.

San Giuseppe Teatini, Corso Vittorio Emanuele/Piazza Pretoria (Piazza Vigliena). Grand baroque interior. Open Mon–Fri 8am–noon, 6–8pm.

San Ignazio all'Olivella, Piazza Olivella. Baroque; frescoes by Novelli. Classical oratory next-door. Open 8–11am.

Santa Maria della Catena, Piazza delle Dogane (off Piazza Marina). Catalan-Gothic with austere interior. Open Mon–Fri 9am–1pm and Sunday services.

Santa Maria della Gancia, Via Alloro. Late Gothic frescoed church. Open 8am–noon and Monday and Saturday 4–6pm.

Santa Maria di Valverde, Piazza Valverde. A Carmelite church; splendid multi-coloured marble nave by Amato.

Santa Zita, Corner of Via Valverde and Squiarcialupo. Sixteenth-century church with works by Gagini. (Overlooks Oratorio di Santa Zita.)

Santo Spirito (also known as dei Vespri), Via dei Vespri. Norman church. The revolt known as the Sicilian Vespers broke out here on 31 March 1282 at the hour of Vespers. Within the S. Orsola. Cemetery. Open daily 8am–2pm.

Santa Teresa della Kalsa, Piazza Kalsa, Corso Vittorio Emanuele. Baroque church built for the Barefoot Carmelites; now linked to Mother Teresa. Check with the tourist office for visiting times.

MUSEUMS AND ART GALLERIES

Museo Archeológico Regionale, Piazza Olivella, tel: 091 6116805. Includes great Classical finds from all over Sicily. One of the richest archaeological collections in Italy and well worth the visit. Open Monday and Thursday 9am–2pm, Tuesday, Wednesday and Friday 9am–2pm and 3–7pm, Saturday and Sunday 9am–1pm.

Museo delle Marionette (International Puppet Museum), Via Butera 1, tel: 091 328060. Large collection from all over the world, particularly of Sicilian puppets. Fascinating overcrowded storerooms downstairs. Puppet shows are also held here. Open Mon–Fri 9am–1pm and 4–7pm, Saturday 9am–1pm.

Museo Etnografico "G. Pitre", Via Duca degli Abruzzi (by Parco della Favorita), tel: 091 7404885. Large collection of Sicilian folklore and customs, including painted carts. Open daily 9am–1pm and Wed 3.30–5.30pm.

Museo Risorgimentale, Piazza San Domenico 1 (near Vucciria), tel: 091 582774. A collection of Garibaldi portraits, medals and sculptures. Open Mon, Wed and Fri 9am–1pm.

Palazzo Abatellis, Via Alloro 4, tel: 091 6164317. The palace dates from 1490 and now houses the Galleria Regionale della Sicilia, which includes medieval and Moorish works as well as Renaissance paintings by Antonello da Messina (The Annunciation, Three Saints). There is also a bust of Eleonora di Aragon by Francesco Laurana on display. Open Mon–Sat 9am–1.30pm, Sun 9am–12.30pm, also Tues, Thur 3–7.30pm.

Palazzo Mirto, Via Merlo 2, tel: 091 6164751. Sixteenth-century palace, lived in until relatively recently and furnished as an aristocratic home. Open Mon–Fri 9am–6.30pm, Sat–Sun 9am–12.30pm.

Politeama, Piazza Politeama. Elegant neoclassical theatre in Pompeiian style. Opera and ballet venue.

Opera dei Pupi e Laboratorio "Figli d'Arte Cuticchio", Via Bara all'Olivella, 48–95, tel: 091 323400. The exhibition displays theatrical tools and posters, stage effects, props, stage machinery, and marionettes. Marionette shows on Sat and Sun at 5.30pm. Book in advance.

Museo Geológico "G.G. Gemmellaro", Corso Tukory 131, tel: 091 7041051. Around 600,000 fossils, documenting Sicily's peerless geological history. Mon–Sat 9am–1pm.

NOTABLE BUILDINGS

Chiosco Ribaudo and **Chiosco Ribaudo**, Piazza Massimo. Two Art Nouveau kiosks in florid, filigree style. Under restoration.

Convento dei Cappuccini, Via Cappuccini, tel: 091 212117. Gruesome catacombs contain

8,000 mummified Palermitans. Mummification continued until 1881. Open daily 9am–noon and 3–5pm. (Take bus 5 or 27.)

La Cuba, Caserma Tukory, Corso Calatafimi, 100. Moorish pleasure pavilion set in army barracks. Open Mon–Sat 9am–1pm, 3–6.30pm.

La Cubola, Corso Calatafimi 575. Tiny Moorish pavilion set in grounds of Villa Napoli. Ask the custodian at Villa Napoli or see the exterior only.

La Ziza, Piazza Guglielmo II Buono, tel: 091 6520269. Built under the Normans but in Arab style. Contains a museum of Arab art. Open Mon–Sat 9am–6.30pm, Sun 9am–12.30pm.

Palazzina Cinese, Piazza Niscemi. Set in Parco della Favorita. Built in 1799. Exotic chinoiserie fantasy. Worth seeing from outside.

Palazzo Aiutamicristo, Via Garibaldi. Catalan-Gothic palace. Walk through the gateway at No. 22 and you can see the lovely arcaded courtyard and delicate loggias.

Palazzo Chiaramonte (or Steri), Piazza Marina 61. Formerly the headquarters of the Inquisition, now houses the University rectorate. Officially closed to the public. With a bit of bravado and a manufactured excuse, it's worth walking into the courtyard and pleading to see the *Sala Magna*, the fine interior with its *mujedar* (coffered) Moorish ceiling.

Palazzo Lampedusa, Via Lampedusa. Bombed rubble remaining from Lampedusa's Palermitan home.

Palazzo Pretorio (delle Aquile), Piazza Pretoria. The former Senate, now the Town Hall. Exterior only.

Palazzo dei Normanni, Piazza Indipendenza, tel: 091 7051111. The palace houses the Sicilian Parliament, the Royal Apartments, Sala di Re Ruggero (King Roger's Room), and the Cappella Palatina (Palatine Chapel) with Byzantine and Arab-Norman mosaics. Open Mon, Fri and Sat 9am–noon.

Palazzo Sclafani, Piazzetta San Giovanni Decollato. Noble palace built in 1330. See facade, arches and doorway.

Porta Nuova, Corso Calatafimi. A grand Spanish gateway decorated with statues of eight great Moors.

Santuario di Santa Rosalia, on Monte Pellegrino. Sanctuary of Palermo's patron saint. Views of the city and the bay. Bus 812 from Palermo. Tel: 091 540326 for opening times.

Teatro Massimo, Piazza Verdi. A neoclassical theatre started by Filippo Basile and completed by his son Ernesto. It is one of the largest opera houses in Europe.

Villa Igiea, Salita Belmonte. Built as a villa by the Florio family in the 19th century. Decorated in Art Nouveau style. Now a luxury hotel: the public rooms can be seen for the cost of a drink at the bar.

Villa Malfitano, Via Dante. Mansion and walled park. Open Mon–Sat 9am–1pm. (Also open for concerts.)

Villa Niscemi (next-door to Palazzina Cinese). Now used as the official residence of the Palermo Mayor. Villa open Sun mornings. The surrounding park open daily till sunset.

PARKS

Orto Botánico, Via Lincoln 2, tel: 091 6173211. One of the leading botanic gardens in Europe. Over 10,000 different species representative of all areas of vegetation in the world. Open Mon–Fri 9am–5pm, Sat–Sun 9am–1pm.

Parco della Favorita, Viale Diana, set on the slopes of Monte Pellegrino. Lovely park laid out by the Bourbons.

Parco d'Orleans, behind Palazzo dei Normanni. Well-maintained park, officially part of the President's domain.

Piazza Marina. Compact but endearing park with hanging banyan trees, set within an historic square.

Villa Bonanno, Piazza della Vittoria. Tatty public gardens with the remains of Roman villas.

Mondello

Grotte dell'Addaura, Monte Pellegrino, tel: 091 6961319; fax: 091 6702078. Prehistoric caves with palaeolithic rock drawings. For information, contact the Palermo Sovrintendenza Archeológica.

Palermo Province

Bagheria

Villa Cattolica, a modern art gallery in a traditional summer villa. The tomb of painter Renato Guttuso is in the grounds. Open Tues–Sun 10am–6pm.

Villa Palagonia. This most bizarre villa is open to the public daily 9am–noon and 4–7pm.

Villa Valguarnera, Piazza Garibaldi. A private residence only visible from beyond the walls.

Baida

Saracen **village church**. Contains a statue of John the Baptist by Gagini. Key from the custodian.

Cáccamo

Castello, Via Termita. Well-restored castle that can be visited on a tour which also includes some churches and a sampling of local food. Tel: 091 545432.

Cefalà Diana

Terme Arabe, Palermo-Agrigento road. Moorish baths. Exterior only viewable.

Cefalù

Tempio di Diana. Built in the 4th-2nd centuries BC. Open to the skies. Makes a good morning or evening stroll, visiting the battered Roman remains and Saracen fortifications. A steepish climb but lovely views.

Duomo. Massively imposing Norman cathedral with Byzantine mosaics. Open daily 8.30am–noon, 3.30–6pm.

Museo Mandralisca, Via Mandralisca. A jumble of archaeological finds and treasures. Paintings include Antonello da Messina's enigmatic *Ritratto di un Ignoto* (*Portrait of an Unknown Man*). Open daily 9am–1.30pm, 3.30–7.30pm.

Monreale

Duomo. Cathedral combining Norman, Saracen and Byzantine architecture in one harmonious whole. One of the most beautiful buildings on the island. The entire ceiling is spectacularly decorated with Byzantine mosaics. Open daily 8am–8pm.

Chiostro (Norman cloisters), next door to the cathedral. Graceful and harmonious. Famous Saracen-style fountain in the southwest corner. Open Mon–Fri 9am–1pm, 3–6.30pm, Sat–Sun 9am–noon.

San Martino delle Scale

Abbazia di San Martino. Benedictine Abbey, tel: 091 418104. Church 16th-century, monastery mainly 17th. Home to a collection of interesting baroque paintings. Open Mon–Fri 9am–noon.

Solunto

A Phoenician and Roman trading post. The scenic **ruins** are open Mon–Fri 9am–6pm, Sat–Sun 9am–noon.

Trápani Province

Trápani

The town was important in the past as a port, and is still the departure point for ferries to the Egadi islands, to Pantelleria and to North Africa. On the edge of the salt beds stretching away towards Mozia and Marsala, the old town is compact and can best be visited on foot. The efficient Trápani provincial tourist office is at Via Sorba 15, tel:0923 27273/27077.

Museo Nazionale Pepoli, Via Agostino Pepoli 200, tel: 0923-531242. In the former Carmelite monastery. Collection includes works by Antonello Gagini and by Titian. Archaeological collection includes objects from Lilibeo, Erice and Selinunte. Open Mon–Fri 9am–6pm, Sat–Sun 9am–noon.

Museo delle Saline (Salt Museum), Salina Culcasi, Nubia. Set in an old mill on the coast 5 km (3 miles) from Trápani. (Call the tourist office for opening times: 0923 27273.) Next to the museum there is a restaurant where you can taste local simple cuisine. Tel: 0923 867142.

Museo Trapanese di Preistoria, Torre di Lugny, tel: 0923 223668. A simple prehistory museum in a coastal Spanish tower. Open 9.30am–12.30pm and 4.30–7.30pm.

Palazzo della Giudecca (Palazzo Ciambra), Via della Giudecca. Impressive 16th-century palace in former Jewish quarter. Worth viewing the exterior.

Santuario dell' Annunziata, Via A. Pepoli, tel: 0923 531242. The star church in Trápani. Rococo interior. Virgin's chapel contains the 14th-century sculpture, *Madonna di Trápani*. Bus 1, 10 or 11 from Piazza Matteotti. Open daily 7.30am–noon, 4–7pm.

Sant'Agostino, Piazza Saturno. Gothic church.

Santa Maria del Gesù, Via Sant' Agostino. Gothic and Renaissance facade. Works by della Robbia and Gagini.

Erice

Castello Pepoli, Viale Conte Pepoli. Exterior only.

Castello di Venere. Medieval (13th-century) castle built on the site of the sanctuary to Venus Erycina. Open daily 8am–2pm, 3–6pm.

Chiesa Madre, Via V. Carvini. Built between the 14th and 16th centuries.

Elymi, Carthaginian and Norman walls. New walls were set into the earlier ones. Can be freely visited.

Museo Civico, Piazza Umberto, tel: 0923 869172. Small museum with Roman and Punic finds. Open daily 8.30am–1.30pm.

Marsala

Duomo, Piazza della Repubblica. Eighteenth-century cathedral dedicated to St Thomas of Canterbury.

Insula Romana, Viale Vittorio Veneto. Remains of a 3rd-century Roman house. Open daily 9am–12.30pm.

Museo degli Arazzi, Via Garraffa 57, tel: 0923 712903. Museum of Flemish tapestries. Open Tues–Sun 9am–1pm, 4–6pm.

Museo Marsala, Lungomare Florio 30, tel: 0923 952535. Contains

exhibits from Mozia and a reconstructed Punic fighting ship. Open daily 9am–1pm, and Wed, Sat and Sun 4–7pm.

San Giovanni, off Viale Sauro (seafront). Church over the Sybil's grotto. Currently closed but check with tourist office.

Stabilimento Florio, Lungomare Florio, tel: 0923 781111. One of the traditional Marsala producers. Tours and tastings. Open 8.30am–1.30pm, closed Fri and Sun.

Mazara del Vallo

Duomo, Piazza della Repubblica, tel: 0923-941919. Open Mon–Sat 8am–8pm, Sun 9am–noon.

Museo Civico, Collegio dei Gesuiti, Piazza Plebescito, tel: 0923 940266. Roman finds. Open Mon–Sat 8.30am–2pm.

Mozia (Motya)

Boats run 9.30am–1pm and 3–6pm to this island in the Stagnone lagoons, the site of a Carthaginian City. Includes parts of the old walls, gate, submerged causeway, necropoli, and dry dock.

Museo Whittaker. Named after the Marsala wine family who own Mozia island, the small museum contains some of the artefacts found on the island. Open daily 9.30am–1pm, 3–6pm.

Segesta

Temple and theatre in wonderful rural setting. Open 9am to 1 hour before sunset. Admission is free but unless you want a 20-minute walk to the theatre, take the paying tourist shuttle from the site car park.

Selinunte

Temples, and much of what was once a great Greek city. Open 9am to 1 hour before sunset. A new entrance and museum now open.

Cave di Cusa, Classical quarries situated 3 km (2 miles) from Campobello, 13 km (8 miles) from Selinunte. Open permanently.

SS Trinita di Delia, in the countryside 3 km (2 miles) west of Selinunte, tel: 0924 82209. An

Arab-Byzantine church. Ring the bell at the adjoining farm to see if it is convenient to visit.

Egadi Islands

The Egadi offer natural sites rather than churches and museums. However, to check temporary sites or activities contact the tourist office, Piazza Madrice 7, Favignana, tel: 0923 921647. Open Mon–Sat 9am–1pm.

Lévanzo

Grotta del Genovese. A cave of prehistoric paintings. You need an appointment so contact the custodian, Signor Giuseppe Castiglione, at Via Calvario 11 (near hydrofoil quay), tel: 0923 924032.

Agrigento City

Valle dei Templi. The site of Greek Akragas and Roman Agrigentum. Temples of Hera (Giunone), Ercole, Concordia, Zeus (Giove Olimpico). Beautifully lit up at night. Western Zone open daily 8.30am–7pm, Eastern Zone permanent access.
Museo Archeológico Regionale, S. Nicola, tel: 0922 401565. Classical museum in the Valle dei Templi. It contains much that has been found on the site, including some *telamones* (gigantic statues), a model reconstruction of the site, and an interesting collection of vases and sculpture. Labels in Italian only; no written guide to exhibits. Open Sun–Tue 9am–1pm; Wed–Sat 9am–1pm and 2–5.30pm.

Agrigento Province

Caos

Casa di Pirandello, Frazione Villaseta, Contrada Caos, tel: 0922 511102. Pirandello museum in the playwright's home in a village outside Agrigento. Open Mon–Fri 9am–1 hour before sunset.

Eraclea Minoa

Greek theatre in a setting above the sea, 30 minutes by car on the road to Sciacca. Open 9am–1 hour before sunset.

Sciacca

Castello Incantanto (Castello Bentivegna), Via Filippo Bentivegna, tel: 0925 993044. Thousands of curious carved stone heads. Open Tues–Sat 10am–noon, 4–6pm.
Pinacoteca e Museo Scaglione, Casa Scaglione, Piazza Duomo, tel: 0925 83089. Open Tues, Thurs and Fri 8am–1pm and 3–7pm.
Stufe di Monte Cronio, Località di Monte Kronio, tel: 0925 26153. Vaporous thermal treatment around a mountain cave with small antiquarium attached. Usually open 8am–1pm but check.

Caltanissetta Province

Although the province is lovely as regards its rugged mountain scenery, it has minimal tourist infrastructure and the fewest number of museums and organised sites of any province.

Caltanissetta

Despite being the capital, there are no "must see" sights. However, the following offer fleeting interest.
Castello di Pietrarossa, western end of town. A ruin. Visible from exterior.
Museo Archeológico, Via Colajanni 3. Bronzes and early sculptures. Open Mon–Sat 9.30am–1pm, 3–7pm
Museo Mineralogico, Viale della Regione 73, tel: 0934 591280. Minerals museum.
Palazzo Moncada, off Corso Umberto, tel: 0934 4111. Feudal mansion which houses city offices.

Gela

Capo Soprano fortifications. (Take Via Manzoni to the sea.) Huge Greek walls. Open 9am–1 hour before sunset.
Museo Archeológico Regionale, Corso Vittorio Emanuele 2, tel: 0933 912626. Classical archaeological museum built over excavations (visible) of ancient acropolis. Open daily 9am–1pm, 3–8pm.

Mussomeli

Castello Manfredonico. Fabulous brooding castle with fine

fortifications. To check opening times call the Biblioteca Comunale (*informazione turistiche*). Tel: 0934 991495.

Enna Province

Enna

Castello di Lombardia, tel: 0935 500962. Perched above the town, the medieval castle looks as unassailable now as when it was first built. Open daily 9am–1pm, 3–5pm.
Duomo. Piazza del Duomo. A mixture of styles, the cathedral contains a beautiful wooden ceiling and various works of art. Open daily 9am–1pm, 4–7pm.
Museo Alessi, tel: 0935 24072. Small, well-designed museum of sacred art. Open Tues–Sun 9am–1pm, 4-7pm.
Torre di Federico II, Giardino Pubblico. A medieval tower and fine views.

Piazza Armerina

Duomo. 17th-century church built over the 15th-century original. With a 15th-century Crucifix by the Master of the Cross of Piazza Armerina.
Roman Villa (Villa Imperiale), tel: 0935 680036. 3rd–4th century villa famous for its mosaics and its completeness. Open 8am–1 hour before sunset.

Aidone

Morgantina. Rural site dating from the Bronze Age. Greek *agora*, luxury houses, theatre, granary and temples. Open daily 9am–1 hour before sunset.
Museo Archeológico, tel: 0935 87307. The museum, in a monastery in the upper part of the village, contains artefacts from the site at Morgantina. Open daily 9am–1.30pm, 3–7.30pm.

Ragusa Province

Ragusa

Ragusa City is more a place for wandering around at a leisurely pace than for visiting specific sights.

Basilica di San Giorgio, Piazza del Duomo, Ragusa Ibla. Masterpiece of Sicilian baroque, designed by Gagliardi.
Duomo di San Pietro, Piazza San Giovanni, Ragusa Alta.
San Giorgio Vecchio, Piazza Odierna, Ragusa Ibla.
San Giuseppe, Piazza Porta Pola, Ragusa Ibla.
Santa Maria delle Scale, Via XXIV Maggio. The Gothic church links Ragusa Alta and Ragusa Ibla. The churches (above) are theoretically open 9am–1pm but in practice tend to open and close at unpredictable times.
Giardino Ibleo, Ragusa Ibla. Peaceful park with three churches.
Museo Archeológico, Palazzo Mediterraneo, Via Natalelli, tel: 0932 622963. Archaeological collection under Hotel Mediterraneo. Bronze Age burial objects, Hellenistic and Roman pottery. Open daily 9am–1pm, 3–6.30pm.

Camarina
Prehistoric and Classical archaeological site on the coast, west of Marina di Ragusa, 34 km (21 miles) southwest of Ragusa, tel: 932 826004. Includes small museum. Open daily 9am–1 hour before sunset.

Castello di Donnafugata
The Moorish-style **castle** is situated 20 km (13 miles) from Ragusa, direction Santa Croce Camarina. (At Donnafugata railway station, take a turning to the right off the main road.) Nineteenth-century palace that combines Venetian gothic with Moorish pastiche. Open Tues–Sun 9am–1pm.

Cava d'Ispica
The prehistoric quarries (*cave*) and tombs occupy a (11-km/7-mile) long valley near Modica. Cava d'Ispica is well-signposted east of Módica: follow signs to *scavi* (archaeological excavations), tel: 0932 951133. Open daily 9am–6.30pm.

Módica
San Giorgio, Módica Alta (Upper Town). Magnificent example of

Sicilian baroque. Open daily 9am–noon, 4–8pm.
Museo Civico, Palazzo dei Mercedari, Via Merce, tel: 0932 945081. Open daily 9am–1pm.
Museo delle Arte e Tradizioni Popolari, Palazzo dei Mercedari, tel: 0932 752747. Folk museum. Open daily 10am–12.30pm, 4.30–7.30pm.

Siracusa City

Parco Archeológico della Neapolis, tel: 0931 66206. Archaeological park containing Greek Theatre, Roman Amphitheatre, the Orecchio di Dionisio (Dionysius' ear), San Nicolò church, Roman baths, the Latomia del Paradiso (Paradise quarries). Open daily, 9am–1 hour before sunset.
Museo Archeológico Paolo Orsi, Villa Landolina, Viale Teocrito, tel: 0931 464022. Well-organised, extensive museum containing finds dating from prehistoric to Roman times. Arguably the best Classical museum in Sicily. Open daily 9am–1.30pm; and 3.30–6.30pm in high season.
Catacombe di San Giovanni. Via San Giovanni, tel: 0931 721665. Fourth-century catacombs. Guided tours only: winter 10am, 11am and noon; summer 10am, 11am, noon, 4pm, 5pm and 6pm. Closed Tues.
Cripta di San Marziano, Basilica di San Giovanni Evangelista, tel: 0931 721665. Catacombs beneath Siracusa's first cathedral. Open 9am–1pm, 2–5pm; closed Tues.
Ginnasio Romano (Roman Gymnasium), Via Elorina, tel: 0931 481111. Open 9am–12.30pm.
Duomo, Piazza del Duomo. Incorporates part of the original 5th-century BC temple to Athena. Became a church in 7th century AD. Open daily 8am–noon, 4–7pm.
Galleria Regionale, Palazzo Bellomo, Via Capodieci, tel: 0931 69511. Mixed collection of Sicilian art housed in a 13th- to 15th-century Gothic palace. Open daily 9am–2pm.
Castello Eurialo, 10 km (6 miles) from Siracusa, on the Ciane river, tel: 0931 711973. Dionysius' 4th-

century BC defensive system. Open daily, 9am–one hour before sunset.

Fonte Ciane
Take a lovely boat trip through the mythical spring where papyrus flourishes. From Siracusa, take a boat from Porto Grande, Foro Italico or Molo Zanagora. This round trip takes 4 hours. Alternatively, go by road: take Viale Ermocrate or Viale Orsi towards Floridia, then turn right at Via Necropoli del Fusco, direction Canicattini Bagni. Make an appointment with the boat guide, Sig. Bella, tel: 0931 69076.

Siracusa Province

Megara Hyblaea
Classical site, tel: 0931 512364. From Siracusa, take Corso Gelone towards Catania. After 20 km (12 miles), a road on the right leads to the Classical site in the shadow of industrial clouds. One of the earliest Greek colonies in Sicily. Open 9am–1 hour before sunset.

Noto
Noto is a museum in itself: a baroque city in which most buildings have equal value.
Palazzo Villadorata, Via Nicolaci. A baroque jewel with extravagant balconies and buttresses.
Palazzo Municipale, **Palazzo Vescovile**, **Palazzo Sant'Alfano**, Piazza Municipio. The buildings around the square complement each other. The yellow stone and the elegance of proportions produce a sense of harmony and tranquillity. However, this did not prevent the last earthquake shaking some foundations.
San Nicolò (**Duomo**), Piazza Municipio. In March 1996 the cathedral's roof and dome collapsed, and the reconstruction and restoration work did not begin until 1999. For further information call Azienda Turismo di Noto (tel: 0931 573779).

Palazzolo Acréide
Zona Archeológica Akrai. Walled park containing a Greek theatre and carvings dedicated to the goddess

Cybele (3rd century BC). Christian places of worship and necropoli also existed in old stone quarries during the Byzantine period. Open daily 9am–1pm, 3–7pm. Also insist on seeing the **Santoni** (strange sculptures of Cybele). These are at a site down the hill and visitors need to be supervised.

Catania City

The city sights embrace baroque and Roman. Some buildings are dilapidated but worth seeing, as are the intimate museums. Many Roman sites are visible from different angles so it is not always necessary to enter the site.
Duomo, Piazza del Duomo. Originally a medieval cathedral, but altered. Most of the present building dates from the 18th century. Recently restored. Open daily 8am–noon, 4–7pm.
Palazzo Biscari, Via Museo Biscari. Ornate baroque mansion. View the exterior only.
Museo Belliniano, Piazza San Francesco 3, tel: 095 7150535. Bellini's house, now a museum containing musical memorabilia. Open Mon–Fri 9am–1pm.
Teatro Romano (**Teatro Greco**), Via Vittorio Emanuele. Classical Greek theatre, overbuilt and enlarged by the Romans. Open daily 8am–1 hour before sunset.
Anfiteatro Romano, Piazza Stesicoro. Remains of the largest amphitheatre in Italy. Closed but visible.
San Nicolò l'Arena, Piazza Dante. The largest church in Sicily, a vast, brooding (and unfinished) 16th-century edifice. Open daily 10am–noon.
Castello Ursino, Piazza Federico di Svevia, tel: 095 345830. Catania's best historical collection of sculpture and paintings (**Museo Civico**, set in a newly restored Hohenstaufen dynastic fortress. Open Tues–Sun 9am–6pm.
Casa Museo G. Verga, Via S. Anna 8, tel: 095 7150598. Literary museum in the former house of Verga. Open Mon–Sat 9am–1pm; Tues, Thurs, Fri also 3–6.30pm.

Orto Botánico dell'Università, Via Antonino Longo 19, tel: 095 430901. Botanical gardens. Open Mon–Sat 9am–1pm.
Porta di Carlo V, Piazza Pardo, Porta Garibaldi. Grand lava-stone Spanish gateway.
Teatro Bellini, Piazza Bellini. Newly restored theatre.
Via Crociferi. A street of fine baroque *palazzi*.
Villa Bellini. Charming gardens to the north of town.

Catania Province

Caltagirone
Museo Civico, Carcere Borbonico, tel: 0933 41315. Small town museum in ex-Bourbon prison. Classical finds and Renaissance ceramics. Open Tues–Fri 9am–1pm.
Museo della Ceramica, Via Roma, tel: 0933 21680. Ceramics museum in the public gardens. Open daily 9am–6.30pm.

Adrano
Ponte Saraceno. Charming medieval Saracen bridge.
Museo Archeológico Normanno, Piazza Umberto, tel: 095 7692660. Eclectic historical collection in a Norman castle. Open daily 8.30am–noon.

Bronte
Castello e Abbazia di Maniace, near Bronte, tel: 095 690018. This 13th-century abbey belonged to Admiral Nelson. Open daily 9am–1pm.
Museo dell'Antica Civiltà, Locale alla Masseria Lombardo, tel: 095 691635. Rural life museum. Open daily 9am–1pm.

Linguaglossa
Museo Etnográfico, Pro Loco, Piazza Annunziata 5, tel: 095 643094. Collection of Etna flora and fauna in local tourist office. Open Mon–Sat 9am–1pm and 4–7.30pm, Sunday 10am–12.30pm.

Nicolosi
Parco dell'Etna, Viale della Regione, tel: 095 914588. Worth

calling and dropping into the park headquarters for information before setting out on a walk through the Etna Natural Park or a climb of Mount Etna's slopes. Also contact Nicolosi tourist office.

Paternò
Castello, Collina Turistica. Medieval castle. Open daily 9am–12.30pm.

Randazzo
Chiesa di San Martino. Fourteenth-century. The bell tower is built of a mixture of lava and limestone.
Chiesa di Santa Maria. Piazza Santa Maria. Norman Hohenstaufen dynastic church with Catalan additions. Tel: 095 921204 for the opening times of church and treasury.

Taormina

Teatro Greco, Via Teatro Greco, tel: 0942 23220. The Greek theatre in one of the world's most perfect natural settings. Open daily 9am–5.30pm.
Badia Vecchia, Via Circonvallazione. Fourteenth-century abbey. Open summer daily 9am–1pm, 4–7pm; winter Mon–Fri 9am–1pm, 4–6pm, Sat 9am–1pm.
Duomo, Piazza del Duomo. Sixteenth-century exterior. Classical concerts in winter. Open daily, 8am–noon, 3.30–6.30pm.
Odeon, Via Teatrino Romano. Small Roman theatre. View over the railings, or see parts of the Odeon exposed in the church of **Santa Caterina**.
Naumachia, Via Naumachia. Possibly a gymnasium in ancient times. Free access.
Palazzo Corvaja, Piazza Vittorio Emanuele. Fifteenth-century palace, now houses the tourist office and various temporary exhibitions. Open daily 8am–2pm and 4–9pm.
Palazzo dei Duchi di San Stefano. Fourteenth-century palace now containing a sculpture museum. Open daily 9am–noon and 3–6pm.
Palazzo Ciampoli, Corso Umberto. Fifteenth-century palace with mullioned windows, now the Hotel Palazzo Vecchio.

San Agostino, Piazza 9 Aprile. Fifteenth-century Gothic church, now a library.
San Domenico, Piazzale San Domenico. Formerly a monastery, now a five-star hotel. Paying guests only.
San Pancrazio, Via San Pancrazio. Built on the site of a Greek temple. For all current church opening times, see the **tourist office** in Palazzo Corvajo, tel: 0942 23243.

Messina Province

Messina
Much was destroyed in the 1908 earthquake but the historic centre and harbour are worth a half-day visit. Ferries leave regularly for the mainland and the Aeolian Islands.
Cimitero, Via Catania (entrance Via Piazza Dante). The city cemetery south of Messina. One of the most picturesque in Southern Italy. Fine views of Calabria.
Duomo, Piazza del Duomo. The cathedral is a superb fake with some original elements. See the clockwork cherubs on the neo-Gothic campanile strike the hours at midday. Open daily 9.30am–7.30pm.
Museo Regionale, Via della Libertà, tel: 090 358716. See Antonello da Messina's Madonna polyptich, and works by Caravaggio. Open daily 9am–2pm.
Santissima Annunziata dei Catalani, Piazza Catalani. One of the few 13th-century buildings in the city to have survived earthquakes. Delicately beautiful. University chapel. Occasionally open for services.

Giardini-Naxos
Scavi (excavations) and **Museo Archeológico**, Capo Schiso, tel: 0942 51001. The remains of the oldest Greek settlement in Sicily. Open daily 9am–1 hour before sunset.

Milazzo
Most visitors see it before sailing off to the Aeolian Islands as this is the main port of embarkation.
Castello, tel: 090 922 1291. Impressive fortifications dating in part from the Hohenstaufen dynastic building of the 13th century and in part from the Spanish of the 15th. Open Tues–Sun 10am–noon, 3–5pm.
Faro, Capo Milazzo. Milazzo lighthouse, sited on a cape at the end of a panoramic drive. Fine views of the Aeolian Islands. View from exterior only.

Patti
Roman Villa, Marina di Patti, tel: 0941 361593. Late-Imperial villa with impressive mosaics. Open daily 9am–1 hour before sunset.

Tindari
Tindaris, Frazione Tindari, tel: 0941 361593. Archaeological park containing Greco-Roman theatre, Augustan basilica, Roman villas, baths, etc. Open 9am–2 hours before sunset. Museum open daily 9am–2pm.
Santuario della Madonna Nero, Piazza Belvedere, tel: 0941 369026. Sanctuary of the Black Madonna. Adjoining the ruins is the kitsch church housing the *madonna nera*, the prized icon.

Aeolian Islands

Apart from on Lípari Island, man-made sights, such as churches and museums, are of only passing interest. It is the natural volcanic sights that command the attention.
Long hikes, climbing volcanoes and leisurely boat trips are recommended on all the islands. There is a volcano to suit everyone but you should check the temperature, altitude and strenuousness of the climb below before embarking on any trip. Boat trips are highly recommended and can be readily booked at the islands' main ports.

Lípari
Castello. The citadel is set on a steep lava rock. Open daily 9am–7pm.
Duomo. The Norman cathedral was rebuilt in the 13th century and has a baroque facade. Open daily 9am–1pm.
Museo Eoliano, located in several buildings around the cathedral, tel: 090 9880174. The best museum on any of the offshore islands, containing finds from the Neolithic era and Bronze Age necropoli; also Greek pottery and terracotta masks. Open daily 9am–2pm, 4–7pm.
Parco Archeológico. It stretches out in front of the Duomo and includes 6th-century BC tombs in the so-called Site of Diana. Open daily 9am–2pm.
Canneto. Obsidian and pumice fields. Bus from Via Vittorio Emanuele in Lípari Town to Canneto. Or drive through Monte Rosa tunnel on the outward journey. Follow the signs to Forgia Vecchi and Pierra to look at the obsidian fields, created by old lava flows. These are the only obsidian deposits known in Europe.

Vulcano
Porto di Levante. The beach includes a yellowish natural pool where visitors wallow in mud. Test the temperature with your hand before going in. Temperatures can be scalding. After rinsing off in the cool sea, see the underwater fumaroles: holes spurting volcanic gases.
Fosse di Vulcano. A climb up a crater from Porto Levante is the star attraction on the island. The climb should take about one hour (293 metres/952 ft) and is fine if you are reasonably fit and have sturdy shoes, a water bottle and some sort of protective clothes. From the top, on clear days, you can enjoy the most spectacular view of all the Aeolian Islands. Do not forget your camera!
Vulcanello. A 30-minute climb to the top of the extinct volcano (124 metres/406 ft). From the summit there is a view of Lípari and Vulcano.

Salina
Monte Fossa delle Felci. The ascent up this extinct volcano (962 metres/3,150 ft) begins at Santa Marina, the port on the east coast of the island.

Panarea

Calcara, San Pietro quay. Mud-bathing in a pool with a hot spring (50°C/122°F). Views of fumaroles and small geysers.

Strómboli

Sciara del Fuoco. The climb to the top of the volcano (926 metres/ 3,040 ft) overlooks Strómboli's active crater. There is a choice between a hectic organised hike to the top and a leisurely night viewing of the fireworks from a boat at the foot of Sciara del Fuoco. Climbing the volcano is permitted only in the company of an official guide (Club Alpino Italiano, tel: 090 986093, Apr–Oct). Sturdy shoes, warm clothes, water, a snack and a flashlight are required, not to mention considerable stamina. At the pace the guides choose to set, it is an arduous climb for all but the fittest. At the top, only about an hour is allowed before the return down the volcano. Volcanic activity is very unpredictable: you may see anything from showers of sparks to virtually nothing.

Strombolicchio. A boat trip from Strómboli town visits this stunning sheer rock a mile offshore. From afar, it looks like a castle.

Filicudi

Grotta del Bue Marino. Mysterious caves sited an hour's boat trip from the island. These are generally treated as part of a complete boat trip around the island. Also ask to see **La Canna**, huge rock obelisks. In a late afternoon light, the caves and rocks take on a surreal glow. Book your trip with fishermen at Filicudi Porto.

Outdoor Activities

Nature Reserves

See the chapter on Sicily's Wild Places (*page 99*) for descriptions of all the regional parks and nature reserves. The principal tourist offices in each province can supply a complete list of reserves, with maps and suggested routes.

The Palermo tourist office (Piazza Castelnuovo 34, tel: 091 583847) has information on the **Zíngaro**, **Ficuzza** and **Monte Pellegrino** reserves. This office can also supply a booklet entitled *14 Aree di Interesse Naturalistico,* on nature reserves and protected areas. The maps are helpful even for non-Italian speakers.

The Siracusa tourist office (Via Maestranza 33, tel: 0931 464255) is the place to go for information on the **Vendicari**, **Necropoli di Pantálica** and **Valle dell'Anapo** reserves. Similarly, the office in Trápani (Piazzetta Saturno, tel: 0923 29000) knows all about the protected areas around Mozia, the **Isola di Mozia**, **Lo Stagnone** and **Saline di Trápani** reserves, as well as **Lo Zíngaro**. There's also an information office within the Zíngaro reserve itself, tel: 0923 26111.

In the Taormina information office (Palazzo Corvaja, Piazza Vittorio Emanuele, tel: 0942 23243), they can tell you about the **Gole dell'Alcántara** reserve, as well as the **Parco dell'Etna**. The Etna park also has an information centre in Nocolosi, at Via Garibaldi 63, tel: 095 911505.

The **Parco delle Madonie** has two information centres, one in Cefalù (Corso Ruggero 77, tel: 0921 421050), the other in Petralia Sottana (Corso Alliata 16, tel: 0921

680478). And the huge **Parco di Nébrodi** has three information offices – in Caronia (Via Ruggero Orlando 126, tel: 0921 333211), in Alcara Li Fusi (Via Ugo Foscolo 1, tel: 0941 793904) and in Cesarò (Strada Nazionale, tel: 0950 696008).

The marine reserve around the **Egadi** Islands is served by the tourist information office in Favignana (Largo Marina 14, tel: 0923 922121), while the **Ustica** marine reserve has an office in the town hall on the main square in Ustica town, tel: 091 8449456.

For more information on any of these reserves, and others still being developed, there are a number of agencies who can help: **Assessorato Regionale Territorio ed Ambiente**, Gruppo Riserve, Palermo, tel: 091 6963842. **Lega Ambiente**, Via XX Settembre 57, Palermo, tel: 091 326875. **CAI** (Club Alpino Italiano), Via Natoli 20, Messina, tel: 090 693196. **Delegazione Sicilia della WWF** (World Wide Fund for Nature), Via P. Calvi, Palermo, tel: 091 322169. **Uff. Conservazione Natura Az. Foreste Demaniali Regione Siciliana**, Via Libertà 9, Palermo, tel: 091 6274235.

Thermal Spas

Many islands and resorts offer the chance to wallow in mud baths or take water cures. These are available at Sciacca (Agrigento Province); Castellammare del Golfo (Trápani Province); or on the Egadi and Aeolian Islands.

Italians and Germans take the therapeutic effects of such water cures very seriously.

Excursions

MOUNT ETNA

How you see Mount Etna will depend on the season, your finances, your transport and time, as well as Etna's current volcanic activity. For those on a limited budget but with a day to spare, the rail route around Etna is recommended. If there is any sort of volcanic activity, an organised tour is recommended from your resort.

Independent travellers will prefer to drive to Etna and take the cable car to the top. If you can afford it, and should Etna's activity merit it, consider hiring a guide. The guides will tell you honestly what you should be able to see on any particular day. In winter it is not possible to reach the summit.

Ferrovia Circumetnea (Etna Railway), tel: 095 374842. This circular rail route runs from Catania to Giarre-Riposto (114 km/71 miles). It skirts Etna's foothills and the volcanic towns of Adrano, Bronte, Linguaglossa, Maletto, Paternò and Randazzo. It is possible to go round the volcano in a day since the journey takes from four to five and a half hours. Book at the Circumetnea office in Catania (Corso delle Province 13). As there is little accommodation in the area, book ahead for an overnight stop. *See also Sports, page 377* for skiing on Etna.

Advice on Ascent: The usual approach is by car, public bus or coach to the Rifugio Sapienza. From there, take the cable car to the summit and explore (with a pre-booked official guide).

Organised Excursion: Etna is accessible on a day trip from Taormina or Catania. But if you are planning to climb Etna, allow for an early start. It is easiest to book an organised excursion with a local operator (e.g. Sun Services at Taormina). Allow at least a morning for the ascent, with an early start. A full-day excursion is more usual, particularly if you want time to explore the Etna foothills.

Independent Excursion: If you wish to travel independently, it is best to book a guide to ensure that you will see volcanic activity in safety. Book an official Italian Alpine Guide from Rifugio Sapienza the day before (*see below*). Check conditions before setting out and plan to be at the refuge early.

Qualified guides are available for hire at Rifugio Sapienza but

negotiate on price, and discuss what you want to see. Also decide which time of day is best, according to season, weather, and the type of volcanic activity you want to see. Overnight, dawn, early morning and sunset are usually the best times to appreciate different aspects of Etna.

Guides: For an official guide at Rifugio Sapienza, tel: 095 914141. For last-minute trips, an official guide, Nino Longo, may be contacted at the centre (during the day) or at home (evenings, tel: 095 7914304). Your guide may speak very limited English. To ensure that there is no linguistic misunderstanding, check which of the following can be seen (and agree on a fixed price): a pit of molten lava (*un pozzo di lava*); a small, secondary but active cone (*piccolo cono erruttivo*); the lava front (*la fronte lavica*); secondary craters (*crateri secondari*).

Costs: The price of a standard organised coach tour of Etna, including a trip to the summit varies greatly. The cost of the cable car (*funivia*) from Rifugio Sapienza to the summit is about 30,000 lire. A personal guide from the Rifugio Sapienza will cost anything from 50,000 lire to 150,000 lire, depending on the duration and complexity of the visit. The cost of the cable car is not included.

Clothing: Protective clothing is advisable for an ascent of Etna, including glasses to protect against sun and volcanic ash, sturdy walking shoes or mountain boots (or skis). Cold mountain temperatures (20°C/68F lower than in Catania) mean that warm clothing is required. Organised Etna excursions often provide protective clothing but check. The summit is snowy from November to March.

EGADI ISLANDS

Lévanzo, Grotta delle Genovese (prehistoric paintings): Necessary to telephone in advance for an appointment with Sig. Castiglione, the custodian of the Grotto, tel: 0923 924032. He will guide those

who wish to make the trip by land or advise on boats for those who wish to reach the cave by sea.

Favignana: The bicycle is the usual means of transport here and can be rented cheaply at the port. The famous, if horrific, seasonal spectacle is *La Mattanza*, the ritual slaughter of tuna. (For details, and to see whether you can stomach it, first read *The Great Tuna Massacre, page 169*.) To follow the *Mattanza* by boat, try to find a willing fisherman at the docks in Favignana.

ALCANTARA GORGE

The Alcántara Gorge consists of rock formed from lava. The rock is black and has formed fascinating and strange crystalline shapes. The river runs for several miles through a deep cut in the ground (*see page 274*).

The place has become a tourist magnet, with coach trips, quite unnecessary lifts down to the river and wellington boots on loan. Nevertheless it is well worth visiting. Both river and rock deserve to be explored and there is an ordinary bar-restaurant on hand for snacks afterwards. You can reach the gorge by car, or by bus from Taormina or Messina. Admission charge.

Beaches

As an island, Sicily offers a vast range of beaches, from volcanic rocks to golden sands. Most beaches in the main resorts charge a fee, in subtle gradations to suit most people's pockets. The beaches on the offshore islands tend to be free, with the notable exception of Panarea. Out of season, many of the beaches are used as rubbish tips and are therefore best seen from a distance.

The tourist season, and the beaches, begin opening in April and the seas are delightful from May until October, with only the tricky month of August to be dealt with.

The "beach season" begins in August, when beaches become

phenomenally crowded in Cefalù, Taormina coast and Mondello, near Palermo. Some public (free) beaches suffer from itinerant traders peddling undesirable junk jewellery and fake Lacoste T-shirts. Also in August, normally pleasant bays, like Castellammare del Golfo (west of Palermo) are taken over by motor launches. Then rages a battle between the sun-worshippers and the speed-freaks.

However, there are compensations in people-watching and in the sophisticated nightlife that spills onto the beaches. Beaches in Mondello are well-equipped with showers, bars and games. However, even in August there are retreats from the crowds. For instance, the long and wide beach of **Marinella di Selinunte** (motorway to Mazzara del Vallo, exit Castelvetrano, follow signposts to Selinunte) offers some tranquillity and clean sea as well as the possibility to have good, fresh and inexpensive seafood under the sheltered terrace of a *trattoria* right on the beach. Also the sandy coast south of Sciacca, around Siculiana Marina and Eraclea Minoa are generally not crowded, clean and rather pleasant.

Recommended beaches: All the offshore islands have lovely, often volcanic, beaches, from which boat trips can easily be arranged. Ustica, the Egadi Islands and the Aeolian Islands are ever-popular with Sicilians and visitors. For swimming, all islands are to be recommended with the exception of the Stagnone Islands, stagnant waters near Mozia. Beaches at Cefalù, Mondello and Taormina are kept extremely clean in season. Beaches south of Siracusa are beatifully unspoilt and even wild near Capo Passero. Beaches between Catania and Taormina, especially those around Aci Trezza and Aci Castello, tend to be rocky, exciting and often well-equipped.

Beaches to avoid: It is easier to say which stretches of coastline to avoid than which to head for. The polluted coast around the so-called Gela Riviera should be avoided at all costs (unless one is there to visit the

impressive Greek walls nearby). The beaches around Porto Empedocle, Agrigento, are also polluted. The beaches north of Siracusa should be treated with caution. Although a cleaning programme is under way, many still suffer from chemical effluents. Avoid the beaches around the ports of Augusta, Messina, Milazzo and Palermo.

Sailing

Palermo province has lovely beaches not too far from Palermo City. Many have exclusive yacht clubs and a sophisticated nightlife. West of Palermo, the stretch of coast from Mondello and Capo Gallo to Isole delle Femmine is a standard yacht excursion. Equally well, east of Palermo, from Romagnolo to Capo Zafferano makes a pleasant boat trip.

The wild stretch of northern coastline from Capo d'Orlando to Cefalù is one of the loveliest in Sicily, particularly near the lagoons below Tindari.

Culture

Performing Arts

There is a wealth of artistic activity in Sicily. Most of the provincial capitals have their own theatre or opera house. Catania and Palermo have their own companies, and present complete seasons of musical and theatrical events. In summer virtually every province stages some form of cultural event, from film festivals to opera and ballet, classical music and theatre to art exhibitions. Many include internationally known companies and artistes.

The following Arts Diary lists a few of the largest and best-known, but expect Palermo, Catania, Siracusa and numerous other cities to stage their own festivals. Details are available through tourist offices, the local press, or the magazine, *Ciao Sicilia*.

Palermo
Anthony, Via Don Orione 16, tel: 091 544766. Cabaret.
Teatro Biondo, Via Roma, tel: 091 582364/7434341. Drama.
Cafè Chantant, Via Stabile 136, tel: 091 586394. Cabaret.
Al Convento, Via Castellana Bandiera 66, tel: 091 6376336. Cabaret.
Teatro Franco Zappalà, Via Autonomia Siciliana, tel: 091 543380/362764. Dialect theatre.
Teatro Golden, Via Terrasanta 60, tel: 091 300609. Classical music.
Teatro Libero Incontroazione, Piazza Marina 38, tel: 091 6174040. Drama.
Teatro Madison, Piazza Don Bosco 13, tel: 091 543740. Cabaret.
Al Massimo, Piazza Verdi 9, tel: 091 589575/589070. Drama, music hall.

Teatro Metropolitan, Viale Strasburgo 356, tel: 091 6886532. Drama, ballet, classical music. Also shows American and British films in the English Film Club, Cinema Metropolitan.

Catania
Teatro Massimo Bellini, Piazza Teatro Massimo, tel: 095 312020. Opera, classical music and ballet.
Teatro Metropolitana, Via S Euplio, tel: 095 322323. Drama, opera, classical music and jazz. Winter concert season from November to June.
Villa Bellini: concerts and other open-air events in the gardens.

Erice
Erice stages the summer **Settimana di Musica Medievale e Rinascimentale** (Medieval and Renaissance music festival) in its lovely churches. For more details, contact Erice tourist office, Via C. A. Pepoli, tel: 0923 869388.

Siracusa
Siracusa is home to the **Istituto Nazionale del Drama Antico** (Institute of Classical Drama) so has home-grown talent to display in the great Greek tragedies. In 1991 German director Jean-Marie Straub filmed *Antigone* in the Greek theatre.

Sicilian Puppet Theatre

Traditional plays performed by puppets (*see page 258*) can still be seen in Acireale, Catania, Palermo and Siracusa.

Palermo
Associazione Figli d'Arte Cuticchio, Via Bara all'Olivella 95, tel: 091 323400. Perhaps the last generation of old family puppeteers. They put on modernised, shortened versions of traditional puppet theatre. Mimmo Cuticchio is one of the few remaining amazing recitors of the *cuntastorie*.
Opera dei Pupi, Vicolo Ragusi 6, tel: 091 329294. Two or three shows weekly at 9pm.

Teatro Bradamante, Via Lombardia 25, tel: 091 6259223. A free show at 10pm most Fridays in summer.
Museo delle Marionette, Via Butera 1. Free shows in summer: check with the museum for details.

Monreale
Munna, Via Kennedy 10. Puppet performances on Sundays in summer.

Acireale
Cooperativa E. Magri, Corso Umberto 113, tel: 095 604521/606272.
Turi Grasso, Via Nazionale 95, tel: 095 7648035.

Siracusa
Opera dei Pupi, Via Nizza 14. In summer there are usually performances on Tuesday, Thursday and Saturday at 9.30pm. Check times with Siracusa tourist office.

Classical Drama

Sicily's Classical theatres often return to their original function, as great settings for Greek drama. The season usually lasts from May to July, with different dramatic cycles performed in the traditional Greek theatres.

Siracusa is home to the Istituto Nazionale del Drama Antico (Institute of Classical Drama) so has home-grown talent to display in the great Greek tragedies. Greek dramas are produced in the Teatro Greco in May and June in alternate years.

Segesta stages Classical (and contemporary) drama in its Greek theatre in odd-numbered years, alternating with Siracusa.

Taormina's Greco-Roman theatre is the venue for an annual festival (July and August) which includes Classical drama, along with opera, dance and music.

Nightlife

Evening Entertainment

Compared with much of Italy, Sicilian nightlife is somewhat introverted, centred on restaurants and private parties rather than mass discos. Even so, the advent of tourism has led to an explosion of bars and clubs on the coastal resorts. Cefalù and Taormina are the main centres for nightlife during the summer, revolving around piano bars and the more sophisticated nightclubs.

It may seem surprising that two such small places monopolise the high life of Sicily to such a degree. After all, Palermo, Catania or Siracusa might seem more natural candidates. But this has a lot to do with the special status of international tourism that Cefalù and Taormina have achieved, both offering a certain level of security at night. Until a few years back the petty criminals that plague the cities actually discouraged people from venturing out in the evenings. Today the situation is radically changing and the cities increasingy belong to their citizens. Nonetheless it is still advisable to avoid venturing into the remote parts of the old cities at night.

An active and interesting cultural life in the big cities like Catania and Palermo has finally taken shape, bringing people back to concerts, cinemas and theatres, and thereby encouraging the opening of new pubs, cafés, piano bars and restaurants. On summer evenings there is a wide choice of events of all kinds. Some events are free or at a token fee.

For a totally different type of nightlife, see Performing Arts page 372. Sicily can offer a wide range:

from avant-garde films to traditional puppet shows. Although there are no major rock venues, open-air concerts take place in Catania and other cities. Evening entertainment often ties in with the local festivities (*see Festivals, page 375*).

Passeggiata

The *passeggiata* (stroll) is an Italian institution that finds favour in Sicily. Mondello is the place to see a nightly parade of Milanese fashion. On summer nights, the offshore islands come alive. In particular, Ustica, the Egadi Islands (especially Lévanzo) and the Aeolian Islands (especially Lípari) are awash with strollers admiring one another.

Young Nightlife

The small coastal resorts in Palermo and Messina provinces abound in clubs catering to the young. Rough and ready video bars and short-lived clubs come and go in Giardini-Naxos (near Taormina) and on most of the north coast resorts. In most towns, the neighbourhood *pizzeria* or *gelateria* is the focus of attention – and a motorbike-riding crowd.

Sophisticated Nightlife

For more sophistication, try piano bars in all the main resorts. In order to fit in, it is best to dress elegantly. Even here, there is a wide range of wealth and style. The resort of Mondello, and particularly the Aeolian island of Panarea, offer spots for the ostentatious jet set. The discreet rich prefer to retreat to the remote island of Pantellería.

City Nightspots

PALERMO

Palermitan high society in particular is relatively closed. Much socialising takes place at private functions, often taking over a nightclub or restaurant for the night. Even so, in the early evening, the upmarket quarter around Viale della Libertà witnesses a *passeggiata* and chic cafés like Roneys are busy. City bars, however, tend to close early and the crowds head to Mondello and the coast. By 10pm the city seems dead.

Bars

The bars and *pasticcerie* on the pedestrianised Principe di Belmonte are the focus of early evening gatherings. Outside this area, jazzy or simple ice-cream parlours prevail:
Gelateria Ilardo, Foro Italico.
Al Gelato, Viale Strasburgo.
Gelato, Piazza Europa 2.
Di Martino Vini, Via Mazzini, is a very popular *panineria* famous for its excellent *panini*.
I Vini d'Oro, Piazza Nascè. More than just a wine bar, this *enoteca* is renowned for its wine tasting. The location is nothing exceptional, a few tables outside, but the service is good and the selection of wines is remarkable.

Clubs and Discos

There are several clubs and discos in Viale Strasburgo, a middle-class residential quarter. Check local for details with your hotel.
Il Cerchio, Viale Strasburgo 312.
Metropolis, Piazza Marina 50.
Kandinsky-Florio, Discesa Tonnara 4 (on the coast at Arenella, near the Hotel Villa Igiea).
Calembour, Via Gerbasi. Disco-dance and Latin American.
Biergarten, Viale Regione Siciliana 6469. Techno music and theme nights.
Gorky Club, Via Ugo La Malfa 95.

Piano bars

The city has many piano bars, including:
Drive Bar, Via del Bersagliere 70.
Blumix, Via Venezia 62. Live music every night.
Grand Hotel des Palmes, Via Roma 396 (city centre).
Malaluna, Via Resurrezione.
Mazzara Escargot, Via Generale Magliocco 15.

Villa Igiea, Salita Belmonte 43/b (out of town; the undoubted star).

MONDELLO

Some socialising is a question of private parties in summer villas. However, **Villa Boscogrande** (Via Tommaso Natale 91, tel: 091 241179) is public, a club set in a dreamy *palazzo* where Visconti filmed scenes for The Leopard. Mondello can also be an inexpensive youth hang-out.
Three popular piano bars are:
Mondello Palace, Viale Principe di Scalea 2.
Thula Club, Viale M di Savoia 102.
Villa Verde, Via Piano Gallo 36.

CATANIA

Catanese nightlife is fairly diverse, revolving around *gelaterie*, bars, discos and clubs. Popular young locations are: **Gelaterie del Duomo**, Piazza del Duomo; **Bar Centrale**, Via Etnea 121; and **Pasticceria Caprice**, Via Etnea 30. These are the places for *gelati* (ice-creams), *arancini* (typical snacks) and *granite* (sorbets).

Discos

Some discos worth investigating are:
Empire, Via Milazzo, tel: 095 375684.
Divina, Via Carnazza 53, tel: 095 399631.
Il Banacher, Via Vampolieri 66 (on the SS 114 near Aci Castello). One of the best-known open-air discos.
Medea Club, Via Medea 2.
Villa Romeo, Via Platemone 20. Latin American music.
Notre Dame, Vulcania. *Pizzeria/discoteca*.

CEFALÙ

Like Taormina, Cefalù's clubs need to be checked on the spot. Piano bars like **Kentia** are popular (Via Nicola Botta 4, tel: 0921 20008).

ERICE

Erice, like Cefalù and Taormina, is another safe pocket. Despite its tiny size, Erice has a number of piano bars and nightclubs. **Blu Notte**, in Via San Rocco is a piano bar and nightclub. **Boccaccio**, in Via dei Misteri, is more of a disco.

SIRACUSA

Much of Siracusa's nightlife is really café life on the island of Ortygia. Most cafés are on Fontana Aretusa, Porta Marina and around the Duomo. Lungomare Alfeo has some lively bars. **Malibu** disco attracts 3,000 for 1970s pop parties and is great fun. For magical live entertainment, the Greek theatre is the stage for Classical drama. Contact the tourist office for information.

TAORMINA

A sophisticated evening is guaranteed in the bars and restaurants of Taormina's hotels. (*See hotels and restaurants under Where To Stay and Eating Out.*) Check the latest clubs locally; clubs change hands at an amazing rate.

Among the more enduring are: **Bella Blu**, Via Guardia Vecchia, tel: 0942 24239.
Septimo, Via San Pancrazio 50, tel: 0942 625522.
L'Ombrello, Piazza Duomo, tel: 0942 23733. Music club.

Gay Nightlife

Taormina is still the focus for the native and foreign gay community. At any time, it should have several gay clubs and bars. **Le Perroquet** (Piazza San Domenico, tel: 24462) is currently popular. There is little of an organised gay scene in Sicily but attitudes are relatively relaxed.

For more information, contact Arci-Gay, a gay organisation in Palermo, tel: 091 324917/8.

Festivals

Special Events

January/February
Agrigento: Almond Fair (runs January to March).
Agrigento: International Folklore Festival (February).
Palermo: Symphony Season continues, Teatro Politeama.

March/April
Catania: Etna Bicycle Race (April).
Catania: Drama, classical music and jazz season.
Palermo: Drama, opera and classical season continues.

May
Caltanissetta: Livestock and Crafts Fair.
Catania: Sicilian Theatre in the World.
Palermo: Panormus Veteran Car Rally.
Palermo: Trade Fair (held between May and June)
Siracusa and Segesta: Classical comedies and tragedies in the Greek theatres. The season runs from May to June. (Siracusa in even-numbered years, Segesta in odd years.)
Taormina: Folk festival and display of Sicilian carts.

June
Catania: Musica Estate. Concert, dance and theatre season lasts until October.
Erice: Estate Ericina. Summer season, including competitions for the most flowery courtyards.
Siracusa and Segesta: Classical comedies and tragedies in Greek theatres.
Taormina: June to mid-September. Taormina Arte, an international festival of cinema, music, opera,

ballet and theatre held in the Greek theatre.

July
Palermo: Palermo di scena. Music, theatre, cinema, ballet through the whole summer.
Agrigento: Settimana Pirandelliana. A week celebrating Pirandello's plays in drama, film and debate.
Catania: Estate a Catania. Music, theatre and cinema during the summer.
Cefalù: Estate Cefaludese. Music and summer puppet shows for everyone.
Enna: Estate Ennese. Summer in Enna, including recitals and concerts in the city castle. Also the Grand Prix del Mediterraneo at Lake Pergusa.
Erice: Festival of Medieval Music, held in town churches.
Palermo: Targa Florio, International Sicily Rally.
Siracusa: Summer season of opera, music and ballet.
Taormina: Prestigious International Film Festival.

August
Agrigento: Persephone Festival.
Enna: Summer festival continues.
Siracusa: Summer Season continues, with music and ballet.
Taormina: Taormina Arte continues.
Palermo: Palermo di Scena continues.
Catania: Estate a Catania continues.

September
Catania: Bellini International Music Prize.
Milo: Table Grapes and Etna Wine Fair.
Palermo: Sicily International Tennis Championships.
Taormina: the last month of the Taormina Arte season.
Palermo: Festival di Palermo sul Novecento. A month of theatre, music, video and cinema.

October/November
Catania: Concert season starts in the Teatro Massimo Bellini.
Catania: Classical concert seasons of the Associazione Musicale Etnea

and Lyceum Club start, until June.
Catania: Jazz concert season of Associazione Catania Jazz e del Brass starts, runs till June.
Catania: Theatre season opens in the Teatro G. Verga, Teatro A. Musco and in the Metropolitan, Ambasciatori, Piccolo Teatro and Nuovo Teatro.
Palermo: Festival di Palermo sul novecento continues.
Monreale: Sacred organ music in the cathedral.
Palermo: The Silent Call of the Earth, international festival of documentary films.

December

Caltagirone: Biennale of Sicilian Ceramics.
Palermo: Fiera del Mediterraneo (Trade Fair).
Palermo: Opera season (Teatro Massimo), runs until May.
Zafferana Etnea: Award of the Brancati literature prize.

The Festive Calendar

Every day of the year somewhere in Sicily a town or village celebrates a religious festival. At Easter, virtually every village has its own traditional celebration. *Ferragosto* (15 August) is also a traditional festival almost everywhere. Other major religious feasts such as All Saints and Christmas produce another crop of celebrations, as does carnival time.

January

There are Epiphany (6 January) festivals all over Sicily.
Caltanissetta: Epiphany pageant evoking the Three Kings.
Mezzojuso: Byzantine procession called A Vulata d'A Palumma.
Piana degli Albanesi: Greek Orthodox rites celebrate Christ's baptism. The women wear traditional dress.

February

Agrigento: first week of February. The almond blossom and folklore festival, held in the Valley of the Temples.
Catania: 1–5 February. Celebration for the city's patron, St Agata. Giant

candles (*Cerei*) are carried through the streets. High points are a procession of 17th-century carriages and another in which the saint's relics are towed by citizens dressed in traditional white gowns.
Sciacca: Carnival, one of the best on the island.
Taormina: Popular Carnival with locals.

March

Acireale: week before Lent. The most famous carnival on the island. A huge procession closes the town centre to traffic, and outdoor concerts and dances take place in the main square.

April/Easter

Holy Week (*Settimana Santa*) is the major religious festival, celebrated all over the island. Virtually every village and town has processions on Palm Sunday, Maundy Thursday and Good Friday.
Aidone: Easter Sunday pantomime meeting between Christ and His mother.
Barrafranca: Another meeting between Christ and the Madonna.
Caltanissetta: Palm Sunday Mass. Maundy Thursday procession of the guilds (*Reale Maestranza*) with the Mysteries (*I Misteri*).
Enna: Holy Week is magnificent; the highlight is the Good Friday processions parading the "urn of the dead Christ".
Gangi: Palm Sunday and Good Friday processions with statues borne aloft by the confraternities.
Marsala: Maundy Thursday. The Mysteries re-enacted by locals in costume.
Mezzojuso: Greek Orthodox celebrations, traditional processions and costumes.
Noto: Good Friday procession called Santa Spina.
Palermo: Greek Orthodox celebrations in La Martorana. Palm branches hung over the doors of churches. Christ's "dead body" paraded by liveried young men.
Petralia Sottana: Palm Sunday "reunion" of Christ and the Madonna.
Piana degli Albanesi: Easter

according to the Byzantine rite. Palm Sunday procession with the bishop on a donkey. 23 April: costumed procession for St George's day.
Prizzi: Easter Sunday Dance of the Devils and Death.
Ragusa: The Mysteries (*I Misteri*) statues in procession.
San Fratello: Good Friday Festival of the Jews.
Trápani: The Mysteries (*I Misteri*). Friday and Saturday recreation of the Passion. Mournful dirges but moving event.

May/July

Agrigento: 1st and 2nd Sundays in June. San Calogero harvest thanksgiving. Rolls shaped like saints are tossed at crowds.
Caltagirone: 24–25 July. Festa di San Giacomo. The 142 steps of Maria del Monte are covered in candles.
Palazzolo Acreide: 29 June. Festival of San Paolo.
Palermo: 10–15 July. U Fistinu. The city's most important festival. Mountain procession to celebrate Santa Rosalia, the patron saint.
Messina: La Varetta. June procession with relics.
Siracusa: July festival of the sea.
Siracusa: First Sunday in May. Festival of Santa Lucia of the Quails (*delle quaglie*), commemorating the miracle of 1646 when the city was saved from starvation by the arrival of quails. A type of wheat porridge (*cuccia*) is eaten.
Taormina: End of May. Display of Sicilian carts and folklore.
Trecastagni: 12 May. Garlic fair and a religious festival; barefoot penitents.

August

Cáccamo: 1–15 August. Historical castle pageant.
Siracusa: 1st Sunday. Boat race (*palio*) round Ortygia island, the five traditional quarters of the city competing enthusiastically.
Gangi: 5 August. Festa della Spiga. Floats, street parties and fireworks.
Messina: 14th. Parade of the Giants, the mythical city founders, followed by barefoot penitents.

Piazza Armerina: 13th–14th. Palio dei Normanni. Jousting tournament and processions in medieval costumes celebrate the victory of the Normans over the Arabs.
Ragusa: 29th. Festival of St John the Baptist.

September

Cáccamo: Lu Tirunfo di la Manna. Festival celebrates manna.
Calasacibetta: 1–3 September. Sagra di Buon Riposo, a folk and food festival, with a livestock market, a race (*Corsa dei Berberi*) and much sausage eating.
Camastra: 9th. San Biagio. Blessing of the harvest. Costumes representing the four seasons. Parade of floats.
Catania: 8 September. Festival of Maria SS Bambina. Fisherman's festival with a procession of boats.
Palermo: 4 September. Pilgrimage to the Grotto of Santa Rosalia, Palermo's patron saint, on Monte Pellegrino.
Tindari: 8 September. Birth of the Virgin, a festival celebrated all over Sicily, especially on the coast.

October–December

Zafferana Etnea. All October. Ottobrata Zafferanese. Gastronomic feast celebrating local produce: grapes, mushrooms, mustard, honey and wine.
Petralia Sottana. 6 October. Sagra delle Castagne. Procession of floats celebrating chestnuts and produce.
Ognissanti (All Saints Day). 1 November celebration everywhere. Presents given to the dead. A strong tradition in Palermo province.
Il Giorno dei Morti (Day of the Dead). 2 November visits to family graves at cemeteries or catacombs. Picnics.
Siracusa: 13 and 20 December, Festival of Santa Lucia, the city's patron saint. Barefoot procession and a borrowed Swedish girl, "Lucia of Sweden".
Natale (Christmas). Cribs (*presepi*) decorated in churches, particularly in Acireale, Palermo Province and Trápani.

Sport

Participant Sports

RIDING

Horse-riding is not really a traditional sport in Sicily: mules rather than horses have traditionally been used to carry loads across the mountains. Nevertheless, riding is catching on, and there are more and more stables from which horses can be hired. Particularly in the Nébrodi and Madonie, trekking over longer distances is growing in popularity. These are some of the stables in Palermo province:
Balestrate: Fattoria Manostalla, C. da Manostalla, tel: 091 8787033.
Castelbuono: Ranch San Guglielmo, loc. San Guglielmo, tel: 092 71150.
Cefalù: Villagrande Ranch, C. da Vallegrande, tel: 0921 420286.
Gratteri: Fattoria Pianetti, C. da Pianetti, tel: 0921 421890.
Montelepre: Don Vito, Piano Aranci, tel: 091 8784111.

SKIING

Ski on black snow with a view of orange trees? Not quite. You would need a very strong telescope to see the orange trees, but they are there. Etna is frequently snow-capped all summer, and the skiing season normally runs from December to April. The snow really is black, at least in patches, where ash, dust and lava from minor eruptions have blown across it. In places, "hot" rocks, those which are still cooling, melt the snow and then stand out through it like lumps of coal.

The views really are spectacular, and perhaps there is an element of bravado in the idea of skiing on a live volcano. Caution: every now and then, Etna really does come to life again, and the skiing areas have to close because of danger from ash or lava flows.

Main ski resorts

Linguaglossa is on the northern side of Etna. The *Autobus della neve* (snow bus) runs every Sunday between January and April from Piano Provenzano, organised by the Ferrovia Circumetnea (see *Attractions, page 362*). General information from the Pro Loco, Piazza Annunziata, tel: 095 643094.
Nicolosi (Rifugio Sapienza) is on the southern side of Etna, above Zafferana Etnea. For information on the pistes, tel: 095 914141.

DIVING

Sicily's coasts are rich in flora and fauna. Both snorkelling and subaqua diving are popular. The island of Ustica is the haunt of subaqua fans. Its coastline is protected and offers spectacular diving in deep water. There are the remains of a wreck visible in one spot. The area around Isola Bella, Taormina, is popular with snorkellers. The Egadi islands, particularly Marettimo, are also a favourite with divers: crystal clear, clean, deep water. Tanks can be filled on most islands, and several, including Ustica, also have decompression chambers available.

Snorkelling can be enjoyed by

Swimming

It is not a problem to find somewhere to swim, whether in the sea, lakes or rivers. The smaller islands offer the cleanest and clearest water (*see Diving, above*). There may be plenty of sea but patches of it are severely polluted (the coasts around Augusta, Gela, Termini Imerese are nobody's choice). For detailed advice on the choicest swimming locations, see *Beaches, page 371*.

Windsurfing

Surf boards can be hired locally. The south coast is the best place for surfing because of the strong dry wind, but conditions in the Mondello bay are also adequate.

anyone who can swim, and it is well worth mastering the art since along Sicily's coasts it gives instant access to an exciting and different world. It is particularly worthwhile wherever there are rocky shorelines, which means the north and the islands.

HIKING

Walks range from peaceful coastal strolls through the nature reserve of Lo Zíngaro on Capo San Vito (Palermo Province) to hikes in the Nébrodi and Madonie mountains. Walks through Sicily's volcanic landscapes are ever-popular. In particular, the Aeolian Islands offer magnificent unspoilt coastal walks.

The excitement of walking on Etna exerts an obvious pull. It is not wise to walk on Etna without a guide: *see Excursions information on guides, page 371.* Etna Trekking (Via Roma 334, Linguaglossa; tel: 095 647592) is an agency that organises hikes. Call the information office in Linguaglossa, tel: 095 643094.

Spectator Sports

MOTOR RACING

If you like racing cars, then investigate Lago Pergusa at Enna. It does not host Formula One events, but races are normally held there at least once a month.

CYCLING

The round Etna bicycle race is held in April. It is an interesting event to take part in, but perhaps more fun is to be standing on the sidelines watching and enjoying the scenery.

Shopping

Shopping Hours

Normal shopping hours during weekdays are 9am–1pm and 4–7.30pm. All shops except those selling food are normally closed on Monday mornings. Food shops close on Wednesday afternoons. In many tourist resorts, the shops are open seven days a week.

Markets

Markets make an invigorating change from the round of museums and churches. Observing what is sold, and how, gives some insight into the life of the less wealthy part of society, and also shows the riches of Sicily's soil.

Palermo

Vucciria Market, in and around Piazza Caracciolo, near the junction of Via Roma and Corso Vittorio Emanuele. Palermo's oldest market: fish, meat, vegetables and almost anything else. Beware of pickpockets. Daily from 8.30am.
Mercato del Capo, around Sant' Agostino, Beati Paoli and Via Porta Carini, behind Teatro Massimo. Second-hand clothes.
Mercato di Ballarò, Via Ballarò, just off Piazza del Carmine. Fruit and vegetables, together with a market selling fabrics and household goods.
Mercato dei Lattarini, Via Calderai, near La Martorana between Via Maqueda and Via Roma. Mixed household market.
Mercato di Via Sant' Agostino, Via Bandiera. In a street which runs from Piazza San Domenico to Via Maqueda. Flea market and second-hand clothes.
Mercato delle Pulci, Piazza Peranni, near the cathedral and behind the

San Giacomo barracks. Antiques, junk, furniture and paintings.

Catania
Pescheria fish market, mornings only, in the Via Dusmet and Porta Uzeda quarter (watch your wallet).
Carlo Alberto market, between Via Pacini, Piazza Stesicoro and Piazza Carlo Alberto. Fruit, vegetables and flea market.

Taormina
Weekly market, Parcheggio Von Gloeden. Every Wednesday 8am–12.30pm.

Clothes

For fashionable clothes, the best bets are Viale della Libertà and Via Ruggero Settimo in Palermo, Via Etnea in Catania and Corso Umberto in Taormina. Here you will find designer clothes from Valentino, Coveri, Gucci and Armani.

For cheaper shopping try Via Maqueda (the continuation of Viale della Libertà) or Via Roma in Palermo, and the side streets off Via Etnea in Catania.

For everyday items, the upmarket chain stores are Coin and Rinascente. Upim and Standa aim at the lower end of the market.

Antiques

Siracusa is renowned for its reproductions of Classical Greek coins. Palermo has a daily antiques market near the Cappucini Catacombs. There are some real treasures here, but also plenty of fakes and rubbish. A Sicilian saying has it that if you arrive here early enough in the morning you can buy back what was stolen from you the night before. The market is unfortunately also a haunt of bag-snatchers, so watch your wallet in every possible sense.

The customs authorities frown on exporting stolen goods, so be wary in your purchases.

Antique Shops
Catania: Bottega Antica, Via XX Settembre 50, tel: 095 501190.

Enna: L'Antiquario, Sant'Agata 100, tel: 0935 500377.
Palermo: Hera, Viale della Libertà 39, tel: 091 322280.

A number of shops around Corso Umberto sell a mixture of antiques and bric-a-brac. You will need some expertise to pick up anything but junk, but browsing is enjoyable.

Art

Most art galleries are concentrated in Catania, Palermo and Siracusa, with a sprinkling in Cefalù and Taormina.
Egadi Islands: Bottega d'Arte, Via Marzamemi 7, Favignana, tel: 0923 921696. Gianni Matto sells his naïve fishing paintings from this workshop.

Books

Books are one of Sicily's happier but lesser-known exports. Bookshops abound in Palermo, Catania and Siracusa. For second-hand books (including lavish books on art and history), try the Quattro Canti area in Palermo, especially the university quarter and Via Roma. **Sellerio**, one home-grown publishers, deserve support for their beautiful books on the island's culture, literature, history and art. Books are available from **Libreria Sellerio di Sellerio Olivia**, Via La Farina 10, Palermo, tel: 091 6254476. **Novecento**, another respected Palermitan publisher, is based at Via Siracusa 7/a, tel: 6256814. The classic **Feltrinelli** bookshop (small selection of books in foreign languages) is in Via Maqueda, 395, tel: 091 587785.

Jewellery

Coral and gold jewellery is made and sold on the island. The best is obtainable from jewellers in Palermo, Catania or Taormina's main shopping areas. Fairly expensive craft jewellery is sold in Cefalù, in shops off Corso Ruggero. Cheaper coral pieces can be bought from tourist shops and stalls in resorts. Traditionally, Trápani was the centre

for coral but although the fantastic coral in the city museum is local, the coral in the shops is imported.

Around Etna: necklaces made from lava make a very interesting and novel present for friends back home. At various other volcanoes, sulphur crystals are sold as souvenirs. Jewellery is sold in Erice, along with other crafts, from woodwork to pottery.

Traditional Crafts

Pottery, puppets and papyrus represent the best of traditional Sicilian handicrafts. They make excellent gifts or souvenirs. Sadly, painted carts, Sicily's other great glory, are harder to transport home.

LACE AND EMBROIDERY

This is best bought from a tiny boutique in the interior, or from an old lady selling it from her home. Elsewhere, in the resorts, it tends to be over-priced and of poor quality.
Catania: Ricamificio Ionio, Viale A Alagona, 37, tel: 095 712 3970.
Palermo: SARAM Di Brancato Gandolfo, Viale Libertà, 230/b, tel: 091 6254152.

POTTERY

Pottery, one of Sicily's glories, has been around for a long time. Kilns from the 3rd century BC have been found around Gela, Siracusa and Catania as well as on Mozia. When the Arabs arrived in Sicily in 827, they introduced glazing techniques used in Persia, Syria and Egypt. Tin-glazed pottery, or majolica, appeared in the Trápani area in 1309.

The devastating 1693 earthquake destroyed much of eastern Sicily as well as razing the ceramics workshops of Caltagirone to the ground. As market demands still had to be satisfied, quality gave way to quantity.

At the end of the 19th century the Sicilian market, led by the Bourbons, became flooded with imported Neapolitan wares. To

stem the flow, a pottery factory was set up in San Stefano di Camastra.

San Stefano Ceramics
Now the best-known ceramics centre in Sicily, San Stefano di Camastra comes into sight behind a jumble of crockery on the Messina-Palermo road. Tiers of dishes, soup tureens and fruit bowls rise at ever increasing heights on each bend in the road, while cracked platters along the roadside testify to cars that have come a cropper among the cauldrons and cake stands.

High-quality local clay and fine workmanship have ensured the town's fame. Styles are very mixed but the authentic ware has a rustic look and feel. Look out, too, for lovely wall tiles decorated with smiling suns and local saints.

Caltagirone Ceramics
Caltagirone ceramics have always been famous for their instantly recognisable animal and floral designs in sky blue and copper green with touches of yellow. Look out for the tall *alberelli*, jars with nipped-in waists once used for storing dry drugs. Also consider acquiring painted tiles, sturdy vases and chunky little stoups.

Some of the newer and more individualistic styles are also highly

Papyrus

Papermaking, and writing and drawing on papyrus, are traditional crafts around Siracusa. The paper is made from the papyrus reeds which have been grown since Classical times. To see the plant in its natural habitat, visit the Fonte Aretusa spring on Ortygia or the river Ciane just outside Siracusa.

Stalls and shops all over the city sell inexpensive examples. These range from copies of Egyptian designs to portraits of your family while you wait. The Museo del Papiro on Viale Teocrito (near the San Giovanni catacombs) can also demonstrate how it is made. Tel: 0931 22100.

attractive. If you can manage the weight, pottery is an ideal gift to take home. In Palermo, buy from De Simone, Via Stabile 133.

PAINTED CARTS

Models of traditional Sicilian carts (*see page 258*) can now be found all over the island, but especially in Bagheria and Palermo province generally. In Aci Sant'Antonio (Catania Province) craftsmen make carts to commission. (The finest are in the local museum.) If you are lucky, you may pick up a painted panel of a cart in a Palermo antique shop but expect to pay a fortune for such painstaking craft work.

RUGS

Erice has a tradition of hand-woven rugs which can be bought in many of the shops there.

STRAW & CANE

Monreale produces traditional straw and cane goods which can be bought directly from the artisans.

PUPPETS (PUPI)

Puppetry's main traditions are in Palermo and some of the best models are still made there. **Vincenzo Argento** (Corso Vittorio Emanuele 445, Palermo; tel: 091 6113680) continues a 160 year-old family tradition. He will make you a *paladino* (paladin or knight) to order in his tiny workshop. After carving the wooden body, he solders on the copper armour and creates the costume with the help of his wife. Open 7.30am–8pm. Argento also organises puppet shows in Palazzo Asmundo, Via Pietro Novelli.

In Taormina, **Francesco and Sabatino del Popolo Lampuri** (Via Luigi Pirandello, 51; tel: 0942 626043) sells inexpensive puppets, with finishing touches added by the family.

Language

Conversation

The language spoken is Italian, supplemented by Sicilian dialects. Dialects may differ enormously within a few villages, and are an essential part of Sicilian culture.

A few examples of Sicilian dialect:

Sicilian	Italian	English
Veni ca	*Vieni qui*	Come here
iddu	*lui*	him
idda	*lei*	her

In large cities and tourist centres you will find many people who speak English, French or German. In fact, due to the massive emigration over the last 100 years, you may meet fluent speakers of these languages, often with a New York, Melbourne, Brussels or Bavarian accent.

One dialect with a difference is that of Piana degli Albanesi in Palermo province: here Albanian is spoken. The population is descended from Albanians who arrived in the 15th century.

Sicilians are deeply hospitable. You will certainly manage without Italian, but learning a little will improve your enjoyment enormously.

Pronunciation is claimed by all Italians to be simple: you pronounce as you read. This is approximately true. A few important rules for English speakers: **c** before **e** or **i** is pronounced **ch**, e.g. *ciao* ("chow"), *mi dispiace* ("mee dispyache"). **Ch** before **i** or **e** is pronounced as **k**, e.g. *la chiesa* ("la kyesa"). **Z** is pronounced as **ts**, e.g. *la coincidenza* ("la coinchidentsa"), and **gli** is pronounced **ly**, e.g. *biglietto* ("bilyetto").

The stress is usually on the penultimate syllable of a word. In this book, where the stress falls elsewhere, we have indicated this with an accent (e.g. Trápani, Cefalù), although Italians often do not bother.

Nouns are either masculine (**il**, plural **i**) or feminine (**la**, plural **le**). Plurals of nouns are most often formed by changing an **o** to an **i** and an **a** to an **e**, e.g. *il panino – i panini*; *la chiesa – le chiese*.

There is, of course, rather more to the language than that, but you can get a surprisingly long way with a mastery of a few basic phrases.

It is well worth buying a good phrase book or dictionary, but the following basics will help you get started.

Basics

Hello (Good day) *Buon giorno*
Good evening *Buona sera*
Good night *Buona notte*
Goodbye *Arrivederci*
Hi/Goodbye (familiar) *Ciao*
Yes *Sì*
No *No*
Thank you *Grazie*
You're welcome *Prego*
Alright, OK *Va bene*
Please *Per favore* or *per piacere*.
Excuse me (get attention) *Scusi* (singular)/*Scusate* (plural)
Excuse me (in a crowd) *Permesso*
Can you show me...? *Puo indicarmi..?*
Can you help me, please? *Puo aiutarmi, per piacere?*
I'm lost *Mi sono perso.*
Sorry *Mi dispiace*
I don't understand *Non capisco*
I am English/American *Sono inglese/americano*
Irish/Canadian *irlandese/canadese*
Do you speak English? *Parla inglese?*
Le piace la Sicilia? **Do you like Sicily?** (you will often be asked)
I love it *Mi piace moltissimo* (correct answer).
It's wonderful *È favolosa* (the alternative answer when asked what you think of Sicily.) Both of these last can equally be applied to food, beaches, the view, etc.

Questions & Answers

I'd like... *Vorrei...*
I'd like that one, please *Vorrei quello lì, per favore*
Is there ...? *C'è (un) ...?*
Do you have ...? *Avete ...?*
Yes, of course *Si, certo*
No, we don't *No, non c'è* (also used to mean: s/he is not here)
Where is the lavatory? *Dov'è il bagno?*
Gentlemen *Signori* or *Uomini*
Ladies *Signore* or *Donne*

Transport

airport *l'aeroporto*
aeroplane *l'aereo*
arrivals *arrivi*
boat *la barca*
bus *il autobus*
bus station *autostazione*
connection *la coincidenza*
departures *le partenze*
ferry *il traghetto*
ferry terminal *stazione marittima*
flight *il volo*
hydrofoil *l'aliscafo*
left luggage *il deposito bagaglio*
no smoking *vietato fumare*
platform *il binario*
port *il porto*
station *la stazione*
railway station *stazione ferrovia*
return ticket *un biglietto di andata e ritorno*
single ticket *un biglietto di andata sola*
sleeping car *la carrozza letti*
stop *la fermata*
taxi *il taxi*
train *il treno*

What time does the train leave? *Quando parte il treno?*
What time does the train arrive? *Quando arriva il treno?*
What time does the bus leave for Monreale? *Quando parte l'autobus per Monreale?*
How long will it take to get there? *Quanto tempo ci vuole per arrivare?*
You need to change at Palermo *Bisogna cambiare a Palermo*
Can you tell me when to get off? *Mi può dire di scendere alla fermata giusta?*
The train is late *Il treno è in ritardo*

Directions

right *a destra*
left *a sinistra*
straight on *sempre diritto*
far away *lontano*
nearby *vicino*
opposite *di fronte*
next to *accanto a*
traffic lights *il semaforo*
junction *l'incrocio, il bivio*
building *il palazzo*
Turn left *Gira a sinistra*
Where is ...? *Dov'è ...?*
Where are ...? *Dove sono...?*
Where is the nearest bank/petrol station/bus stop/hotel/garage? *Dov'è la banca/il benzinaio/la fermata di autobus/l'albergo/l'officina più vicino?*
Can you show me where I am on the map? *Puó indicarmi sulla cartina dove mi trovo?*
How do I get there? *Come si può andare?*
You're on the wrong road. *E sulla strada sbagliata.*

Road Signs

Alt **Stop**
Attenzione **Caution**
Caduta massi **Danger of falling rocks**
Deviazione **Diversion**
Divieto di campeggio **No camping allowed**
Divieto di passaggio **No entry**
Divieto di sosta, Sosta vietata **No parking**
Galleria **Tunnel**
Incrocio **Crossroads**
Limite di velocità **Speed limit**
Passaggio a livello **Railway crossing**
Parcheggio **Parking**
Pericolo **Danger**
Pericolo di incendio **Danger of fire**
Rallentare **Slow down**
Rimozione forzata **Parked cars will be towed away**
Semaforo **Traffic lights**
Senso unico **One way street**
Sentiero **Footpath**
Strada interrotta **Road blocked**
Strada senza uscita **Dead end**
Vietato il sorpasso **No overtaking**

Shopping

How much does it cost? *Quanto costa?*
(half) a kilo *un (mezzo) kilo*
100 grams *un etto*
200 grams *due etti*
a little *un pochino*
Give me some of those. *Mi dia alcuni di quelli lì*
That's enough *Basta così*
That's too expensive *E troppo caro*
It's too small *E troppo piccolo*
It's too big *E troppo grande*

Numbers

1	Uno	**12**	Dodici	**50**	Cinquanta
2	Due	**13**	Tredici	**60**	Sessanta
3	Tre	**14**	Quattordici	**70**	Settanta
4	Quattro	**15**	Quindici	**80**	Ottanta
5	Cinque	**16**	Sedici	**90**	Novanta
6	Sei	**17**	Diciassette	**100**	Cento
7	Sette	**18**	Diciotto	**200**	Duecento
8	Otto	**19**	Diciannove	**500**	Cinquecento
9	Nove	**20**	Venti	**1,000**	Mille
10	Dieci	**30**	Trenta	**2,000**	Duemila
11	Undici	**40**	Quaranta	**1,000,000**	Milione

I like it *Mi piace*
I don't like it *Non mi piace*
I'll take it *Lo prendo*

Hotel

I'd like *Vorrei*
a single/double room (with a double bed) *una camera singola/doppia (con letto matrimoniale)*
with bath/shower *con bagno/doccia*
for one night *per una notte*
How much is it? *Quanto costa?*
Is breakfast included? *E compresa la colazione?*
half/full board *mezza pensione/pensione completa*
key *la chiave*
towel *un asciugamano*
toilet paper *la carta igienica*
Do you have a room with a balcony/view of the sea? *C'è una camera con balcone/una vista del mare?*
Can I see the room? *Posso vedere la camera?*
Is it a quiet room? *E una stanza tranquilla?*
We have one with a double bed *Ne abbiamo una matrimoniale.*
Can I have the bill, please? *Posso avere il conto, per favore?*

Bar Notices

You will often see these signs at a bar:
*Prezzo in terrazza/*Terrace price (often double what you pay standing at the bar)
*Si prende lo scontrino alla cassa/*First pay at the cash desk, then take the receipt to the bar to be served.

Bar Snacks & Drinks

(*See also Restaurant Menus on page 352.*)
coffee *un caffè*
un espresso (**small, strong and black**)
un cappuccino (**with hot, frothy milk**)
un corretto (**with alcohol**)
tea *un thè*

lemon tea *un thè con limone*
fresh orange *una spremuta di arancia*
lemon juice *una spremuta di limone*
(mineral) water *acqua (minerale)*
ice *ghiaccio*
red/white wine *vino rosso/bianco*
beer *una birra*
milk *latte*
bottle *una bottiglia*
ice-cream *un gelato*
cone *un cono*
pastry *una pasta*
sandwich *un tramezzino*
roll *un panino*

Finding the Sights

Custode **Custodian**
Sacristano **Sacristan**
Suonare il campanello **Ring the bell**
Abbazia **Abbey**
Aperto **Open**
Chiuso **Closed**
Chiesa **Church**
Entrata **Entrance**
Monastero **Monastery**
Museo **Museum**
Ruderi **Ruins**
Scavi **Excavations/archaeological site**
Spiaggia **Beach**
Tempio **Temple**

Is it possible to see the church? *E possibile visitare la chiesa?*
Where can I find the custodian/sacristan/key? *Dovè posso trovare il custode/il sacristano/la chiave?*
We have come a long way just to see ... *Siamo venuti da lontano proprio per visitare ...*
It is really a pity it is closed *E veramente peccato che sia chiuso.*
(The last two should be tried if entry seems a problem!)

Further Reading

Literature

Gesualdo Bufalino: *Argo il Cieco* (*Blind Argus*), Sellerio, Palermo. *Blind Argus* and *Night's Lies*, Harvill.
Lara Cardella: *Volevo i Pantaloni*, Mondadori. A bizarre account of a young girl's struggles with rural prejudice.
Andrea Camilleri: *La forma dell'acqua*, *Il cane di terracotta*, *Il Ladro di merendine*, *La voce del violino*, Sellerio. 4 detective stories written in Sicilian vernacular language have become best-sellers in Italy.
Vincenzo Consolo: *Le Pietre di Pantalica*.
David Gilmour: *The Last Leopard: A Life of Giuseppe di Lampedusa*, Quartet.
D.H Lawrence: *Sicilian Carousel*, Marlowe.
Dacia Maraini: *Bagheria* and *The Silent Duchess*.
Luigi Pirandello: *Six Characters in Search of an Author*, Methuen.
Mary Renault: *The Mask of Apollo*, Sceptre. A novel set in ancient Siracusa.
Leonardo Sciascia: *The Day of the Owl*, Paladin.
Leonardo Sciascia: *Sicilian Uncles*, Carcanet.
Leonardo Sciascia: *The Wine-Dark Sea*, Paladin.
Leonardo Sciascia: *La Sicilia Come Metafora*, Saggi.
Giuseppe Tomasi di Lampedusa: *The Leopard*, Collins.
Giovann Verga, i. *I Malavoglia* (*House by the Medlar Tree*), Dedalus.
Elio Vittorini: *Conversation in Sicily*, Quartet.

History and Culture

Luigi Barzini: *The Italians*, Penguin.
Giuseppe Bonomo: *Pitrè la Sicilia e i Siciliani*, Sellerio, Palermo.

Academic study of Sicilian folklore.

Antonino Buttitta: *Easter in Sicily*, Sicilian Tourist Service, Palermo. An introduction to Sicilian festivals.

Finley and Mack Smith: *History of Sicily*, Chatto & Windus. The best overall Sicilian history.

Gay Marks: *Le Mie Isole*, Edizioni La Ziza, Palermo. Personal account.

Nino Muccioli: *Leggende e Racconti Popolari della Sicilia*, Newton Compton, Rome. Legends and festivals.

John Julius Norwich: *Kingdom in the South*. The Norman period (out of print, available through libraries).

Regione Sicilia. *Archaeology in Sicily*, D'Agostini, Italy.

Crime and Society

Pino Arlacchi: *Gli Uomini del Disonore*, Mondadori. An account of the Mafia through the eyes of Antonino Calderone, a *pentito* from Catania.

Anton Blok: *The Mafia of a Sicilian Village*, Harper & Row.

Danilo Dolci: *Sicilian Lives*, Writers & Readers.

Giovanni Falcone: *Men of Honour, the Truth about the Mafia*, Little, Brown. Judge Falcone's testament.

Norman Lewis: *The Honoured Society*, Eland Press. A colourful if exaggerated account of the wartime Mafia.

Saverio Lodato: *Potenti*, Garzanti, Italy. An analysis of the Mafia's curent support within Sicily's institutions.

Clare Longrigg: *Mafia Women*, Vintage. The changing role of women in la Cosa Nostra.

Gavin Maxwell: *Ten Pains of Death*, Alan Sutton. An account of the people the author met while living in Scopello in the 1950s,

Gavin Maxwell: *God Protect me from my Friends* (out of print but available through libraries). A biography of the legendary bandit Salvatore Guiliano.

Mario Puzo: *The Godfather*, Pan (UK) or Putnam (US).

Mario Puzo: *The Sicilian*, Bantam Books.

Peter Robb: *Midnight in Sicily*, Panther. Insights on art, food, history, travel and the Mafia.

Gaia Servadio: *To a Different World*, Hamish Hamilton.

Tim Shawcross: *The War against the Mafia*, Mainstream.

Clare Sterling: *The Mafia*, Grafton. Analysis of the Mafia, particularly the "Pizza Connection".

Travel and General

Giuseppe Bellafiore: *Palermo*, Bess, Palermo.

Vincent Cronin: *The Golden Honeycomb*, Granada.

Paul Duncan: *Sicily*, John Murray.

Giuseppe Fava: *I Siciliani*, Cappelli Editore.

Dominique Fernandez: *Le Radeau de la Gorgone*, Grasset, France. Personal account of architecture and people.

J.W. Goethe: *Italian Journey 1786–1788*, Penguin.

de Maupassant, Guy. *Voyage en Sicile*, Edrisi, Palermo.

Fiona Pitt-Kethley: *Journeys to the Underworld*, Abacus. Bawdy account of her island adventures.

Mary Taylor Simeti: *On Persephone's Island*, Penguin.

Mary Taylor Simeti: *Sicilian Food*, Random Century (first published as *Pomp and Sustenance*).

ART & PHOTO CREDITS

All photography by
Lyle Lawson unless otherwise
stated

AKG London 19, 51, 54, 140T,
144T
V. Arcomano/Marka 129
the art archive 302T
Jenny Bennathan 99, 102
M. Capovilla/Marka 29
Carlo Chinca 73, 89, 126, 167T,
168, 169
Nevio Doz/Marka 34
Robert Fried 286, 287, 289
C. Garrubba/Marka 119
Glyn Genin 22, 90, 91, 92, 120,
123T, 124T, 128T, 130R, 139T,
142T, 145, 152T, 156T, 160T, 173,
175, 175T, 179, 180, 187, 189,
191, 198T, 210T, 214T, 226T,
229T, 232, 232T, 239, 243, 244T,
253, 254, 261, 262T, 263, 265,
268, 269, 271, 272, 273, 275,
276T, 277, 281, 282, 288T, 292,
292T, 299T, 303, 308, 309T, 313,
314T, 315
F. Giaccone/Marka 100, 123,
218T, 256T
Wilhelm von Gloeden/AKG 293
Ronald Grant Archive 94, 95, 96,
97L, 97R
John Heseltine 5B, 128, 240, 247
Michael Jenner 4/5, 98, 103

Magnum 78, 79, 80, 81
**Museo Internazionale della
Marionette** 2B
Axel Poignant Archive 4B, 270T
Stiken/Marka 306T
Topham Picturepoint 82, 83

Picture Spreads

Pages 30/31:
Top row left to right:
G.Allegretti/Marka,
M. Cristofori/Marka; John
Heseltine, M. Capovilla/Marka.
Centre row:
John Heseltine, Glyn Genin.
Bottom row:
M. Capovilla/Marka,
M. Christofori/Marka, Glyn Genin,
S. Pitamitz/Marka,
M. Capovilla/Marka

Pages 132/133:
Top row left to right:
John Heseltine, John Heseltine,
M. Mazzola/Marka, John Heseltine.
Centre top:
F. Giaconne/Marka.
Centre bottom:
F. Lovino/Marka.
Bottom row:
John Heseltine, R.G.Everts/Marka,
John Heseltine, F. Giaconne/Marka.

Pages 192/193:
Top row left to right:
Glyn Genin, A. Korda/Marka,
Axel Poignant Archive.
Centre row:
P. Ongaro/Marka,
F. Giaccone/Marka,
F. Giaccone/Marka.
Bottom row:
Axel Poignant Archive,
F. Giaccone/Marka,
F. Giaccone/Marka.

Pages 258/259:
Top row left to right:
P. Ongaro/Marka, L. Fioroni/Marka,
Axel Poignant Archive,
F. Pizzochero/Marka.
Centre row:
P. Ongaro/Marka, Axel Poignant
Archive, Glyn Genin.
Bottom row:
F. Giaccone/Marka, Museo
Internazionale della Marionette.

Small cover pictures all by Lyle
Lawson

Map Production John Scott
© 2000 Apa Publications GmbH & Co.
Verlag KG (Singapore branch)

INSIGHT GUIDE
SICILY

Cartographic Editor **Zoë Goodwin**
Production **Stuart A Everitt**
Design Consultants
Carlotta Junger, Graham Mitchener
Picture Research **Hilary Genin,
Monica Allende**

Index

Numbers in italics refer to photographs

A
B
C
D
E
F
G
H
I
J
a
b
c
d
e
f
g
h
i
j
k
l

☀ INSIGHT GUIDES

The world's largest collection of visual travel guides

A range of guides and maps to meet every travel need

Insight Guides

This classic series gives you the complete picture of a destination through expert, well written and informative text and stunning photography. Each book is an ideal background information and travel planner, serves as an on-the-spot companion – and is a superb visual souvenir of a trip. Nearly 200 titles.

Insight Pocket Guides

focus on the best choices for places to see and things to do, picked by our local correspondents. They are ideal for visitors new to a destination. To help readers follow the routes easily, the books contain full-size pull-out maps. 120 titles.

Insight Maps

are designed to complement the guides. They provide full mapping of major cities, regions and countries, and their laminated finish makes them easy to fold and gives them durability. 60 titles.

Insight Compact Guides

are convenient, comprehensive reference books, modestly priced. The text, photographs and maps are all carefully cross-referenced, making the books ideal for on-the-spot use when in a destination. 120 titles.

Different travellers have different needs. Since 1970, Insight Guides has been meeting these needs with a range of practical and stimulating guidebooks and maps

"I was first drawn to the Insight Guides by the excellent "Nepal" volume. I can think of no book which so effectively captures the essence of a country. Out of these pages leaped the Nepal I know – the captivating charm of a people and their culture. I've since discovered and enjoyed the entire Insight Guide series. Each volume deals with a country in the same sensitive depth, which is nowhere more evident than in the superb photography."

Sir Edmund Hillary

✵ INSIGHT GUIDES

The world's largest collection of visual travel guides

Insight Guides – the Classic Series
that puts you in the picture

Alaska	China	Hong Kong	Montreal	Seattle
Alsace	Cologne	Hungary	Morocco	Sicily
Amazon Wildlife	Continental Europe		Moscow	Singapore
American Southwest	Corsica	Iceland	Munich	South Africa
Amsterdam	Costa Rica	India		South America
Argentina	Crete	India's Western	Namibia	South Tyrol
Asia, East	Cuba	Himalaya	Native America	Southeast Asia
Asia, South	Cyprus	India, South	Nepal	Wildlife
Asia, Southeast	Czech & Slovak	Indian Wildlife	Netherlands	Spain
Athens	Republics	Indonesia	New England	Spain, Northern
Atlanta		Ireland	New Orleans	Spain, Southern
Australia	Delhi, Jaipur & Agra	Israel	New York City	Sri Lanka
Austria	Denmark	Istanbul	New York State	Sweden
	Dominican Republic	Italy	New Zealand	Switzerland
Bahamas	Dresden	Italy, Northern	Nile	Sydney
Bali	Dublin	Italy, Southern	Normandy	Syria & Lebanon
Baltic States	Düsseldorf		Norway	
Bangkok		Jamaica		Taiwan
Barbados	East African Wildlife	Japan	Old South	Tenerife
Barcelona	Eastern Europe	Java	Oman & The UAE	Texas
Bay of Naples	Ecuador	Jerusalem	Oxford	Thailand
Beijing	Edinburgh	Jordan		Tokyo
Belgium	Egypt		Pacific Northwest	Trinidad & Tobago
Belize	England	Kathmandu	Pakistan	Tunisia
Berlin		Kenya	Paris	Turkey
Bermuda	Finland	Korea	Peru	Turkish Coast
Boston	Florence		Philadelphia	Tuscany
Brazil	Florida	Laos & Cambodia	Philippines	
Brittany	France	Lisbon	Poland	Umbria
Brussels	France, Southwest	Loire Valley	Portugal	USA: On The Road
Budapest	Frankfurt	London	Prague	USA: Western States
Buenos Aires	French Riviera	Los Angeles	Provence	US National Parks: East
Burgundy			Puerto Rico	US National Parks: West
Burma (Myanmar)	Gambia & Senegal	Madeira		
	Germany	Madrid	Rajasthan	Vancouver
Cairo	Glasgow	Malaysia	Rhine	Venezuela
Calcutta	Gran Canaria	Mallorca & Ibiza	Rio de Janeiro	Venice
California	Great Barrier Reef	Malta	Rockies	Vienna
California, Northern	Great Britain	Marine Life of the	Rome	Vietnam
California, Southern	Greece	South China Sea	Russia	
Canada	Greek Islands	Mauritius, Réunion		Wales
Caribbean	Guatemala, Belize &	& Seychelles	St Petersburg	Washington DC
Catalonia	Yucatán	Melbourne	San Francisco	Waterways of Europe
Channel Islands		Mexico City	Sardinia	Wild West
Chicago	Hamburg	Mexico	Scandinavia	
Chile	Hawaii	Miami	Scotland	Yemen

Complementing the above titles are 120 easy-to-carry Insight Compact Guides, 120 Insight Pocket Guides with full-size pull-out maps and more than 100 laminated easy-fold Insight Maps